PFKNR

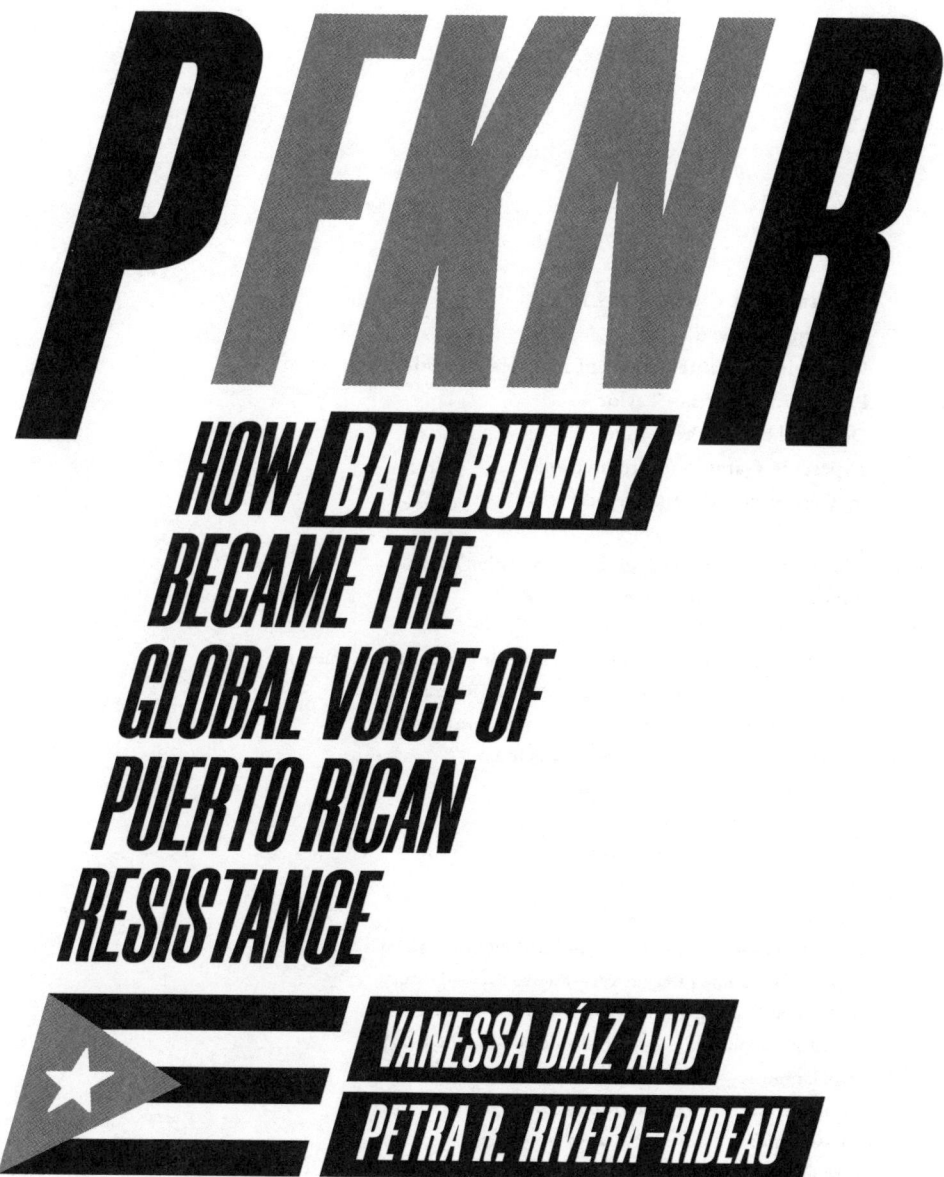

PFKNR

HOW BAD BUNNY BECAME THE GLOBAL VOICE OF PUERTO RICAN RESISTANCE

VANESSA DÍAZ AND
PETRA R. RIVERA-RIDEAU

DUKE UNIVERSITY PRESS / DURHAM AND LONDON / 2026

© 2026 DUKE UNIVERSITY PRESS
Printed in the United States of America on acid-free paper ∞
Project Editor: Ihsan Taylor
Designed by Matthew Tauch
Typeset in Garamond Premier Pro
by Westchester Publishing Services

Library of Congress Cataloging-in-Publication Data
Names: Díaz, Vanessa, [date] author. | Rivera-
Rideau, Petra R., [date] author.
Title: P FKN R : how Bad Bunny became the global voice of Puerto
Rican resistance / Vanessa Díaz and Petra R. Rivera-Rideau.
Description: Durham : Duke University Press, 2026. |
Includes bibliographical references and index.
Identifiers: LCCN 2025031598 (print)
LCCN 2025031599 (ebook)
ISBN 9781478033332 (paperback)
ISBN 9781478029885 (hardcover)
ISBN 9781478062097 (ebook)
Subjects: LCSH: Bad Bunny, 1994– | Bad Bunny, 1994—Criticism
and interpretation. | Reggaetón—Puerto Rico—History
and criticism. | Trap (Music)—Puerto Rico—History and
criticism. | Popular music—Social aspects—Puerto Rico. |
Popular music—Political aspects—Puerto Rico. | Hur-
ricane Maria, 2017. | Puerto Rico—History—1998
Classification: LCC ML420.B11057 D539 2026
(print) | LCC ML420.B11057 (ebook)
LC record available at https://lccn.loc.gov/2025031598
LC ebook record available at https://lccn.loc.gov/2025031599

Cover art: Illustration by Matthew Tauch, based
on a photograph by Thais Llorca Lezcano.

ESTE LIBRO VA DEDICADO A:

Anacaona, Clemente, Rafael, y Adrian,
y a todos los nenes de Borikén dentro de
Puerto Rico y en la diaspora.

Y PARA NUESTROS QUERIDOS PADRES,

Eugenio Rivera Jr. y Woodrow Díaz Jr.

"SOY GRANDE PORQUE VENGO DE UN LUGAR PEQUEÑO. SOY LEYENDA PORQUE SOY PUERTORRIQUEÑO. AQUÍ NACÍ, Y AQUÍ ME MUERO."

BENITO ANTONIO MARTÍNEZ OCASIO, A.K.A. BAD BUNNY

CONTENTS

INTRODUCTION

"¿QUIÉN TÚ ERES?": UNDERSTANDING BAD BUNNY AND RESISTANCE IN PUERTO RICO

It was December 2024, and Bad Bunny was wrapping up his 2025 album *DeBÍ TiRAR MáS FOToS* when he realized that the title track was not working out. Inspiration struck after Bad Bunny and his longtime collaborator and producer MAG joined a parranda to celebrate the Christmas holiday. Similar to Christmas carolers, Puerto Rican parrandas are groups of people going door-to-door singing holiday songs, accompanied by musicians with instruments such as the cuatro, güiro, and panderetas (handheld drums used in the Puerto Rican folkloric genre of plena).

MAG returned to the hotel after the parranda and couldn't sleep. "I was hearing bomba and plena circulating in my head," he recounted. "Then, at 8 a.m., with pitorro coming out of my breath, I thought, what if we try plena, but in our own way.[1] So I sent a voice note to Benito [a.k.a. Bad Bunny] and he was like, 'Eso me gusta mucho.'"[2] They promptly headed to the studio to record the new song. "DtMF" opens with melodic synth chords, setting the stage for Bad Bunny's powerful, raw vocals. The two saw the need for some live instrumentation. Bad Bunny invited a group of young musicians whom he affectionately calls "los sobrinos" (the nieces and nephews). They were students or recent graduates of Puerto Rico's public music schools, the Escuela Libre de la Música and the Escuela Pablo Casals, and had already contributed to other tracks on the album. These young musicians were essential in creating the call-and-response vocals and percussion that are associated with plena, a traditional Afro–Puerto Rican musical genre. MAG recalled the communal recording process: "I was singing, Benito was singing. Everybody was in the live room having the best time. We recorded a live plena, and it was just this celebratory, beautiful moment. It was the most beautiful session I've ever been a part of."

Little did they know that "DtMF" would thrust Puerto Rican plena onto the global stage. "DtMF" swiftly reached number one on the top two music streaming platforms in the world—Apple Music and Spotify. By January 21, 2025, just a few weeks after the release of *DeBÍ TiRAR MáS FOToS*, the plena fusion song reached number one on Billboard's Global 200 chart, the chart that measures songs' worldwide streaming and sales.[3] Prior to "DtMF," no plena song had ever entered the charts, let alone reached number one. In fact, given the folkloric nature of the genre, it is likely that most people outside of Puerto Rico and the Puerto Rican diaspora had never even heard of plena. "I didn't expect this reaction, this reception," MAG explained. "What's happening with 'DtMF' feels like a cultural movement. And it feels like the world is hugging us and Puerto Rico, and in such a beautiful way."

The song's success—and that of the album as a whole—was hardly surprising given Bad Bunny's dizzying array of accomplishments as one of the top artists in the world. *DeBÍ TiRAR MáS FOToS* was his fourth album to reach number one on the Billboard 200. In fact, the first Spanish-language album to ever debut at number one on the chart was Bad Bunny's 2020 album *El Último Tour del Mundo*.[4] Remarkably, every single one of his eight studio albums has reached number one on the Billboard Latin Albums chart. More than one hundred of Bad Bunny's songs have reached the Billboard Hot 100, including fifteen songs that have made it into the Top 10 of the chart; this is a particularly notable achievement given that Spanish-language songs rarely make it that high.[5] In fact, from 2020 to 2022,

1.1 Bad Bunny, wearing a suit reminiscent of those worn by salsa icon Héctor Lavoe, performs "BAILE INoLVIDABLE" and "DtMF" with a live salsa band, including Los Sobrinos, during the SNL50: The Homecoming Concert at Radio City Music Hall on February 14, 2025. Peacock/NBC Universal via Getty Images.

Bad Bunny became the most streamed artist on Spotify for three years in a row, beating out the likes of Beyoncé, Taylor Swift, and Harry Styles.[6]

In addition to these trailblazing chart metrics, Bad Bunny has repeatedly broken barriers for Latin music and Spanish-language artists in the United States. Cumulatively, Bad Bunny has received over forty nominations for Grammys and Latin Grammys, becoming the first Spanish-language artist to earn a Grammy nomination for Album of the Year for his 2022 album *Un Verano Sin Ti*.[7] *Un Verano Sin Ti* became the most streamed album in the history of Spotify, and it received numerous accolades, including its ranking as number nine in *Rolling Stone*'s top albums of the twenty-first century.[8] The album's success also paved the way for Bad Bunny to be the first artist in history to stage two separate $100 million-grossing tours in less than twelve months (El Último Tour and the World's Hottest Tour, both in 2022).[9] On the heels of these tours, Bad Bunny became the first Spanish-language Latino artist to headline Coachella in 2023.[10] In 2024, Bad Bunny's Most Wanted Tour was the seventh-highest-grossing tour in the United States, earning over $200 million.[11] In the summer of 2025, Bad Bunny performed a historic residency in Puerto Rico. Bad Bunny is indeed a bona fide superstar.

Although many have celebrated Bad Bunny's success in the US mainstream, others have questioned whether his fame has distanced him from his Puerto Rican roots and communities. These criticisms came to the fore with his 2023 album, *Nadie Sabe Lo Que Va a Pasar Mañana* (often referred to as *Nadie Sabe*), which immediately preceded his 2025 *DeBÍ TiRAR MáS FOTOS*. Bad Bunny presented *Nadie Sabe* as an album for his "real fans" and harkened back to his days as a Latin trap artist.[12] The album's lyrics spoke of Bad Bunny's discomfort with fame while simultaneously boasting of his riches and success. Bad Bunny released *Nadie Sabe* after having relocated briefly to Los Angeles, where he lived in a modern mansion off the Sunset Strip. There, he started a romance with the supermodel and reality star Kendall Jenner, who has faced criticism for appropriating Mexican culture in the marketing of her tequila brand 818.[13] The move to Los Angeles, hobnobbing with US movie stars, dating a member of the Kardashian-Jenner family, and complaining about his fame made many fans surmise that Bad Bunny had eroded his commitment to Puerto Rico and to Latinos more broadly.[14]

What fans *didn't* know is that alongside this Latin trap record, Bad Bunny had also conceived of and begun working on *DeBÍ TiRAR MáS FOTOS*, which, upon its release, many reviewers would call a "love letter to Puerto Rico."[15] Bad Bunny is known for fusing genres in unique and unexpected ways; however, *DeBÍ TiRAR MáS FOTOS* marked the first time that the artist blended more traditional Puerto Rican genres like plena, bomba, and salsa into his characteristic reggaetón and trap sound. He also highlighted a plethora of young Puerto Rican artists like Dei V, RaiNao, and Chuwi in addition to Los Sobrinos and Los Pleneros de la Cresta.

But it was more than the music that made *DeBÍ TiRAR MáS FOTOS* Bad Bunny's most Puerto Rican album yet. *DeBÍ TiRAR MáS FOTOS* is perhaps Bad Bunny's most politicized work to date. The album celebrates Puerto Rican resilience and joy while simultaneously offering a searing political critique of US colonialism in Puerto Rico. The media campaign leading up to the album's release on the day before the important Puerto Rican holiday Three Kings' Day (January 6) included a twelve-minute short film that starred Puerto Rican actor and film director Jacobo Morales and an animated sapo concho, which is a critically endangered crested toad that is endemic to Puerto Rico. Like many of the lyrics of the album, the short film tackled gentrification in Puerto Rico, which, as we discuss later in this book, is devastating to the archipelago's culture, land, and people. *DeBÍ TiRAR MáS*

FOToS was as much a musical masterpiece as it was a political rallying cry, one firmly rooted in the culture, concerns, and traditions of Puerto Ricans. As we described in our album review for *Latina*, "The album draws from the long history of Puerto Rican music-making as a form of resistance, particularly against U.S. colonialism, and the use of art and dance to tell stories of everyday Puerto Rican life, joy, and struggle."[16] For those who remained skeptical, *DeBÍ TiRAR MáS FOToS* underscored that Bad Bunny was still committed to Puerto Rico and Puerto Ricans, and that he would continue to utilize his platform to shed light on the issues facing his homeland.

Bad Bunny was born in 1994 in Vega Baja, Puerto Rico, the eldest son of a truck driver and a schoolteacher. His life has been marked by a series of political, economic, and social crises in Puerto Rico, including a ruinous debt crisis, failing infrastructure, and pervasive governmental corruption. At the same time, the past thirty years of Puerto Rican history have also revealed the innovation and self-determination of Puerto Ricans in the face of their ongoing colonial realities. It is undeniable that colonialism and the acute moments of crises in Puerto Rico have shaped his life both as Benito Antonio Martínez Ocasio, in many ways a typical Puerto Rican millennial with working-class origins, and as Bad Bunny, the distinctive world-renowned artist. As opposed to growing distant from his roots in his ascent, Bad Bunny's success is in large part *because* of his unapologetic championing of his homeland and *through* the intimate connections he maintains to Puerto Rico.

Many of the people we interviewed for this book observed how incredible it is that Puerto Rico, a tiny island just thirty-five by one hundred miles, could produce such an abundance of huge pop culture figures. From baseball icon Roberto Clemente to salsero Ismael Rivera to pop superstar Ricky Martin, legendary Puerto Ricans have made their mark in the United States and around the world. Jowell, of the popular reggaetón duo Jowell y Randy (a group that also is one of Bad Bunny's own musical influences), told us, "Many times people like you ask us, 'Look, what is so special about Puerto Rico that makes our music special?' It is such a small island and yet somehow it is a powerhouse in culture, music, and art." Another reggaetón and Latin trap artist, De La Ghetto, told us, "Everywhere I go, people ask me, 'man, how can such a small island like Puerto Rico produce so many athletes and musicians?' That's the question they ask me in other countries. And I just say, 'Cabrón, I don't know!'" For music producer Eduardo Cabra, Bad Bunny's success is indebted in part to his Puerto Rican roots. Eduardo, who produced the song "WELTiTA" on

DeBÍ TiRAR MáS FOToS, told us, "It is no coincidence that Bad Bunny is Puerto Rican."

We borrow the title of our book *P FKN R* from Bad Bunny's anthem to Puerto Rico on his 2020 album *YHLQMDLG*.[17] Short for "Puerto Fuckin' Rico," P FKN R itself reflects the impacts of US colonialism on Puerto Rican Spanish and culture. As linguistic anthropologist Jonathan Rosa notes, it is an example of expletive infixation that indicates deep knowledge of, and familiarity with, English linguistic norms that come as a result of over one hundred years of US colonial rule.[18] But P FKN R is not just a reflection of US cultural imposition. P FKN R is a ubiquitous phrase in Bad Bunny's repertoire because it embodies the struggles and joy of Puerto Rican life. It reflects the duality of life in the archipelago, wherein FKN refers to both the positive and the negative. It is an expression of both pride in Puerto Ricanness and frustration with the problems wrought by colonialism on the archipelago. This duality informs the magnificent art that has emerged from Puerto Rico and that contributes to the many evolving forms of daily resistance to oppression and colonialism that are part of Puerto Rican life.

Resistance is not a monolithic concept. Instead, resistance can take on many different forms to serve the particular circumstances and needs of resistors. In the case of Puerto Rico, its more than five hundred years (and counting) of colonialism—first at the hands of Spain and then the United States—has created a situation in which continuous resistance is the only option. As historian Jorell Meléndez-Badillo explains, from the moment Spanish colonizers arrived on the shores of Puerto Rico, the Indigenous Taíno people of Borikén—or what is now referred to as Puerto Rico— "realized that the colonizers were not to be trusted."[19] For this reason, Meléndez-Badillo refers to the Taínos as "the people who resisted conquest by Columbus."[20] And so began the centuries-long resistance to colonization. Puerto Ricans have engaged in different types of resistance, from music and dance, to visual art and poetry, to organized protests and armed rebellion, to simply holding up a Puerto Rican flag (which at one point under American rule could land Puerto Ricans in prison).[21] The phrase P FKN R is itself an exhibition of that resistance. Despite the infixation of the colonizer's language in the middle of PR, P FKN R is prideful, powerful, and forceful.

P FKN R—as a title, as a mantra, as a way of life—also opens a space to honor the vulgar. As a reggaetón artist, Bad Bunny has been subject to the same cultural paranoia and concerns that have always impacted the genre.

Since the early days of his career, Bad Bunny has been publicly accused of being, in part, responsible for societal problems in Puerto Rico.[22] Kacho López Mari, a renowned film director and producer who has directed several projects for Bad Bunny, told us in an interview that one of the most impressive things about Bad Bunny is the range of topics he covers in his songs, from the socially conscious to the vulgar: "He doesn't give a fuck. He's going to talk about sexual stuff. He doesn't hesitate to get explicit, very explicit. But the way I see it, that's the way he talks, and the world is able to consume it and somehow connect with that message. The truth is that he says it in a way that is very much his own. He is a musical genius." In media coverage of Bad Bunny's historic 2022 concerts in Puerto Rico, parents who brought their teenagers to the concert looked beyond the vulgarity of some of his lyrics, acknowledging that his work is part of a historical movement of young people in Puerto Rico, and they wanted their children to be connected to that history.[23]

Vulgarity, or perceptions of vulgarity, were also key to the 2019 mass uprisings in Puerto Rico (also known as the Verano Boricua), which included perreo as protest. Perreo, the dance associated with reggaetón, is typically danced back-to-front, with the person in the front provocatively gyrating their hips against their partner's pelvis. The term perreo presumably comes from the Spanish word "perro," or dog, because it is said to mimic the sexual act between dogs. The explicit nature of perreo has made the dance a subject of concern, scorn, and even a censorship campaign.[24] At the same time, others have also considered perreo a space of liberation and freedom.[25] In this spirit, the (mostly queer) youths who convened on the steps of the iconic cathedral in Old San Juan to dance perreo were intentional in their audacity and "fearless vulgarity" during the mass protests in 2019.[26] Since queerness has historically been equated with vulgarity, Bad Bunny's often gender nonconforming presentation of self, along with his advocacy for issues like ending gender-based violence that disproportionately impact women and LGBTQ+ folks, has contributed to perceptions of him as vulgar. Although reggaetón has rightly been accused of being misogynistic and homophobic, reggaetón's relationship to vulgarity and broader social unacceptability has, at the same time, connected it to queerness.[27] Reggaetón has never been interested in respectability. Instead, reggaetón disrupts the associations between Puerto Ricanness and respectability while also shining light on the ongoing colonial realities facing the archipelago.[28]

Thus, taking cues from the pioneering Puerto Rican reggaetón artists who came before him, Bad Bunny has maintained that his music is not the reason for Puerto Rico's social woes. In 2018, the now disgraced governor Ricardo Rosselló requested via social media that Bad Bunny add a third night to his spring 2019 concerts at El Coliseo de Puerto Rico José Miguel Agrelot (locally called "El Choli"), Puerto Rico's largest indoor concert venue. In response, a Puerto Rican school teacher took to social media to critique Bad Bunny, accusing his vulgar, uncouth lyrics as contributing to a "generation of idiots" in Puerto Rico.[29] When the teacher's social media post went viral, Bad Bunny posted a multipage statement to his Instagram account to respond to both her and Rosselló. In response to Rosselló's request, he said: "My dignity as a Boricua won't allow it, knowing that there are much more important issues than me performing a third concert."[30] He was referencing the numerous problems plaguing Puerto Rico, from the ongoing debt crisis to the inept government response to Hurricane María. Then, Bad Bunny thanked the teacher for her service to the community but also held her accountable in her role as an educator of Puerto Rico's youths: "Know that this artist you're criticizing is just another product of the educational system of my country, so you and your colleagues have also contributed to a successful plan of creating a 'generation of idiots.' . . . [One] where they tell you that Christopher Columbus is a hero and is good, but it is bad to want to know more than the teachers and ask difficult questions."[31] This incident demonstrates how Bad Bunny turns the accusations of vulgarity around to show that the real vulgarities happen at the level of state failure, colonial policies, and racist and classist attitudes that mark Puerto Rican society.

Bad Bunny has effectively utilized his platform to express the pride and the frustration encapsulated in the phrase P FKN R. He always represents Puerto Rico, which is partially what makes him so admired and respected by his peers. "Other people would have kept it neutral, because [they're] trying to be global and [they're] trying to get more ears," Marissa Lopez, head of Latin Artist Relations for Apple Music, who has collaborated with Bad Bunny and his team on several album rollouts, told us. "But Benito beats to his own drum." Bad Bunny's producer MAG explained to us that when Bad Bunny "started showing where he stands politically about things that are happening on the island," it endeared him more to Puerto Ricans both in Puerto Rico and the diaspora. Reggaetón artist Jowell explained to us that part of Bad Bunny's appeal is that he constantly represents Puerto Rico: "Well, I think Bad Bunny is like the maximum expression of Puerto Rico. . . . He said, no matter how big I am, I'm always going to keep writing in Puerto Rico, talking about Puerto Rico, talking about the culture of Puerto Rico, which I think is something that is interesting for the whole world." As Kacho told us, "Benito uses Puerto Rican identity as a jumping off point for everything. He is truly inspired by it. There's something impressive about his ability to see the value and the potential in Puerto Ricanness. With it, Boricua creation has been able to conquer the world on a global level."

Since 2020, Bad Bunny has dominated global popular culture with his groundbreaking albums, historic performances, and dazzling chart stats. For Gus Lopez, veteran music executive and founder of reggaetón label Machete Music, Bad Bunny's unique voice, brilliant stage presence, connection with the audience, and unconventional approach make him a "once in a generation artist. He does everything you are not supposed to do, and it works! Then, on top of that, he's a beast on stage." Tainy, Bad Bunny's longtime collaborator and producer who is himself a legend in reggaetón, similarly sees Bad Bunny as a groundbreaking artist of their generation. Reflecting on the significance of Bad Bunny performing in US mainstream spaces like the *Tonight Show with Jimmy Fallon*, Tainy told us:

> It's not normal for a Latin artist to be in those [US mainstream spaces]. It is important not just for Puerto Rico, but also Latin America. He's an artist who's famous right now. He's made it. He's making his money and he's doing his thing, but at the end of the day we can understand that he is a human being like any other person who knows the different circumstances that people live in. And you can see that he's someone so important, coming from our country, but also watching over the country. These are the things that separate him from other artists.

Tainy's view that Bad Bunny is a global icon not just for Puerto Rico but also for Latin America resonates with many, as does the fact that his politics have been instrumental in his rise. Bad Bunny himself regularly underscores that he intends to live in Puerto Rico forever. As he told Puerto Rican podcaster Anthony Cáceres, who goes by the nickname "El Tony," "I live here, I own property here, thank God I can afford it. If I need a property somewhere, let's say in LA because I'm making a couple of movies, so for work reasons, anyone who asks me 'Where do you live?' I don't say, 'I live in LA' or 'I live in New York.' I say, 'I live in Puerto Rico.' Right now, I'm sleeping in LA, but I live in Puerto Rico. It's different."[32] Bad

Bunny still works with his high school friends, and he is still connected to his community of Almirante Sur in the municipality of Vega Baja. In 2023, he told *Billboard*:

> I like to be connected with people. And when I say "connected," it's not "Ah I want to share this with my fans." No, it's "What's happening in Puerto Rico?" If I were still working at the supermarket, how would I view things? I want to feel that connection. . . . Maybe I'm not walking around in the streets anymore, but I'm aware of what's happening in the street. My friends are all there. They all live in their hometowns, where they've always lived, and everyone is still the same and they have their families and the same friends they've had for years like I do. If someone in the neighborhood dies, I know. If someone gets pregnant, I also find out.[33]

In a similar vein, Bad Bunny told El Tony that, even though he has achieved so much success that he could live anywhere in the world, he wants to stay in Puerto Rico and live among Puerto Ricans. He said, "I don't want to live in [the municipality of] Dorado where I have a house with a pool. I don't want to live in a bubble where everything is fine when I know that beyond the gates, things aren't good. . . . If I ever have kids, man, I don't want to raise them in a little golf resort. I want to let them go out into the neighborhood, not live in a bubble."[34] Bad Bunny's references to Dorado and golf resorts point to the intensive gentrification happening in Puerto Rico. Laws like Act 60 paved the way for wealthy Americans to move to Puerto Rico and settle in areas like the highly gentrified seaside town of Dorado, where luxury buildings and exclusive resorts have displaced Puerto Ricans and cut off public access points to local beaches.[35] As a multimillionaire, Bad Bunny is one of the few Puerto Ricans who can actually afford to live in places like Dorado, but he prefers to stay in the "neighborhood," around his fellow Puerto Ricans.

Bad Bunny has deftly utilized his platform as a global superstar to advocate for Puerto Rico, building on the long tradition of infusing joy and protest into his music as a form of resistance. This is what makes him such an effective spokesperson for Puerto Rico. Pablo Batista, who has worked with reggaetón artists since the genre's earliest days, told us, "Everything that Benito has done to this day is always meaningful to Puerto Rico. For the first time, we have someone that can tell the world what we are feeling and is not a government person that has his own agenda. . . . If we're fucked, he will tell you that, 'Hey, we're fucked. We need help.'" It is clear from our interviews with producers, artists, and other industry figures that Bad Bunny has become increasingly intentional and open about using his work and his enormous platform to advocate for Puerto Rico, calling out its failing infrastructure or endemic corruption while also expressing utmost pride in and hope for Puerto Rico.[36] *P FKN R* demonstrates how Bad Bunny's work, from his earliest days as a SoundCloud rapper to his current global superstar status, reflects and helps to shape the discourse on Puerto Rican life over the past thirty years. His art is part of a long history of Puerto Rican resistance.

BRIEF PRIMER ON PUERTO RICAN HISTORY

When Bad Bunny released *DeBÍ TiRAR MáS FOToS*, his team hired historian Jorell Meléndez-Badillo to write text that would be displayed in the YouTube visualizers for each song on the album. Visualizers are streamed visuals such as a series of photographs or a scene that are loosely connected to an album's theme, appearing on screen while a song's audio plays.[37] For *DeBÍ TiRAR MáS FOToS*, Bad Bunny wanted the visualizers for each song to contain a different history lesson about Puerto Rico that fans could read while listening to the song. He wanted to leverage his platform to shed light on aspects of Puerto Rican history that even he, as someone educated in Puerto Rican public schools, never learned. Meléndez-Badillo wrote text about a wide range of topics, from the Grito de Lares in 1868, in which Puerto Ricans attempted to overthrow the Spanish, to the creation of the Puerto Rican flag, to early twentieth-century labor activism, to the growth of the Puerto Rican diaspora.[38] Blending popular culture with direct educational content was not only a clever idea; it also provided important context and information with which to interpret the songs on the album. Similarly, our goal with this book is to enlist Bad Bunny's work to shed light on both the many crises facing Puerto Rico and their roots in Puerto Rico's colonial relationship with the United States. Although a full, detailed account of Puerto Rican history is beyond the scope of this book, in the following paragraphs we provide some basic background about Puerto Rico since 1898, when the United States established itself as a global power and Puerto Rico became one of its most important territories.[39]

The United States obtained Puerto Rico—along with Guam, the Philippines, and Cuba—from Spain at the end of the Spanish-American War in

1898. After a brief military government, the Foraker Act in 1900 established a new government, led by a governor who was appointed by the US president, alongside Puerto Rican elected officials in the Puerto Rican house of representatives. Still, the matter of what to do with the Puerto Rican population remained a problem for many US politicians and elites who saw Puerto Ricans as racially inferior and unassimilable into the United States.[40] Shortly after the Foraker Act, a series of US Supreme Court cases known as the Insular Cases (1901–22) established Puerto Rico as a territory that was "foreign in a domestic sense," meaning that Puerto Rico was a "domestic" possession of the United States but too "foreign" to actually be integrated into the country.[41]

Citizenship was one of the most critical complexities of this arrangement. Puerto Ricans were not US citizens, nor were they citizens of any other country (because Puerto Rico was not a sovereign state). In 1917, the US Congress passed the Jones-Shafroth Act that enforced US citizenship on all Puerto Ricans, including those born and raised in the archipelago. However, Puerto Ricans' citizenship to this day does not grant full civic rights to people living in the archipelago of Puerto Rico. For instance, Puerto Ricans cannot vote in US presidential elections, nor do they have voting representation in the US Congress; however, Puerto Ricans are eligible for the military draft.[42] In fact, legal historian Sam Erman refers to Puerto Ricans as "almost citizens," meaning that despite being classified as US citizens, the US never intended to grant them full citizenship rights.[43]

In 1948, things shifted slightly when Puerto Ricans were, for the first time, permitted to elect their own governor—a seasoned politician named Luis Muñoz Marín, who served four consecutive terms from 1949 to 1965. Under his leadership, Puerto Rico passed its own constitution in 1952 and established a new political status: the Estado Libre Asociado (ELA), or Free Associated State. For Muñoz Marín and other supporters of the ELA, this seemed like a great compromise that would grant Puerto Rico autonomy while maintaining its ties to the United States. Muñoz Marín's administration and the US government claimed that the ELA was not a colonial arrangement but rather a unique "compact" into which both parties had entered voluntarily, an argument they made in front of the United Nations General Assembly to remove Puerto Rico from the list of non-self-governing territories.[44] However, in practice, ELA status only further entrenched US colonial rule in Puerto Rico. For example, when Puerto Rico sent its 1952 constitution to the US Congress for approval, Congress not only eliminated some of the policies the constitution included—those granting free education, housing security, and the like—but also ensured that, at the end of the day, the United States would always have the final say when it came to Puerto Rico.[45] The US Constitution supersedes anything written in the Puerto Rican constitution, and the US Congress retains the right to modify or reject any legislation in Puerto Rico.[46]

Throughout this time, Puerto Ricans also resisted US colonialism. Major pro-independence leaders, most notably Pedro Albizu Campos, emerged in the mid-twentieth century to encourage Puerto Ricans to fight for their sovereignty. Others participated in acts of armed resistance, such as when Blanca Canales led a small uprising in the town of Jayuya in 1950, or when four activists—Lolita Lebrón, Rafael Cancel Miranda, Andrés Figueroa Cordero, and Irving Flores—fired gunshots from the Capitol rotunda during a meeting of the US Congress in 1954.[47] In addition, students, union workers, feminists, and people in the Puerto Rican diaspora mobilized around workers' rights, reproductive rights, US military actions, and environmental justice.[48] These movements have faced repression from the United States and even from the Puerto Rican government; and yet, as we show throughout this book, mobilizations, organizing, and protest continue to be important facets of Puerto Rican life.

This context is necessary for understanding how the current moment in Puerto Rico has shaped Bad Bunny's work. The ongoing debt crisis, the aftermath of Hurricane María and other natural disasters, the massive gentrification and displacement taking place on the archipelago, and the more recent dramatic cuts to social services such as healthcare and education all have their roots in this long colonial history. What's more, Bad Bunny's work is also part of this long history of resistance in Puerto Rico. Whether by leaving his tour in Europe in 2019 to join protests to oust then-governor Ricardo Rosselló, or by adding a twenty-two-minute documentary about gentrification at the end of his 2022 music video for "El Apagón," or by incorporating imagery and lyrical references to Puerto Rican independence in his 2025 song "LA MuDANZA," Bad Bunny has increasingly used his platform to advocate for Puerto Rico.

1

LAS COSAS ESTÁN EMPEORANDO: PUERTO RICO IN THE ERA OF "SOY PEOR"

Rafael Castillo Torres, better known by his artist name De La Ghetto, started recording rap music in 2005, when he was about twenty-one years old, with his contemporary Austin Agustín Santos, better known by his artist name Arcángel. (While they were only the duo Arcángel y De La Ghetto for about a year, they have continued to work together periodically.) Over the next two decades, De La Ghetto would create a new Spanish-language rap and R&B sound that would become the basis of Latin trap. In many ways, Arcángel y De La Ghetto were ahead of their time, fusing hip-hop beats and R&B riffs with Spanish-language lyrics at a time when the more Caribbean-based reggaetón ruled the airwaves.

Bad Bunny then took Latin trap to new heights. As De La Ghetto told us from his home in Orlando, Florida, "Bad [Bunny] brought [the genre] to a global level . . . the number one artist in the world." Bad Bunny, in De La Ghetto's telling, was gracious about building on the work of earlier Latin trap artists. He recalled what it was like to realize that Bad Bunny and others in this new generation of rappers were so impacted by his work: "They looked at me like, 'Damn! De La Ghetto!' . . . when they were in the studio they listened to us. We sang at their prom."

In 2023, Bad Bunny called De La Ghetto to talk about making a new song together. The two had collaborated on the 2016 hit "Caile," which also featured artists Bryant Myers and Zion. At the time of "Caile"'s release, Bad Bunny had been a new trap star who had yet to record an album. By 2023, Bad Bunny had become one of the biggest artists not only in Latin trap but in the world. When he called, De La Ghetto explained, "I just felt like, you know, Batman was calling me, like, all the DC heroes. 'Bro, there's a problem, come to New York.'"

De La Ghetto arrived at the studio in New York to record with Bad Bunny, Tainy, Arcángel, and Ñengo Flow (another Puerto Rican artist who began in the mid-2000s). According to De La Ghetto, the vibe in the studio was electric. Everybody "left [their egos] outside the door" to support Bad Bunny and his idea to create a song that celebrated life in Puerto Rico's working-class barrios and caseríos (public housing developments). The song would become a new anthem for Puerto Rico—"ACHO PR."

Bad Bunny released the music video for "ACHO PR" on March 10, 2024—his thirtieth birthday. The nearly twelve-minute video documents the making of the song. Viewers see De La Ghetto, Arcángel, and Ñengo Flow arrive at the studio in Manhattan. Between the footage of each of them rapping their verses, everyone singing happy birthday to De La Ghetto and Bad Bunny's close friend and creative director Janthony Oliveras, and the group joking around and hanging out, fans get a rare glimpse into Bad Bunny's creative process.[1]

Bad Bunny is more than just a rapper. He is also a widely respected producer and songwriter. His creative partners and producers MAG and Tainy both told us how much they love that he actively participates in all aspects of the production. MAG told us, "I've been fortunate enough in my career to have been in the room with some of the best songwriters of all time. Benito is probably the best writer I've ever been in the room with." Tainy similarly described feeling completely in awe when he first met Bad Bunny: "I understood after talking with him that all the music he had put out were his own beats. And that also blew my mind because I was listening to this super cool music from this new young kid from Puerto Rico, and, well, I thought I could tell that there were other producers involved or whatever, but then to see that these production ideas also came from him was like, 'Damn, this isn't normal!'" De La Ghetto told us, "I would say that he was like a Puerto Rican Kanye [West] in the sense that he raps, he mixes, and he did his own beats." The music video for "ACHO PR" shows Bad Bunny working on beats on the computer with Tainy, listening to recordings-in-progress on his headphones, and offering Ñengo Flow, De La Ghetto, and Arcángel tips on their verses and vocal delivery.

Bad Bunny's feedback was one of the things that De La Ghetto loved most about the process of recording "ACHO PR." He recalled, "[Bad Bunny] helped us out a little bit, like he would listen to our verses, like 'let me listen to that, dadadadada, I like that, change that,' papapapa, and we just all did the record together." It was a true exchange. "I would say something, he liked it, he would tell me something, and it was just working back and forth," De La Ghetto said. Sometimes Bad Bunny's tips for the current recording were based on the older artists' previous songs, reflecting his deep knowledge of their catalogs. De La Ghetto remembered a time when he wasn't sure what Bad Bunny meant. He remembered saying, "'Ah, bro, what do you mean? Let me hear you out, what do you want? ¿Qué tú quieres?'" Bad Bunny's response was, "'Cabrón, remember on that track what you did, when you first started, yo, remember that flow?'"

Bad Bunny could make those recommendations because he was a true student of these artists who came before him. "Benito says it all the time, like, we're his inspirations, me, Arcángel, Jowell y Randy," De La Ghetto told us. The recording includes such a statement: after Ñengo Flow's verse in "ACHO PR." Bad Bunny says, "Cabrón, eso fue lo que me crié escuchando desde chamaquito, a Arca, De La, Ñengo. Papi, que están aquí se siente muy cabrón, de verdad, de corazón" (Damn, this was what I grew up listening to from when I was a little boy, Arcángel, De La Ghetto, Ñengo. Papi, it feels amazing that they're here, for real, from the heart).

De La Ghetto had always known that he had been an inspiration to Bad Bunny, but the depth of that influence was not clear to De La Ghetto until they recorded "ACHO PR." He recalled that during the recording process, Bad Bunny told him that the song "Solo y Vacio" on De La Ghetto's 2008 album *Masacre Musical* had been important to him. De La Ghetto told us that Bad Bunny said: "'I had this girlfriend and she dumped me. Bro, I would listen to that song every night before I went to bed, I listened to it every night, and every night I cried. I cried to that song.'" De La Ghetto was amazed. "These are things I never thought about when I first did the record. But then, thinking about it now, it's like, wow, look, Benito listened to that song, that was one of his favorite records."

Such information is vindicating for De La Ghetto. For years, he had been told that rap and R&B in Spanish would never sell. "I got a lot of criticism from a lot of people," he told us. People told him that he was too Americanized, trying to do too much rap, too much Spanglish, too little reggaetón. But, he persevered, becoming one of the founders of the Latin trap sound. "I always knew this style would be a hit," he told us.

De La Ghetto started rapping in 2005, when Bad Bunny was only about eleven years old. It wasn't just skepticism from other rappers and producers that made these early years difficult for De La Ghetto. This was also the time when the Puerto Rican economy, which was already struggling due to decades of colonial fiscal policy that profoundly disadvantaged Puerto Rico, began to enter a deep recession. De La Ghetto told us he felt this crisis very acutely. In 2006, the tax breaks that many US companies enjoyed in Puerto Rico disappeared, and thousands of Puerto Ricans lost their jobs.[2] This unleashed what historian Jorell Meléndez-Badillo calls a "fiscal disaster."[3] During Bad Bunny's formative years and De La Ghetto's early career, Puerto Rico saw an even more intense phase of austerity that plunged the archipelago further into crisis. By the time Bad Bunny released his first single "Diles" in 2016, Puerto Rico faced an unprecedented political and economic crisis. This was the backdrop for the rise of Latin trap, a genre that represented the barrios and caseríos described in "ACHO PR," and for the rise of Bad Bunny.

On November 3, 2024, Bad Bunny appeared at the Festival de Esperanza (Festival of Hope) in San Juan to support Juan Dalmau, the pro-independence gubernatorial candidate. Dalmau ran as part of a new political alliance, La Alianza, comprising the Puerto Rican Independence Party and the Movimiento Victoria Ciudadana (Citizen's Victory Movement). The race was historic because it was the first time that a pro-independence candidate actually had a shot at winning the governorship. Bad Bunny and many of his peers, including reggaetón artists Young Miko, Residente, Rauw Alejandro, and Jowell y Randy, among others, actively supported Dalmau. Many of these artists are part of a generation of Puerto Ricans who had grown up under the shadow of Puerto Rico's debt crisis. In his speech at the festival, Bad Bunny talked about being part of a generation that was disillusioned with the status quo and wanted a change. He stated, "I'm part of the generation born during one of the most corrupt administrations this country has seen. Nobody told me this. I was born here, I was raised here, and I live here. I lived through it."[4]

Indeed, Bad Bunny's lifetime has witnessed some of the most important problems leading up to the current debt crisis. He was born in Bayamón in 1994, just two years after President Bill Clinton eliminated Section 936 of the US tax code. In 1976, the US Congress codified Section 936 at the behest of Puerto Rican Governor Rafael Hernández Colón.[5] Section 936 exempted US corporations doing business in Puerto Rico from paying federal taxes on their profits, even after transferring the funds back into the United States. It allowed corporations to move patents and other assets to Puerto Rico to avoid federal taxes on those, as well. What's more, it exempted these corporations from paying taxes upon liquidation, which meant that assets and profits could be passed to corporate officers and shareholders without tax liability.

In a video interview from his office in Puerto Rico, Alejandro García Padilla (governor of Puerto Rico from 2013 to 2017) told us that he considered Section 936 a successful intervention because the 1970s oil crisis would have caused an economic recession in Puerto Rico without it. In the 1960s, the Puerto Rican government had made significant investments in increasing oil refining for export into the United States. However, Arab states imposed an embargo on United States oil in 1973. In response, the United States lifted restrictions on foreign oil imports, which placed Puerto Rico at a strategic disadvantage. This move, along with local environmental activism challenging the oil project, decimated the economic potential of Puerto Rico's oil refineries.[6] The archipelago's economy entered a severe recession, with unemployment hovering around 20 percent in 1976.[7] García Padilla credited Section 936 with bringing factories, jobs, and investment to Puerto Rico. Some manufacturers, such as pharmaceutical companies, relocated to Puerto Rico, providing jobs to the local population. However, researchers have demonstrated that Section 936's tax breaks were primarily successful in drawing capital rather than factories to the archipelago and that, as a result, it created substantially fewer jobs than its architects had promised.[8] Section 936 did not happen in a vacuum; instead, it was simply the latest in a longer history of implementing policies that bolstered Puerto Rico's economic dependency on the United States and that ensured capital would flow from Puerto Rico into the hands of US corporations.[9] In the case of Section 936, critics like Meléndez-Badillo argue that it "consolidated Puerto Rico's dependence on foreign investment."[10] In the long term, it would eventually prove to be an unsustainable economic plan with disastrous results for Puerto Rico.

In 1992, the United States, Mexico, and Canada approved the North American Free Trade Agreement (NAFTA), which created a free-trade zone across the region. And with that, Puerto Rico's advantages over other Latin American countries in terms of a low-cost labor force and favorable financial conditions for US companies effectively dissipated.[11] Clinton's phaseout of Section 936 began in 1996. He maintained that this legislation unfairly allowed corporations to avoid paying federal taxes, thus increasing the US national deficit. The Puerto Rican governor at the time, Pedro Rosselló, a member of the pro-statehood party, supported the elimination of Section 936 as well. According to García Padilla, Rosselló believed that Section 936 was incompatible with Puerto Rico eventually becoming a state since the policy was viable only if Puerto Rico remained a colony.[12] The phaseout of Section 936 between 1996 and 2006 proved to be another devastating blow to Puerto Rico. Thousands of Puerto Ricans lost their jobs when many of the corporations that had benefited from the tax code left.[13]

However, even with the end of Section 936, US investors still enjoyed several financial benefits that made investments in Puerto Rico attractive, especially in relation to Puerto Rican bonds. The Puerto Rican government has used bonds since the 1940s to fund operations, selling them to US entities. Bonds are, essentially, IOUs that government agencies issue to creditors in order to borrow funds. These government bonds are considered safe because governments usually pay their debts. Puerto Rico's bonds are understood to be particularly safe. Puerto Rico, unlike other US municipalities, cannot access Chapter 9 bankruptcy, and the territory's constitution requires the repayment of its public debt over all other financial obligations. Furthermore, creditors do not pay local or federal taxes on any of their earnings from Puerto Rican bonds.[14] Investors thus know they will always be repaid, and they will always profit.

According to García Padilla, Puerto Rican deficit spending continued at a rapid clip after the phaseout of Section 936 in 2006 cut off tax revenue. He explained that the Puerto Rican government "began to take out new loans in 2006 without any way to repay it. So, they took out loans that they paid later on with more loans." Thus, Puerto Rico plunged into a deeper debt crisis. García Padilla said that this policy resulted in the accumulation of $40 billion of debt between 2006 and 2012—twice the amount that Puerto Rico had accumulated from 1940 to 2006.

Discussions of the Puerto Rican debt in the US media also blamed Puerto Ricans themselves for amassing such a large amount of debt, calling Puerto Rico a "welfare island." This accusation posited that Puerto Ricans irresponsibly entered into copious amounts of debt because of their alleged laziness and poor lifestyle.[15] However, Puerto Rico's colonial status meant it had few options. As a colony, Puerto Rico was not only barred from declaring bankruptcy in US courts; it could also neither borrow from nor enter into financial agreements with organizations like the International Monetary Fund as a sovereign nation would. The archipelago is beholden to the United States for its finances. From this perspective, the irresponsible party is not Puerto Rico but instead the US financial institutions that continued to loan money to Puerto Rico. They knew that repaying the loans would present serious financial hardships for Puerto Ricans; and yet these vulture funds disregarded this fact because they also knew that, no matter what, Puerto Rico would have to pay them back.

In addition to extensive borrowing to fund basic government operations, several Puerto Rican administrations implemented severe austerity measures. In the 1990s, the administration of Governor Pedro Rosselló promoted the privatization of public services and drastic cuts to the public sector, a practice that continued with subsequent administrations, regardless of political party. In 2008, García Padilla's predecessor Luis Fortuño immediately implemented far-reaching austerity measures, including mass layoffs of public-sector employees, which sparked significant protests around the archipelago.[16]

As a preteen, Bad Bunny likely witnessed some of the mass mobilizations that occurred during Fortuño's administration, and many students in his generation took the cuts to public schools personally. Political scientist José Laguarta Ramírez notes that, given the scale of public service cuts, the singer probably experienced at least one school closure that lasted a few days or more. Bad Bunny's mother, Lysaurie Ocasio, worked as a schoolteacher, and Laguarte Ramírez points out that, with respect to the mobilizations, "It seems likely that there would have been some sympathy in the household."[17] A 2020 *Pitchfork* article mentions that Bad Bunny's mother was out of work for a period when he was fifteen; although the article does not state exactly why, the timing (2009) coincides with the passage of Law 7 during Fortuño's administration, which laid off thirty thousand public employees.[18] Bad Bunny acknowledged this outright in 2024 during his speech at the

Festival de Esperanza when he stated, "At 18, in my ignorance, blinded by bipartisanship, my first vote went to one of the biggest contributors to the debt the people now have to pay—a traitor who left over 30,000 families, including mine, without work," referring to Fortuño.

In addition to such dramatic austerity measures, Fortuño's administration helped pass Act 20 and Act 22 in 2012, both of which provided US investors incentives to relocate to Puerto Rico by offering a low tax rate of 4 percent and exempting them from any capital gains tax.[19] In essence, Act 20 and Act 22 gave individuals the types of tax credits that Section 936 had previously extended to US corporations, with the hope of luring high-net-worth Americans to Puerto Rico. Writer Ed Morales points out that despite assumptions that the relocation of wealthy Americans to Puerto Rico would spur economic growth, "there is no mechanism to ensure that a significant portion of their investment goes to Puerto Rican economic development."[20] Furthermore, while Fortuño's administration justified slashing funding for public services like the University of Puerto Rico as a way of addressing the debt, he also thrust the archipelago deeper into debt. Puerto Rico accumulated an additional $16 billion in debt during Fortuño's tenure from 2009 to 2013.[21]

Although García Padilla did not share Fortuño's party affiliation, he also implemented austerity measures, supported US investment in Puerto Rico, and continued borrowing in an effort to stave off greater economic turmoil. For instance, Meléndez-Badillo notes that "one of García Padilla's first acts was to privatize the Luis Muñoz Marín Airport" in 2013.[22] This controversial move made Puerto Rico's main airport the only fully privatized airport in the United States and its territories.[23] Meléndez-Badillo also points out that García Padilla's administration significantly reduced union power, wages, and benefits for government employees, the largest employment sector in Puerto Rico.[24] Thus, austerity measures, privatization, and excessive borrowing remained a problem even during García Padilla's administration.

Just two years into García Padilla's administration, Puerto Rican bonds received a rating of "junk status." Normally junk bonds have a very high risk of default. For investors willing to take the risk, these junk bonds have a very high rate of return. However, Puerto Rico's constitutional requirement to repay its debts above all else meant that the normally risky junk bond rating would lead to big profits for investors, even though this also virtually guaranteed that Puerto Ricans would suffer. Hospitals, schools, and retirement accounts were all at risk because whatever money existed in Puerto Rico's coffers went right into the hands of US banks and hedge funds.

García Padilla told us that by May of 2015, he knew that Puerto Rico would not be able to make its next debt repayment. He had proposed a series of measures that he thought could help, including a Value Added Tax that he had hoped would allow Puerto Rico to avoid default, but the legislature would not pass it. He also tried to work with federal entities. As García Padilla told us, "We also proposed alternatives to the federal treasury, alternatives that they did not accept. We proposed alternatives to [the US] Congress, alternatives that they did not accept." His hands were tied.

On June 28, 2015, García Padilla gave what Ed Morales called one of the most consequential gubernatorial addresses in Puerto Rico's history.[25] Sitting at his desk, García Padilla stated in a somber tone that Puerto Rico could not pay off its $72 billion debt. "This is not politics, this is math," he declared.[26] The money was simply not there. Puerto Rico was on the precipice of an unprecedented financial crisis and needed some kind of relief.

The governor's declaration that Puerto Rico was bound for default caught the attention of many people in the United States, including government officials and, especially, those managers of hedge funds and other financial institutions who expected to be repaid. Consequently, the discussion of how to resolve this crisis prioritized how to make it possible to pay back Puerto Rico's creditors. On June 30, 2016, President Barack Obama signed a bipartisan bill called PROMESA, which was presented as a "generous" opportunity for Puerto Rico to get its finances in order. PROMESA created the Fiscal Oversight and Management Board (FOMB), commonly referred to as "La Junta" in Puerto Rico. Per the bill, the US president appoints La Junta's seven voting members. Obama's appointees, including the four Puerto Rican members, had strong ties to the financial sector; in some cases, those ties were to the same banks that profited from Puerto Rico's debt.[27] The bill stipulates that Puerto Rico's governor participates as a nonvoting member of La Junta.

García Padilla told us that La Junta was a "problem" imposed upon Puerto Rico that US Republicans in Congress required as a condition for passing PROMESA. Certainly the installation of La Junta reified the colonial relationship between Puerto Rico and the United States. Political scientist Pedro Cabán argues that "PROMESA was a legal instrument devised by the federal government to deprive the insular administration of authority to manage Puerto Rico's political economy."[28] La Junta had full control over Puerto Rico's economic restructuring, and PROMESA gave La

Junta the unilateral power to block "any new law, executive order, joint resolution, rule, or regulation" that it deemed would interfere with the new "Fiscal Plan."[29] Thus, PROMESA further entrenched the long-standing colonial arrangement that made the United States the primary decision-maker for Puerto Rico. Further, a series of US Supreme Court decisions since 2016 have reinforced Puerto Rico's lack of sovereignty, including a 2023 case that protected La Junta from obligations to release documents about its operations, even though this withholding of documents violated Puerto Rico's constitution.[30]

Although García Padilla sees La Junta as a problem, he has an optimistic view of PROMESA's impact on Puerto Rico. He told us, "Without PROMESA, Puerto Rico would have hit rock bottom. Puerto Rico did not hit rock bottom." He elaborated, "One realizes that having the protection against lawsuits that, after all, a bankruptcy law permits, they couldn't seize our accounts. It meant the banks didn't collapse, the credit unions didn't collapse. . . . It meant business stayed open, it meant that the typical Puerto Rican family wouldn't improve their quality of life really, but their quality of life wouldn't get worse, either."

Not everyone agrees. Many activists, scholars, and everyday Puerto Ricans believed that the debt itself was illegal under the Puerto Rican constitution, as it exceeded Puerto Rico's constitutional debt limit. In 2015, under pressure from citizen groups, García Padilla signed Law 97 to create a Commission for the Comprehensive Audit of Puerto Rico's Public Debt. The commission was to comprise independent citizens who would examine the legality of outstanding debts. However, this commission never formed, and García Padilla's successor, Ricardo "Ricky" Rosselló (the son of former Governor Pedro Rosselló), ultimately voided the legislation.[31] At the time of this writing, there has still not been an audit of Puerto Rico's debt.

While García Padilla had hoped that Puerto Ricans' lives would not worsen with PROMESA, the reality is that the aftermath of PROMESA has been exceptionally harsh, with negative effects compounding over time. Severe austerity measures continue. Diminishment of public services includes the closure of hundreds of schools, while the minimum wage has been reduced and the cost of living has increased.[32] The privatization of public services like Puerto Rico's electrical grid has worsened service rather than produce the cost savings and improvements that were promised. As author Carina del Valle Schorske discussed with us in an interview, Bad Bunny likely felt the economic aspects of PROMESA in other ways as well. She said he "was in the age group whose minimum wage was lowered below $5 by PROMESA," adding that he was also "a college drop-out of a public university that isn't free anymore," referring to Bad Bunny's enrollment in the University of Puerto Rico (UPR) in Arecibo for a few years before dedicating himself fully to music. In other words, Bad Bunny was one of thousands of young people in Puerto Rico directly impacted by cuts to their schools, diminished job prospects, and a deteriorating quality of life due to the severe economic crisis faced by the archipelago.

Multiple mass strikes and student-led protests against cuts to UPR occurred throughout Bad Bunny's high school and college years, even before the first massive set of cuts by La Junta took place in 2017.[33] Laguarta Ramírez attributes Bad Bunny's political discourse to a general identification with Puerto Ricans' history of political and cultural resistance to US colonialism that may have gotten its strength from observing these strikes and protests.[34] In a 2019 episode of musical artist Residente's YouTube show *El Influence[R]*, Bad Bunny agreed with Residente that UPR should never be privatized, stating that his two years there had been invaluable for his personal development and as a musician.[35]

As Carina explained to us, for members of Bad Bunny's generation, decolonization is "not some kind of abstract idea." From crumbling infrastructure and barriers to auditing government debt, they see decolonization as a matter of "looking at specific parts of the archipelago's functioning that could be decolonized." This does not mean that young people in Puerto Rico are not concerned with questions of status; rather, it means that they are instead driven by the very material realities of ongoing colonialism in Puerto Rico that have always impacted Puerto Ricans. Growing up over the past three decades, this generation has experienced a rapid and dramatic decrease in their quality of life and in the opportunities available to them. The imposition of La Junta in Puerto Rico in 2016 made it impossible to ignore the connections between the everyday struggles of Puerto Ricans and the long history of US colonialism in the archipelago. This is the sociopolitical context that shaped Bad Bunny's formative years, and the creation of his genre Latin trap.

De La Ghetto remembers what it was like before he made it big. He began his singing career in 2005, just one year before Section 936 ended completely. Times were tough. He told us:

I'm a guy from PR. I lived in the barrio. I know what it's like to work, I know what it's like to catch the bus, I know what it's like to struggle. I lived that my whole life. De verdad, I've seen it all. Before I did music, I felt like there was no hope. I was going to work all my life, or sell drugs, or just party and bullshit. There wasn't a government [youth] program for sports or music or acting. There was nothing. There was no help. It was like in the summer, we would do nothing with our lives. And I was one in a million.

De La Ghetto was born in New York City but moved to Puerto Rico when he was eight years old. In the early 2000s, he was living in La Perla, a historic working-class neighborhood along the shore, just outside of the city walls of Old San Juan. His godmother had gotten him a scholarship to study sound engineering. De La Ghetto always wanted to be a producer like his idols, hip-hop producers Timbaland and Dr. Dre.

At the time, Old San Juan started its "martes de galería" (Tuesday art night), where people would come to drink, hang out, and visit the local art galleries the first Tuesday of every month. Martes de galería ended early. Afterward, attendees, mostly college students who did not live in La Perla, would hang out there at a place called La Placita, a small plaza outside of a bodega.[36] De La Ghetto saw an opportunity. He explained, "That gave me the idea of setting up DJs, and people who would want to do spoken word, music, whatever. It was like making a platform to help these people show-case their art." After getting permission from the bodega owner to use La Placita for his shows, De La Ghetto connected with a local DJ group that had equipment, microphones, and a sound system, and the group began an open mic night following martes de galería.

De La Ghetto was shy and avoided the limelight. But one Tuesday, he decided to take a chance. "I was working in a kitchen in Old San Juan," he recalled. "So I left a little early and went down to La Perla. It was open mic, so I went in my kitchen clothes and began to improvise on stage."

When his set ended, a man from the audience approached him. This man worked for reggaetón artist Zion who had just started a record label called Baby Records. After a quick phone call during which De La Ghetto sang a cappella, Zion decided to sign him. "My [stage] name was Rafael de la Ghetto," De La Ghetto told us. "It was longer, like, inspired by Fresh Prince [of Bel Air] and Will Smith. So when I met Zion he was like, 'That name is too long. Ponte De La Ghetto.'" And so began the recording career of De La Ghetto.

As he recounted to us, De La Ghetto started working as a solo artist for Baby Records while still living in La Perla. He started hearing about Arcángel from Arcángel's classmates in night school. De La Ghetto said that people said to him, "'There's this new kid, Arcángel, you should meet him,' and vice versa they said the same thing to Arcángel. 'You should meet this guy, he's a kid from New York too, he likes the same music.'" Eventually, the two met and immediately hit it off. "When we started talking it was like wow, we had a lot in common. He's Dominican, raised in Puerto Rico. I'm half Dominican raised in Puerto Rico. We were both born in New York. We just hit it off muy rápido, ¿entiendes?"

The two decided to start making music together as a duo in 2005. At that time, reggaetón was becoming increasingly popular on a global level. But Arcángel y De La Ghetto had a different kind of vision. Their main inspirations were hip-hop and R&B coming out of the United States. De La Ghetto explained, "I always thought, ven acá, how come no one is doing this American flow in Spanish? Because in Puerto Rico, you know, they love New York rappers, LA rappers." He recalled songs like 50 Cent's "In Da Club" being incredibly popular in Puerto Rico in 2003: "I remember seeing the same people in the street, a lot of people who don't even know English, bumpin' to 50 [Cent] and I was like, yo, I can do that in Spanish."

To that end, Arcángel y De La Ghetto envisioned a more hip-hop and R&B sound than the dancehall-inflected sounds of reggaetón. De La Ghetto told us, "We started listening to Gucci Mane, Young Jeezy, all those rappers. Like, vamos a hacer eso, let's do that, you know, in Spanish. Let's do this R&B shit in Spanish, let's Americanize it a little bit more. And that's what we really wanted to do." They went to the studio where De La Ghetto had an instrumental recording of Dr. Dre's *The Chronic 2001*. Arcángel y De La Ghetto wrote what he described to us as a "hip-hop joint" called "Traficando a Mi Manera" based on one of those tracks, and it became an instant hit on the streets. Arcángel y De La Ghetto got on several important reggaetón compilations. Their songs like "Ven Pégate" with Zion on Naldo's album *Sangre Nueva* (2005), and "La Fanática" on powerhouse reggaetón producers Luny Tunes and Tainy's *Más Flow: Los Benjamins* (2006) thrust them into the spotlight.

Despite Arcángel y De La Ghetto's short time as a duo, they had made an indelible impact on the Latin music scene, essentially creating Latin trap. Trap is a subgenre of rap that emerged from Atlanta, Georgia, in the late 1990s and early 2000s. Trap's style is characterized by a slow sustained baseline (often played on a synthesizer) and rapid hi-hat cymbals over which artists rap with a slowed down, sometimes mumbly and often monotonous vocal style. The term trap comes from local Atlanta slang for a house that was the center of drug dealers' operations. De La Ghetto described trap music from Atlanta as "more ratchet, more like in the crackhouse and shooting [up], you know, where they shoot dope in their veins. So it was more like cooking crack, shooting up, drug dealing, more hardcore in Atlanta" compared to Latin trap.

The first Spanish-language trap song that gained serious traction in Puerto Rico was 2009's "El Pistolón Remix" produced by DJ Blas and recorded by Yaga y Mackie with Randy, Arcángel, and De La Ghetto. Like Atlanta-based trap, "El Pistolón" (The big pistol) talks about life in the streets and brags about the artists' prowess in the rap game. The song also reflected the more street-oriented sounds of trap during a time when reggaetón had become significantly more commercialized. Reggaetón, and its precursor, underground, emerged in the late 1980s and early 1990s as Puerto Rican DJs mixed together Jamaican dancehall, Panamanian reggae en español, and hip-hop.[37] Puerto Rican DJs like DJ Negro and DJ Playero created a new sound that blended these genres together to create the backbone of modern reggaetón. At its core, underground was party music, but many artists stated that their music spoke to the realities of life in poor, urban neighborhoods, including violence and drugs. These associations were so stark that at one point underground became the subject of a censorship campaign that, though unsuccessful, reiterated stereotypes of urban, working-class communities as centers of drugs and crime.[38]

Despite these attempts at censorship, underground and reggaetón could not be stopped. In fact, these censorship campaigns unwittingly gave the music publicity and taught DJs and artists that tweaking their language could expand their audience. Reggaetón continued to grow, gaining traction across Puerto Rico, the diaspora, and other places in Latin America. Daddy Yankee's 2004 global crossover hit "Gasolina" thrust reggaetón into the mainstream Latin music scene. However, by about 2010, Apple Music's Jerry Pullés describes that reggaetón entered a "dry spell." Few new reggaetón artists emerged, and many established artists were putting out records with what Jerry described as a "tropical edge . . . this party, fun, tropical, merengue-ish vibe." The release of massive hits such as Enrique Iglesias, Gente de Zona, and Descemer Bueno's "Bailando" (2014) and Luis Fonsi and Daddy Yankee's "Despacito" (2017) thrust reggaetón-pop fusions into the mainstream.[39] A new reggaetón sound came out of Colombia with the rise of artists like J Balvin, Maluma, and Karol G, who produced what many described as a softer, romantic style of reggaetón more palatable to mainstream audiences.[40] For some, this shift in reggaetón's style and aesthetics to more pop-inflected sounds and lyrics distanced the genre from its roots.[41]

In this context, some saw Latin trap as a return to the streetwise sounds and themes of original reggaetón. Farruko, who had already established himself as a reggaetón singer, explained to *Billboard* that trap was "the closest expression of the street, what people are living in this new generation."[42] Similarly, Ozuna described Latin trap lyrics as "the raw lyrics of the streets."[43] Latin trap surged in Puerto Rico during the profound uncertainty of the post-2006 economic recession that disproportionately impacted the urban poor. Many cultural critics and fans alike claimed that, with reggaetón going more mainstream, Latin trap songs returned to the themes that had previously dominated reggaetón, including drug dealing, violence, and life in the streets.

De La Ghetto told us that Latin trap coming out of Puerto Rico differed from trap in Atlanta because it was "the same street stuff, but doing it a little more pretty. We also sang it a little more for the girls. It was more sexual. We were rapping and singing, ¿me entiende'? We were doing more melodies, more choruses, más cantaíto." While the beats sounded more like Atlanta trap, this sing-songy element could be traced back to Arcángel y De La Ghetto's early work, such as the first song they ever wrote together called "Traficando a Mi Manera." But it was the success of their song "El Pistolón" that inspired a new generation of Latin trap artists who adopted this style in the early 2010s, including Anuel AA, Bryant Myers, and Ozuna.[44]

One breakout song was Bryant Myers's hit "La Esclava" (The woman slave) with a remix featuring artists Anonimus, Anuel AA, and Almighty. This was a very sexually explicit song that talked about a woman who liked rough sex. "La Esclava" exemplifies many of the sonic characteristics that De La Ghetto described as typical of Latin trap—a sung chorus interspersed with slow, melodic rapped verses and very explicit lyrics.

Both Jerry and De La Ghetto identify "La Esclava" as one of the songs that made Latin trap popular to a wider audience. Still, Latin trap was distributed primarily through informal channels such as via pirated CDs or on free digital platforms like SoundCloud. For instance, Jerry told us about how he followed the development of Latin trap on "user-generated websites where, you know, like do-it-yourself-type artists, unsigned, independent artists were making their own music and uploading it. It wasn't living in the regular DSPs [Digital Streaming Platforms]" like

Spotify or Apple Music. The explicit content made it difficult to distribute the music on radio or more formal channels.

Then, in 2016, Latin trap had a second breakout hit: "La Ocasión," produced by DJ Luian and Mambo Kingz, and featuring De La Ghetto, Arcángel, Ozuna, and Anuel AA. Jerry explained that "La Esclava" is "a little bit like the template that 'La Ocasión' was based on. 'La Ocasión' is like the super polished version of it." Like "La Esclava," "La Ocasión" is about sex, but the lyrics are a bit less explicit. This helped to make it the first Latin trap song to chart on Billboard. Jerry recalled, "It was a very important moment in the genre because it had two established artists, Arcángel and De La Ghetto, who always dipped their feet in R&B and trap type songs way before 'La Ocasión,' and then it was also Ozuna and Anuel AA who were kind of unknown artists at the time." According to De La Ghetto, DJ Luian came up with the idea to do "La Ocasión" after hearing "La Esclava." De La Ghetto sang the line "no sé, porque no quiere darme la oportunidad" (I don't know why you don't want to give me the opportunity) for the opening of "La Ocasión," and DJ Luian composed the beat around it with Ozuna singing the hook. De La Ghetto remembers that he was in New York when DJ Luian called him about putting the song together. De La Ghetto shared a melody with him, and DJ Luian liked it. De La Ghetto told us, "So, the next day I got to Puerto Rico and I went straight to the studio and I recorded the intro and did my verse. And then Anuel tiró, Arcángel tiró. We didn't even know it would be such a big hit."

"La Ocasión" was released at the perfect time when streaming platforms were starting to dominate music distribution. In fact, in 2015, revenue from DSPs like Spotify and Apple Music surpassed sales of records or downloadable MP3s.[45] De La Ghetto explained to us that the release of "La Ocasión" during this time period "made the Latin trap market explode. All the major labels, all the playlists were like, 'Yo what is this?' We were the ones that changed even radio programming and digital programming. Because until that time it was just reggaetón, there never was a trap in Spanish category."

At Apple Music, Jerry had been waiting for just the right moment to release a new Latin trap playlist. He already knew that, as he told us, "there was a moment happening there, and this was music that was underrepresented, was not getting played on mainstream terrestrial radio stations, or any radio stations really. And no DSP had any dedicated space to curate the best of that music." The success of "La Ocasión" revealed that there was a wider audience for Latin trap that would consume it in more formal channels. Not only did "La Ocasión" give Jerry something to justify the creation of his playlist, it also gave the playlist its name. At the end of the song, De La Ghetto ad libs, "Trap Kings!" Jerry took that phrase and made it the title of Apple Music's inaugural Latin trap playlist—"Trap Kingz."

"Trap Kingz" was the first DSP playlist dedicated to Latin trap. For Jerry, "Trap Kingz" created a much needed space for a genre that was quickly becoming one of the most popular in the Latin music scene. "I think it kind of validated the [Latin trap] movement for a lot of people," he explained. "Because at the time, at least I wasn't aware of anybody else, you know, any other major platform dedicating any space to that genre. Definitely traditional radio was not going to touch that music at all. It took them years to support any of that music. But it feels great to see that those artists had a home, and I think it probably encouraged some artists who were afraid to dip their toes into it to do trap music because now there's a playlist for it." Not only did they find a home, but "Trap Kingz" quickly became the number one Latin music playlist on Apple Music. By January 2017, "Trap Kingz" had spawned an Apple One (at the time called Beats One) radio show of the same name that featured the hottest Latin trap songs of the day. Apple's radio team envisioned an artist host who would reflect on the genre's growth, tell stories about the artists, and overall become the face of the "Trap Kingz" brand. Jerry immediately thought of the artist who had quickly become the most popular rapper on the playlist: a young guy from Vega Baja, Puerto Rico, who went by the name Bad Bunny.

Before he was Bad Bunny, he was Benito Antonio Martínez Ocasio, a regular guy from a regular family in Vega Baja, Puerto Rico. Vega Baja is a town right smack in the middle of Puerto Rico's northern coast. The Puerto Rican tourism website recommends visiting Vega Baja for the town's natural beauty. In fifty-five square miles, Vega Baja's northern edge borders the Caribbean Sea, and is home to gorgeous beaches including Puerto Nuevo, which is considered one of the cleanest beaches in all the Caribbean. The southern part of Vega Baja borders the mountainous municipality of Morovis.

Bad Bunny is from the Almirante Sur neighborhood, which is closer to the Morovis side of town. In February 2018, Jerry traveled with Bad Bunny and his team to Vega Baja to shoot a brief documentary in preparation for Bad Bunny's Apple Music Up Next campaign. The documentary takes viewers on a ride along mountain roads surrounded by lush, tropical vegetation and rolling hills. The video was shot in the places that Bad Bunny frequented like the local beach and the basketball court. It also featured cameos from old friends, many of whom still work with him, and rare interviews with his brothers, Bernie and Bysael, and his mother, Lysaurie Ocasio. The documentary featured a guy on the cusp of global superstardom—someone who already had the eyes and ears of his homeland but who, Jerry rightly predicted, was about to take off into the stratosphere.[46]

But no matter how big Bad Bunny gets, it is Vega Baja that he calls home. He grew up in a pretty typical Puerto Rican family. As Bad Bunny told Carina del Valle Schorske in an interview for the *New York Times Magazine*, his was a "normal family caught up in the quotidian."[47] His mother is a devout Catholic, and she brought her three sons to church regularly. Bad Bunny's first experience singing for an audience was in the local church choir, something that music critic Suzy Exposito said makes him distinct from other Latin trap or reggaetón artists. She said, "It's no surprise he grew up singing church songs, and a lot of the best singers do."[48]

Still, Bad Bunny had no formal musical training. And as someone growing up in the relatively sleepy town of Vega Baja, he was not connected to the reggaetón and Latin trap scenes. Instead, he found his way into music via the internet. Carina noted that Bad Bunny and his friend Ormani Pérez learned how to use the heavily pirated music production software Fruity Loops (now known as FL Studio) that provides basic elements like special effects, sounds, and instrumentals to develop beats.[49] In the early years, pioneering reggaetón producers like Luny Tunes and DJ Blass created the genre's signature sounds with Fruity Loops. This software was easily accessible in part because pirated versions circulated across Puerto Rico; production software is otherwise too expensive for everyday people to use. Beyond easy access, though, reggaetón producer Tainy told us that Fruity Loops was popular because it was relatively easy to use and understand, even for people without any formal musical or technical training. For young people like Bad Bunny and Ormani, Fruity Loops provided an accessible and user-friendly option with which to dabble in making their own music.

In addition to perusing the internet, Bad Bunny and his friends would take occasional trips into the San Juan metropolitan area. They especially enjoyed Plaza Las Américas, a massive mall in the San Juan metro area, where they would go a few times a year to check out the latest music in the record stores. But this was just an occasional indulgence. "You have to remember, I was just a country kid," Bad Bunny told Carina del Valle Schorske in an interview for the *New York Times Magazine*.[50]

Later, while studying at UPR and working at the grocery store chain Econo, Bad Bunny began making a name for himself locally, producing his own songs and writing his own rhymes. In between classes and bagging groceries, Bad Bunny uploaded his new songs to SoundCloud, an internet platform that enables artists to post songs for free.

In 2016, Bad Bunny released a song on SoundCloud that would change his life forever—"Diles" (Tell them). The song is a slow, sexy trap song about a man who knows how to sexually please a woman. Bad Bunny created the beat himself and recorded his own vocals. The song took off. One day, while working on a project in Colombia, De La Ghetto visited a barber. He told us, "I was shooting a video out there, and my barber was like, 'Bro, listen to this song by Bad Bunny.'" It was "Diles," and De La Ghetto loved it. "I met with [DJ] Luian and said, 'Bro, have you heard this kid Bad Bunny?' And Luian said, 'Bro, I heard his name around.' And I told Luian, 'Bro, sign him, I don't think that's a bad idea.'" DJ Luian took the advice and signed Bad Bunny to his label, Hear This Music. Hear This Music released a remix of "Diles" that featured verses by some of Puerto Rico's hottest Latin trap stars including Farruko, Arcángel, Ñengo Flow, and Ozuna. This was Bad Bunny's first official single backed by an actual record label, and it swiftly climbed the charts.

Back in Miami, Jerry heard the "Diles" remix right when it came out and was determined to add it to "Trap Kingz." Unable to use music not already on Apple's platform, he frequently had to reach out directly to artists to ask if he could include their music on his playlists. Before the release of the new "Diles" remix in August 2016, Jerry communicated briefly with Bad Bunny about adding his music to "Trap Kingz." Jerry had noticed that Bad Bunny's songs would show up on Apple Music, but then they would disappear without warning. Jerry sent Bad Bunny a message on Instagram and asked the young artist to reach out to him via email. Bad Bunny actually did, responding "Aquí estamos. ¡Saludos! (Here we are. Greetings!). Jerry wrote back, "I wanted to reach out to you because we received some Bad Bunny songs a few weeks ago, but they are no longer available on Apple Music. I don't know why they disappeared, but I wanted to know if they'll come back soon because I had two of them on my playlist and I would love to put them back on it again."

A short while later, Bad Bunny emailed back. "Honestly, I have no idea which of my songs are on Apple Music or if they'll come back, etc.," he replied. Jerry learned that Bad Bunny was not aware of his songs on the platform—turns out that bootleggers had uploaded his songs onto the service, which was why they were regularly removed. But with the new version of "Diles" released in August 2016, Jerry finally had a Bad Bunny song he could use.

Bad Bunny's music quickly became the most popular on the "Trap Kingz" playlist. Just six weeks after Hear This Music released "Diles," Bad Bunny had a new song, "Tú No Vives Así" with Arcángel. Produced by DJ Luian and the Mambo Kingz, the song features a classic trap beat punctuated by gunshots throughout the chorus. Jerry immediately added it to the "Trap Kingz" playlist. Then, in December of the same year, Bad Bunny released "Soy Peor." The success of this third song solidified Bad Bunny's position as the leader of the playlist and of Latin trap more broadly. "Anything I put on there with his voice on it, it was going to work," Jerry said in an interview with us. Even if it was just a small feature on another person's song, Bad Bunny's work would instantly become popular. Bad Bunny's success on the playlist showed that he was poised to be the next major Latin trap star.

"Soy Peor" is a classic Latin trap beat that foregrounds a decelerated syncopated hi-hat with a deep bass line, layered with slow synth chords. Rather than the more sexually explicit lyrics, "Soy Peor" is a sad breakup song. Bad Bunny tells his old love interest to move along—"sigue tu camino que sin ti me va mejor" (keep it moving because without you I'm doing better). But then there's a twist because, despite trying to move on and claiming he's better off, Bad Bunny can't seem to get the girl out of his mind. "Si antes yo era un hijueputa ahora soy peor / ahora soy peor, ahora soy peor por ti" (If I was a son of a bitch before, now I'm worse / Now I'm worse, now I'm worse because of you). Jerry thought these lyrics distinguished Bad Bunny from the typical themes in Latin trap. Communications scholar Luis Rivera-Figueroa argues that most Latin trap in Puerto Rico involves "pornographic aesthetics, sexual encounter narrative formula, and depictions of male dominance through sexual conquest."[51] Instead, Jerry noted that "the concept and content of ["Soy Peor"] was not the type of stuff that's in a typical Latin trap song. It's a song about failing and being vulnerable, and he's talking about a breakup and how losing this woman changed him and made him a different person. But, it's presented in this hard trap way. . . . That was just a moment like, 'this guy is different from all the other guys.'"

Jerry also loved "Soy Peor," noting, "melodically, that song can probably be recorded in many other genres and still be a hit." "Soy Peor" was a slow song that easily showcased Bad Bunny's smooth baritone voice. Suzy Exposito describes Bad Bunny's voice as unique within the Latin trap scene: "He doesn't sound like every other guy in Latin trap or reggaetón. Especially when he sings in his higher register, there's something very brassy about his voice. His cadence, it reminds me of the way a trumpet might sound and that's something that is so distinct to him, just the fullness of his voice."[52] Similarly, producer MAG told us that the first thing that drew him to Bad Bunny as a fan was his voice. "The tone in his voice grabbed me right away. It wasn't the tone that we were used to hearing in reggaetón, or he was making trap at the time, so that grabbed me. There was like this baritone thing to his vocal and also his melodies, his range melodically." Bad Bunny's distinctive voice, emotional lyrics, and unique melodies differentiated him from the typical trap sound.

Bad Bunny quickly became the face and voice of Latin trap. By then, he had left his original record label and joined the independent label Rimas, which he signed onto shortly after the success of "Diles" in 2016, with the label's owner Noah Assad as his new manager. Noah was already known in Latin trap circles. Noah told *Billboard* that he "would do anything to make a dollar in the music industry. I was a road manager, I would book artists, I had a studio and I would rent it."[53] In fact, Jerry first met Noah when Noah became the primary contact for another future superstar who started in the trap world, Ozuna. Eventually, at just twenty-four years old, Noah cofounded his own label Rimas Entertainment in 2014. Noah's initial plan for Rimas involved using YouTube to promote local artists and help them claim assets through the platform.[54] Rimas thus centered its initial marketing strategies on maximizing the reach of YouTube's algorithm to distribute music, especially Latin trap, by Puerto Rican artists.[55]

Noah loved Bad Bunny's distinctive voice, gender-bending look, and unique personality. Noah devised a strategy for Bad Bunny to rapidly release back-to-back singles (accompanied by budget videos created for $5,000 to $10,000) and key features on other artists' songs that would quickly gain traction online.[56] By the time Apple Music selected Bad Bunny for Up Next, Bad Bunny had already amassed a significant fan base even without an album.

Jerry invited Noah out to dinner in Los Angeles, where he pitched the idea that Up Next would be a great platform to expand Bad Bunny's reach even further. Bad Bunny had grown so popular that some at Apple questioned if he was really "up and coming," or if he was actually an established artist not suitable for the Up Next series. But Jerry persevered and convinced Apple to include Bad Bunny, arguing that while he was already very popular in the Spanish-speaking world, he had not yet been introduced to other audiences. As part of the campaign, Bad Bunny performed an intimate concert in a small venue in Miami in March of 2018. As Jerry recalled, "He was growing so fast that by the time we did that party, he was already performing in much bigger venues." Even in the three months between the approval of Bad Bunny as the new Up Next artist and the concert, his star rose exponentially.

The concert, then, was a uniquely intimate experience for many of his fans. On a small stage with just his friend Ormani (who started going by the artist name DJ Orma) backing him up, Bad Bunny performed his hits for a few hundred fans. In the video of the concert, the camera pans over fans recording the performance, FaceTiming shocked friends as they streamed him live. He sang his verses on collaborations like "Sensualidad" with Prince Royce and J Balvin, and "Krippy Kush" by Farruko, along with his own songs like "Diles," "Chambea," and "Soy Peor." At the end, he brought out De La Ghetto to sing their joint hit, "Caile," from when, as De La Ghetto put it, "Bad Bunny was super green." Despite having so many hits, Bad Bunny hadn't yet released an album. His first one would not come out until Christmas Eve later in 2018. And yet, his fans knew every word.

Between songs, Bad Bunny effusively thanked his fans and attributed his success to "all the Latinos who support me."[57] The connection to Latino communities was even more pronounced in the mini-documentary that Apple released about Bad Bunny's life as part of the Up Next campaign. By this time, Hurricane María had sharpened Puerto Rico's crisis, and he talked about his pain observing it from afar and shared what had become a viral freestyle video extolling the resilience of Puerto Ricans to overcome such a massive tragedy. In these moments, we catch a glimpse of future Bad Bunny's continuous advocacy for Puerto Ricans and Latinos everywhere.

The growth of Latin trap that had started ten years earlier with Arcángel y De La Ghetto had finally earned the respect it deserved. De La Ghetto is proud of his role in innovating the genre but sees its growth as a group effort: "Arcángel and I started [Latin trap] in Puerto Rico, but after us this generation with Bryant Myers, Anuel AA, Bad Bunny, Eladio Carrión, Myke Towers, they created the movement. . . . Everybody opened the door bit by bit until Bad Bunny came and opened it up completely." Bad Bunny's rise would be so meteoric, so groundbreaking, that he could have become an enigma the way of Prince or untouchable like Beyoncé. But instead, Bad Bunny is more or less the same guy, a theme reiterated in almost every retrospective and every interview. In Apple Music's Up Next, we see the beginnings of Bad Bunny the superstar, not only his fame and popularity but also his gender-bending performances, his political commentary, and his authenticity. These aspects of Bad Bunny's persona have only grown as his platform has expanded to a wider audience.

Indeed, Bad Bunny's entourage today includes many of the same people he hung out with growing up. Ormani (now DJ Orma) serves as Bad Bunny's official tour DJ; together, they produced the massive hit "Safaera" (from his 2020 album *YHLQMDLG*) using Fruity Loops. Bad Bunny also grew up with his sound engineer, Beto "La Paciencia" Rosado, who has helped record his voice since the very beginning. Another childhood friend named Jomo Dávila works as his official photographer and assistant. And then there's Janthony Oliveras, a tall, skinny guy with curly hair. Bad Bunny met Janthony during their time at UPR's Arecibo campus. Janthony helped Bad Bunny become more stylish, picking out outfits for Bad Bunny's early shows, and eventually became the artist's creative director. In 2022, Janthony told podcaster Chente Ydrach that he was like Bad Bunny's "second brain"—the person who knew Bad Bunny's wants and tastes best, and who helped bring the rapper's ideas to fruition.[58] Bad Bunny keeps his friends close. As Noah Assad told *Rolling Stone*, "To this day, he's with his eight best friends, and they're working. They're not his entourage, they're his family."[59] In fact, when Spotify released a video of the dinner they hosted to celebrate Bad Bunny's incomparable twelve songs that each surpassed one billion streams, the group of people he invited to dine with him included all his childhood friends along with his brothers, Bysael and Bernie. (The only more recent industry friends who were at the table were his longtime collaborators and producers, Tainy and MAG).[60]

Unfortunately, Puerto Rico has not enjoyed the same success as Latin trap or those closest to Bad Bunny. De La Ghetto acknowledged this in his conversation with us, saying that when he goes back to Puerto Rico, he sees many of the same problems he saw years ago. In his old neighborhood, he sees "the same people working the same jobs, not doing anything. The system needs a very drastic change." But this is not actually surprising in the context of US colonialism. PROMESA's promise of improving Puerto Ricans' lives was a ruse to hide the reality that the true winners would be the same US corporations and elites that had always benefited from colonial policy in Puerto Rico. But a new crisis was about to happen: a historic hurricane would prompt Bad Bunny to begin using his larger platform to advocate for his homeland.

2

¿"ESTAMOS BIEN"?: HURRICANE MARÍA AND UNNATURAL DISASTER IN PUERTO RICO

Bad Bunny made his television debut performing "Estamos Bien" on NBC's *Tonight Show with Jimmy Fallon* on September 26, 2018. María, a strong Category 4 hurricane, had made landfall in Puerto Rico a year and six days before the appearance. This storm was the deadliest and most costly hurricane in Puerto Rican history. *Tonight Show* audiences were reminded of this fact with the words, "On September 20, 2017, Puerto Rico was exposed to the full force of nature's ferocity," which appeared on-screen just before Bad Bunny took the stage. Then, black-and-white footage of the storm's destruction played, and Bad Bunny took the stage.[1]

Uncharacteristically speaking in English, Bad Bunny was determined to communicate with the mainstream American audience to which he had newfound access at this moment: "After one year of the hurricane, there's still people without electricity in their homes. More than 3,000 people died and [President Donald] Trump is still in denial. But you know what, estamos bien." The statement was a reference to Trump's dismissal of the hurricane's significant death toll and, more broadly, to his administration's failure to fully mitigate the storm's devastation.[2]

The video footage screening behind Bad Bunny then switched from the hurricane's destruction to images of a beautiful Puerto Rico—Bad Bunny with his friends, happy families, Puerto Rican beaches, the countryside, and clips from the music video for his song, "Estamos Bien." The singer's eclectic style was in evidence: painted nails, small oval sunglasses, hoop earrings, and a long jacket.

This performance exemplified the simultaneous frustration and celebration inherent to the phrase P FKN R. It was ironic but also bold, reminding viewers that despite the dehumanizing rhetoric from the Trump administration, Puerto Ricans were still here and doing more than just surviving. It both drew attention to the dire situation in Puerto Rico and told a general audience who likely did not know much about the archipelago that the spirit of its people remained strong. But the final message was one of hope. In a diversion from the song's recorded lyrics, Bad Bunny spoke directly to the people of Puerto Rico: "Estamos bien, y vamos a estar mejor, Puerto Rico" (We're good and we're going to be better, Puerto Rico), he concluded.

For many viewers it was their first glimpse of Bad Bunny. Perhaps it was a risk for a young artist being introduced to the US mainstream for the first time to use this platform to criticize how the federal government had failed Puerto Ricans. When Bad Bunny spoke with Petra during a Harvard University event in 2019, he told her that using his platform in this way was not a difficult decision. He knew that the world was not seeing what was happening on the ground in Puerto Rico, and this was his chance to show them. Bad Bunny was on tour in Europe when Hurricane María hit, and like so many of us in the Puerto Rican diaspora, he found himself struggling to process the news and reach his family. His newfound visibility as a singer on the *Tonight Show* gave Bad Bunny the opportunity to shed light on the devastation and despair that so many Puerto Ricans on and off the archipelago felt in the aftermath of Hurricane María.

Legendary reggaetón producer Tainy produced the song "Estamos Bien." He told us in an interview that the *Tonight Show* performance

> influenced the affection that everyone has for [Bad Bunny], especially people from Puerto Rico. He has never been that person who forgot where he came from. It's very risky and different to use such big platforms

to give these messages and make it genuine. But there are certain artists who define a generation, and they are going to play an important role in getting certain messages across. They think, "Maybe my music or my songs aren't going to talk about this all the time, but as soon as I can do something to contribute, I know that I have millions of eyes on me and I'm going to do something. That's important to me."

Tainy suggested that Bad Bunny's commitment to political action is unusual since many artists often feel uncertain about the most effective ways to use their platforms. In this context, Bad Bunny's performance was especially moving for Tainy. He told us, "It made me proud as a Puerto Rican to have someone representing that way. And it's cool to say that I worked with someone like that."

Bad Bunny's debut on the *Tonight Show* was the first demonstration of his political power. Clearly, he did not do it because he wanted to be viewed as an activist or because he had ambitions to become a politician or a political leader. Rather, as he told Petra in 2019, Bad Bunny acted because he felt he had no choice but to stand up for Puerto Rico. The frustration that Bad Bunny worked hard to communicate in his first appearance on US mainland television demonstrated his willingness to take a stance on political matters. This broadcast performance of "Estamos Bien"—a song that speaks specifically to Puerto Rican realities—was more directly and forcefully political than any song or video he had ever delivered.

To date, Hurricane María was one of the most devastating catastrophes to occur in Bad Bunny's lifetime as well as in modern Puerto Rican history. The hurricane and its aftermath laid bare, in the most clear and public way, Puerto Rico's undeniable status as a colony. US colonial policy had left Puerto Rico's infrastructure and Puerto Ricans themselves in a dire state. The impact of the storm cannot be divorced from Puerto Rico's longer colonial history.[3] As author Jean Hostetler-Díaz explains, Hurricane María revealed how tenuous life in the archipelago had really become, how misconduct and mismanagement had destroyed the state apparatus; it clarified beyond any doubt what it meant to be a colony.[4]

The disparate treatment of American citizens was in plain sight.

When María hit, Puerto Ricans were already dealing with massive destruction from Hurricane Irma, the Category 5 hurricane that had hit the archipelago just two weeks earlier. While María was a slightly weaker storm when it made landfall in Puerto Rico, María lasted much longer than Irma and impacted the entire archipelago. With sustained winds of up to 155 miles per hour and more than forty inches of rainfall, it left at least $100 billion dollars in damage.[5] The smaller Puerto Rican islands of Vieques and Culebra were terribly damaged, and as of this writing eight years later, Vieques remains without a hospital.[6] The archipelago's power grid was completely destroyed. About 80 percent of Puerto Rico's agriculture was lost.[7] Nearly 800,000 homes were damaged, and thousands of homes were demolished. In the first few months after the hurricane, more than 300,000 Puerto Ricans left the archipelago in desperation, making it one of the largest migrations of Puerto Ricans to the US mainland in history.[8] Many more migrated in the years following María.[9]

In the aftermath of the hurricane, Vanessa's close friend Alex, who lives in Guaynabo, Puerto Rico, got in touch. He would sit in his car to use air conditioning for a few minutes, charge his phone, and call her. Via social media, she shared his accounts about life after the hurricane at his request:

> Vanessa, Puerto Rico is destroyed. Things are dire. We don't have food. There's no water anywhere. I went to get water today at a river. And if the river is polluted, it's going to spread disease. People are showering in the river. There's trash everywhere. It's been a week. We aren't getting help. No light. No water. I'm driving through the street and it's just pure black. The line to get gas is so huge. And Donald Trump is talking about the NFL?[10] There are fucking people dying here. People with dialysis can't get dialysis. People like my grandpa who need their insulin to stay cold can't because there is no ice.[11]

Alex's reflections demonstrate the profound neglect on the part of the US and Puerto Rican governments in their responses to María. One particularly ineffective agency was the Federal Emergency Management Agency (FEMA), which is charged with helping US states and territories manage disasters. Of the Puerto Ricans who applied for FEMA funding to help rebuild homes, about 62 percent were denied assistance.[12] National Public Radio's 2018 story "How FEMA Failed to Help Victims of Hurricanes in Puerto Rico Recover" outlined how the federal government was desperately needed to help the archipelago, documenting the massive number of people struggling with no roof over their heads, no food, and no clean water.[13] Anthropologist Sarah Molinari documented that even when FEMA did respond to those who applied for assistance, limited funding, bureaucratic processes, and significant delays led to a form of "disaster assistance fatigue" for many Puerto Ricans who remained without basic resources long after the storm had passed.[14] In July 2020, the Associated Press reported that "not a single repair or rebuilding job" of the relatively small number of houses that were granted federal funding had been completed.[15] When we visited Puerto Rico three years later, we saw countless homes that still had blue tarps instead of roofs.

US government officials, including those from FEMA, consistently downplayed the gravity of the calamity and the incompetence of the US response. FEMA Director Brock Long went so far as to tell Fox News that the response to Hurricane María in Puerto Rico was "the most logistically challenging event the United States has ever seen," adding that the government was "moving and pushing as fast as the situation allows."[16] The fact that Puerto Rico is an archipelago was used as an excuse to justify the incompetent and inhumane response by the US government. While it may be true that the extent of María's destruction presented unique challenges for relief efforts, as one of the most powerful nations in the world, the United States had access to resources, equipment, and the labor force necessary to improve the situation. As Alex told Vanessa, "The US Army can go and invade Iraq and take over a big ass country in a week, but we can't clean shit up in PR. We can invade Afghanistan, but we had a disaster and we can't get water or put light back on for the Puerto Rican people."[17] When Florida and Texas were hit by Hurricane Irma and Hurricane Harvey, around the same time as María, the federal response was significantly more efficient and effective there than in Puerto Rico.[18] For example, FEMA installed 100,000 roof tarps in Florida within a week of Irma.[19] One hundred days after María, only 30,000 roof tarps had been installed in Puerto Rico, and promises of more were never realized.[20]

Instead of tarps, water, food, or other necessary supplies, President Donald Trump arrived in Puerto Rico for a quick five-hour visit two weeks after the storm to distribute "beautiful, soft [paper] towels. Very good towels."[21] At one point, Trump claimed that the Puerto Ricans with whom he visited no longer needed solar-powered flashlights—this at a time when only about 7 percent of the archipelago actually had power.[22] At the same time, Trump expressed extreme contempt for Puerto Rico and its people whom he accused of not being self-sufficient problem-solvers or grateful recipients of the aid he claimed had arrived in Puerto Rico. For instance, in the days following the paper towel incident, Trump tweeted:

Texas & Florida are doing great but Puerto Rico, which was already suffering from broken infrastructure & massive debt, is in deep trouble.

. . . It's [*sic*] old electrical grid, which was in terrible shape, was devastated. Much of the Island was destroyed, with billions of dollars. . . .

. . . owed to Wall Street and the banks which, sadly, must be dealt with. Food, water and medical are top priorities—and doing well.[23]

Rather than acknowledging that Puerto Rico has been a victim of divestment and extraction, Trump continually kicked the colony while it was down, blaming its government and its people for the situation, claiming that Puerto Rico was a drain on the US economy. Puerto Ricans, he wrote, wanted "everything done for them," reifying centuries old racist stereotypes of the generous Uncle Sam giving handouts to his pesky, poor, uncouth dark-skinned colonial children.[24]

Still, Trump was not the only person blaming Puerto Ricans. For instance, rather than admit their systematic failures at providing aid, FEMA officials claimed that a lack of resolve and a cultural proclivity for "waiting for things to happen" prevented Puerto Ricans from accessing aid.[25] As anthropologist Hilda Lloréns describes, US media coverage generally depicted Puerto Ricans as helpless Black and Brown people fleeing the chaotic and "disastrous tropics."[26] This combination of coverage that focused on natural disasters and drew from stereotypes of exotic, savage, and tropical places helped bolster the US government's self-image as altruistic and doing all it could, even when nothing could have been further from the truth.[27]

In one of Alex's phone calls to Vanessa, he emphasized the devastating impact of the lack of federal response in the wake of the hurricane: "I haven't seen federal help. When Texas was hit, there were resources. As American citizens, we should be getting help. The Puerto Rican people, they are the ones cleaning this shit up. They are the ones cutting up the trees. But we don't have the proper supplies. So it's very slow. Everything that has happened, we organized it. The people. Not FEMA."[28] Alex was right. Instead of government assistance in the aftermath of the storm, Puerto Ricans took matters into their own hands. To the extent possible, Puerto Ricans cleared their own debris, hauled their own water, created their own energy infrastructures, and created and/or strengthened existing mutual aid programs.[29] For example, Oscar Carrion from the town of Canóvanas began rewiring power lines to restore power. Using YouTube tutorials for guidance,

2.1 In this 1898 cartoon titled "Will wear the stars and stripes," a tall, white Uncle Sam dressed in the quintessential American stars and stripes suit offers a smaller version of his suit to a much shorter, dark-skinned caricature of a Puerto Rican man wearing only underwear and a hat that says "Porto Rico." The tropes shown here were common in cartoons of this era and promulgated the idea that Puerto Ricans (and all Latin American and Caribbean peoples) were racially inferior, poor, un-educated, and desperately in need of support from the United States. This discourse was meant to justify holding Puerto Rico as a colony and to legitimize continued US intervention across the Americas. Illustrated by Charles Lewis Bartholomew. Originally published in *Minneapolis Journal*, May 7, 1898. Library of Congress.

he risked his life daily without gloves and without any experience working as an electrician, and he restored power to thousands in the area.[30]

While some people like Trump claimed Puerto Ricans were ungrateful and lazy, others praised Puerto Ricans' resilience in the face of the storm. However, anthropologist Yarimar Bonilla has critiqued this notion of resilience. She stated, "The much-touted resilience of Puerto Ricans . . . needs to be itself understood as a form of trauma: years of abandonment by local and federal governments have forced communities to take care of themselves. . . . This is wonderful but also troubling, given the super-human capacity for resilience that is now expected of [Puerto Ricans]."[31] Even Puerto Ricans were subject to this line of thinking; journalist Benjamín Torres Gotay found that Puerto Ricans after the storm felt resigned to the fact that government help would be minimal, at best.[32] Bonilla similarly points out that the phrase #PuertoRicoSeLevanta (Puerto Rico Rises) became a popular slogan to celebrate the resiliency of the Puerto Rican people in the wake of the hurricane. However, as she argues, the people's resilience should not be used to excuse the lack of resilience in Puerto Rico's infrastructure.[33] Ultimately, as historian Jorell Meléndez-Badillo has written, "focusing on resilience ignores the fact that people who had suffered multiple traumas were doing what they needed to survive. . . . For many, María painfully revealed that the U.S. government continued to view Puerto Ricans as second-class citizens at best, lazy and in need of saving at worst."[34]

Hurricane María exposed the colonial realities in Puerto Rico, from the archipelago's crumbling infrastructure to the racist discourses that informed the US government's response to the disaster. Colonialism functions in part by presenting the colonized as disposable. Perhaps nothing made the disposability of Puerto Ricans clearer than the tremendous death toll of María. When Trump visited Puerto Rico, he praised Governor Ricardo Rosselló's administration for avoiding mass casualties, claiming that only sixteen people had died as a result of the storm.[35] However, as time wore on, it became increasingly apparent that this number was profoundly inaccurate. In many ways, the aftermath of the storm became even more deadly than the storm itself. One day, Alex explained to Vanessa, "People are really struggling. People are dying because there aren't [any] services. [The government is] hiding it. People are struggling. They are committing suicide.[36] I'm telling you because I'm here and I know what's going on."[37] To this day, we do not know exactly how many people died as a result of Hurricane María and its aftermath due to the US government's failure to provide basic needs, such as food, clean water, or power for life-saving medical devices and medications.[38] The Puerto Rican government has reported varying numbers, but most Puerto Ricans accept the statistic provided by a Harvard public health study that determined a *minimum* of 4,645 people lost their lives as a result of the hurricane.[39]

In July 2018, shortly after the publication of the Harvard study, hundreds of Puerto Ricans placed pairs of shoes in front of Puerto Rico's capitol building to protest the Puerto Rican government's claim at the time that only sixty-four people had died from María. Each pair of shoes represented a deceased loved one. When those loved ones' shoes had been lost, people left a pair of their own.[40] On September 21, 2024, seven years after María, Bad Bunny revealed on X (formerly Twitter) that he, too, had left his own shoes at the memorial:

> Wow! For many years, every time I see a photo of this day [of the shoe protest], I look for a while to see if I can find the pair I left there. I never recorded it, nor did I post photos, nor did I publish anything; not even for my own memories. No one noticed nor realized that I went there, nor did I tell anyone. Today I finally found them in this photo. And wow! I got so emotional seeing them and my eyes watered, but more than the significance of the act itself, these [shoes] were really special to me. They were the sneakers I used the first time I was on the stage at El Choli (Farruko's concert in 2016), a day I'll never forget. I'll never stop being grateful to and returning the love that this land has given me. For this reason I will always be here.[41]

Back in the United States, the Puerto Rican diaspora was mobilizing to find relatives, to access information, and to send supplies to their communities in the archipelago. Like many other Puerto Ricans in the United States, Vanessa posted desperate social media messages trying to find anyone on the west coast of Puerto Rico who could help her track down her family members, including her grandfather (who had been in a hospital awaiting surgery when the hurricane hit) and her aunt (who had been holed up at their family home with minimal food and water). With no way to contact family members for a week, she posted social media messages in the hope that someone on the ground would see them and give her an update.[42] In those days, Facebook was a hub of activity for the Puerto Rican diaspora, with people exchanging information and sharing the deep sadness for so many who couldn't contact their families. There was tremendous guilt from not being there, in Puerto Rico, to offer support, but there was also the recognition that if we had been there, we would have just been another drain on resources. This contributed to a sense of helplessness and confusion stemming from wanting to help and not knowing how best to do so. After waiting for ten days, Vanessa's family was finally able to marshal their connections and resources to secure passage for her grandfather and

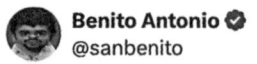

Benito Antonio ✓
@sanbenito

wow! por muchos años cada vez que me salían las distintas fotos de este día, me quedaba mirando un rato a ver si encontraba el par mío que dejé allí. Nunca grabé, ni tiré foto, ni publiqué nada; ni tan siquiera para mi de recuerdo. Nadie se enteró ni se dió cuenta de que fui, ni si quiera se lo conté a alguien. Hoy por fin las acabo de ver en esta foto. Y wow! Me emocioné mucho al verlas y se me aguaron los ojos, pues ademas del significado del acto, eran muy especiales para mi. Fueron las tennis que utilicé la primera vez que me trepé en la tarima del choli (concierto de farruko en el 2016), día que nunca olvidaré. Nunca voy a parar de agradecer y devolver el amor que me ha dado esta tierra. Por eso siempre voy a estar aquí.

"Fueron 5 mil que dejaron morir, y eso nunca se nos va a olvidar..."

Translate post

2.2 Bad Bunny's post on the social media platform X (formerly Twitter) from September 21, 2024, conveys his shock over spotting his shoes in a photo of the impromptu 2018 Hurricane María memorial, in which individuals placed pairs of shoes across the marble plaza outside the Capitolio government building in San Juan to demand a proper count of those who died as a result of the hurricane. The shoes Bad Bunny placed at the memorial were those he had worn during his first performance at El Choli in Puerto Rico in 2016. Image from X @sanbenito.

aunt to the United States on a Royal Caribbean cruise ship (the company stepped up by providing supplies and transportation at a time when the US government claimed that access to Puerto Rico was impossible).[43]

Just like Vanessa, Bad Bunny was also waiting to hear news from his family. When María hit, Bad Bunny had just arrived in Europe after weeks of touring in Latin America and the United States. This placed Bad Bunny, if temporarily, in the diaspora. He posted a message on Instagram that reflected the feelings of many people in the diaspora at the time: "You don't know how difficult it is for me to be so far from my home and be unable to do anything. My body is in Europe, but my soul and mind are in Puerto Rico with all of you. I still haven't even been able to talk to my mom and I swear that this hurts me the most. . . . It breaks my soul to see all the images of my beautiful island. But I know we will recuperate soon. *PUERTO RICO TE AMO*!!"[44] Bad Bunny has subsequently described his guilt for not experiencing María in Puerto Rico. For instance, in a 2020 interview, Bad Bunny reflected on what it felt like to experience the hurricane outside of Puerto Rico when his entire family and all his friends were back in the archipelago. He described that for Puerto Ricans outside of Puerto Rico, "they suffered greatly in a different way: the uncertainty, the discomfort of wondering what's happening and wondering 'where is my family?'"[45]

Just a few days after María, Bad Bunny expressed this sentiment in an impromptu rap he posted on Instagram, called "Mi Puerto Rico"—My Puerto Rico.[46] The rap brilliantly captured the everyday sorrow, anger, and fear that many Puerto Ricans off and on the archipelago felt. It opened with a line that expressed the dread of not knowing whether family members were alive or dead: "Otro dia que no sé de mami" (Another day with no word from mama). The song continued by offering a sense of hope for the future:

> Otra tarima que me trepo con el nudo en la garganta
> Dicen que Dios no manda pruebas si uno no la aguanta
> Por eso sé que Puerto Rico de esta se levanta
> Y el árbol se planta, la flor vuelve y crece
> Somos la estrella que alumbra aunque estemos sin luz seis meses.[47]

> I climb up another stage with a lump in my throat
> They say God doesn't test those who can't take it
> That's how I know Puerto Rico will rise above this
> And the trees seed and the flowers grow and return.
> We are the star that shines even without power for six months.

In many ways, these lyrics reiterate the idea of resilience that is criticized by Yarimar Bonilla and other scholars. At the same time, Bad Bunny's words reflected a sentiment that many Puerto Ricans could relate to—something that Bonilla has called "hopeful pessimism" that "opens our eyes to the hard tasks required to transform the here and now."[48] The song's message of perseverance in the wake of disaster spoke to the hope that Bad Bunny and others could grasp onto in this impossible situation. While individuals' resilience cannot be used as a cover for governmental neglect, the reality is also that hope is critical to the possibility of imagining brighter futures.

"Mi Puerto Rico" takes on a more mournful tone consistent with hopeful pessimism. But during this time, other songs emerged that helped many people cope with the aftermath of the hurricane, sometimes even providing a moment of levity in a time of crisis. People played music while waiting in long lines for everything from gas to water to entry into a sparsely stocked grocery store. One such song was "Te Boté," a Latin trap song released on December 1, 2017, just a few months after María. Artist manager and former reggaetón promoter Pablo Batista recalled that in the immediate aftermath of María, he couldn't go anywhere in Puerto Rico without hearing "Te Boté." He described the song as a "soundtrack of you going [out] and looking for gas, or going in and spending two hours to do the grocery shopping. If you go ask a Puerto Rican that was on the island when 'Te Boté' came out, they will tell you a story of what they were doing during post-María times." Pablo explained that, left without the internet, Puerto Ricans had only the radio to entertain them. He recalled that "Te Boté" was "played like three times every hour" on the local station. He opined that "if you're living in Puerto Rico and you ask about what song you listen[ed] to the most during post-María times, eight of ten people would tell you 'Te Boté.'"

"Te Boté" is a Latin trap song produced, performed, and written by José "Young Martino" Martín Velásquez, with contributions by Puerto Rican rappers Nio García, Darell, and Casper Mágico. Young Martino, Nio, and Casper were storm refugees, and the four rappers came together in Orlando, Florida, to make music to relieve their anxiety. In an interview with *Rolling Stone* Casper explained that "Te Boté" was "a song that was born from ruin, just out of nothing." Nio added it was a response to the struggles of communicating with people in Puerto Rico at the time. "We were in darkness, in a depression, and we wanted something that would move people," he said.[49]

The artists channeled their emotions into what would become a massively successful song. In 2019, Young Martino told *Billboard* that when "Casper asked me to create some beats, a rhythm, and just like that, with no piano or instrument, a beat came out of my brain. I programmed it, a melody followed, then the base of the track, and we started humming with Nio what would become the intro." Young Martino combined this melody with Casper's vocals to create the song.[50] Casper and Nio uploaded a preview of the song to Instagram, and it quickly went viral. The initial version of the song had nearly sixty million YouTube views in less than three months.[51]

Another Latin trap star, Ozuna, reached out to Casper about doing a remix. Then, Bad Bunny and reggaetón veteran Nicky Jam were brought into conversations about the new version of the hit track. On April 13, 2018, the remixed version of "Te Boté"—featuring Ozuna, Bad Bunny, and Nicky Jam—catapulted it to new heights. The song has racked up billions of views on YouTube, and it quickly reached number one on Billboard's Hot Latin Songs chart where it stayed for fourteen weeks. "Te Boté" even peaked at number thirty-six on the Billboard Hot 100 chart.[52] This is no small feat, considering that the remix is all in Spanish and more than seven minutes long.

The song was a dark, *despecho*: part of a genre of songs about heartbreak and vengeance. The remix was Latin trap-meets-reggaetón, and all the rappers were Puerto Rican. It was a stark contrast to the feel-good, sexual, corny, tropical sounding Latin pop–reggaetón fusion songs like Luis Fonsi and Daddy Yankee's 2017 hit "Despacito," whose bilingual remix featured Justin Bieber. Media outlets had reported that "Despacito" was an anthem for post-María life. For instance, a *Tampa Bay Times* article about the cruise ship that brought Vanessa's aunt and grandfather back into the United States described the song playing when the ship came into port in Fort Lauderdale, Florida: "At the port, hundreds of desperate family members carried their own flags, signs, and chanted 'Puerto Rico se levanta'—Puerto Rico rises—as evacuees started trickling out of the ship at about 9:30 a.m. Luis Fonsi's anthem to the Island of Enchantment, 'Despacito,' played in the background."[53]

But back in Puerto Rico, it was "Te Boté" that was the post-María anthem. For Pablo, the song was significant not only because it dominated the airwaves but also because it resonated with Puerto Ricans at a time when they needed something positive. He told us, "'Te Boté' reflects that time that we were struggling after María. It was like, you know María hit us, fucking destroyed us. You wake up and, you know, in between the clouds you will see that ray of light? That was what 'Te Boté' was like. It came out at a time [when] we needed something like that."

Although "Te Boté" is, at its heart, a breakup song, it also expresses a powerful tone of freedom instead of sadness. Rather than rapping about wanting their ex back, the rappers say good riddance. "Te boté" means I threw you out. I disposed of you. In one of the many iterations of the chorus, Darell and Nio rap:

Bebé, yo te boté
Te di banda y te solté
Pa'l carajo te mandé
De mi vida te saqué

Baby I threw you out
I let you go and released you
I sent you to hell
I got you out of my life

Casper's verse follows with, "Pa'l carajo te boté / Yo sin ti me siento bien / Ya no sufro por amore,' ahora rompo corazones'" (I sent you to hell / Without you I feel good / I no longer suffer for lovers, now I break hearts). On the surface, "Te Boté" seems like nothing more than a typical song about dumping someone and moving on. But considering the sentiments out of which the song was born and the conditions to which Puerto Ricans were subjected in the aftermath of the storm due to the US government's inaction, it is easy to understand how this song could take on a motivational, and even political, connotation. In the context of extreme abandonment after Hurricane María, it is natural to read "Te Boté" as a song about the uselessness of the United States. The United States is like the dysfunctional lover who needs to be removed from Puerto Ricans' lives because they would be better off without them.

At first blush, it seems unlikely that "Te Boté" would become a song that would speak to the experience of Hurricane María. But, from its inception, "Te Boté" was intimately connected to María. Young Martino, Casper, and Nio García initially recorded it as they grappled with their own anxiety and anger about the storm, and these emotions were exacerbated by the failure of the US government to respond properly and humanely to the crisis. The song was so tied to the hurricane in people's minds that Pablo heard a rumor that the remix was recorded in a studio powered by a generator. Whether or not this is true, it indicates just how embedded "Te Boté" is in Puerto Rico's collective memory about Hurricane María. It is clear that the sentiment of the song provided an outlet for their frustrations about the hurricane and its aftermath in the archipelago. While songs like "Te Boté" and "Mi Puerto Rico" were the initial soundtrack of Puerto Rican life on the ground immediately after María, there was another song brewing that would help to sound out Puerto Ricans' hopeful pessimism to the rest of the world: Bad Bunny's "Estamos Bien."

A few months after the "Te Boté" remix dominated airwaves, Puerto Ricans got a new hit. Bad Bunny's "Estamos Bien" dropped on June 28, 2018. It was a different kind of sound and a different kind of song for him. While his hits prior to "Estamos Bien" were harder Latin trap songs, "Estamos Bien" opens with the sound of a choir and has a brighter and more upbeat tone. The song was the result of the combustion of the quick and explosive growth of his popularity, along with the vast destruction of his homeland while he was away. Just like the artists who created "Te Boté," Bad Bunny channeled the overwhelming moment into music. The result was this anthem about himself, and about the realities of life in post-María Puerto Rico. Like "Te Boté," the song's lyrics are relatively typical for a Latin trap song, boasting about money and flashy cars. But in the context of María, it took on a whole new meaning, one that Bad Bunny and his producer Marco Efraín Masís Fernández, better known by his artist name Tainy, never anticipated.

To understand the reverence Bad Bunny and other artists have for Tainy, we just have to listen to what Bad Bunny himself said on stage at the concert celebrating Tainy's album *Data* in January of 2024: "Puerto Rico, you're watching the best artist of el género urbano in history. And I'm not talking about me. I'm talking about Tainy."[54] Bad Bunny knows he gets a tremendous amount of shine as an artist, but he gives a lot of that credit to Tainy. Indeed, Tainy has played a critical role in the development of reggaetón. Although he began producing as a young teen, Tainy's vast repertoire covers the entire trajectory of the commercialization of reggaetón from the mid-2000s to the present.[55] Put another way, Tainy made many of the songs that Bad Bunny heard when he was coming up, and now the two collaborate to make some of the most important hits in the contemporary reggaetón scene.

2.3 Tainy and Bad Bunny perform together on January 5, 2024, at the concert promoting Tainy's album *Data* at El Choli in San Juan. Photo by Luis M. Medina Leandry.

Tainy's studio is a small bungalow on a quiet Miami street. The interior walls are decorated with plaques celebrating his myriad platinum hits with Bad Bunny. In an hours-long interview at his studio, Tainy told us about his career, which began when he was only fourteen. Tainy's eclectic sound comes from his eclectic influences: US pop, hip-hop, and rock, from the Beatles to Biggie Smalls, Linkin Park, Eminem, Aerosmith, Timbaland, and the Neptunes. Raised in a very religious home by his Dominican mother in Puerto Rico, he wasn't allowed to listen to the burgeoning genre of reggaetón at home, but he took every opportunity he could to listen to it at school or while visiting friends. Yet his religious upbringing unexpectedly helped launch his career when he met one of his friends and mentors, producer Josías de la Cruz, better known as the accomplished reggaetón producer Nely el Arma Secreta, at church. Tainy credits Nely with teaching him "what it is to make rhythm." Nely helped Tainy get a bootleg copy of the Fruity Loops production software that was commonly used in early reggaetón production. Tainy's mom scraped together the funds to buy him a computer, and he got straight to work. Trips to the studio with Nely helped Tainy develop his craft. He told us that in the studio, he felt like he was in "another world and there was no one there, only [Nely]. I sat in the back, without asking any questions. I didn't talk much so as not to bother, but what I wanted was to absorb everything I could." Tainy would share his beats with Nely at church, and Nely would give him honest feedback.

Nely shared Tainy's music with reggaetón powerhouse production duo Luny Tunes when Tainy was only fourteen years old. At the time, Luny Tunes, a duo of Francisco Saldaña and Victor Cabrera, were the biggest producers in the business. They were responsible for many of reggaetón's massive hits, like Daddy Yankee's "Gasolina," Tego Calderón's "Métele Sazón," and Wisin y Yandel's "Rakata." Luny Tunes liked the material Nely shared with them, and they invited Tainy to their studio. Saldaña offered to sign Tainy on the spot. Tainy's mom was waiting in the car outside, and he ran out to get her approval on the contract.

That moment changed Tainy's life. He joined the small group of producers who became the architects of the sound of reggaetón. Tainy recalls that reggaetón stars like Wisin y Yandel, Don Omar, Héctor el Father, Alexis y Fido, and Zion y Lennox would often casually hang out at the studio while Tainy worked in the small upstairs studio space "getting experimental" with the production equipment he didn't have access to at home. Working alongside producers who were twice his age, the pioneers of reggaetón, Tainy honed his craft and started to create his own unique sound.

While he had already contributed to many popular songs, Tainy's first major hit was "Pam Pam" by reggaetón duo Wisin y Yandel in 2006. The song has some of the classic synth sounds of early reggaetón that Tainy blended with the catchy hook from the 1989 hit, "Lambada." For Tainy, working with Yandel, in particular, introduced him to new ways of incorporating melodies into his beats. Yandel wanted to incorporate "Lambada" into a song, and he sang the melody for Tainy (Tainy told us that he realized he had heard the melody, but at that time never knew what it was). From there, Tainy told us, "I could kind of recreate it and add different elements to it to make it a little more reggaetón." "Pam Pam" launched Tainy into the spotlight.

The young producer quickly became a mainstay in reggaetón. At age seventeen, Tainy coproduced the 2006 album *Más Flow: Los Benjamins* with his mentors Luny Tunes. The album featured a diverse array of artists, from Daddy Yankee to merengue star Tony Tún Tún, to Latin pop supergroup RBD, thus creating a bridge between reggaetón and other Latin genres. Since then, Tainy has become one of the biggest producers in Latin music with numerous accolades—including Grammys, BMI

2.4 Tainy performs in El Choli on January 5, 2024.
Photo by Luis M. Medina Leandry.

Awards, and Billboard Awards—in part due to his openness to bridging and blending genres and, by extension, for helping the iconic artists he works with like Bad Bunny to blend genres as well.

The first song that Tainy produced in which Bad Bunny was featured was also one of Tainy's biggest hits ever—Cardi B's "I Like It," which came out in May 2018. But Bad Bunny and Tainy didn't meet during the production of that song; instead, they were first introduced on a group chat by José Álvaro Osorio Balvín (known by his artist name J Balvin). Bad Bunny had asked J Balvin to make the connection. Then, as Pablo, who manages Tainy, tells it, "Noah [Assad] hit Tainy, like, 'Hey, can you come to Puerto Rico and go into the mountains and work with [Bad Bunny]?'" From there, Bad Bunny and Tainy began what would become one of the most important creative partnerships in reggaetón history.

Tainy described an instant sense of connection when he and Bad Bunny finally met to produce "Estamos Bien." By that time, Tainy already had worked with a who's who of reggaetón; but collaborating with someone closer in age to himself meant that he and Bad Bunny understood each other in a way that was very different from the pioneering artists he worked with when he was a teenager. He explained, "It was cool to have someone like him younger than me, but closer to my generation, who grew up listening to the same things." When working with older artists, Tainy explained that he felt he had little in common with them. Bad Bunny and Tainy are less than five years apart in age. As Tainy said, they had "similar tastes" that made him "feel more comfortable at the time." He recalled that working with Bad Bunny made him feel he could experiment openly with musical ideas in a truly collaborative way. As he said, "I can propose [new ideas] because I no longer feel afraid that maybe they won't hear what I hear."

As much as Bad Bunny reveres Tainy, Tainy is equally awed by working with Bad Bunny, who, in addition to being an excellent lyricist, is also a producer in his own right: "All the music [Bad Bunny] was putting out were beats from him. And that also blew my mind. . . . It helps me to be able to have conversations on the production side with someone who understands it. That's what happened with 'Estamos Bien.' He said, 'It's just that chorus from the beginning and . . . I had nowhere to take it.' I came in like, 'OK, I would do this percussion. I would add this piano here.' But the initial idea came from him and that happened [with other songs] on *X 100PRE*."

Bad Bunny had already begun many of the songs on *X 100PRE* when the two met, but he needed his new teammate, Tainy, to help bring them to completion. The pair's organic, collaborative approach was evident from "Estamos Bien" onward. "It's not just me proposing things," Tainy told us. "He teaches me too. . . . It was just as fun as that exchange of ideas and being kind of in sync." He and Bad Bunny made music that inspired them both. While Bad Bunny has worked with other producers throughout his artistic evolution, Tainy remains a constant—present in the production of each of his albums, if to varying extents. As Tainy told us, the degree to which he and Bad Bunny are "connected" through their creative process is "something different and it ends up being a revolution."

Not only do Tainy and Bad Bunny's collaborations make a musical "revolution," they also center and honor Puerto Rico in their work, even if they don't necessarily intend for every one of their songs to be "political." Puerto Rico's colonial status and ongoing crises necessarily makes their work political. To Tainy, Puerto Rico is "stuck." Referring to the many ongoing crises facing the archipelago, he explained, "many difficult things have happened. But at the same time there is that sense that no matter what happens, there will always be a voice of the community or the people. . . . They will always go out and fight for their people and in some way move forward from catastrophes like María." Like Bad Bunny, Tainy says he has endless love for "the country where I was born, which gave me so many ideas and so much influence."

Tainy said the songs he and Bad Bunny make together stay relevant because the focus of their music is how they make people feel, and how they reflect the emotion they're trying to convey through the song—often about issues that are particular to Puerto Rico or Puerto Rican realities. "Being able to make people feel something different, even if it may take time at first, it can be really intense, or strange, or just different, but it always ends up being special." From the content of the song to the sound of the beat, "Estamos Bien," which music critic Suzy Exposito called "electropsych bliss," is definitely special.[56]

As therapeutic as the new process of production was for Tainy, the creation of "Estamos Bien" was a turning point for Bad Bunny as well. He was emerging from what he recalls as a "dark" time, with a "period of dark moments and depressive episodes."[57] Although *X 100PRE* was his first album, Bad Bunny's numerous successful singles had already catapulted him into the spotlight, and the rapid rise to fame was jarring for the new artist. In a 2018 interview with Puerto Rican influencers and podcasters Molusco and Chente Ydrach, Bad Bunny talked about his struggles with adjusting to fame, saying "I wasn't ready."[58] He also wasn't ready for the music business itself. He told them, "The music is beautiful. But the business, the industry está cabrón, es una mierda" (It's fucked, it's bullshit). A month before he recorded "Estamos Bien" in 2018, he "disconnected from everything." The remedy was escape and time with loved ones: "I rented a house for my friends, my brothers for a month. We rented equipment to make music. . . . I spent time with my family. I was trying to understand why I wasn't content, with all the success, and fame."[59]

The song "Estamos Bien" emerged from this experience. The song boasts: "Hoy me levanté contento, hoy me levanté feliz / Aunque dicen por ahí que están hablando de mí, hey / Joda, que se joda, que se joda, hey" (Today I woke up content, I woke up happy / Even though they're saying they're talking about me, hey / Fuck it, fuck it, fuck it, hey). On an Instagram live celebrating the release of *X 100PRE*, Bad Bunny expressed that he had taken the time to reflect on people and things that were "toxic in his life." He sought to distance himself from people who "did not have the same passion for music, have the same vision of the world, same mission for love, for what art was, who did not have the same philosophy of life" as he did.[60] While Bad Bunny had signed with record label Rimas in 2016, he was still making music with Hear This Music until *X 100PRE* was released in 2018. It's difficult not to interpret some of this language as related to the breakup of his partnership with Hear This Music, particularly because his

Hear This Music contract did not permit him to have a studio album. He said he was now surrounding himself with "people who love me for who I am, not for who I have become or what the world projects about me."[61] As he started doing things the way he wanted to, "the inspiration for his music came faster."[62] It seemed that all these issues—grappling with fame and managing his business dealings—combined with the myriad problems facing Puerto Rico had been too much.

"Estamos Bien" responded to these issues with lyrics that were simultaneously inspirational and open about the realities of life at a time when Puerto Ricans needed both an acknowledgment of their problems and hope for the future:

> Dime qué esperas tú
> Si alguien puede, eres tú
> Aunque pa' casa no ha llega'o la luz
> Gracias a Dios porque tengo salud . . .
> No te preocupes, estamos bien
> Con o sin billetes de 100

> Tell me what are you waiting for
> If someone can do it, it's you
> Even though power still hasn't come back on at home
> Thank God that I have health . . .
> Don't worry, we're good
> With or without $100 bills

This message of resilience is not the same sort that scholar Yarimar Bonilla critiqued in the aftermath of the hurricane. Rather than suggesting that Puerto Ricans can naturally withstand anything, in his lyrics Bad Bunny references resilience to offer hope to his community. Even without electricity or money, he and his people will be ok.

Reflecting on what made "Estamos Bien" so powerful, Pablo told us:

At that point, he allowed himself to open up and tell everyone what he was feeling. Remember, we're coming out of Hurricane María, so we're struggling. So that song gave everyone a 'Yeah, we're struggling, but *estamos bien*.' With or without money, *estamos bien*. We're Puerto Ricans. We're proud Puerto Ricans. We are happy to be Puerto Ricans and there has been nothing ever to stop us. Not a Spanish government, not an

American government. Not putting us in the biggest disadvantage ever with the Jones Act.[63] Nothing has stopped us. Like [one of] the fucking biggest hurricanes ever recorded just pass over us and we're still here, so. . . . He gave a new breath to people in Puerto Rico. And it became a song that every Puerto Rican will sing at the top of their lungs. Because it reminds us that, hey, we're gonna get through all this bullshit. That was a Puerto Rican song.

Pablo's comments clarify how and why Bad Bunny's music represents the broader theme of Puerto Rican resistance, and not just the resilience that is demanded of Puerto Ricans at every turn.[64] Resistance can take many forms. Bad Bunny's approach is his own, but it resonates with Puerto Ricans. This is why he used his platform on the *Tonight Show* to address the state of things in Puerto Rico one year after Hurricane María. This is why he directly admonished President Trump. He knows who he is, where he comes from, and what he stands for, even if he can't stand for everything and everyone. Even if he is flawed, like all people. He arrived at this place as an artist, as a reluctant spokesperson for Puerto Rico, in part through his relationship with Tainy. Tainy helped solidify the sound of Bad Bunny, and that sound brings with it the history in which Tainy was so steeped. Together, they shaped the contemporary sound of resistance on the archipelago.

3

"EL PUEBLO NO AGUANTA MÁS INJUSTICIA": BAD BUNNY AND EL VERANO BORICUA

On the night of July 24, 2019, Vanessa arrived at Los Angeles International Airport for the first leg of two flights she had to take to get to San Juan, Puerto Rico. She was heeding a call on social media by many public figures, including Bad Bunny and Ricky Martin, to join a mass protest there. For ten days, in what may have been the largest protests in Puerto Rican history, thousands of Puerto Ricans had been calling for then-Governor Ricardo "Ricky" Rosselló to resign.[1]

As she waited to board her flight, a television tuned to CNN was visible from the gate. The banner across the screen read: "Breaking News: Puerto Rico Governor to Resign." Vanessa was wearing a shirt she had just made that said "Ricky Renuncia" above a photo taken a few days prior of Bad Bunny at the protests holding the Puerto Rican flag. As she watched Ricky renunciando (resigning) on live television, she began to cheer. There were no signs that there were other Puerto Ricans in the vicinity, and people gawked at the noise. But she boarded the flight hopeful, invigorated, and in disbelief. The Puerto Rican people—our people—had just forced out the governor.

The immediate impetus for the protests was the release by Puerto Rico's Center for Investigative Journalism on July 13, 2019 (the day before the protests began), of nearly 900 pages of digital chats between Rosselló and his top aides and cabinet members.[2] The release of the unfiltered chats, which was quickly dubbed "RickyLeaks" and "Chat gate," exposed messages mocking those who died as a result of Hurricane María as well as messages containing misogynistic comments, homophobic slurs, racism, and classism. In one exchange with former Director of Finance Christian Sobrino Vega in which he and the governor discussed the growing number of bodies accumulating at the forensic institute following Hurricane María, Rosselló callously joked, "Don't we have some corpses to feed our crows?" This was the ultimate sinvergüenza, a term for extreme shamelessness that no English word can capture. After several years of extreme hardship, the chats pushed Puerto Ricans over the edge. As scholar Marisol LeBrón put it, the protests were a matter of life and death.[3]

Bad Bunny decided to interrupt his European tour to return home to Puerto Rico and participate in the protests. "My people need me!!! And I need them," he declared in the caption for a video he posted on Instagram on July 15, 2019.[4] Later that year, at an event at Harvard University, Bad Bunny told Petra that he didn't think twice about canceling his tour dates to participate in the protests. He felt it was his civic duty as a Puerto Rican and wanted to witness something so historic.

In a post on Twitter, on July 15, 2019, Bad Bunny implored: "HEY, PUERTO RICO! I'm going down to the island and I would love to see you with me and the other people that are in the streets!! These government people think we're afraid and we're going to show them that they are very wrong!!"[5] On July 18, in a caption below an Instagram video, he proclaimed: "THE PEOPLE ARE THE ONLY VICTIMS HERE! NO ONE ELSE! YOU'RE EITHER WITH THE CORRUPT ABUSIVE GOVERNMENT OR YOU'RE WITH THE PEOPLE!! THERE IS NO IN BETWEEN!!! WE WON'T REST! WE WON'T QUIT! WE CAN'T FORGET! THIS IS NOT JUST ABOUT NOW! THIS IS DECADES! BUT THE ASSHOLE RICKY ROSSELLO [*sic*] FILLED THE CUP! AND NOW HE WILL FEEL THE FULL FURY OF OUR PEOPLE! THIS IS HISTORIC! I'LL SAY IT AGAIN, WHEN THEY TELL OUR HISTORY TWENTY YEARS FROM NOW, WHAT SIDE ARE YOU GOING TO BE ON? PUERTO RICO, WE AREN'T GOING TO

QUIT, DAMMIT!"[6] The fury of Bad Bunny and all Puerto Ricans had reached a breaking point. The pride of Puerto Rico was at stake.

"A mí me hizo Puerto Rico," the artist declared in the accompanying video he posted to Instagram. Puerto Rico made me. "This isn't about revolutionaries, this is about everybody, all Puerto Ricans, have to go out to the street no matter their race, their religion, their political ideology."[7]

With fists up and flags waving, Bad Bunny, along with Puerto Rican musical artists Residente, iLe, and Ricky Martin, among others, showed their solidarity in the struggle from the back of a white pickup truck that carried a very large amplifier. Dressed all in black with his then-signature (prepandemic) mask, Bad Bunny stood atop the amplifier and brandished a Puerto Rican flag that included a light blue triangle, a version widely acknowledged as a pro-independence flag. This image of Bad Bunny became one of the most iconic of the protest and made Bad Bunny the most visible celebrity figure who participated. On July 22, the date of the largest protest that drew nearly one-third of the archipelago's entire population, Bad Bunny was present again, proudly waving the same flag, alongside Residente, musician Ednita Nazario, boxing champion Tito Trinidad, and other prominent Puerto Rican figures.

As Vanessa made her way to Puerto Rico, protesters continued to surround the governor's mansion even after Rosselló announced his resignation. The streets of Old San Juan filled with creative hand-painted protest signs, melodic chants simultaneously demanding and celebrating the resignation, and countless mini-concerts and dance parties featuring everything from bomba, to plena, to reggaetón. But there were also vast numbers of police in riot gear who were quick to act aggressively toward the protesters. Bad Bunny posted to Instagram, "Let's use this strength that we have taken and fight for what is right! Let us keep removing the corrupt politicians who abuse the people and build a better Puerto Rico! To the politicians you are a witness that the times where the people were blinded by your lies and manipulations have passed!!! Your time is running out!! Get to work for the country in an honest and committed way, or else you will feel our strength and fury!!! PUERTO RICO!!! I LOVE YOU!!! I am motherfucking proud of you!!! Of us!!! I believe in my country! I believe in my generation! The generation of: YO NO ME DEJO!!!"[8] He also joined the protests on July 24, riding on a truck and dressed in a pink sweatsuit; he was accompanied by fellow reggaetón stars Wisin of the duo Wisin y Yandel, Nicky Jam, and Residente.

3.1 Iconic protest image of Bad Bunny holding the Puerto Rican flag standing atop a large amplifier, which was positioned on top of a white pickup truck directly in front of El Capitolio—the government building that houses Puerto Rico's senate and house of representatives. Just below him on the pickup are the artists iLe, Residente, and Ricky Martin. Bad Bunny is holding the version of the Puerto Rican flag with a light-blue triangle; this flag is widely recognized as a pro-independence flag. Photo by Joe Raedle/Getty Images.

When Vanessa finally landed in Puerto Rico on July 25, 2019, protesters remained in the streets despite the fact that Rosselló had already announced his impending resignation. The protesters sought to keep up the pressure to prevent people intimately involved in Rosselló's administration, such as Secretary of Justice Wanda Vázquez Garced and Acting Secretary of State Pedro Pierluisi, from succeeding Rosselló. The people did not trust anyone who had participated in Rosselló's administration. When Vanessa joined the protests in Old San Juan that afternoon, she learned new protest chants about Vázquez Garced and Pierluisi like, "Pierluisi, Pierluisi, culpable por la crisis" (Pierluisi is to blame for the crisis). She saw the people's art on the walls of the historic buildings with text like "Vamo' Pa' Ti, Wanda" (We're coming for you, Wanda). After centuries of struggle and more recent economic and (un)natural disasters, the people had reached a breaking point. This historic summer of 2019 became known as the Verano Boricua, or the Boricua Summer.[9] It was one of the most important mobilizations in Puerto Rican history, and one that would help shape the lives and attitudes of Bad Bunny and others in his generation.

Reflecting on his time as governor, in a 2021 *New York Times* profile, Rosselló did not admit his failure as a leader that provoked the mass protests and his eventual ouster. Instead, Rosselló said his decision to resign came from something much smaller—a single pothole.[10] The seemingly infinite number of potholes (boquetes) in Puerto Rico and the generally poor condition of roads there, which have severely worsened since Hurricane María, is a quintessential feature of Puerto Rican life at this point. In fact, several of Bad Bunny's songs reference potholes, such as 2018's "Estamos Bien" ("La Mercedes en PR recogiendo boquete" [The Mercedes hitting potholes in PR]), 2022's "El Apagón" ("Cogiendo to' lo hoyo" [Hitting all the potholes]), and 2025's "BOKeTE," which is titled after the infamous potholes. Rosselló told the *New York Times* that it was not the loss of support of the Puerto Rican people that prompted his resignation; instead, it was a time when he and his family drove over a pothole and his young daughter thought it was a gunshot.[11] Ironically, as the governor, these potholes are—if indirectly—his responsibility to fix. So, if it really was a pothole that moved him to resign, it was his own fault. But in reality, everything was his fault. Rather than steward Puerto Rico through myriad crises, Rosselló worsened them with his drastic austerity measures, his willful neglect of different hardships, and his administration's massive corruption scandals.

If Rosselló struggled to connect these dots, the Puerto Rican people did not. In response to Rosselló's disregard for Puerto Rican citizens prior to the release of the chat, the feminist group La Colectiva Feminista en Construcción (known locally as La Cole) mobilized its members and their collaborators to spark the beginnings of these protests. For several years prior to the Verano Boricua, La Cole had already been organizing around many issues that affected ordinary Puerto Ricans, from the imposition of La Junta to the inadequate government response to Hurricane María, to the devastating impact of gender-based violence on the archipelago. As philosopher Rocío Zambrana describes, La Cole utilized Black feminist tactics in their organizing that called attention to the interconnectedness of colonialism, racism, and misogyny.[12] Members of La Cole are widely recognized as the key organizers who drew the masses to the streets. Scholar Marisol LeBrón notes: "It was the radical, intersectional vision of a life affirming future for Puerto Rico put forward by queer and feminist organizers that resulted in convening people for one of the largest, if not the largest, protests in Puerto Rico's history."[13] La Cole spokesperson Zoán Dávila-Roldán told the *New York Times* that the uprising of 2019 was a "long time coming."[14] The chats were the final straw in a "culmination of decades of grievances with the island's leadership."[15]

From the moment that Vanessa landed in San Juan that summer, she found Puerto Ricans eager to talk about what was happening there. A border patrol officer she encountered at the airport saw Vanessa's "Ricky Renuncia" shirt and approached her to talk about what was happening on the streets. "Somos una colonia" (We are a colony), the agent declared, waving over another agent to talk to Vanessa about their takes on the ongoing uprising. Vanessa's Uber driver in San Juan a few days later told her, "We have to have a third party in power because we have no faith or trust in the two main parties. I had no water or power for seven months after María, and I live in the [San Juan] metro area." A restaurant worker in Rincón told Vanessa that the protests gave her goosebumps and said, "Those of us who weren't in San Juan were protesting in our own neighborhoods. So the protests were even bigger than what we saw in the media." On the radio, people called in to express their opinions and, often, their concerns that, despite the protests, nothing meaningful would change. There was a dramatic sense of pride and indignation, hope and worry.

The many crises Puerto Rico has experienced over the last several years all stem from the archipelago's colonial status. Rosselló's predecessor, Alejandro García Padilla—who faced his own experiences with backlash during his term as governor—expressed his disgust with the behavior of Rosselló and his cronies. In an interview with us, García Padilla shared his perspective on the development of the protests as well as his horror at the chats, which he said were "barbaric, completely vulgar." He noted that the chats revealed a level of "hypocrisy" on the part of the Rosselló administration that Puerto Ricans could not accept. According to García Padilla, Rosselló's government would promote a set of "conservative" values while "internally, they are mocking women, mocking gay people, mocking fat people, mocking dead people. In a moment when the country is suffering, [Rosselló] wanted to project sensitivity, but his team showed insensitivity."

The chats clearly offended everyone and galvanized the public. As García Padilla explained, "The summer of 2019 was different [from prior protests] because it wasn't about one issue. It was about all issues.

It was everyone against [Rosselló]. There were religious people, atheists, young people, old people, statehood supporters, those who believe in independence [for Puerto Rico], commonwealth supporters, because you read the chat and everyone could find something offensive. No one was left unoffended." Similarly, Puerto Rican singer and activist Ileana Cabra Joglar, better known as iLe, told us that the chats made it impossible for people to ignore the corruption that has long plagued Puerto Rico. Puerto Ricans were sick of business as usual, and they were not afraid to take the streets.

As iLe recalled, the massive crowds in the Verano Boricua protested in creative and fun ways. The question was not: What *are* Puerto Ricans doing to protest? It was: What *aren't* Puerto Rican people doing to protest? From yoga sessions in front of the governor's mansion, to catchy slogans chanted alongside rhythmic cacerolazos (banging pots and pans), to bomba dancing and drumming, to perreo combativo on the steps of the cathedral in Old San Juan, Puerto Rican protesters utilized innovative tactics as the days of the protest wore on. And while the protests were certainly scary at times due to police efforts to suppress them, the overwhelming sense was one of deeply connected community members who, while indignant, were also having fun.[16]

One of the most impressive spectacles of the protests was when the motorcyclist Misael González Trinidad mobilized thousands of other motorcyclists to join the July 17 protests in Old San Juan. Better known as El Rey Charlie, González Trinidad has a huge following on social media and across Puerto Rico. He had previously rallied many supporters to protest issues like the increased criminalization of working-class men on the archipelago.[17] For the Verano Boricua, he stopped by caseríos (public housing developments) on his way to Old San Juan to recruit additional protesters. Activist Lale Namerrow Pastor commented, "When they arrived in San Juan it was one of the most impressive things I've ever seen. Thousands of motorcycles."[18] El Rey Charlie's crew was so large that police could not stop them from entering the narrow streets of Old San Juan that lead to the governor's home.[19] It was exactly this kind of spontaneous display of massive solidarity across groups, including some who did not typically engage in political protest, that made the Verano Boricua so powerful.[20]

Puerto Rican celebrities' participation also made the mass demonstration feel different from past uprisings. Puerto Rican pop star Ricky Martin's presence was made especially meaningful by the fact that Rosselló and his cabinet members and aides directed homophobic slurs and jokes at Martin in the chats. On July 16, Martin posted a video to social media in which he denounced the governor and pleaded for folks to join him in the streets. He publicly shared that he was feeling: "Frustrated. Angry. I feel such a terrible tension in my chest and like nothing can free me from this anxiety. The only option is to be in Puerto Rico and say 'I am present' at the march." He then described the protest route, which would begin at the Capitol and end at the governor's residence where protesters would "let Ricardo Rosselló know that we do not want him in power, that we are tired. Puerto Rico has suffered so much, and we can't tolerate these cynical leaders any longer."[21] That same day, Bad Bunny posted a video to his social media accounts also calling for people to "hit the streets" for the same protest.[22]

The participation by both artists as well as by salsa singers La India and Danny Rivera and Academy Award–winning actor Benicio del Toro, on Wednesday, July 17, gave important visibility to the protests, especially in the US mainstream media. For instance, on that day journalist Núria Net published an article in *Rolling Stone* titled "Why Bad Bunny Wants Puerto Rican Youth to Take the Streets." While the article used Bad Bunny as a hook, the bulk of the reporting was about the protests themselves and the scandals surrounding Rosselló and his administration.[23] Similarly, an Associated Press video report about the July 22 protest demonstrated this dynamic between the artists and other protesters. While the video's headline mentioned Ricky Martin and Bad Bunny, short clips of celebrities were interspersed with meaningful statements from other protesters. One protester said: "I want the government to know that we are tired of the corruption, that we are tired of them depriving us of services, that people are dying of hunger, there are children without school." Another said, "I feel angry, but my way of showing my anger is marching with all of my fellow Puerto Ricans, with all my compatriots."[24]

Arguably the hypervisibility of these celebrities overshadowed the work of groups like La Cole, but there is no way to know if the media would have given organizers this attention without celebrity involvement. Former Governor García Padilla told us that the artists "were the spokespeople of what people wanted to express. I believe that the protests of the summer of '19 were not protests of artists. They were protests of the people, where the artists were invigorators as spokespeople. And that was fundamental to the success of the protests." The artists themselves also made it clear that the protests were never about them. Instead, like all the other Puerto Ricans protesting that July, they wanted to bring attention to the injustices Puerto Rico has suffered and to create change collectively.

3.2 This image of the protests against Governor Ricardo Rosselló is emblematic of the community-oriented nature, diversity, and popularity of the 2019 #RickyRenuncia movement. One sign reads "FUERA CORRUPTOS HOMOFÓBICOS" (Get out corrupt homophobes), referencing the homophobia evident in Rosselló's chats. Photo courtesy of Gabi Pérez-Silver.

René Pérez Joglar, better known as Residente, told the *New York Times*, "People are there because they are upset, not because they want to see artists."[25] Artists helped draw the attention of the international media that, more often than not, otherwise ignored Puerto Rican matters; however, in Puerto Rico, the crowds amassed to protest, not to see the celebrities.

What's more, celebrities had as much reason to be angry as every other Puerto Rican. Bad Bunny's passion as part of a younger generation of Puerto Ricans was evident when, in announcing he was canceling his European tour to join the protest, he wrote on Instagram: "They've made us believe that those who take to the streets to speak up are crazy, criminals, troublemakers. Let's show them that today's generation demands respect. . . . The country doesn't belong to them, it belongs to all of us."[26] Young people, celebrities or not, played a huge role in making the protests successful. Citing legal scholar Ariadna Godreau Aubert, Marisol LeBrón notes that these protesters had grown up "during Puerto Rico's 'lost decade' when . . . the government enacted selective austerity on an increasingly vulnerable population while enticing foreign nationals to treat

Puerto Rico as their own personal tropical paradise and tax haven."[27] This generation—Bad Bunny's generation—took to the streets to show the government and the world that enough was enough.

Tainy, Bad Bunny's close friend and collaborator, did not participate in the protests, but he reflected on them with us later. He said, "There's power in unity. Just as it was with the [ousting of the] governor and seeing that the entire population came out. . . . It's something special that a country can unite for the same cause." Interestingly, it was music, and reggaetón in particular, that unified Puerto Ricans during the protests.

It was profoundly palpable that, on the streets, people necessarily felt frustration, anger, and indignation alongside joy, love, and pleasure, often to the beat or chants of reggaetón hits. In our interview with iLe, she explained the role of music in Puerto Rican culture: "[M]usic in Puerto Rico is an act of resistance and we vent a lot through music, whether it be the movement in dance, but also plena, bomba, those are also our ways of letting off steam and uniting." As iLe noted, in addition to music, different styles of dance played a crucial role in the protests. This centrality of dance "showcased how embodied pleasure should be a vital and necessary component of political protest," LeBrón writes.[28]

Perreo, the dance associated with reggaetón, played an important role in the Verano Boricua. For many of reggaetón's critics, perreo represents the sexual deviance and promiscuity that they believe is inherent in the genre. Critics have admonished perreo for allegedly promoting inappropriate sexual behavior among Puerto Rican youth, especially young women.[29] These virulent criticisms of perreo ultimately represented the dance and the working-class Black communities that created it as fundamentally distinct from the respectability associated with Puerto Rican nationhood.

But not everyone saw perreo as oppressive or immoral. For some, perreo could be a space of liberation, self-expression, and joy. Performance studies scholar Ramón Rivera-Servera posits that perreo could be part of a "working-class feminist and queer politics" that counters the emphasis on modesty and respectability associated with dominant Puerto Rican society, including in "white middle-class Puerto Rican feminism."[30] In this context, perreo directly contradicts the heteronormative and patriarchal systems that structure Puerto Rican society. It is an expression of recognition and liberation for the marginalized communities that were targeted in Rosselló's chats.

Puerto Rican activists have drawn on perreo in their work. For example, in the years leading up to 2019, La Cole organized an annual event called "Si no puedo perrear, no es mi revolución" (If I can't dance perreo, it's not my revolution). The online invitation for the event declared that the space would be one free of anti-Black violence, racism, lesbophobia, transphobia, homophobia, sexism, or harassment. It invited attendees to come get down on the dance floor and "desculonizar."[31] The term is a play on the word *descolonizar* (decolonize); *culo* means ass. Thus to desculonizar is to engage the body and bodily movement in resistance practices. It was one of many events that addressed dance as an anti-colonial practice, especially for members of LGBTQ+ groups.[32]

"Hoy ganó el perreo" (Today perreo won) was spray-painted on the walls of Old San Juan when Vanessa joined tireless protesters the morning after the announcement of Rosselló's resignation. It was just a few feet from where queer DJs Perra Mística and Kaya Té made history when they convened the perreo combativo. As Rosselló prepared to resign, people gathered on the steps of the Cathedral of San Juan for a perreo intenso, a big perreo party. There, hundreds gathered to dance perreo together. Puerto Rican multimedia artist Karla Claudio-Betancourt created a one-minute video to memorialize the occasion.[33] In the video, viewers see a diverse group of young people dancing perreo on the storied cathedral steps. Women with women, men with men, women and men, trans and nonbinary folks, all dancing together. Some wear shirts and headgear with #RickyRenuncia, while others wear sequins or party clothes. One person wears a revealing Puerto Rican flag bikini bottom, and she shakes her mostly bare ass on the steps of the cathedral (an image that has become so iconic that Bad Bunny includes it in some of his videos).

Those front-and-center at the bold and prideful perreo combativo were the very same groups that have suffered discrimination, exclusion, and violence in Puerto Rico for decades. Rocío Zambrana writes that perreo combativo's "irreverence" presented a type of protest that may not have caused systemic change, but that became a kind of "subversive interruption" that forcefully rejected the respectability politics that defined hegemonic Puerto Ricanness.[34] These protesters took the vulgarities of the chat and enacted them as a means of expressing their own identities, pleasures, joy, and humanity. This form of protest turned the tables on Rosselló, his cronies, and reggaetón's critics by making perreo an inclusive

3.3 This is one of the most iconic images that emerged from the perreo combativo that took place on the steps of Old San Juan's historic cathedral after Ricardo Rosselló announced his plan to resign on July 24, 2019. The convergence of the symbolism of a protester's (dancer's) near-bare butt (with a hint of the Puerto Rican flag peeking out from between the person's butt cheeks) twerking on the steps of a famed Catholic church underscores the layered and subversive nature of this queer, women-led, dance-based protest and celebration. Screen shot from "El Apagón," video directed by Kacho López Mari.

and liberatory space. On the steps of the cathedral, these protesters enacted the very fears that reggaetón would corrupt Puerto Rican society to make instead a profound and patriotic statement about Puerto Rico being a place for everyone. The true corruptors were the politicians like Ricky Rosselló.

The perceived crudeness and irreverence associated with reggaetón and perreo that provoked censorship campaigns against the genres made them the perfect fodder for creative slogans and protest tactics in 2019. Several slogans utilized in the protests referenced reggaetón. Similar to perreo combativo, one slogan, "Sin Perreo, No Hay Revolución" (There's no revolution without perreo), depicted perreo as an inherently revolutionary act. Another played on a famous quote from Puerto Rican independence leader Pedro Albizu Campos, "Cuando la tiranía es ley, la revolución es orden" (When tyranny rules, revolution is warranted), replacing the word revolution so that it stated, "Cuando la tiranía es ley, el perreo es orden" (When tyranny rules, perreo is warranted).

In addition to these slogans, protesters cleverly utilized reggaetón lyrics in their chants, as well. It is ironic that the power of the people's perreo intenso brought down Ricardo Rosselló, given that his father, Pedro Rosselló, played a major role in attempting to censor the music during his own governorship in the 1990s. At that time, much of the censorship efforts focused on lyrics, particularly those about sex and violence. In this vein, the protesters drew from the very types of lyrics and songs that would-be reggaetón censors targeted decades earlier.[35] This meant singing songs like Daddy Yankee and Nicky Jam's 2001 "En la Cama" (In Bed), which explicitly detailed sex acts and referenced women's body parts. The chorus of this song declares, "Yo quiero la combi completa / ¿Qué? / Chocha, culo, tetas" (I want the whole package / What? / Pussy, ass, tits). In 2019, protesters transformed the song into a call and response; someone would yell into the bullhorn, "Yo quiero la combi completa," and the crowd would respond, "¿Qué? ¡Ricky renuncia, puñeta!"(What? Ricky, resign, damn it!).[36] It's unclear when this chant first took hold during the Verano Boricua, but on July 17, it was Residente shouting the first half and eliciting the crowd's response.[37]

Another use of a reggaetón lyric in the protest was a sign quoting the 2003 song "Mami Yo Quisiera Quedarme," by Yandel featuring Alexis. This sign was documented in Lale Namerrow Pastor's 2020 documentary *Landfall*, which recounts the torments of the archipelago from Hurricane María through the Verano Boricua.[38] The original song talks about a man who wants to be with his girlfriend, but the pull of the streets is too strong: "Mami yo quisiera quedarme pero la calle me llama / No me esperas que llego tarde / La calle está que arde" (Mami I wish I could stay but the streets are calling me / Don't wait up for me / The streets are hot).[39] The song continues with the singer describing various weaponry and experiences with gun violence. The sign pictured in *Landfall* transforms the song from a macho song about gun violence into a call to join the masses in the streets.

And it wasn't just older reggaetón tracks that took center stage at the protests. The post–Hurricane María trap anthem "Te Boté" became an anthem once again during the Verano Boricua. The masses of protesters could be heard singing "Te Boté" as they celebrated Rosselló's resignation in the streets of Old San Juan.[40] As mentioned in chapter 2, "Te Boté" can mean "I dumped you," but it also means to kick someone out, to throw away, or to fire; and Puerto Ricans had quite literally kicked out Rosselló.

The day after this celebration in the streets, Vanessa photographed a sign that used the word *botó*. It said, "Ricky no renunció fue el pueblo que lo botó por ser: corrupto, homofóbico, misógino, machista" (Ricky didn't resign, the people threw him out for being corrupt, homophobic, misogynist, male chauvinist).[41] Given the relevance of "Te Boté" during these significant moments for Puerto Rican people, the choice of verb certainly seemed like a reference to the song protesters had been singing the day before.

Tainy's manager Pablo Batista, who began his career when early reggaetón songs like "En La Cama" were popular, told us that Puerto Ricans' usage of reggaetón lyrics and perreo combativo during the protests "shows how clever we are. . . . Puerto Ricans make something out of nothing real quick. . . . So, like, yeah, we're gonna stand here, and we're gonna perrear and we are gonna combat this with perreo." During the Verano Boricua, the repurposing of the songs and the perreo that originally provoked such angst due to their perceived vulgarity took on a new meaning of defiance. They highlighted that the true vulgarity was not reggaetón, nor was it the working-class or Black or queer communities that used it in protest. Instead, the real vulgarity was in the statements of Rosselló and his cronies, both for their language in the chats and the policies that actively marginalized these groups and furthered the colonial project in Puerto Rico. A new anthem arose that explicitly called out this contradiction: "Afilando los Cuchillos" (Sharpening the knives), by Residente, Bad Bunny, and iLe. It was the (unofficial) song of the summer.

Released at 9 a.m. on July 17, 2019, "Afilando los Cuchillos" was the piercing musical critique of the Puerto Rican government that the people wanted and needed as the mass protests continued. Whereas songs like "En La Cama" were recycled for the protest, "Afilando los Cuchillos" was created precisely for this moment, documenting not just the artists' feelings but also what was happening in the streets of Puerto Rico in real time. For instance, Residente opens the track with lines he wrote about the crowds who came with El Rey Charlie: "Llegó la hora de un combo de miles en motoras / Patrullando las 24 horas, boricua de cora' / Con el puño arriba, a la conquista" (The time has come of a group of thousands in motorcycles / Patrolling 24 hours, Boricua from the heart / With the fist up, toward victory). The night this song came out, the streets of San Juan saw the largest gathering of protesting motorcyclists.

In his verse, Bad Bunny directly addresses the chats, calling attention to Rosselló's mocking of the dead from Hurricane María and his rampant homophobia. Bad Bunny repeatedly calls for Ricky to leave, and notes that the whole world will hear of his corruption and immorality:

> Y que se enteren to's los continente'
> Que Ricardo Rosselló es un incompetente
> Homofóbico, embustero, delincuente
> A ti nadie te quiere, ni tu propia gente

> And let all the continents know
> That Ricardo Rosselló is incompetent
> Homophobic, liar, delinquent
> Nobody loves you, not even your own people

Bad Bunny's lines show that the audience for the rap was not only the Puerto Rican protesters but really the entire world. Like their ability to attract mainstream media coverage, these artists would use their star power to draw global attention to Rosselló's incompetence and corruption. Whether by documenting what happened on the ground as Residente did with El Rey Charlie, or by expressing the anger and frustration of Puerto Ricans as Bad Bunny did in his bars, their creation of "Afilando los Cuchillos" brought further attention to the protests.

The song eviscerated Rosselló and his administration for its corruption. Residente drew a direct line between Ricky Rosselló's corruption and that of his father, Pedro Rosselló, "Tú eres hijo del cabrón más corrupto de la historia" (You are the son of the most corrupt bastard in history). In fact, more than eighty people from Pedro Rosselló's administration faced corruption charges, and many went to prison.[42] Making such an explicit connection between the two Rosselló administrations underscored that the chats were but one incident in a pattern of corruption that began long before 2019. The call for Rosselló's ouster was further heightened by iLe's haunting chorus in "Afilando los Cuchillos," stating that the people were sharpening their knives so that they could "arrancar la maleza del plantío / pa' que ninguno se aproveche de lo mío" (pull out the weeds from the crops / so no one can take advantage of what's mine). "Afilando los Cuchillos" was a warning to would-be Puerto Rican politicians that the people were fed up and would no longer accept the type of corruption and abuses they had experienced before.

The song's minimalist sound and flow highlighted Residente and Bad Bunny's rap and lyrical skills, along with iLe's unique and powerful voice. The song also came together very rapidly and with little time to beef up the production quality or instrumentals. In an episode of Residente's YouTube show *El Influence[R]*, Residente and Bad Bunny spoke about the writing of the song just a few weeks after the protest. Residente recalled, "'Afilando los Cuchillos' was like we were so pissed off as Boricuas, we were connected. Everything was honestly really fast. The song was really what we were feeling in the moment, and we put it out quickly. There was no time to think beyond the fact that we were pissed at what was happening in the country. That night we didn't sleep."[43] Turning to Bad Bunny, Residente said, "You were in Ibiza, and you flew like eight or nine hours to get to Puerto Rico. I was in the US [mainland]. We didn't know what each of us were going to write. And it was great because we didn't have any overlap in what we were saying. . . . It was like each of us said what we wanted to say and in the end we ended up sharing different things."[44] Similarly, when we talked with iLe about the process of creating the song, she explained that it was "very spontaneous." Residente contacted iLe and Bad Bunny to record "Afilando los Cuchillos." Each of them recorded their parts separately around the theme of "sharpening the knives." iLe recalled that they hadn't heard each other's parts until the song was all put together.

On *El Influence[R]*, Bad Bunny explained that he sent his verse to the producers at "two in the morning, so that [the song] could come out at 9 a.m."[45] As Residente said in the lyrics of the song, "Esto salió temprano pa' que te lo desayunes" (the song came out early so that you [referring to Rosselló] could have it for breakfast). Residente, Bad Bunny, and iLe released the track on YouTube, making it accessible for free to anybody anywhere in the world. Then, on the same morning the track debuted, the three hit the streets together, and immediately heard the new song everywhere they went.

Right away, the artists felt the significance and the impact of the song. "When you see that people were looking for that song, because it was simply giving words to that historic moment that we were living, it was super powerful," iLe told us. For iLe, hearing their song at the protest affirmed that each artist had effectively used their music to make a mark on the protests in their own way.

"Afilando los Cuchillos" amassed more than 2.5 million views within a day of being posted to YouTube.[46] iLe told us, "In moments like that, we always look for a place to feel safe. And there are times when songs are just

3.4 Residente, Bad Bunny, and iLe attend the July 17, 2019, Verano Boricua protests in San Juan that ousted Governor Ricardo Rosselló. Photo courtesy of Thais Llorca.

that. It's like they help us feel accompanied, to feel safe like, 'Ok. This is what we have to do. Like, we're going to stay here [and protest].' It gives you that push that sometimes one needs to stay those extra hours on the street, to look for other creative ways to protest, so that more people keep coming. They are motivators. So, yes, that moment will always be there for history."

That summer, Residente had stated publicly that he would record a perreo track if Rosselló resigned, and he kept his promise.[47] Bad Bunny joined him, releasing a song called "Bellacoso" [Super horny] the day after Rosselló resigned, reflecting both artists' versatility and range. "Bellacoso" is more of a party anthem than "Afilando los Cuchillos." On the surface, its lyrics seem like an irreverent description of casual sex. But the song made references to the scandal with the chats, particularly with the first line of the chorus "Bien bellacoso pero sin acoso" (Very horny but without harassment). Residente later explained to *Rolling Stone* that the song was about consent but also about inclusivity and joy in protest, much like La Cole's organizing along with the Verano Boricua protests themselves.[48] The music video featured dancers from diverse backgrounds: men, women, Black, white, straight, queer, fat, thin, and everything in between. Thus, it reflected the wide range of people who had been mocked and ridiculed in Rosselló's chats. But, like the perreo combativo, in "Bellacoso," these groups were celebrating together and having fun. The song represented the balance of the protest—the anger and fight, alongside the fun and joy—and the ways that the Puerto Rican people pushed back to show that it was actually Rosselló and his cronies who were the vulgar ones.

In the episode of *El Influence[R]* on which Bad Bunny was a guest, Residente recalled their meeting in 2017 as "love at first sight."[49] He told the audience, "I admire [Bad Bunny] and if people don't understand why I admire him then they don't have the capacity to admire what I admire." He explained that he doesn't collaborate with people he doesn't admire. "For me to do music for my album with someone, there must be a connection. For someone to enter my house, my album, there must be some kind of admiration . . . for those who don't understand it, they will understand it in the future."[50] Bad Bunny has likewise openly acknowledged Residente as one of his most important musical influences.[51] For example, when asked in a 2024 *Vogue* interview what his favorite lyrics by another artist were, Bad Bunny immediately identified Calle 13's 2008 song "La Perla."[52]

Just as Bad Bunny's career builds from the success of Latin trap pioneers like De La Ghetto and Arcángel, Residente and his group, Calle 13, which he founded with his siblings iLe and Eduardo Cabra, have been an ongoing influence on Bad Bunny as an artist. In a 2018 interview about Bad Bunny's first album, *X 100PRE*, YouTube personalities Chente and Molusco asked him about his relationship to Residente, noting that not only had the two artists been seen together often after first connecting late in 2017, but as Molusco notes, they seemed to have a similar approach. Molusco said: "We see that Residente doesn't always do the same thing. When he records, he records what fulfills him. And when we asked you a question at the start of this interview, you basically said you're taking the same approach. So I'm wondering if talking to Residente. . . . Maybe he was able to influence you to think about doing something a lot different on this album than what people are used to getting from Bad Bunny."[53] Bad Bunny reinforced that his approach to *X 100PRE* was to do what came naturally to him during a difficult time in his life. However, he confirmed Residente's impact as well, in line with what Molusco had observed. Bad Bunny stated, "[Residente] has influenced me in terms of maybe making me feel more secure [in this approach]. . . . He told me, 'Cabrón, I realize that you have the ability to . . . make your lyrics better.'

And so he gave me the advice that I can stop singing about stuff without meaning, that I can sing about something with more substance." In a 2022 interview, Residente said that he and Bad Bunny talk every day, but that Bad Bunny's artistic choices are his own. Residente is just there to guide him when he asks for support. "He's doing it . . . by himself but, yeah, I'm there. He knows. And sometimes he asks [for advice] and I answer . . . as I told you, we talk a lot."[54] Thus, Residente has served as an informal mentor to Bad Bunny.

What Residente and Calle 13 modeled for Bad Bunny and other young musicians is how to create popular, danceable hits and songs with extensive political commentary. Eduardo Cabra, the brother of Residente and iLe (known as "Visitante" in his Calle 13 days), told us that a cornerstone of the group's approach was that they "had a coherence between what was said offstage and what was sung on stage." Residente and his siblings came from a politically active family that advocated for Puerto Rican independence. Even early in their career, they did not shy away from making direct political commentary. For instance, in 2005, the group released "Querido FBI" (Dear FBI), which was an almost instantaneous response to the FBI's killing of Filiberto Ojeda Ríos, the Puerto Rican pro-independence revolutionary leader and cofounder of the militant group Los Macheteros.[55] In 2009, Puerto Rican officials canceled a Calle 13 concert after Residente criticized then-Governor Luis Fortuño's plans to lay off 17,000 state employees. Wearing a shirt that said, "Viva Puerto Rico Libre," meaning long live a free/independent Puerto Rico, Residente called Fortuño a "hijo de la gran puta" (a son of a bitch) at the Latin American MTV awards.[56] As a result, the band was banned from performing in Puerto Rico for more than three years.[57]

In many ways, Calle 13's forthright political critique was somewhat of an anomaly within mid-2000s reggaetón and música urbana. One exception is Tego Calderón, whose lyrics often explicitly addressed social and political issues in Puerto Rico, including the effects of US colonialism.[58] However, reggaetón's relative silence on independence is not surprising given the history of repression of expressions of Puerto Rican pride and independence. Puerto Ricans have never enjoyed First Amendment protections for speech against US domination of the archipelago. Repression of pro-independence sentiments included the mass arrests of activists, US government surveillance of those who supported or even discussed independence, and even outright massacres, such as the Masacre de Ponce in 1937, during which the US-appointed governor of Puerto Rico ordered the police to target a peaceful protest against the imprisonment of independence leader Pedro Albizu Campos.[59] Calle 13's immense global popularity and critical acclaim (for instance, they are the most decorated artists in the history of the Latin Grammys to date) meant that moves to censor them brought this continued history of repression, which has so often been covered up, to light at an international level.

Calle 13 exemplified not only a distinct kind of political engagement for a younger generation of reggaetoneros but also a performance style that disrupted, and sometimes openly mocked, the respectability politics associated with Puerto Ricanness. In fact, while Bad Bunny is known for his "do whatever I want" attitude, one might say that it was Calle 13, and Residente in particular, that modeled that attitude for him. Residente's lyrics have always incorporated satire, humor, and irreverence. Scholar and cultural critic Frances Negrón-Muntaner has called Calle 13's style a "poetry of filth" that borrows from surrealist elements to upend the status quo, whether that be the hypermasculine and commercial aesthetics of reggaetón or the political situation in Puerto Rico.[60] Similarly, anthropologist Hilda Lloréns argues that Calle 13's work counters the respectability politics that undergirds Puerto Rican nationalism and gender roles (albeit in ways that sometimes reproduce the very same problems Calle 13 purports to critique).[61] "One of the best things about Calle 13 is that they're like those guys at the back of the class making awful jokes that everyone knows carry a grain of truth. Residente knows where people are vulnerable and inconsistent, and there he strikes," journalist Anne Hoffman once wrote in an article for NPR.[62] Eduardo confirmed to us that Calle 13 was intentional about pushing buttons. "It was like it [our work] created discomfort and also promoted discomfort." The goal was to disrupt expectations and contribute to cultural shifts.

iLe told us that, although artists should not be required to participate in social and political advocacy, it is important for artists to think about ways to creatively engage with issues that are meaningful to them. She explained that doing so shows solidarity with those impacted by and mobilizing around various social issues, and perhaps it encourages others with similar platforms to do the same. In many ways, this is what Calle 13 did for artists like Bad Bunny who grew up listening to their music. Bad Bunny is part of a newer generation of Puerto Ricans who imagine a different kind of future for their homeland. This experience, combined with the lessons learned by groups like Calle 13 before him, has helped Bad Bunny become an especially forceful voice in contemporary Puerto Rico.

✦

Unfortunately, the protests stopped short of changing the system, even if they massively disrupted it. On August 7, 2019, Wanda Vázquez Garced, secretary of justice in the Rosselló administration, was sworn in as governor to complete Rosselló's term. Then, in 2021, Pedro Pierluisi, another member of Ricky Rosselló's administration, became the twelfth elected governor of Puerto Rico. Little has changed. Despite these ongoing problems, iLe told us that the protests nonetheless offered hope for a different future.

Interestingly, whereas Calle 13 received backlash and censorship for their outwardly political stances earlier in the group's career, Bad Bunny's political engagement has actually bolstered his reputation rather than hindered it. Given the massively popular nature of the Ricky Renuncia movement, Bad Bunny's visibility during the 2019 protests increased his popularity among Puerto Ricans on and off the island. It sealed his position as a spokesperson for the archipelago, even if that was not his goal. All this happened at a particularly important moment in Bad Bunny's career, as he was preparing to release another album—*YHLQMDLG*, which stands for *Yo Hago Lo Que Me Da La Gana* (I do whatever I want). The phrase has come to represent much of Bad Bunny's attitude, style, and musical evolution as his career has progressed, which, like Residente before him, blends sharp political critique with a kind of humor and cockiness. The Verano Boricua showed that in many ways Puerto Ricans have long used playfulness and joy as part of their protest traditions. Bad Bunny would marshal this attitude, along with his unique musical fusions and clever lyrics, to continue to push the envelope.

4

"¿POR QUÉ NO PUEDO SER ASÍ?": BAD BUNNY AND GENDER POLITICS

In 2019, a student group at Harvard called No Label arranged for Bad Bunny to visit their campus just before he kicked off the last leg of his X 100PRE Tour at the Agganis Arena in Boston. They invited Petra, a recognized expert in reggaetón, to moderate the conversation. Most stars receive hefty speaker fees to talk to college groups. Bad Bunny agreed to be in conversation for one hour for free to talk about his work.

He also allowed for some time to see the Harvard campus and to talk with Petra informally before they sat down in front of an audience of students. Petra arrived at the Harvard Art Museum ahead of Bad Bunny. The No Label students lounged by the stone steps to the museum, nervously checking their phones. Petra shifted back and forth to keep warm on the crisp fall day. Hoping to exude a cool professor vibe, she had chosen to wear her new plum-colored jeans with a white leather jacket more suited for Southern California than a gusty, overcast New England fall afternoon. Bad Bunny's publicist, Sujeylee Solá, arrived soon after Petra did, and she let everyone know that the star and his team were caught in traffic but that they would be there shortly. Petra made small talk with the police escort, who said he was awed by this assignment. He usually escorted international heads of state, US congressional representatives, and the like; this was the first time he worked with a famous musician and a fellow Latino at Harvard.

Eventually a few conspicuous large, black SUVS pulled up, and several casually dressed, skater-looking Puerto Rican guys stepped out. Bad Bunny got out of the last car. He was tall. He wore a casual striped cotton collared shirt, cargo pants, and hiking boots, along with a small pair of flashy, uber-thin rectangular spectacles and a ratty baseball cap. He didn't look much different from the college students who walked by.

The No Label students showed the group around campus as a way of welcoming Bad Bunny and his entourage. The group had hoped to be inconspicuous, but they were anything but—about a dozen people speaking Spanish, walking through Harvard Yard with a police officer in tow. Still, no one bothered them. Bad Bunny and Petra awkwardly made small talk about things like Fruity Loops and his album *Oasis*, which had been recorded with Colombian reggaetón star J Balvin and released four months earlier. Petra asked him if he was nervous, and he responded, unequivocally, yes. He said that speaking at Harvard was much more nerve-wracking than performing in arenas. She expressed to him how important he and his work were to college students, including her own, mentioning that just that week she had already graded several papers analyzing the gender politics of his music video for the *X 100PRE* song "Caro."

"¡En serio!" he exclaimed, seeming genuinely shocked.

But it was true. Petra's students at Wellesley College were particularly attracted to "Caro" because of the music video, in which Bad Bunny morphed into an androgynous woman played by Puerto Rican model Jazmyne Joy. The gender fluidity in the video stood out in a Latin music scene that tends to be firmly entrenched in gender binaries, and in which queer representations are few and far between.

"Caro" was just one of many times in Bad Bunny's career when he pushed the envelope around questions of gender, masculinity, and queerness in Latin music. This is especially critical within the Latin trap scene, where hypermasculinity is central to the ethos of the genre.[1] From early on, Bad Bunny aesthetically distinguished himself from other Latin trap artists by embracing brightly colored and more fitted clothing, as opposed to the baggy athletic jerseys and jeans associated with the genre. He painted his nails (in fact, "Caro" begins with a scene of Bad Bunny getting his nails painted), which is an increasingly accepted practice for young men now, but which at the time was considered quite controversial. In

4.1 Still shot from the video for the single "Caro," from Bad Bunny's 2018 album *X 100PRE*. At the time, few men painted their nails in the reggaetón or Latin trap scene; however, Bad Bunny incorporated painted nails as part of his overall signature style. This opening scene featuring a woman giving Bad Bunny a manicure challenged many of the norms associated with masculinity in reggaetón. Video directed by Fernando Lugo and Bad Bunny.

2018, Bad Bunny was denied service at a nail salon in Spain because they declared that they did not paint men's nails, and he was not shy about expressing his frustration with the situation on social media.[2] In an interview with us, Apple Music's Latin Programmer Jerry Pullés reflected, "I remember there were tons of people on the internet just talking about a man painting his nails like 'Oh my God! Oh my God!' And now any male artist would paint nails and you don't even think twice about it." Eddie Santiago, the former head of US Latin at Spotify, noted in an interview with us that Bad Bunny "was unapologetic in challenging gender norms. It started with 'small things'"—nail polish, wearing female-presenting clothing, and jewelry. "He just likes to wear cool shit and cool shit doesn't really have a gender tied to it," Eddie explained.

Bad Bunny has famously said that he admires women's clothing for its diversity of styles, and he chooses to wear what he feels most comfortable in above all else. The artist told *Allure* in 2021, "Going shopping with my mom was one of my favorite things because I would get lost in the women's department, seeing the combinations, the colors, the cuts, the designs. And then it was my turn to buy clothes and it was boring as hell. The same jeans and T-shirts, jeans and T-shirts in different sizes. The women had it all!" Of purses he told *Allure*, "For women there are so many different types, colors, shapes, designs. . . . And what do men get? A beat-up old wallet to stuff in your pocket."[3] He has worn clothing designed for women on the covers of high fashion magazines like *Harper's Bazaar* and *Allure*. In 2022, he debuted at the Met Gala with an outfit that combined the tailored men's collared shirt and tie with a jacket that had the puffed sleeves more characteristic of women's clothing and a long matching skirt. The sides of his head were shaved, and his longer hair on the top was straightened and styled in an updo adorned with gold leaf barrettes.[4]

Veteran Latin trap artist De La Ghetto credits Bad Bunny's fashion sense for shifting the image of Latin trap artists as super macho guys from la calle. De La Ghetto told us, "Our genre in Puerto Rico is very machista, ¿entiende'? Bad Bunny broke that stereotype, like 'Yo, what do you mean I can wear my shorty short pants all the way up, you know, to my knees?' I can rock shorts with Vans and no socks. You know, I'm me, let me be me. I don't have to be like everybody else with the same chain, with the same haircut, with the same attitude, entiende'? I was like, 'Wow, qué bueno, he gave us a chance to breathe.' He changed everything. He practically created a whole new genre."

Bad Bunny contests gender norms in other ways as well. In 2023 he received the Vanguard Award from GLAAD for promoting acceptance of LGBTQ+ communities in the media, reflecting the profound impact that Bad Bunny has made in pushing conversations about gender identity and sexuality forward. He has also spoken up about the crisis of gender-based violence. This is significant in the context of Latin trap and reggaetón as well as in Puerto Rico, where gender-based violence and femicides (or the killing of women, often by domestic partners) is a serious problem. Bad Bunny's contesting of gender norms and bringing attention to gender-based violence is an integral part of his politics, even if he does not frame it as such. To be sure, like a lot of reggaetón (and other popular music), Bad Bunny's lyrics can be interpreted as objectifying women, something for which he has received criticism by cultural critics and scholars.[5] Nevertheless, Bad Bunny's speaking out on issues related to gender inequality and violence, and his own gender presentation and performances, are a central aspect of his music as resistance.

4.2 Bad Bunny attends the 2022 Gilded Age–themed Met Gala in a custom-made outfit designed by Riccardo Tisci for Burberry. The outfit combines elements of both men's and women's fashion trends from Puerto Rico in the late 1800s. He wore his hair in a more feminine-style updo. The iconic outfit exemplifies how Bad Bunny often resists mainstream gender norms in his own fashion choices. Kevin Mazur/Getty Images Entertainment via Getty Images.

Back at the Harvard event, Bad Bunny and Petra were settled into their seats on stage. Students had prepared questions for him in advance about his music and activism. After a brief discussion of his song "Estamos Bien" and the Verano Boricua protests of 2019, they turned to questions of gender politics in reggaetón. Bad Bunny and Petra both balked at the students' question about why reggaetón was so misogynistic. Petra felt validated when Bad Bunny repeated what she frequently tells her own students—that reggaetón indeed deserves criticism for its misogyny, but that this is a reflection of sexism in society at large, not only the music itself. Bad Bunny himself has received criticism for having misogynistic lyrics. He mentioned that he learned from critique and took the time to hear where others were coming from. Bad Bunny explained that he reflected on his upbringing in a machista society and how, just like with his work in the 2019 protests, he could use his platform to represent women as agents in their own stories, while also acknowledging men's vulnerability and feelings.

For some fans, this vulnerability and attention to feelings is evident from Bad Bunny's very first hits. For instance, recall Jerry Pullés's comments in chapter 1 about one of Bad Bunny's first singles "Soy Peor," in which he expressed heartache and vulnerability in a way that distinguished him from other Latin trap artists at the time. Another early hit, Bad Bunny's 2019 single "Callaíta," similarly evokes feeling in its lyrics and sound that differentiates it from many other reggaetón hits. The song developed after Tainy sent Bad Bunny a beat he produced. Tainy told us that "Callaíta" is one of the songs that he feels marked a milestone in his own career. He said that the song "opened a new stage in my career where I could make my own music as an artist, not just as a producer of other artists' records. I could make a new sound, and I felt like I could continue experimenting more." In his production of the song, Tainy brought together sounds that one might not typically hear in reggaetón. As he told us, "I tried a combination of percussion that is not the traditional one [for reggaetón], and types of chords, combining them with that emotion, that feeling. . . . When it came out, it was really different from the way that reggaetón or [música urbana] normally sounds. But it sounded good to me."

Tainy showed the song to Bad Bunny, who connected with it right away. Bad Bunny returned the completed song two days later. Tainy said, "He could understand exactly the emotion or the feeling that I wanted to convey in the music, and he executed it in lyrics and melodies." "Callaíta" begins with the distant calls of seagulls and waves crashing, and then an organ starts to play. Bad Bunny told *Vanity Fair* that "'Callaíta' . . . is a song

I never get tired of. The intro track is such a beautiful melody," referring to the melodies that Tainy created.[6] In her review of the single, Suzy Exposito wrote in *Rolling Stone*, "The song encapsulates some of the most telltale signs of the impending beach-faring season: the hiss of crashing waves, distant cries of seagulls and carnivalesque echoes of a steam organ. Altogether, they make for a spellbinding collage-turned-reggaetón lullaby."[7]

The ethereal sounds that Tainy created made "Callaíta" stand out in the crowded field of reggaetón. But it was also the story that Bad Bunny told in the lyrics that fostered this lullaby feeling. The song describes a young woman who is usually *callaíta* (quiet, but in an endearing way), but who, at heart, is actually *atrevida*—or more daring than she seems. Bad Bunny sings,

Ella es callaíta
Pero p'al sexo, es atrevida, yo sé
Marihuana y bebida
Gozándose la vida como es

She's quiet
But daring at sex, I know
Marijuana and drinks
Enjoying life as it comes

This is a familiar reggaetón plot. From Calle 13 to Don Omar to CNCO, many reggaetón artists tell the story of a respectable, often studious young woman who becomes her wilder self when she dances perreo.[8] But in "Callaíta," there is a plot twist. Bad Bunny sings: "Ella no era así, ella no era así, no sé que la dañó" (She wasn't like this, she wasn't like this, I don't know what hurt her). Whether "así" (this) refers to her quietness or her daringness is ambiguous.

This ambiguity is significant. While many songs celebrate the notion that dancing perreo makes women daring, the focus on women dancing perreo has also been used to attack reggaetón, reflecting a sexual double standard that "Callaíta" effectively resists. In 2002, Puerto Rican Senator Velda González initiated the Anti-Pornography Campaign that primarily targeted sexual content in reggaetón music videos, though González claimed it addressed pornographic content in the media generally. Proponents of the Anti-Pornography Campaign were especially concerned that these music videos might negatively affect young women's self-esteem and sexual behavior, potentially "corrupting" them and leading them to have premarital sex or to do drugs. Tellingly, it did not raise concerns about the impact of reggaetón on young men.[9] Tainy's manager Pablo Batista remembers the reaction that reggaetón fans and artists had to the campaign. He told us that they wondered why the Anti-Pornography Campaign targeted reggaetón singers rather than the actual drug dealers and criminals who committed violence. He told us that González and her supporters "were wasting [their] time. [They were] wasting police resources following us, when you had drug trafficking everywhere." Pablo's comments reflect a common sentiment among reggaetón artists and fans at the time who regularly retorted that the real threats facing young people in Puerto Rico were poverty, inadequate housing, poor education, and other systemic inequalities rather than reggaetón.[10] However, the Anti-Pornography Campaign instead doubled down on depicting reggaetón itself as posing a danger to Puerto Rican youth. Following the logic of the Anti-Pornography Campaign, it is reggaetón that has damaged the protagonist of "Callaíta" who enjoys vices like drinking, weed, and perreo. In contrast, Bad Bunny tells an entirely different story, one of a woman with a history, potentially a painful one, one that either made her more quiet or more daring—or both.

For the music video, Bad Bunny wanted a fun vibe. His team contacted Grammy-winning reggaetón music video director Kacho López Mari after seeing an ad for Medalla beer that Kacho made showing young people hanging out and having fun. As Kacho told us from his San Juan office, the only direction that Bad Bunny gave him was that "Callaíta" should show the "perfect summer." The music video focuses on a young woman played by Puerto Rican model Natalia García. Her friends pick her up at home to go to a local bar. There, they dance, drink, and have fun. When we see García dancing, she is often smiling, surrounded by friends, and dancing perreo on her own terms.[11] Bad Bunny notices her from his seat at the bar, and while they exchange glances, he does not pursue her. The two eventually meet up at a late-night beach party, where they dance in a playful way, barely even touching each other. One of the iconic images from the "Callaíta" music video is a beautiful, old-fashioned carousel lit up against the night sky with waves crashing in the background.[12] García seems totally free as she rides the carousel with her friends and, later, with Bad Bunny himself, leaning against his shoulder as Bad Bunny gives her a warm embrace. The carousel, with its invocation of youth and fun, suggests a kind of innocence and calm. Overall, the music video's imagery matches the lyrics that emphasize the woman's inner thoughts, feelings,

4.3 In this still shot from the music video for "Callaíta," model Natalia García joyfully dances with friends at a beach party with the brightly lit carousel in the background. This moment exemplifies her innocent playfulness, and contrasts starkly with the ways in which the Anti-Pornography Campaign portrayed reggaetón and perreo as always dangerous and threatening to women. Video directed by Kacho López Mari.

and motivations rather than her body and sex appeal. This directly contradicts the Anti-Pornography Campaign's assumption that perreo is always dangerous and threatening to women.

Of course, if the carousel's image is whimsical and carefree, getting it to the set was not. In his *Vanity Fair* interview, Bad Bunny acknowledged this: "I want a carousel in front of the beach. I know that I'm not going to be the one who has to take it [there]. Poor guys had to work their asses off to get that carousel on that beach. But I was surprised when I got there and saw the carousel. I said, 'Oh wow!'"[13] The video was filmed in Playa Caracoles, a nature preserve in Arecibo, on the north coast of Puerto Rico. Because it was a protected area, Kacho's team could not bring trucks onto the beach, nor could they move any sand. It took them two days to carry in the equipment and materials they needed, including large planks of wood to create a base on which they could put the carousel. The carousel was brought in from a company in San Juan, and they had to use a giant construction crane to place it onto the beach from the parking lot. The efforts were worth it, as the image of the carousel became one of the most iconic associated with Bad Bunny's career, making the unique song even more memorable.

Both the video and the song "Callaíta" contrast with the typical portrayal of women in reggaetón, including, at times, by Bad Bunny himself. That said, Bad Bunny often subverts reggaetón's typical gender representations even in songs that on the surface appear to conform to them. The song "La Difícil" included on *YHLQMDLG* describes a woman who loves to party, do drugs, and have sex with different men because she doesn't want a relationship. She is so sexy and flirtatious that everyone—men and women—all want to get with her. In many respects, she is the archetypal reggaetón woman, given her insatiable sexual appetite. She is also ogled by everyone around her. Yet she is in charge of her own sexuality, the agent of her own pleasure. She decides which men she dates; she tells them what she likes and how she likes to be touched, and she is in full control of their encounters.

The music video for "La Difícil," directed by Cliqua and Stillz, complicates this narrative even further. Bad Bunny debuted the video on February 28, 2020, the day before *YHLQMDLG*'s release. The video begins with a very young mother, played by Miami model and podcaster La Yuli, braiding her daughter's hair on the couch. The camera cuts to a dressing room reminiscent of one in a strip club, where the young mother joins other women putting on their makeup in front of a huge, brightly lit mirror. It turns out that these are the video models for Bad Bunny's latest video. They dance perreo in the background while he performs. As the narrative progresses, we see the young mother take care of her daughter between gigs like sexy photo shoots, other music videos, or working in a nightclub. In one particularly jarring moment, she auditions for something, dancing before a black screen as a panel of men watch her hips and butt. She never seems especially happy at work, always giving a very serious and sometimes blank expression while she dances and meets the various men who might hire her for jobs. But with her child, the young mother laughs, smiles, and has fun doing everyday things like brushing their teeth or washing clothes in the laundromat. The video ends with the young mom, still clad in a glittery sequin minidress, cuddling in bed with her daughter.[14]

Women such as the video's protagonist—who dance provocatively, whether as strippers, exotic dancers, or music video models—figure prominently in the discourse surrounding reggaetón. Indeed, female dancers were the focus of the Anti-Pornography Campaign. Everyone from politicians to social workers maligned music video dancers. One reggaetón music video director's defense of his videos was that hiring strippers for music videos took them out of the club, implying that strippers were, in fact, the danger to themselves and society that the Anti-Pornography Campaign made them out to be. All these narratives implied that women who dance perreo are inherently problematic and hypersexual, dangerous role models for young women, and lacking in agency themselves.[15]

In the video for "La Difícil," Bad Bunny plays a rapper who consistently hits on women and, like the other men in the video, is completely oblivious to the trials and tribulations that the young mother faces. From the point of view of his character, the dancers might be exactly what the Anti-Pornography Campaign claims. Yet the video's focus on the young mother reveals a different story. She is not actually obsessed with her own sexual pleasure; she pretends to be the woman the song depicts in order to earn money to take care of her daughter. That she resorts to this kind of work to support her family could be an implicit critique of sex work and related jobs as exploiting vulnerable women. At the same time, combined with the lyrics, the video presents a more complex and nuanced understanding of women's agency in these spaces.[16]

Indeed, Bad Bunny frequently gives agency to the female protagonists in his songs by focusing on their desires, whether sexual or otherwise, and many of his music videos amplify that agency in the presentation of the songs. Bad Bunny is very intentional about prioritizing videos in order to give greater meaning to his songs. As Kacho described to us, many record labels have decreased their investment in music videos, and many artists now make only short-form videos that can be easily accessed on internet platforms like TikTok and Instagram. In contrast, Bad Bunny has actually invested *more* in his music videos over time. Bad Bunny's videos continue to provide meaning to his songs; he uses music videos to make socially relevant statements. This allows his pronounced commentaries on gender to have a greater impact.

As part of their public conversation at Harvard, Bad Bunny and Petra played a series of Bad Bunny's music video clips, discussing each one before playing the next. One of those clips was the 2018 single "Solo de Mí." The song is slow, propelled by a piano with a reggaetón beat in the background. In it, Bad Bunny shows his emo side, singing about the end of a relationship; but instead of a mournful lament, the lyrics describe someone who is happy to reclaim their freedom. The chorus begins the song: "No me vuelvas a decir 'bebé' / Yo no soy tuyo ni de nadie, yo soy solo de mí" (You won't call me baby again / I'm not yours or anybody else's, I'm only mine).

Much like "Callaíta" and "La Difícil," the message of "Solo de Mí" becomes all the more powerful in relation to the music video. It too centers on a young woman, played by Venezuelan actress Laura Chimaras, who wears a sequined black jacket with just a black bra underneath. She mouths the lyrics, which are sung in Bad Bunny's voice, into an old-fashioned microphone in front of a sparkly blue curtain. Chimaras begins with her eyes cast downward as she sings the chorus, but when the beat drops, a light shines on her and she starts looking into the camera. Right before the first verse begins, her head flings sharply to the left as if she has been punched. She looks back at the camera, gingerly puts her hair behind her ear, and a dark bruise starts to form on her cheek. As the song progresses, the violence continues and she develops a black eye and a bloody nose. She stares more defiantly into the camera after each punch. But then, not quite two minutes in, she hunches forward and sticks her hands straight out at the camera. When she puts them down, her wounds have healed and she smiles into the camera while she declares that she doesn't belong to anyone but herself. The video shifts as a kalimba starts to play and a harder dembow beat kicks in. As the end of the song morphs into more of a party track, the video features Chimaras partying with Bad Bunny and his friends at a club.[17]

Bad Bunny has openly described the video as a commentary on domestic violence. Literary scholar Elena Valdez writes that some aspects of the video reinforce patriarchal norms (e.g., Chimaras's revealing outfit, her being the only woman in a nightclub surrounded by men), stating that this could be a "male version of what women's liberation should be."[18] Yet she argues that the music video is also a feminist text. Valdez commented that Bad Bunny's director's credit in the video was a "personal declaration from the artist" about the necessity for serious action to address gender-based violence in Puerto Rico.[19]

One of the things that keeps a superstar like Bad Bunny on the roster of a smaller independent record label like Rimas is that it allows him to retain creative control of his music and videos. In 2019, Bad Bunny told Petra that "Solo de Mí" was one of the most important videos he had made to date. He said he had deliberately chosen to keep the video simple and focus on the woman's experience, even as he acknowledged that the lyrics were told from the male perspective (in addition to being sung in his voice, the lyrics are masculine, e.g., "no soy *tuyo*" instead of *tuya*). In a 2018 interview with Chente Ydrach and Molusco, Bad Bunny explained more about the concept of the video, which he released after the song. "The song is amazing," he told them. "Listen and interpret it how you want. And then, BOOM! I change your mind completely with this concept and message [of the video]. And that's how it was. And the whole world was like, 'What?' Because the song is un despecho.[20] I don't want you in my life anymore, etc. And then we get hype and go off. But then it takes on another meaning."[21] Bad Bunny's strategy for the release of the video for "Solo de Mí" amplified his political messaging about gender-based violence in Puerto Rico without compromising its mass appeal.

In their introduction to a special issue on gender-based violence in Puerto Rico in *CENTRO: Journal of the Center for Puerto Rican Studies*, Diana Aramburu and Tania Carrasquillo Hernández give a sense of the scope of the problem on the archipelago: in a population of just over 3 million people there were seventy-nine femicides in Puerto Rico in 2022, including fifteen attributed to intimate partner violence. This is a shocking increase from fifty-nine femicides in 2021.[22] Activists, analysts, and scholars argue, however, that these numbers are likely inaccurate because of underreporting and the government's unwillingness to seriously account for the problem.[23]

Vilma González Castro directs Coordinadora Paz para las Mujeres, which is a coalition of organizations in Puerto Rico dedicated to ending gender-based violence by providing services and education to victims and communities. She notes that overlapping crises like the debt crisis, Hurricane María, and COVID-19 exacerbated what was already a high rate of gender-based violence in Puerto Rico.[24] Colonialism makes stress the baseline condition of the population.[25] The debt crisis limited funds for social services and support. Hurricane María destroyed infrastructure needed to access women in rural communities. The isolation of COVID-19 presented new opportunities for gender-based violence to flourish. In January of 2021, Governor Pedro Pierluisi signed Executive Order 2021-013, declaring a state of emergency regarding gender-based violence. The order created a committee of government agencies and other organizations to tackle the crisis.[26]

For some activists, Pierluisi's declaration was too little too late. Feminist organizations had been protesting and calling on Puerto Rico's government to address femicide for years. In 2018, La Cole camped out in front of the governor's mansion, La Fortaleza, to demand that then-Governor Ricky Rosselló address gender-based violence. Rosselló never met with them. Instead, on November 25 (the UN's International Day for the Elimination of Violence against Women, which coincided with the last day of La Cole's protest), the police arrived and attacked protesters with pepper spray and batons.[27]

Bad Bunny released "Solo de Mí" one month later. Simultaneously, he made an announcement on his Instagram account denouncing gender-based violence:

I'm not sure if cockfighting is abuse, but gender-based violence against women and the absurd number of women who are murdered every month DEFINITELY IS. When are we going to prioritize what really matters? . . . IT'S TIME TO TAKE ACTION NOW! I know that there will be a lot of opinions, but I'll just say that for something to start, everyone has to do their part and what they can, WE DON'T WANT ANY MORE DEATHS! Respect women, respect men, respect your neighbors, respect life! LESS VIOLENCE, MORE PERREO! (AND ONLY IF SHE WANTS IT, IF NOT LEAVE HER TO PERREAR ALONE AND DON'T FUCK WITH HER.)[28]

Then, in January, Bad Bunny and Residente showed up at La Fortaleza to demand a meeting with Rosselló about violence in Puerto Rico (it is unclear to what extent gender-based violence was discussed in the meeting). Residente told *Rolling Stone* that he and Bad Bunny circled La Fortaleza for hours, taking pictures with the security guards and trying to obtain permission to enter the building. According to Residente, what finally gained them entry was that he sent the governor a direct message on Twitter asking for the meeting, and Rosselló agreed.[29] The three men talked about many of the overlapping crises on the archipelago, including austerity, education, and, especially, violence.[30] In a *Rolling Stone* interview, Residente mentioned that he was particularly interested in supporting the "feminist movement" in Puerto Rico and the work of La Cole.

For their part, La Cole expressed their rage at Rosselló's hypocrisy. They wrote on Facebook, "Ricardo Rosselló welcomed Residente and Bad Bunny to speak about violence in the country, but DIDN'T welcome us when we were camped out in front of La Fortaleza for three days demanding he declare a state of emergency about gender-based violence. Perhaps the governor only meets with men, or is he only here for the faranduleo [show]?? Keep disrespecting the women of this country; machista violence is also the responsibility of the state."[31] In her analysis of these events, Elena Valdez referenced this clear disrespect shown by Rosselló for his constituents, which she argues is intimately tied to the rampant misogyny in Puerto Rico.[32]

Since then, Bad Bunny has continued to use his art and performance to address issues pertinent to gender equality and to ally himself with groups marginalized on the basis of sex and gender identities. For instance, he repeated his message about women's bodily autonomy in his 2020 hit song "Yo Perreo Sola" on *YHLQMDLG*. The music video set included a neon sign that read "Ni Una Menos," or "not one [woman] less," a slogan that originated during massive protests in Argentina against gender-based violence in 2015 and that quickly took hold across the Americas.[33]

The murder of Alexa Negrón Luciano, a Black homeless trans woman who was brutally killed on February 24, 2020, in Toa Baja, Puerto Rico, was another occasion on which Bad Bunny spoke out. Negrón Luciano was shot in a park in Toa Baja; a video uploaded to social media subsequently showed a group of men harassing her before she was killed.[34] Negrón Luciano's murder is different from intimate partner violence—in this case, she was killed by people she did not know.[35] Still, as Vilma González notes, violence against trans people stems from the same structural inequities and gender ideologies as other forms of gender-based violence.[36] Trans women in Puerto Rico face disproportionately high levels of economic insecurity, homelessness, and violence.[37] Puerto Rico has only recently begun including violence against trans women in their statistics, and such violence is vastly underreported.[38] In fact, Negrón Luciano was the first of six known trans people killed in Puerto Rico in 2020 alone.[39]

Three days after Negrón Luciano's death, on February 27, Bad Bunny appeared on the *Tonight Show with Jimmy Fallon* to perform his new song "Ignorantes" with Panamanian singer Sech. The song is classic emo Bad Bunny with lyrics about a break-up. The music video already advocated for queer equality by portraying both queer and heterosexual couples struggling to manage their relationships. The song was a hit, debuting at number three on Billboard's Hot Latin Songs chart and even breaking into the Hot 100 in its first week.[40] For the *Tonight Show* performance, Bad Bunny wore a black skirt with boots, a white T-shirt, and a light-pink jacket. As he sang, the jacket slowly slipped off his shoulders to reveal the words, "Mataron a Alexa, no a un hombre con falda" (They killed Alexa, not a man in a skirt). Misgendering is endemic in Puerto Rico, where investigators and the media frequently misgender or deadname trans victims of violence.[41] Bad Bunny's message was both a pointed response to US media outlets ignoring the case and a criticism of investigators and media outlets in Puerto Rico that reported that Alexa was a "man in a skirt."

Bad Bunny's reputation for speaking out about gender-based violence is so strong that people sometimes interpret his work to be about gender-based violence even when it is not. One example is the song "Andrea" from his 2022 album *Un Verano Sin Ti*. "Andrea" was one of the last songs recorded for the album. Its lyrics are similar to songs like "Callaíta" that describe a woman striving for autonomy. "Andrea" tells the story of a woman named Andrea who hopes for a better future with a loving partner who respects and supports her. The lyrics imply that she has experienced intimate partner violence: "A la buena, beso y abrazo / A la mala, botellazo sin soltar el vaso" (The good way: a kiss and a hug/The bad way: hitting with a bottle without dropping the glass). Later, Bad Bunny raps:

> Ella no quiere una flor, solo quiere que no la marchiten
> Que cuando compre pan, no le piten
> Que no le pregunten qué hizo ayer
> Y un futuro lindo le inviten
> Que le den respeto y nunca se lo quiten

> She doesn't want a flower, just to not whither
> To not get catcalled when she goes out
> To not get asked what she did yesterday
> And to be invited to have a nice future
> To have respect and never get it taken away from her

Here, Bad Bunny paints the picture of a woman who desires a better future in which, above all, she is respected and recognized for who she is. Bad Bunny wrote the verses; for the chorus, however, he enlisted the help of Buscabulla, a Puerto Rican indie pop duo composed of spouses Luis Alfredo del Valle and Raquel Berríos, who blend electronic synth sounds with tropical rhythms. In the chorus, vocalist Berríos continues the story about Andrea's quest for respect and autonomy when she sings, "Quiero alguien que se atreva, que se atreva y me entienda a mí" (I want somebody who is not afraid, who is not afraid and who understands me).

"Andrea" had a major impact. Media outlets such as *People en Español* and Yahoo News reported that it specifically referenced the case of Andrea Ruiz Costas.[42] Ruiz Costas was a thirty-five-year-old woman who had sought legal protection from her abusive ex-boyfriend Miguel Ocasio Santiago. In 2021, she took advantage of the new law signed by Governor Pierluisi meant to address domestic violence. Ruiz Costas asked the court to arrest Ocasio Santiago, who she said threatened and stalked her; but the judge ruled that there was "no cause" to do so. Shortly afterward, on April 28, 2021, her body was found on the side of the road. Ocasio Santiago had assaulted her with a knife and then burned her body so badly that she could be identified only via dental records. Miguel Ocasio Santiago confessed to the killing, and subsequently committed suicide while in prison awaiting trial for first-degree murder.[43] Ruiz Costas's murder galvanized

Puerto Ricans who demanded the release of the audio tapes of her court hearing in order to understand just how this could happen, especially in the wake of Pierluisi's state of emergency declaration. As the newspaper *El Nuevo Día* reported, although the government claimed that they were prioritizing this issue, the Puerto Rican courts denied the majority of petitions for protective orders despite 2021 being a record year for femicides.[44]

Given Bad Bunny's previous advocacy around gender violence and the massive publicity surrounding the case, many people believed "Andrea" was actually about Ruiz Costas. Even Buscabulla thought this was a possibility. Del Valle told NPR, "It's an image that's put in your mind, obviously, if you're Puerto Rican. You knew about the case. You know how horrible it was. It was very visceral, you know?" His partner, Raquel Berríos, recalled, "Benito never really clarified if it was about Andrea." However, Berríos said, "When I was writing the [chorus], I kind of had it in the back of mind, but I wasn't completely sure."[45]

Producer MAG described how the song was written, and the use of the name is clearly coincidental. MAG and Bad Bunny were in Miami putting the finishing touches on *Un Verano Sin Ti*. Bad Bunny was editing vocals on the computer while MAG was going through some new "ideas" because he felt the album was "missing something." He was reviewing a track he described as "my attempt at making a Buscabulla beat. I titled it 'Buscabulla-type beat.' So I'm listening to that in my ear, and Benito turns around and was like '¿Qué es eso?' And I was like, 'Esto es una idea que tengo . . .' And he was like 'Let me hear it, let me hear it again.' I don't know how he heard it because it was playing so low and I had my phone to my ear." MAG played the beat for him. MAG recalled that after he went home for the night, Bad Bunny "ended up writing and recording himself that night. He was obsessed with the beat. The next day, we're back together, and he's like 'I've been writing, and I recorded to that track.'" But the song lacked a chorus. Bad Bunny asked MAG if they could contact Buscabulla even though it was very late at night. So MAG sent the couple a DM on Instagram telling them Bad Bunny, whom they had never met, wanted to talk to them. They agreed to have a late-night impromptu FaceTime. After the call, Buscabulla made the chorus and recorded an extended instrumental to close out the song.

Bad Bunny has stated that the song was not about Andrea Ruiz Costas. He told Chente Ydrach, "I really don't know how to feel about [the erroneous assumption that it is about Ruiz Costas]. I know it went viral and even came out in the news." Bad Bunny was not necessarily opposed to the association people made between his song "Andrea" and Ruiz Costas. That said, he explained, "The person I'm talking about in the song could easily be Andrea, the woman that was murdered, just as it could be a million other women that have been victims of gender-based violence." The Andrea of his song was meant to be relatable, he said. "I love that many women have found themselves identified with it and perhaps the family members of Andrea can identify her with it. . . . The reality and purpose of the song is that the Andrea from the song is still alive and wants to stay alive."[46]

The fact that so many people, including his collaborators, assumed Bad Bunny's "Andrea" was Andrea Ruiz Costas is indicative of his well-established reputation as an advocate for ending gender-based violence. Since his earliest hits, Bad Bunny has called attention to gender-based violence and to femicides, in particular, in Puerto Rico. This is all the more significant within the context of reggaetón, a genre in which many songs and music videos promote deeply misogynistic messages. Still, as Bad Bunny and Petra discussed at Harvard, reggaetón itself is not responsible for the misogyny, violence, homophobia, and transphobia that pervade Puerto Rican (and other) societies.

Activists in Puerto Rico correctly do not point to reggaetón as the thing that causes gender-based violence; instead, they talk about the structural inequalities, deep-seated cultural norms, and the lack of crucial resources, especially given the colonial relationship with the United States, as key factors in perpetuating the problem. Nonetheless, given reggaetón's reputation as an especially misogynistic genre, it is significant that a male reggaetón artist has chosen to use his platform to actively speak out against gender-based violence in all its forms.

Although Bad Bunny was amazed when Petra told him many of her students wrote papers about the video for his song "Caro," Petra was never surprised. The gender-bending music video switches back and forth between Bad Bunny playing himself and androgynous Puerto Rican model Jazmyne Joy playing Bad Bunny, both styled and dressed identically so that sometimes it is difficult to tell who's who. For many of our students, this was a refreshing departure from the hypermasculine "barriocentric macho" of reggaetón obsessed with cars, money, and girls.[47] "Caro" is a self-love anthem that declares that everyone, regardless of their background, is valuable in their own way. This message is amplified in the song by the video's "Easter egg" moment, a surprise interlude featuring Ricky Martin. Soft chords play in the background and Bad Bunny sings

¿Por qué no puedo ser así?
¿En qué te hago daño a ti?
¿En qué te hago daño a ti?
Yo solamente soy feliz

Why can't I be like this?
How am I hurting you?
How am I hurting you?
I'm just happy

Bad Bunny stands silhouetted against the setting sun as men and women run past him. Ricky Martin's voice comes in to harmonize with "solamente soy feliz" as Bad Bunny repeats the refrain. These lines talk back to those who would argue that queerness presents a serious threat to the social order. This is emphasized by the visuals that accompany this moment in the song; at one point, a woman kisses Bad Bunny's cheek, and a few seconds later a bearded man does the same. The interlude ends with Martin's voice crooning "solamente" as the image fades back into Jazmyne Joy–turned–Bad Bunny rapping atop a car with their friends.

One might read Ricky Martin's participation on *X 100PRE* as merely an established Puerto Rican global star endorsing one who is up and coming. Ricky Martin's international success has made him a global Puerto Rican icon, perhaps the most popular one until Bad Bunny. At the same time, Martin's bubblegum pop and ballads, and his upper-class blanquito positionality make him, in many ways, the opposite of the type of streetwise, and often nonwhite, hypermasculine figure associated with reggaetón.[48]

On the other hand, including Martin's voice on these particular lyrics with these specific images in the music video makes a profound statement that aligns Bad Bunny with open support for LGBTQ+ communities. Ricky Martin began his career in the boy band Menudo. He then established a solo career in both Spanish-language and English-language pop music. Throughout his 2010 memoir *Me*, Martin writes about the extreme pressure he felt to present himself as a heterosexual man throughout much of his career, fearing that his fan base and his community would ostracize him if he came out.[49] Puerto Rico's anti-sodomy laws were not repealed until 2003, and same-sex desire has long been stigmatized as the product of US colonial influence.[50] Puerto Rico recognized same-sex marriage rights in 2015 and the right to change gender identities on all official documents in 2018, but the history of exclusion and marginalization of the LGBTQ+ community in Puerto Rico is long.[51] While Puerto Rico has presented itself as a haven for queer tourists in the Caribbean, queer Puerto Rican citizens continue to face structural and physical violence.

Martin came out in 2010. As scholar Lawrence La Fountain-Stokes describes, it was a huge moment in Puerto Rican culture, and Martin endured significant backlash from many Puerto Rican elites.[52] American studies scholar Edward Chamberlain notes that Martin's social media presence as an openly gay Puerto Rican icon who speaks freely about humanitarian and social justice issues is far from superficial; instead, it stakes a claim for LGBTQ+ belonging in the Puerto Rican context.[53]

Martin has repeatedly lauded Bad Bunny for supporting LGBTQ+ communities. It was Martin who presented Bad Bunny's GLAAD Vanguard Award in 2023, praising him for "loudly standing with trans women and the entire community and telling every fan to let LGBTQ+ people dance, love, and live lives authentically."[54] In subsequent interviews, Martin has continued to celebrate Bad Bunny's allyship. On a March 2024 appearance on the *Kelly Clarkson Show*, Martin said:

> Isn't it incredible what Bad Bunny's doing? I wish I had that. I mean, it's a different generation. I was very afraid of being myself. I was afraid of being judged, and I was afraid of losing my career just sharing who I am and how I love. And now you have a generation of great artists, very talented artists, who are like, I don't care, if I want to wear a skirt, I'm gonna wear a skirt. If I want to paint my nails, I paint my nails and I'm an ally to the LGBTQ+ community. How lucky they are. How lucky are we to have this force of young people that are talking to young people about how important it is to just be.[55]

As Suzy Exposito notes in her 2020 *Rolling Stone* cover story about Bad Bunny, Ricky Martin "arguably set the scene for Bad Bunny to be free in many ways that, during [Martin's] own breakthrough moment, he could not."[56]

"Caro" was the first of many representations of queerness in Bad Bunny's work, including the depiction of LGBTQ+ couples in the video for "Ignorantes" and his gender-bending outfits. But nothing received as much attention as his music video for "Yo Perreo Sola" from *YHLQMDLG*. Like many of his other songs, "Yo Perreo Sola" celebrates women's agency, in this case focusing on respecting women's choice to dance perreo alone without unwanted sexual advances. For the video, Bad Bunny dressed in full drag, complete with artificial breasts and three different outfits, including what has since become an iconic red latex bodysuit. Never before had a reggaetón star dressed and performed in full drag.

The internet was abuzz. Some people suggested that Bad Bunny was queerbaiting—that is, adopting queer aesthetics or identities for profit rather than to express authentic queerness. Queerbaiting is a form of cultural appropriation by people who have never grappled with the lived realities that impact actual queer people. Bad Bunny has never explicitly identified as queer, although he did suggest his sexuality was fluid when he told the *Los Angeles Times* in 2020, "I don't know if in 20 years I will like a man. One never knows in life."[57] Then, he added, "But at the moment I am heterosexual and I like women."[58] His two most visible relationships have been with women (Gabriela Berlingeri and Kendall Jenner).

In a widely circulated editorial in the *Guardian*, Andre Wheeler expressed frustration with the tremendous praise Bad Bunny received in the wake of the music video, arguing that the artist's embrace of queer aesthetics endeared him to mainstream audiences. Wheeler argued that Bad Bunny should not receive so much attention when the actual queer people who pioneered these aesthetics did not. He wrote, "We need to approach this kind of celebrity activity with the same kind of skepticism and scrutiny we apply to the brands and businesses for their Pride campaigns. Because if allyship so easily leads to higher record sales and Twitter trending topics, is it really a pure, selfless kind of support?"[59] Similarly, scholar Verónica Dávila Ellis argues that Bad Bunny's position as a cisgender heterosexual man affords him certain privileges to engage in drag performance and other gender nonconforming representations that other people are not able to do.[60]

Critics and fans also admonished Bad Bunny for not giving Puerto Rican trap rapper Nesi—a woman—a featured credit on "Yo Perreo Sola"; instead, Nesi received only a writing credit. Nesi recorded the opening vocals and some of the chorus for the track. Nesi said publicly that she was not bothered, and Bad Bunny argued that he wrote the lines she sang, such that her voice could be that of "any girl."[61] Critics argued that this was incorrect, that Nesi's voice actually made the track a hit. Verónica Dávila Ellis wrote in her review of *YHLQMDLG* that Bad Bunny had undermined his own "attempts at feminist lyrics by perpetuating the historical occlusion of women collaborators and contributors in reggaetón."[62]

In 2024, Bad Bunny's ex-girlfriend Carliz de la Cruz won $40 million in damages after he used her voice without her permission on one of his taglines in several songs.[63] The issue is broader than Bad Bunny, and it is broader than credit. Women have sung some of the most famous hooks and lines in reggaetón hits, often without receiving credit, sometimes also to the detriment of their own careers.[64] For example, reggaetón singer Glory recorded many of the most recognizable lines in songs like Daddy Yankee's "Gasolina" and Don Omar's "Dale, Don, Dale" that thrust reggaetón into the global spotlight. Her own career never took off, and cultural critic Félix Jiménez argues that this is in part because she was never taken seriously as a performer in her own right since her role seemed to be to be that of a sexy woman available to men.[65] Other uncredited reggaetón women include Jenny la Sexy Voz, who sang vocals on hits by a who's who of reggaetón—including Wisin y Yandel, Héctor el Father, Alexis y Fido, Daddy Yankee, and others—but who never achieved a successful solo career.[66] Credits would not only legitimize and acknowledge these women's participation in the genre and give them greater visibility; they also carry royalties.[67] Men experience this sometimes. Bad Bunny did not credit Ricky Martin on "Caro," and Bad Bunny himself did not receive credit for his vocals on Karol G's "Provenza." However, the stakes for established male musicians like Bad Bunny and Ricky Martin are much lower than for women like Nesi, Glory, and Jenny la Sexy Voz, who are trying to make it in an industry and a genre that routinely marginalize women.

Other critics suggested that "Yo Perreo Sola" appropriated a message previously recorded by a woman—Ivy Queen's 2004 classic "Quiero Bailar," which declared that just because a woman danced perreo did not mean that she was sexually available. At the end of the music video for "Yo Perreo Sola," the words "si no quiere perrear contigo, respeta, ella perrea sola" (If she doesn't want to dance with you, respect that, she dances alone) appear in red against a black backdrop, a message very similar to that of "Quiero Bailar." For some, these controversies made the message of gender inclusivity fall flat, and some questioned whether the whole video deserved the praise it received. Bad Bunny eventually recorded a remix that included Ivy Queen and Nesi, this time with feature credits; but for some critics, the harm had already been done.

Others nonetheless lauded "Yo Perreo Sola" as an important and necessary antidote to the machismo and heteronormativity that dominates the reggaetón and Latin music scenes. Historian Julio Capó Jr. responded to Wheeler's assertions that Bad Bunny did not deserve to be called a queer icon with an essay titled "Bad Bunny Is Queer to Me."[68] In it he argued that queerness need not be "reduce[d]" to "sexual identity." Wheeler, Capó argues, focused only on the US mainstream. Capó writes, "To whom has [Bad Bunny] recently become an ally, however? The mainstream, perhaps, but not for many Latinx and Latin American and Caribbean audiences." In other words, if mainstream critics assumed that Bad Bunny had only just begun advocating for LGBTQ+ communities when it became fashionable to do so, it was because they were unfamiliar with his earlier work like "Caro" or "Ignorantes." Bad Bunny's allyship must be understood in relation to the long histories of queer activism and representation in Puerto Rico. Capó thus calls for understanding Bad Bunny's work in cultural context and with a more expansive understanding of queerness.

Debates about whether or not Bad Bunny engaged in queerbaiting resurfaced in the 2022 MTV Video Music Awards (VMAs). During a televised live performance of "Tití Me Preguntó" from Yankee Stadium, Bad Bunny kissed two of his dancers—one woman and one man. Once again, the internet buzzed with criticism that it was just for show. In *Out* magazine, Bernardo Sim admonished these critics, stating that Bad Bunny's kiss was about his long-standing attempt to counter the stereotype of Latino men as machista and homophobic and "actively telling and showing men how to loosen up and get comfortable with themselves—or at least how to stop being prejudiced *machistas*—which feels like a completely different intention and context than queerbaiting."[69]

While Sim makes an important point, he also misses key cultural references in this performance. For instance, Bad Bunny shared kisses with a woman and a man years earlier in "Caro," something that mainstream critics may have missed but that certainly was not lost on Bad Bunny's long-term fans. What's more, the VMAs kiss responded to a controversy that had occurred in Puerto Rico just one week before the awards show, when Puerto Rican trans woman rapper Villano Antillano (a.k.a. la Villana) kissed Dominican artist Tokischa, a bisexual rapper, during a performance at a local nightclub. They received tremendous backlash from artists and the general public; NPR reported that the backlash "was so vicious it included death threats."[70] Villano Antillano described the response on Twitter: "I want to be clear, with respect and an incredible sense of responsibility, the amount of messages I've received telling me I'll be murdered like Kevin Fret; for being loud-mouthed, for being a whore."[71] Kevin Fret was the first openly gay trap artist in Puerto Rico who was tragically murdered while riding his motorcycle through San Juan in 2019; his murder remains unsolved.[72] For some fans, Bad Bunny's kiss at the VMAs expressed support for la Villana and Tokischa, something he referenced again in the lyrics to his song "Baticano" from his 2023 album *Nadie Sabe lo que va a Pasar Mañana*: "Me beso con Villana, me beso con Tokischa / el que no le guste, je, es porque no chicha" (I kiss Villana, I kiss Tokischa / whoever doesn't like it, ha, it's because they don't have sex).

As Villano Antillano has stated in multiple interviews, the transphobia of the music industry has made it profoundly difficult for her to access resources and opportunities that she might have if she were not a trans woman.[73] However, Bad Bunny has long supported her. He invited her to share the stage with him at his historic concerts at El Choli in August of 2022. In 2023, *Rolling Stone* magazine's Future 25, a list of up and coming artists that Bad Bunny helped to curate as that year's Future of Music cover star, included a major profile of Villano Antillano. Bad Bunny told *Rolling Stone*, "I like Villano's lyrics a lot. . . . I've been listening to Villano for a long time. . . . I was telling the guys, like, 'This goes so hard.'"[74]

Nor is Villano Antillano the only queer artist Bad Bunny has supported. He also invited Young Miko, a lesbian rapper from Puerto Rico, to share the stage at El Choli, and he also selected her as an up-and-coming artist for *Rolling Stone*'s 2023 Future of Music issue. For both of these artists Bad Bunny acted the part of hype man while they sang their own hits on stage, thus giving them the opportunity to really showcase their own talent. At the closing concert for his Most Wanted Tour in San Juan in 2024, Young Miko told Bad Bunny that he had changed her life by sharing his platform with her at El Choli just two years prior, and the two exchanged a warm embrace.[75]

An endorsement by one of the biggest stars in the world has undoubtedly played a huge role in elevating the careers of queer artists like Young Miko and Villano Antillano. Jerry Pullés of Apple Music noted that at the most basic level, "it obviously helps that he's supportive of their music on his platforms, whether it be reposting one of their songs or inviting one of them to appear on a song." Similarly, Eddie Santiago, the former head of US Latin at Spotify, noted that Spotify began paying more attention to Young Miko and Villano Antillano after Bad Bunny featured them in his concerts for *Un Verano Sin Ti* in Puerto Rico. Eddie told us that after Villano Antillano and Young Miko performed alongside Bad Bunny, there was a "huge spike in consumption" of their music on Spotify. "The Bad Bunny co-sign was very valuable," he explained. Bad Bunny's endorsement made these artists difficult to ignore. As Eddie recalled in our conversation,

"It informed trends and made us as a platform pay attention to these moments, and react accordingly."

Central to the discussion of queerbaiting is whether artists approach queerness only for their own benefit. Bad Bunny has clearly opened doors for artists like Young Miko and Villano Antillano within a genre, an industry, and a society that is profoundly homophobic and transphobic. This is part of his overall expansion of reggaetón's gender politics. In his fashion choices, performances, and endorsements of other artists, Bad Bunny routinely creates space for the acknowledgment and celebration of queerness. His unapologetic stance is a far cry from the anxiety that Ricky Martin felt twenty years before. Some of these changes stem directly from the legal victories that have granted LGBTQ+ people greater rights in Puerto Rico and elsewhere. Eddie Santiago also credits the attitudes of Generation Z, which he claims is "much more inclusive than all of the generations before them." At the same time, LGBTQ+ artists remain profoundly underrepresented in reggaetón, Latin music, and popular music as a whole. In this context, Bad Bunny's gender-bending and queer friendly stances make a powerful statement that challenges misogyny, homophobia, transphobia, and toxic masculinity.

One of the most memorable exchanges from Petra's conversation with Bad Bunny at Harvard was when the event organizers asked him a question about masculinity. They asked whether Bad Bunny could explain how to be a better man. Bad Bunny's reaction was immediate: "That's impossible, I can't tell anybody how to be." This sense that everyone should be free to be themselves is his guiding ethos, and he routinely strives to create a welcoming and inclusive environment at his concerts, within the reggaetón genre, and in the music business generally. Reflecting on his career in a 2023 *Vanity Fair* interview, Bad Bunny noted that no matter how he has evolved artistically, he has always wanted "to convey a clear feeling of embracing everyone and that everyone feels comfortable in my space, at my concerts, while listening to my music."[76]

Throughout his career, Bad Bunny has routinely created narratives and representations that address gender and sexuality as part of his overall social justice work, whether in his music videos, his fashion choices, his performances, his lyrics, or in his supporting and uplifting new queer artists. At the same time, Bad Bunny, like all artists, is rife with contradictions. He has reproduced misogynistic lyrics that objectify women, sometimes in ways that foreground respectability politics and classist stereotypes of working-class women.[77] His not crediting women like Nesi reproduces some of the gender inequities that remain entrenched within the Latin music industry. Overall, some have argued that his push for a different type of gender politics is limited, whether by broader societal expectations, his own biases, or perhaps both.[78]

Despite these contradictions, others have seen a key shift in how contemporary male artists, especially reggaetón artists, represent their own masculinity. Typically, male reggaetón artists have not expressed emotional vulnerability, let alone worn a skirt, or painted their nails. Eddie described these choices by Bad Bunny as "the first step of making queer culture acceptable in the traditional heteronormative [Latin music] space." This shift is part of Bad Bunny's legacy—he not only actively supports artists like Young Miko and Villano Antillano, he also has changed cultural norms in a way that enables other queer artists to gain entrance into the music scene. One example is the up-and-coming artist La Cruz, an openly gay reggaetón singer from Venezuela, whom Eddie now helps manage. Eddie sees a direct link between Bad Bunny's "unapologetic" gender politics and La Cruz's success. He described La Cruz's look as "more of a typical heterosexual masculine-presenting male. . . . If you line him up with other reggaetón artists, he fits the scope of what society expects that would look like." However, La Cruz's lyrics speak about same-sex male desire, and he features other masculine-presenting male dancers' perreando in his videos. Eddie attributed La Cruz's success to Bad Bunny's work that expanded ideas of masculinity in reggaetón. He explained, "It's a machismo dominated culture. Queerness is seen as a weakness in a sense. Bunny flipped that narrative with the approach of, 'Well who are you to say what's cool and what's not cool? I'm going to unapologetically do what I think is cool,' which we saw with *Yo Hago Lo Que Me Da La Gana*. That project cemented his stance, and he never folded or succumbed to any of the criticism. His approach empowers artists like La Cruz to unapologetically be authentic to who they are and to their own artistry." New artists like La Cruz, Eddie said, reflected a "domino effect of essentially what Benito set in motion."

Bad Bunny is certainly not perfect, and his art alone will not totally rid society of homophobia, transphobia, and misogyny. However, his work has played a critical role in calling out violence and misogyny in Puerto Rico and other Latino cultures. This has been key to how his music and artistry has engaged in a politics of resistance since the very early days of his career. In fact, Bad Bunny's social impact and artistic power comes from this resistance, which is often expressed through his refusal to accommodate a mainstream white, heteronormative, English-speaking audience, or even a conservative Latino one. Despite the contradictions in his work, Bad Bunny ultimately has opened a more inclusive space within a musical genre and a society that have long marginalized women and the LGBTQ+ community, among others. Whether through featuring two men perreando in his dance crew, using his platform to support artists like Villano Antillano, or writing stories with complex women characters in his lyrics, Bad Bunny's engagement with gender issues is intrinsic to his overall politics of resistance.

5

"EL MUNDO ES MÍO": BAD BUNNY BEYOND EL BORINQUEN

YHLQMDLG never had a proper tour because the world shut down for the COVID-19 pandemic in March 2020, just two weeks after the album's release. Like everyone else, Bad Bunny was stuck at home. Holed up in a rented Airbnb in San Juan with his then-girlfriend Gabriela Berlingeri, he spent much of his days playing games, taking selfies, and chatting with friends on WhatsApp. He did fill some of his time working on the surprise album *Las Que No Iban a Salir* in May.[1] These were songs that literally were never going to come out. They had been considered for *YHLQMDLG*, but since they were not going to be used, Bad Bunny had not recorded vocals. He explained to Puerto Rican podcaster Chente Ydrach that he had simply played some of these tracks on an Instagram live—as he had done to promote *YHLQMDLG*—and then people began requesting that he release the songs. Bad Bunny headed to his engineer's home, laid down his own vocals, and two days later released the record.[2]

More than three thousand miles away in Los Angeles, Marcos Borrero was also stuck at home. Marcos had made a name for himself as the producer MAG. MAG was signed by Max Martin, one of the most legendary pop producers in the world. As a producer, MAG participated in sessions with other writers and producers, creating demos and pitching them to artists at a rapid clip. With no one in the studio due to the pandemic, MAG found himself with time to make his own music for the first time in years. On a video call with us from his studio in Miami in June 2024, MAG recalled, "I was back at square one. I just started making beats and getting everything out of my system. There was a freedom creatively when the world shut down." Some of the songs he wrote reflected the anxiety of those early pandemic times. "Everything felt very dark, gloomy, and sad," he told us. He was working on some guitar riffs from his good friend Mick Coogan and began "fusing them with new genres and sounds."

One day, MAG was in the shower, trying to figure out his next steps. He told us about his thinking at that time: "I had all this music I was making, and I thought to myself, 'What am I going to do with all this?'" He had folders on his computer dedicated to artists he hoped to work with one day, each folder containing new beats and songs he thought might be suited to them. Bad Bunny's name was on one of the folders. "Benito was one of my favorite artists," MAG explained to us. "I was really inspired by the music that he was making. So somewhere in my brain, I thought, let me just make these ideas because I think if one day the opportunity ever presented itself, I think we could complement each other musically."

MAG had been acquainted with Bad Bunny's manager Noah Assad for years, and they had crossed paths at industry events around Los Angeles. MAG realized that the pandemic might just be his chance to get the beats from his Bad Bunny folder to the artist himself. He said, "Something clicked, and I thought to myself, 'I can reach out to Noah right now and at least ask.' I didn't know Benito's process, I didn't know what he was doing, but what I did know was that no artist was touring and every artist was stuck at home somewhere. So I thought, well, let me just reach out to Noah and ask him if Benito's open to receiving track ideas and instrumentals and stuff."

MAG sent Noah more than twenty ideas, which Noah then passed along to Bad Bunny. MAG was floored when Noah got back to him and said "hold everything"—meaning, don't share those tracks with anyone else—because Bad Bunny may be interested. MAG told us, "I thought to myself, there's no way that I'm holding everything, like what is this? Are you scamming me right now? You're not gonna use everything!" But it was true. As MAG told us, "It turned out that he played everything for Benito, and Benito loved it, and asked to hold everything. He wanted to work on all the ideas I sent him."

At first, MAG would send completed instrumentals to Noah, who would pass them on to Bad Bunny. Bad Bunny then recorded his vocals on MAG's tracks. But then Noah and Bad Bunny invited MAG to come down to Puerto Rico and work together on additional tracks in person. As MAG explained to us, "I remember Noah calling and telling me that [Bad Bunny] was trying to find a producer he could work closely with in person. Of course, he already had an incredible trajectory. He had done so much incredible music with Tainy and others. But he was looking for a producer to sit down with and create things from scratch that could bring his ideas to life." Although Noah had met MAG, he had no idea when he first passed MAG's materials on to Bad Bunny that MAG was such an accomplished producer. But at this point the answer seemed obvious: MAG and Bad Bunny would need to meet in person.

In July 2020, MAG and his wife packed up their stuff and took a harrowing flight from Los Angeles to Puerto Rico in the midst of the ongoing COVID pandemic. MAG laughed when he told us that the flight was "terrifying! There were like all of six people on this massive airplane, and I'm sitting there and I'm looking back, and there's just empty rows like twenty rows down. There's one guy with his mask on, also looking at me scared." Initially, Puerto Rico had some of the strictest curfews and social distancing rules anywhere in the United States or its territories. As MAG recalled, "When we got to San Juan, there's all these people in like astronaut suits coming over to test me. You had to do COVID tests. It was a whole thing." Luckily, MAG made it through and eventually crossed the island to Rincón where he, Bad Bunny, and a few of Bad Bunny's friends established a COVID bubble. Stuck together in Rincón, safe from the virus raging around them, MAG and Bad Bunny produced what became the very first Spanish-language album to debut as number one on Billboard's 200 chart: *El Último Tour del Mundo* (The last tour in the world).[3]

Bad Bunny told Chente that he named his album *El Último Tour del Mundo* because "when you saw the news, it seemed like it was the end of the world. So I named it *El Último Tour del Mundo* not because it is my last tour, but because it's the last tour in general, after this tour no one is going on tour again."[4] But in fact the album was the beginning of a major shift in Bad Bunny's career. It broke numerous records that wouldn't be broken again until Bad Bunny released his fifth solo studio album, *Un Verano Sin Ti*, in 2022. *El Último Tour del Mundo* thrust Bad Bunny onto the global music scene, enabling him to reach heights that no Latin artist had ever attained. And it was the beginning of a dynamic creative partnership between MAG and Bad Bunny that would have an indelible impact on both their lives.

MAG and Bad Bunny's time in Puerto Rico together was fruitful. The first idea that they worked on together was based on a guitar chord progression that Bad Bunny had created using an app on his phone that he had received from Residente. MAG recalled that Bad Bunny told him, "'I want to do a song based on these chords' and he whips out that app. And I'm like, 'What the fuck is that? That's amazing!' And then I opened my voice recorder, and I took a voice note of him playing out those chords one by one, and then I imported that into my computer. And we had a chord progression to write from."

The song that came from those chords was "Trellas," a sci-fi themed, sad rock-pop ballad. The 2:37 minute song starts with slow guitar chords and an echoey synth. Bad Bunny's voice sounds like it's coming from far away. He sings about looking out at the stars and wishing for his lost lover, then traveling through the universe, to Mars and to the moon, looking for someone like his ex. The ethereal, spacey sounds match the mournful timbre of his voice. As MAG noted, "Trellas" is "a sadder, gloomy song."

From there, *El Último Tour del Mundo* took shape as a softer, more somber album that reflected the "gloomy time" MAG and Bad Bunny experienced during the pandemic. This vibe even permeates those songs that might be considered party songs, like the album's lead single and biggest hit, the Tainy-produced "Dákiti," which became the first Latin song to ever hold the number one spot on both the Billboard Global 200 chart and the Billboard Global Excl. US chart (a spot it held on both charts for two weeks).[5] As MAG described: "Even 'Dákiti' is a dark song, like it's a party anthem, but it's still like, you know, minor chords and gloomy." Minor chords have a long association with sad songs, whereas major chords tend to be used for celebratory songs, particularly in Western music. Similarly, "Yo Visto Así" lyrically expresses some of the inspirational self-love attitude from *YHLQMDLG*, but in a minor key that connected to the times: Everyone should love themselves and do what they want because it felt like the world was ending.

For MAG, this vibe and rock-oriented sound felt like a risk for Bad Bunny who had spent most of his career making danceable club records: "It was just crazy because the world shut down, but Benito's music up to that point was made for like the clubs and the parties, and none of that was happening." Even Bad Bunny's first pandemic-era album, *Las Que No Iban a Salir,* was a party record. Gary Suarez gave it four stars in *Rolling Stone*, praising it while noting that it was "a 10-song dive into Bad Bunny's hard-drive of set-aside, previously discarded, or otherwise unreleased songs."[6] Critics hailed not only its excellence but also its timing in providing a moment of levity during the horror of the pandemic. Bad Bunny told music critic Suzy Exposito in 2020 that the album had "no real meaning behind" it. "I just thought, 'Damn. What people need is entertainment.'"[7]

Months later, when *El Último Tour del Mundo* was released, Bad Bunny told Leila Cobo of *Billboard* that it was a more "sentimental album" that reflected the pandemic moment. He continued, "I laugh because people told me I kept on releasing *perreo* at a time when people couldn't go out and party, and I said, 'OK, now you can't complain.' This is an album for you to stay at home, chill, having a beer, a glass of wine, paying attention to the lyrics. It's a bit more rock 'n' roll, a lot of guitars—there's one song that only has guitar—it's more musical, has more fusions, and also reggaetón and rap."[8] These rock and reggaetón musical fusions created a new sound for música urbana that helped propel *El Último Tour del Mundo* up the charts and earned it the 2022 Grammy for Best Música Urbana album. It was an all the more fitting recognition of the historical significance of the album's sonic innovations as the category was new for the Grammys.

In addition to inaugurating a Grammy category, *El Último Tour del Mundo* had significance as the beginning of the musical partnership between MAG and Bad Bunny. MAG expressed delight in Bad Bunny's openness to experimenting with new sounds and ideas, and he enjoyed working with an artist who also had experience producing songs. MAG told us that despite his years of hit productions, he believes he has "grown so much as a producer working with" Bad Bunny. MAG told us that he had a special rapport with Bad Bunny when it came to songwriting and producing. He recalled, "With Benito, there was almost instant creative chemistry. We'd be working on something in the room together, and he'd say like 'Yo creo que en esta parte debemos de cambiar esto y meter . . .' [I think that we should change this part and put in . . .], and I could finish the sentence and say, 'This is what you wanted to add?' And he'd say, 'Yes!' And vice versa."

MAG said that this chemistry even works from afar. When they are not in the same city, they often exchange voice notes. "He'll sometimes just send me a voice note and tell me, 'Mira, MAG, ponle esto en esta parte del tema' [Hey, MAG, put this in that part of the song] and he'll

5.1 Bad Bunny and producer MAG appear in deep discussion amid a sea of music production equipment while working on an album. The image was posted to MAG's Instagram account on the same day that *DeBÍ TiRAR MáS FOToS* was released January 5, 2025. Photo by Robinson Florian via Instagram @itz_mag.

send me a clip, or he'll tell me to look for a sample he wants to add, and I do it." At other times, Bad Bunny will present an idea that seems completely unexpected, but it totally works. As MAG said, "He always just wants to push the boundary and try something different, try something that hasn't been done. There's been multiple songs where we've had something going on and he's like 'Okay, now we're gonna take this section and we're gonna make it like this.' And I'm just like, what the fuck are you talking about? And then a hit comes out."

El Último Tour del Mundo itself is a testament, too, to the ways that MAG has contributed to Bad Bunny's artistic development. Part of what made the album a surprise was that Bad Bunny himself was not planning on releasing another pandemic album. He was inspired by the tracks MAG had sent for him. This inspiration continues. MAG said he occasionally sends Bad Bunny ideas that they haven't talked about together but that he feels Bad Bunny would sound good on. The seed that became a surprise track called "WHERE SHE GOES" released in May 2023 was an example. When it appeared on the album *Nadie Sabe Lo Que Va a Pasar Mañana* later that year, many critics commented on the unexpected Jersey Club beat in the song.[9] In fact, *Vibe* listed "WHERE SHE GOES" as one of the "most influential" Jersey Club songs of all time. In their description, journalists Amber Corinne and Regina Cho asked, "Who knew Spanish lyrics could fit so seamlessly over a Jersey Club beat?"[10]

MAG knew. As he explained to us, "Jersey Club has been part of northeast culture like in New Jersey, New York City, for years. It's been a genre way before it became like a mainstream thing. . . . I thought, 'Wow! It would be amazing to hear a Spanish language Jersey Club song!' It hadn't been done." He created the track and sent it to Bad Bunny who recorded the vocals. The unique fusion debuted at number one on the Billboard Global 200 chart.[11]

Their collaborative creative process and mutual respect are what makes Bad Bunny and MAG's partnership so fruitful. Ultimately, as MAG told us, "There's a lot of trust between Benito and me." This trust enables the two to take new kinds of musical risks. Both Tainy and MAG's descriptions about their creative chemistry with Bad Bunny demonstrate the literal magic in their music-making processes. Thus, Bad Bunny's relationship to both of his main producers has clearly been key to the explosive success of his music, and the way that he works together in harmony with them on many projects expands the sound and scope of música urbana.

We first met MAG in person in Miami at a Mexican restaurant on a humid June evening. Laughing over tacos, he noted that one of the first questions he had heard that Bad Bunny asked after listening to his demo pack was, "Is this producer Puerto Rican?" This was not particularly surprising, as Bad Bunny often collaborates with Puerto Ricans from the archipelago like Tainy. But MAG grew up in New York City. His father is from the western city of Mayagüez, not far from where he and Bad Bunny established their COVID bubble to make *El Último Tour del Mundo*.

MAG, then, is a Nuyorican: both New Yorker and Puerto Rican. He grew up in Brooklyn rather than in Puerto Rico, and like Tainy, his mother is Dominican. This background contributes to the unique perspectives that MAG brings to Bad Bunny's sound. Their song "NUEVAYoL" from Bad Bunny's 2025 album *DeBÍ TiRAR MáS FOToS* exemplifies the blend.

The song starts with a sample from "Un Verano en Nueva York," a 1975 hit from the Puerto Rican salsa band El Gran Combo de Puerto Rico, one of the most important salsa bands in Puerto Rican history.[12] After the opening melody of the salsa classic plays, the beat drops, and the song turns into a mash-up of Puerto Rican salsa and Dominican dembow. MAG and Bad Bunny made "NUEVAYoL" in January 2023, two full years before *DeBÍ TiRAR MáS FOToS* was released. For MAG, emphasizing New York and bringing together sounds from his Dominican and Puerto Rican backgrounds made the song the ultimate "love letter to my hometown." In fact, MAG told us that, "There's a little bit of New York City in everything I do." Another example is "Tití Me Preguntó" from *Un Verano Sin Ti* (2022), one of the biggest hits of both MAG's and Bad Bunny's careers. Critics and fans alike lauded the song for its blend of dembow, hip-hop, and even an old-school Antony Santos bachata sample. MAG described this fusion as a natural reflection of his experience living in New York City: "The way I visualize 'Tití Me Preguntó' is, if you're walking down New York City for seven streets, if you could put all those sounds in a blender—what all these cars are passing by listening to."

MAG grew up surrounded by sounds. He heard music from his Puerto Rican father and his Dominican mother. His father was a guitarist. His older sisters introduced him to late 1990s pop of the Backstreet Boys, Celine Dion, 'N Sync, and Britney Spears. Outside, young Marcos played drums in his church band, and he would hear "cars coming down the street blasting hip-hop and bachata, dancehall."

All these sounds became an obsession for the budding producer, who would spend his afternoons working on music. Like Tainy and Bad Bunny, MAG taught himself how to produce songs at home using a pirated copy of the production software Fruity Loops. "I became a bedroom producer, making these full tracks," he explained to us. He would come home from school, set up his laptop in his attic bedroom in his parents' Brooklyn apartment, and use what he learned about rhythmic structure as a drummer to start making up some tracks. Eventually, MAG also got a keyboard, and began teaching himself to play chords that would round out his beats.

After high school, MAG started taking classes at a trade school for music production, where he specialized in sound engineering. But his heart was in creating music more than the technical stuff he was learning in class. MAG started making friends at the school who would go on to intern for major music executives around the country. Even though most of his friends were "just getting coffee for an A&R [that is, a talent scout] that doesn't even know their name," many asked MAG to pass along his tracks so they could show them to their bosses. He was nervous, but he complied, eventually landing meetings with some executives. One of them, Andrew Luftman, took a special interest in MAG's work. MAG told us, "He started critiquing [my songs]. . . . I'll play him stuff, and he'll like, put the audio in his office and be like, 'Go home and fix this and come back and I'll try and listen to it again.'"

Luftman came from the pop world and worked closely with Benny Blanco, a hotshot producer who worked with major pop acts like Britney Spears, Maroon 5, and Justin Bieber, and whose career MAG had been following closely. Blanco got ahold of MAG's work from Luftman, and he loved it. This connection led to more A&R meetings, including with some big names in Los Angeles. Eventually, MAG's tracks made their way to Savan Kotecha, a songwriter who had just partnered with Max Martin. Martin is one of the most prolific pop producers of our time, with the most number one hits on Billboard's Hot 100 of any producer in history.[13] Martin loved MAG's work and invited him out to Los Angeles, where, at the age of twenty-two, the native New Yorker moved to make it in the music business.

MAG said he was a "sponge" under Martin's tutelage, "learning about song structure, melodies, production, what makes things catchy." He worked on a team churning out pop hits. And then, Max Martin gave him a demo to work on. That song was rapper Flo Rida's 2015 hit "My House," which spread like wildfire when various sports arenas and teams adopted the minimalist dance-pop song for their stadium anthems, becoming a major breakthrough in MAG's career. He told us that his experience in Top 40 "gave me a different approach when I started working in Latin." This is part of what made *El Último Tour del Mundo* so successful, and reviewers applauded the album's blend of rock and pop with reggaetón and trap.

US Latinos have always contributed to the development of Latin music. However, Latin music is also talked about as something that comes directly from Latin America itself, with no influence from other places.[14] As scholars such as Iván A. Ramos, Ignacio Corona, and Deborah Pacini Hernandez note, such narratives erase the many circuits of exchange and musical influence that extend across national and linguistic boundaries.[15] Latin music and US popular music genres like pop, hip-hop, and rock have long influenced each other. MAG's experiences as a US Latino involved in the pop world is not an anomaly in and of itself, nor is his incorporation of pop elements in his Latin productions. In fact, reggaetón is a music that emerged from several streams of migration and cultural exchange across the Caribbean basin. Many reggaetón artists have deep connections to the Puerto Rican diaspora as well. Artists like De La Ghetto, Arcángel, and underground pioneer Vico C were all born in New York, while others like Ivy Queen lived there as young adults. The iconic reggaetón production duo Luny Tunes met while working in a dining hall at Harvard University in Massachusetts, the state where reggaetón pioneer Nicky Jam and Jowell of the reggaetón duo Jowell y Randy were born. Tego Calderón and Rauw Alejandro spent some of their formative years in Florida. Bad Bunny's family is also part of the diaspora. Although Bad Bunny was born and raised in Puerto Rico, the artist's first time on an airplane was to visit his grandparents on the US mainland.[16] Trap singer De La Ghetto explained to us that his connections to New York always influenced how he made his own music back in Puerto Rico. "I was two steps ahead of a lot of people in Puerto Rico because I knew both languages [English and Spanish], and I would listen to hip-hop, American music, Spanish music, too, but I always listened to more American music," he told us in an interview. De La Ghetto sees Puerto Rican musical development as intimately tied to US musical elements and traditions. He explained, "Puerto Rico is very Americanized. We have culture from New York that goes back to the 1930s. You know, Puerto Rico has always been an island that absorbs American music." Of course, this is due in no small part to Puerto Rico's status as a US colony. But Puerto Ricans moving back and forth between the US and the archipelago, like De La Ghetto, or diasporic Puerto Ricans like MAG, have played a critical role in Puerto Rico's musical development, including that of reggaetón and Latin trap.

Bad Bunny's global success with *El Último Tour del Mundo* quickly solidified his position as one of the best-known Puerto Rican musical icons of the past several decades in the US mainstream market, as much as in the Latin one. MAG recalls that one of the album's early singles, "Yo Visto Así," marked a turning point for his understanding of the album's reach. He told us that, for the first time, despite Bad Bunny continuing to record only in Spanish, "white people that I knew were saying, 'Man, this Bad Bunny guy is pretty cool!' and started listening. And that for me was like eye opening. It was like, 'Holy shit, we just reached an entirely different audience!'"

MAG's influence on Bad Bunny's music is significant not only because of the unique pop blends he brings to their projects but also because of his perspective as a Nuyorican. This matters because the Puerto Rican diaspora has not always been seamlessly integrated into perceptions of Puerto Rican national culture. Puerto Rican cultural nationalism has often reproduced very rigid understandings of what it means to be authentically Puerto Rican. In turn, they exclude cultural practices or identity expressions from the US diaspora.[17] Race and class stereotypes of Nuyoricans are common in Puerto Rico.[18] In his study of Nuyoricans who returned to the island, Juan Flores described their experience: "They are outsiders and 'others' whose presence all too often spurs resentment, ridicule, and fear, and even disdain and social discrimination with clear racial and class undertones. Yet at the same time, their presence also elicits fascination, engagement, and change."[19] Among the criticisms of the Puerto Rican diaspora is that they are not "authentically" Puerto Rican because of not having grown up in the archipelago.

Both of us are Puerto Ricans born in the diaspora, and we have experienced what Flores describes. Incidentally, both of our fathers came with their parents from Puerto Rico as babies in 1948. As part of the state-sponsored migration known as "Operation Bootstrap," Petra's family relocated to Lorain, Ohio, and Vanessa's to East Harlem, or "El Barrio," in New York City.[20] In addition to promising tax exemptions and cheap labor to US manufacturers who relocated to Puerto Rico, Operation Bootstrap sought to increase migration out of Puerto Rico, resulting in the largest airborne migration in US history. This policy responded to the alleged "overpopulation" of Puerto Rico. Since the very beginning of colonial rule, US officials had lamented this supposed overpopulation of poor Puerto Ricans and saw migration as a key strategy to ameliorate this so-called problem.[21] As a result, Operation Bootstrap took many Puerto Ricans away from their homeland.[22] US recruiters came to Puerto Rico to find laborers to work in the United States. In 1947, the Puerto Rican government created the Bureau of Employment and Migration. This office, along with the Migration Division in the United States, helped facilitate Puerto Ricans' migration to the United States by securing labor contracts with US companies. In fact, this is how Petra's grandfather came to the United States from Ponce; he was recruited by the S. G. Friedman Labor Agency to work for the National Tube Company's steel mill in Lorain, Ohio.[23] Although the Migration Division offered language and culture classes to migrants to ease their transition, many Puerto Ricans struggled, facing racism, linguistic discrimination, poverty, and in many instances poor working conditions.[24]

Both of our families moved back and forth between the US mainland and Puerto Rico many times as they struggled with finances, securing livable housing, and finding resources for their respective families. Migration, including movement back and forth between Puerto Rico and the US mainland, is a central aspect of the Puerto Rican experience. It has also left a lasting mark on Puerto Rican culture on the archipelago, whether in language, music, literature, or any number of what Juan Flores terms "cultural remittances"—the cultural innovations of the diaspora that make their way back to the homeland.[25] For this reason, scholars like Jorge Duany have argued that the diaspora constitutes a critical part of the Puerto Rican nation.[26] What's more, there are more Puerto Ricans living on the US mainland than in Puerto Rico. A 2022 study from the University of Connecticut found that about two-thirds of all Puerto Ricans live in one of the fifty states or the District of Columbia.[27] From this perspective, it is even more crucial that perhaps the biggest Puerto Rican musical icon in decades, if not ever, not only performs in a genre indebted, in part, to the Puerto Rican diaspora, but also has a sound that is actively shaped and influenced by a diasporic Puerto Rican/Dominican from Brooklyn.

MAG described his feelings to us about going home after one month of quarantining and working with Bad Bunny: "Maybe two people in my life knew that I was working on an album with him. I couldn't talk about it. Not being able to talk about it with my friends before it [came out] was really hard." Bad Bunny wanted this to be another of his surprise albums. There would be small clues about the upcoming release of *El Último Tour del Mundo* on November 27, 2020—subtle ones, perhaps recognizable only to his biggest fans—but nothing explicit. MAG knew almost nothing about Bad Bunny's plans to promote the album, only that it would use particular imagery and that he was to keep it a secret.

The ongoing pandemic meant that the roll-out of the album required completely new tactics in almost every other respect. Eddie Santiago, former head of US Latin at Spotify, worked on the streaming service's campaign to promote the album. "We were still under the pandemic lockdown, following the restrictions [so] we didn't host content shoots," he told us in an interview. Instead, they relied on "witty billboards" to promote the record. Each of Bad Bunny's albums has a visual theme attached to it, like the eyeball of *X 100PRE* and the boy on the bike for *YHLQMDLG*. The alignment of each album with a particular visual icon contributes to its overall feel. For *El Último Tour del Mundo*, that image is a semitruck with a license plate that features the letters YHLQMDLG.

5.2 This is the cover of *El Último Tour del Mundo*. Note that the truck's hood bears a tiny logo with the name of the album on it, and the license plate reads "San Juan" with the letters YHLQMDLG below it. The semitruck became the primary symbol associated with the album. Bad Bunny incorporated it into his iconic performances promoting the album, including performing an entire concert on top of a semitruck driving through New York City in advance of the album's release. He also included an actual truck as part of his set design during P FKN R concerts in San Juan. Album cover designed by Stillz.

MAG knew about this choice during the production of the album. He told us that he "draw[s] inspiration" from the visuals associated with the album he's working on.

The first single was the Tainy-produced reggaetón smash hit "Dákiti" featuring Jhayco that was released in October 2020. The end of the song's music video featured a truck speeding down a desert road, followed by the text "El Último Tour del Mundo," an Easter egg for Bad Bunny's album. Spotify took this imagery and used it in the campaign leading up to the album's release. "When you listen to a song [on Spotify], there's a video clip, known as a canvas, in the background," Eddie explained to us. At the time, "the feature was new. We partnered with his team to upload those few seconds [of the music video] as the song's canvas. It became a moment and started conversations as fans wondered, 'What does this mean? What is "El Último Tour del Mundo"?'"

On September 20, 2020, the third anniversary of Hurricane María hitting Puerto Rico, Bad Bunny performed his first concert since COVID atop an eighteen-wheeler driving through the Bronx and upper Manhattan. Fans in New York could see him cruising through neighborhoods atop the truck. Those of us not in New York watched a live stream sponsored by Verizon and Uforia/Univision as part of their Hispanic Heritage Month programming.

This event brought the community together on this significant date in Puerto Rican history, one associated with the ongoing growth of the Puerto Rican diaspora in the United States mainland. In the first year after the hurricane, the inhumane and incompetent government response to Hurricane María forced an estimated 160,000 Puerto Ricans to flee the devastation in search of basic needs for survival.[28] As Bad Bunny explained in a pre-recorded interview that was broadcast as part of the concert livestream, "Nobody in Puerto Rico and nobody who has Puerto Rican blood will forget that date. It's good not to forget this date and know that it changed us so that people remember and don't do the same things. I say to the government that in the next elections, this has put a target on you."[29] That the New York-based concert took place on the anniversary of Hurricane María, and that Bad Bunny spoke directly to the date's significance, emphasized the deep connection between the diaspora and the archipelago. His outspokenness about the struggles in his homeland as part of the interview for the concert was yet another reminder of Bad Bunny's continuous commitment to Puerto Rico even as his global star rose to new heights.

The public did not yet know about *El Último Tour del Mundo* or that it would be associated with the image of a truck. The concert made evident how much Bad Bunny recognized the importance of the Puerto Rican diaspora as constituting not only his fans but also integral members of the Puerto Rican nation.[30] MAG told us that the truck concert was "in a way ... one of the biggest performances we've ever seen in New York, and he's done Yankee Stadium. But he was going from neighborhood to neighborhood, like performing, and managing not to get hit by streetlights." Indeed, the production was a huge effort. Univision had proposed the idea for the concert to Bad Bunny's team. Noah Assad reflected that the proposal seemed "too good to be true"; Univision had done the bulk of the legwork already, and Bad Bunny and his team brought their creative vision to the project.[31] The truck was a custom design to match the silver color of New York City's classic subway cars. Livestream hosts Brea Frank, Damaris Díaz, and El Shino Aguakate praised the logistical feat that made this concert happen—cameras on all the street corners, motorcycles following along to capture images from the street, and a helicopter flying above for aerial shots. On the live feed, we could see small crowds of people chasing the truck down the street to catch a glimpse of the star. Atop the truck, Bad Bunny sang his hits from *X 100PRE* and *YHLQMDLG*, along with some of his earlier singles. Some of his collaborators joined virtually. Viewers of the livestream could watch Bad Bunny duet from the truck and watch live video of his collaborators performing in their hometowns, including Sech in Panama City, Mora in San Juan, and J Balvin in Medellín, Colombia.

Many artists had done virtual concerts during the pandemic lockdown. While Bad Bunny did several Instagram lives, singing along to his prerecorded hits, he was not interested in doing a virtual concert. In his prerecorded interview for the truck concert special, Bad Bunny said, "For me, it was really hard to imagine doing a concert without an audience." He explained, "But in this moment, like, maybe, accepting our new reality, the idea is to be able to, I don't know, unite people, families, doing what we can. And I think that it could be cool in some way, I hope that I can feel the energy and euphoria of the crowd even if they're far away."[32] One of the things that has made Bad Bunny feel so authentic are his genuine expressions of gratitude for his fans during performances. This truck concert was another way to express this gratitude, and an attempt to foster these interactions given the restrictions from the ongoing pandemic.

Rather than put on a show in front of one of New York City's iconic landmarks like Times Square or Rockefeller Center, Bad Bunny performed as the truck rolled through the neighborhoods that comprise a major part of the city's Puerto Rican and Dominican diasporas. He began near Yankee Stadium, which is in the Highbridge and Concourse neighborhoods of the Bronx and has some of the highest concentrations of Puerto Ricans and Dominicans in New York City.[33] Then he continued through the historically Dominican neighborhood of Washington Heights. Finally, he ended up in Harlem just outside Harlem Hospital on 135th Street. There he performed "Yo Perreo Sola" in front of an adoring crowd. But first he thanked first responders who, "have sacrificed their lives, giving everything for the health of the city."[34]

Bad Bunny's truck concert celebrated these Puerto Rican and Dominican communities that are often invisible save for stereotypical portrayals of them as "problem" populations. Although historically Puerto Ricans settled across the country, by the mid-twentieth century, New York City became home to the largest Puerto Rican diaspora in the United States, and it has remained so until recently.[35] New York Puerto Ricans have been framed by people in power in the city as a "problem" that threatens New Yorkers' safety, stability, and wallets. Whether in policy proposals or popular culture, New York Puerto Ricans were and continue to be frequently represented as hypersexual, violent, foreign, and/or lazy.[36] Such racist stereotypes obscure how structural racism and inequality have imposed substandard housing, inadequate healthcare, high rates of unemployment, and failing schools on the community. As yet another example of this structural inequality, Bronx neighborhoods like Highbridge and Concourse had the highest rates of COVID infection, death, and hospitalization in New York during the pandemic.[37] The conditions in these neighborhoods reflect the history of racial and class discrimination that Puerto Ricans in New York have endured for more than one hundred years.

Bad Bunny says that the Puerto Rican and Dominican communities of New York make him feel like he's back home in Puerto Rico.[38] Riding through them emphasized the importance of the diaspora in understanding Puerto Rican identity, culture, and politics. That the concert took place three years to the day that Hurricane María hit Puerto Rico emphasized the deep connection between the diaspora and the archipelago. That Bad Bunny could pull off such a spectacle also made clear that he was a star with the resources and clout of any English-speaking singer. Still, he chose to speak directly to those communities that had always supported him. It was yet another reminder of Bad Bunny's continuous commitment to Puerto Rico even as his global star rose to new heights.

MAG told us that he had buzzed with anticipation after the truck concert: "I think I saw that, and I was excited and anxious and nervous thinking about what was about to unfold." The truck concert enabled Bad Bunny to interact with fans for the first time since finishing *YHLQMDLG*; but with the impending release of *El Último Tour del Mundo*, Bad Bunny was itching to have a conventional tour. In November 2020, he told *ET*, "For 2021, I think right now my biggest dream is to have a concert with a lot of people. That's the only thing I want. I know that it's hard, but that's my only goal right now, really."[39]

And he delivered. In August 2021, the artist announced a set of concerts that would take place later that year at Hiram Bithorn Stadium, a baseball stadium built in the 1960s and named for the first Puerto Rican player in Major League Baseball. Tickets sold out in just thirty minutes.[40] After tickets sold out so quickly for the shows, Bad Bunny and his team decided to sell tickets to watch parties of the shows; these were to be held in Puerto Rico's other major venue, the Coliseo de Puerto Rico José Miguel Agrelot (commonly referred to as "El Choli"), which also sold out its 18,000-person capacity.[41] The historic set of concerts, which Bad Bunny called "P FKN R," took place on December 10 and 11, 2021. Bad Bunny told podcaster Chente Ydrach that it was the biggest concert of his career: "Nobody knows the number of people because there's the [venue] capacity, and they fit double. Crazy. . . . So the exact number of people who entered, no one really knows."[42] *Rolling Stone* and *Billboard* reported that 40,000 attended the concert each night, while outlets like *New York Times* and *Vox* estimated 60,000 fans.[43] These numbers did not include the 18,000 people who watched the livestream at El Choli.[44]

As Bad Bunny said, "It sounds tough to say this but neither Hiram Bithorn nor any venue in Puerto Rico was prepared for an event of this magnitude, like, they weren't ready."[45] Media reported long lines with people waiting up to four hours to enter the stadium, dehydrated fans fainting en masse, and even a small fire that occurred on set during night one.[46] Bad Bunny told Chente that he felt sick in the days immediately preceding the concert, maybe because of stress, and so he could not do a full rehearsal before the show.[47]

What's more, despite mandating that concertgoers show vaccine cards, the concert would become one of the first major superspreaders of Puerto Rico's COVID outbreak. Puerto Rico had had some of the most restrictive COVID-19 protocols of any US state or territory, along with one of the most successful vaccination campaigns (at the time of the concert, 85 percent of Puerto Ricans had been vaccinated).[48] But after the Bad Bunny concert, an estimated 2,000 people were reportedly infected at the event, and the story served as a warning that vaccines were not providing protection against infection from the emergent Omicron variant.[49]

Despite these setbacks, the P FKN R concert was one of the most historic concerts Puerto Rico had ever seen. It reportedly cost $10 million dollars to put on.[50] At a press conference preceding the show, Bad Bunny's manager Noah Assad, who produced the event, stated "We are doing this without any economic benefit. We are doing it as a give-back for everything Puerto Rico has done for us."[51] Noah later told students at the University of Puerto Rico that they incurred a loss of upward of $3 million on the P FKN R concerts, but that it was worth it.[52] Ticket prices were low to make the concert accessible, with the cheapest seats at just $30 and the most expensive at $125.[53] Travis Shirley, the production and lighting designer for the shows, said, "It was a four-week load-in for a two-night show and was [declared] the largest in Puerto Rican history.[54] They said they wanted it to be the Super Bowl of Puerto Rico and that is exactly what it was in terms of size and scope."[55] Building the scaffolding around the stage alone took one month.[56] The set even included a massive semitruck that drove onto the stage for the last few songs, then was raised sixteen feet up into the air. Bad Bunny performed atop the raised truck with several guests including Myke Towers, Romeo Santos, and Arcángel.[57] At the end of the concert, streets in San Juan were closed so Bad Bunny could rapidly make his way to El Choli and greet fans there.[58]

Jessica Roiz of *Billboard* called the event "Badchella" because of its "Coachella-inspired aesthetics," referring to the iconic Coachella Valley Music and Arts Festival held annually in Indio, California. The area surrounding Hiram Bithorn was an extravaganza. There was a museum, located inside the Coliseo Roberto Clemente adjacent to Hiram Bithorn, that displayed artifacts like Bad Bunny's numerous awards, his Bugatti, outfits he had worn in music videos and industry events, and enormous reproductions of magazine covers featuring the artist.[59] In their *Rolling Stone* review, Jhoni Jackson described it as a "superb playground for any Bad Bunny lover." Jackson noted that the museum included "two giant inflatables: one an air-filled, astoundingly hyperrealistic model of his face, the other more in keeping with the Sergio Vazquez-made artwork of *X 100PRE*, Bad Bunny's groundbreaking 2018 debut LP, cartoon-like with his tongue as a slide down which folks could swoosh through and bounce out."[60] Roiz noted that the "carnival atmosphere" extended "outside of the stadium . . . with various food trucks, a live DJ, a carousel, a merchandise booth and different Bad Bunny stations for cute photo ops."[61] Chente called the event "un jangueo del proporciones bíblicas" (a hang-out of biblical proportions).[62] Media outlets encouraged fans to arrive early and dress comfortably. Puerto Rican newspaper *El Nuevo Día* even encouraged attendees to wear sneakers so that they could enjoy the long event.[63]

MAG watched the concert from the middle of the stadium floor. He wanted to experience it with the fans. He had never before witnessed such

5.3 Bad Bunny performs during the P FKN R concert in December 2021 at the Hiram Bithorn Stadium in San Juan. Photo courtesy of Thais Llorca.

a huge crowd singing his songs. It was a moving experience. "It was very special to be on the island and just experience the people singing these songs that weren't reggaetón songs, like 'Yo Visto Así' and 'Maldita Pobreza.' One section of the concert felt like this rock concert almost," he told us. The musical risks that he and Bad Bunny took had paid off. For MAG, this was evident not only in the album's record-breaking success but also in the reactions of fans in Puerto Rico. "To see Puerto Rico just embracing that and loving it, even though it wasn't just perreo, was really special and was confirmation that we created something special, even though we didn't do what was easy and safe. It was very rewarding," he said. The production was also awe inspiring. "I remember the truck pulling in and Arcángel showing up, and just like, it was crazy. Wow."

The concert began with a nearly seven-minute-long video introduction. Reflecting Bad Bunny's similarly intense affection for his island fans and for Puerto Rico itself, the lengthy introductory video was a love letter to the archipelago. MAG stood in the middle of the general admission crowd and watched when the video started right around midnight. "It was just goosebumps, chills, tears," he told us. "I remember my blood rushing through my body. It was beautiful and so moving. There were a lot of tears." In their conversation about the concert on his YouTube show,

Chente shared a similar sentiment with Bad Bunny, saying that the video "was a tearjerker."[64]

Bad Bunny told Chente that the introductory video "was made with a lot of love, a lot of pride." Narrated by Academy award-winning Puerto Rican actor Benicio del Toro, the video celebrated the history, culture, and pride of Puerto Ricans everywhere. It begins, "This is the chronicle of a star that jumped out from the depths of a great volcano under the ocean into another galaxy. It's the chronicle of a legend that represents what is in these coordinates. From up above, celestial beings painted an archipelago below." The screen shows images of Puerto Rican flora and fauna, especially the patriotic symbol the coquí, a tiny tree frog with a distinct "ko-kee" sound that is native only in Puerto Rico.[65] "Nació una raza recia" (A strong people were born). The video continues with images of a long list of Puerto Rican "legends" from both the archipelago and the diaspora: athletes (e.g., baseball players Roberto Clemente and Hiram Bithorn, boxers Tito Trinidad and Miguel Cotto, Olympic athletes Mónica Puig, Carlos Arroyo, Adriana Díaz, and Jasmine Camacho-Quinn); musicians (e.g., Ismael Rivera, Ruth Fernández, Ednita Nazario, Héctor Lavoe, Daddy Yankee, Lucecita Benitez, Tito Puente, Rafael Cepeda, Ricky Martin, and iLe); actors (e.g., Miriam Colón, Raúl Juliá, and Benicio del Toro); and writers (e.g., Mayra Santos Febres and Pedro Pietri). The introductory video also highlights important political figures like US Supreme Court Justice Sonia Sotomayor and activist Antonia Pantoja. It prominently spotlights key individuals involved in resistance—from Agüeybaná, the cacique (chief) of the Indigenous Taíno people who fought the Spanish, to twentieth-century leaders who fought for the independence of Puerto Rico from the United States, such as Pedro Albizu Campos, Lolita Lebrón, and Blanca Canales.[66] Interspersed with these Puerto Rican icons are images of Puerto Ricans living their everyday lives, from present-day people driving kids to school and selling pastelillos from a kiosko, to historical images of laborers cutting sugar cane and children playing in the countryside. The video showcases the long history of political protest in Puerto Rico, including protests to oust the US Navy from the island of Vieques, protests to save the University of Puerto Rico from privatization, and of course, the iconic 2019 protests of the Verano Boricua. The last thirty seconds place Bad Bunny as the latest luminary to come out of Puerto Rico. It concludes with an image of Bad Bunny and Jennifer Lopez (arguably the most famous contemporary Nuyorican) posing in front of the feathered Puerto Rican flag cape that she wore during their 2020 Super

Bowl performance. The screen goes black and the crowd cheers. Then, Benicio del Toro comes on the screen and says, "Being legendary comes naturally to us because in the end, no matter the achievement, there is no greater pride than saying '¡Yo soy de P FKN R!'" I am from P FKN R.[67]

The introductory video was an homage to the beauty, genius, and resistance of Puerto Ricans. This theme was also captured by calling the concert P FKN R, which was not only the title of the shows but also the title of one of Bad Bunny's anthems to Puerto Rico. The song "P FKN R" features Arcángel and Kendo Kaponi. It is an ode to Puerto Rico, especially the low-income barrios and caseríos that were the birthplace of reggaetón. The lyrics reference places like Juana Matos, a caserío in San Juan, and Villa Palmeras, a low-income neighborhood in Santurce. The song also references Puerto Rican icons like NBA star J. J. Barrea, salsero Ismael Rivera, and rapper Vico C. The lyrics have a lot of the braggadocio and hypermasculine fronting typical of Latin trap and reggaetón when the artists praise their jewelry, designer clothes, cars, and money. They also rap about drugs, guns, crime, and, in the case of Kendo Kaponi, his time in prison. The lyrics celebrate figures in the neighborhood like maleantes (thugs), prostitutes, crack addicts, and drug dealers.

On the surface, "P FKN R" reproduces many of the stereotypes associated with reggaetón and Latin trap from their early days. But at its heart, "P FKN R" is a song of defiance. The song begins with Bad Bunny singing "Si no sabes de donde soy, no me ronque, no" (If you don't know where I'm from, don't come at me, no). He then declares, "Yo soy de P FKN R" (I'm from P fuckin' R). While some might consider this aggressive attitude to be crude or even violent, it can also be an expression of pride. It is a warning to those who would "roncar" to Puerto Rico that they shouldn't because Puerto Rico is ready to defend itself. Although in Spanish, the term *roncar* translates to "to snore," in reggaetón *roncar* refers to declaring one's superiority through bragging about yourself or dissing a rival.[68] In this vein, Bad Bunny directly challenges the stereotype of Puerto Rico and Puerto Ricans as docile, which has been used to dismiss Puerto Ricans' long history of resistance to colonialism. In "P FKN R," Bad Bunny, Arcángel, and Kendo Kaponi represent themselves and their communities as always ready to defend their turf. Moreover, the song celebrates people from barrios, caseríos, and the working class—those communities that are the most impacted by the austerity measures and colonial policies put in place both by La Junta and by Puerto Rican government officials like Ricardo Rosselló and Pedro Pierluisi. "P FKN R" is thus a song of defiance and community, one that celebrates the agency, resilience, and power of Puerto Rico. In his May 2020 Instagram about *YHLQMDLG*, Bad Bunny proclaimed: "Don't mess with me if you come from some cold place because here [Puerto Rico] it gets hot for real." As he played the song, he screamed, "Yo soy de P fucking R!"[69]

This is precisely the sentiment that pervaded the P FKN R concerts. Chente made a thirty-five-minute video about his experience attending the concert. When the show finally starts, we hear Chente react to the first few seconds of the introductory video with, "This is an homage to Boricuas, homage to PR. P FKN R!"[70] And this is exactly what the concert was. With this concert, Bad Bunny hoped to create a spectacle that would lift people's spirits and show his gratitude to the Puerto Rican fans who had supported him all these years.

P FKN R cemented Bad Bunny's position as a global representative for Puerto Rico. He was already one of the most successful Puerto Rican musicians of all time. Adding MAG to his team helped Bad Bunny take reggaetón to new heights and in unexpected directions. It is no accident that 2020 was the first year Bad Bunny became the most streamed artist on Spotify; it was the year he released three different albums and, with *El Último Tour del Mundo*, the year he broke a new barrier for Spanish-language music. But even with this new status as a global Puerto Rican star, he remained committed to creating music for Puerto Rico and Puerto Ricans. His riding on a truck through some of the historic epicenters of Puerto Rican life in New York and his staging of an unprecedented extravaganza in San Juan for his P FKN R concerts showed that.

In many ways, this dedication makes Bad Bunny even more of an anomaly within the global cultural marketplace than his Puerto Rican roots do. It can be difficult to remain connected to one's community of origin while climbing the charts over and over again, especially if that community is far from the halls of power or the epicenters of global stardom. But as his star has risen to ever-growing heights, it appears that Bad Bunny's global success only made him even more committed to Puerto Rico and Puerto Ricans everywhere.

In 2021, it felt impossible to imagine that Bad Bunny would be able to top the success of *El Último Tour del Mundo* or the P FKN R concerts—but we would quickly realize that, while he celebrated Puerto Rico and gave back to his fans on the archipelago and the diaspora, he was also planning what would become one of his biggest takeovers in global music history.

6

"PUERTO RICO ESTÁ BIEN CABRÓN": THE PARTY IS THE PROTEST

Bad Bunny's fifth solo studio album, *Un Verano Sin Ti*, which translates to "A Summer Without You," was released on May 6, 2022.[1] A soundtrack to a summer day in the Caribbean, the album opens with the sound of the sea and seagulls calling as a synthesized steel drum beat kicks in, just before Bad Bunny's voice, softly singing, welcomes us to his masterpiece of an album with "Moscow Mule." While the song never loses its beachy, Caribbean feel, the track turns into a low-key reggaetón song with the classic *boom-ch-boom-chick* beat. We then move from the soft perreo vibes of "Moscow Mule" to the mysterious opening of "Después de la Playa," with its psychedelic, entrancing, experimental sound. Bad Bunny's lyrics ponder what he and his companion should do after they leave the beach (as they ride his surfboard, he suggests they get soaking wet again, but this time in his bed). Suddenly, the song comes to a brief pause and Bad Bunny asks if we're going to get into a mambo. After shouting "¡Zumba!," the track shifts to an explosive live instrumental mambo-merengue, unlike anything we had heard from the artist before. The album builds on a broad array of Caribbean sounds, but this song takes us directly to the Dominican Republic, with good reason.

"Whatever location we're in when we're together, we capture the magic of that location and the energy that's there, and really feed off of each other creatively," MAG, who produced most of *Un Verano Sin Ti*, including the two opening tracks, explained to us in an interview. "There's something special about grabbing that and putting that into a song." MAG and Bad Bunny lived in the Dominican Republic for about a month while creating the album. At first, "Después de la Playa" was just an extended version of the intro synth. But then, Bad Bunny had the idea to switch gears; MAG recalled that Bad Bunny told him, "Ok, this is going to start with synths and electronic, but then we'll make it a mambo song." MAG told us that they "went into [the city of] Santiago to this pretty small studio right in the middle of the city." At the studio they met up with Dominican merengue composer Luis Daniel Frías Felix (better known by his artist name Dahian "El Apechao") who MAG said had done a few projects that had caught their attention. El Apechao convened a team of musicians, and MAG described to us what happened when they came together in the small studio with Bad Bunny: "They just crammed everybody in there. And we recorded a full mambo band." When the band heard the song for the first time with Bad Bunny in the studio, MAG said the musicians were "kind of looking at each other like, 'Is [Bad Bunny] really here?' Because he had his face covered. And then he lifted [his mask] and introduced himself." Bad Bunny explained to everyone, "'I have this idea that I started and I would like to have you guys like play on it!' So he plays them the song. And he tells them, 'And then here is where I want you guys to come in!' Then he plays the song a second time and then they were like, 'Okay, cool!' So they only heard the song two times. We're ten minutes in and then they are like, 'Play it again!' And this time, maybe the third time, they start jamming. And they just started just playing what it was. We had what we needed by the third take. It was incredible." The result was a merengue-mambo fusion that feels like a live Dominican party. This improvisational moment, which led to one of the biggest hits of the album, is representative of the spontaneity, the playfulness, the community-oriented nature, and the Caribbean vibes of *Un Verano Sin Ti*.

The massive hit "Tití Me Preguntó" also took shape in the Dominican Republic. On the track, the iconic voice of the titi (a Puerto Rican colloquial term for aunt) was the voice of an *actual* titi of one of their friends, Dominican musician Tito Flow.[2] Bad Bunny wrote a script for her to record as a voice note on her cell phone that MAG then incorporated into the song. MAG told us that although the song blended the sounds of his New York City neighborhood, it was still a summer beach song: "There might be a couple that don't feel beachy, but they somehow feel like the summer. It feels like a block party in New York in the summer. Whatever environment the summer is for you, [the album] somehow captures [it] in whatever part of the world you're in. But the root of it is a Puerto Rican beach."

Bad Bunny's vision for the album was clear: it was all summer vibes, sitting on the beach with your friends, drinking a beer. MAG told us, "Benito would talk about this when we were making the album. It was something that started while you're on the beach. And then after a beach day, you're going to the club, or vice versa, like you leave the club and you wanna end up going to the beach and catching the sunrise . . . when you think of that, that balance of high energy, but also more beautiful elements more melodic emotional elements, I think you get this perfect summer album."

These qualities are palpable at first listen. The album feels like a communal Puerto Rican beach party, certainly; but it is also full of protest and resistance, love and heartbreak, hopes, dreams, and disappointments. And the songs tell these stories in ways that are unique to the Puerto Rican experience. From the genres and instruments used to tell the stories, to the songs like "El Apagón" that talk about the daily struggle for access to electricity in Puerto Rico, this album captures the highs and lows of life in the archipelago, which has always felt substantial influence not just from the United States but also from the Dominican Republic. Not only are MAG and Tainy, the two main producers on *Un Verano Sin Ti*, both half Dominican, but Dominican music has had an important impact on Bad Bunny's musical development as well as on that of reggaetón more generally.[3]

Although *El Último Tour del Mundo* had broken numerous records, nobody could have been prepared for how massively popular and culturally significant *Un Verano Sin Ti* would instantly become. Just three days after its release, *Un Verano Sin Ti* set the record for most single-day streams—at 183 million—and it also debuted at number one on Apple Music.[4] Just two weeks after its release date, *Un Verano Sin Ti* debuted at number one on the Billboard 200 chart, and then it spent an additional thirteen weeks at the top of the list. This was only the second album of any genre to spend this many weeks at number one.[5] Furthermore, every single one of the twenty-two new tracks on the album charted simultaneously on the Billboard Hot 100 chart, including four in the top ten (the exception to this was the "Callaíta," which had been previously released as a single in 2019).[6] These numbers are even more remarkable considering that all these songs are in Spanish. In fact, *Un Verano Sin Ti* was only the second all-Spanish-language album ever to reach number one on the sixty-six-year-old chart; and the first was *El Último Tour del Mundo*.[7] In November 2022, it was announced that *Un Verano Sin Ti* was the first Spanish-language album in history to be nominated for Grammy's Album of the Year award.[8] By 2023, it became the most streamed album in Spotify history.[9] Years later, at the time of this writing, it still holds that record.

"I didn't have any idea that statistically, and charts-wise, it was going to be as big as it was," MAG told us as we discussed the massive success of *Un Verano Sin Ti*. He continued:

> What I did know is how the album felt. I sat with a lot of these songs for months before the album came out. One or two of them I had maybe a year before the album came out. When we're working on an album, I'm listening to our reference or our demos constantly. I'm constantly listening to see what can be improved. While we were creating [the songs] there was a feeling that we had, and the feeling that I would get. I knew we gave everything to this album. We would feel that when we listened back to the songs. And that alone was fulfilling. That it was going to be the most streamed album of all time in less than two years of it being released? No, I don't think any of us predicted that. But we knew we created something special because of how much love we poured into it, into every song.

These record-breaking moments for a Spanish-language album by a Latin trap and reggaetón artist on an independent Puerto Rican label had never before seemed possible. Up to that point, Latin music, and reggaetón in particular, had been disregarded consistently by the American music industry.

By all accounts, *Un Verano Sin Ti* is a musical masterpiece. Reviews referred to the album, which features a wide-ranging assortment of blended musical genres demonstrating the expansive possibilities of Bad Bunny's musical innovation, as a "love letter" to Puerto Rico and to the Caribbean more broadly.[10] As music journalist Suzy Exposito told Vanessa, "With every song he sharpens his focus on the island so he's not just painting a visual picture, a sonic picture, but he's giving us a lot of context for the island that he lives in."[11] It takes only one listen, and close attention to the lyrics, to see the truth in this assessment. Despite the beach party theme, *Un Verano Sin Ti* also includes searing political critiques of the myriad crises in Puerto Rico. The album addresses issues like gentrification, austerity, and the failing Puerto Rican infrastructure. The album exemplifies the essence of P FKN R: It is an ode to the beauty of Puerto Rico and a commentary on the ongoing impacts of colonialism in the archipelago.

One crucial factor that made *Un Verano Sin Ti* so unique is that it was built from the synergistic creative partnerships Bad Bunny developed with both Tainy and MAG. As MAG recounted, "Benito said it best. *Un Verano [Sin Ti]* is like 'un granito de Tainy y un granito de MAG' [a bit of Tainy and a bit of MAG] and our worlds. We have different styles. I think a lot of Tainy's stuff on the album has more emotion, like if you listen to 'Ojitos Lindos' or 'Yo No Soy Celoso,' but then you balance that with my high energy tracks like 'Efecto' or 'Tití Me Preguntó,' you get this beautiful balance." Together with Bad Bunny, MAG and Tainy created a wildly imaginative, and very Caribbean album, with fusions and samples of reggaetón, cumbia, bomba, bachata, mambo, merengue, reggae, soca, dembow, and more.

Bad Bunny and his team already had a knack for blending different genres together in unique ways, but even so, *Un Verano Sin Ti* added some truly unexpected sounds. While Bad Bunny had previously dabbled in a bossa nova style with "Si Yo Veo a Tu Mamá" on *YHLQMDLG*, *Un Verano Sin Ti* included a complete, original bossa nova song titled "Yo No Soy Celoso." The track stands out for its guitar, melodic elements, whistled refrain, and the absence of a standard reggaetón beat. Tainy told us that he "made the beat specifically for [Bad Bunny]," but he was initially reluctant to show him. Tainy recalled that he went to Puerto Rico to show Bad Bunny a few of his ideas, and the beat for "Yo No Soy Celoso" was among them. He felt the beat had "something cool there," but Tainy still had some doubts about it, especially because he had never done a bossa nova beat before, and he wasn't even sure Bad Bunny would be interested. In fact, he originally did not intend to play the beat for Bad Bunny. Sitting in the studio, Tainy explained:

> I always like to lower the volume when I'm not sure what I have in the folder or what I want to share. I lower the volume so that maybe only I can hear it. So I start to kind of scroll to see which [beat] is which because [the tracks] were all called the same thing. And he heard a little bit from that song and I stopped it quickly. And he said, "Hey, hey, hey, what's that?"

And so he heard that little bit and he tells me to leave it playing in a loop. So then I see him get motivated. Because maybe he has an idea that connects perfectly with that track, and he's mumbling and moving. So, for me that was another cool moment, because it reaffirms that we're connected in a certain way.

At the end of the process, the song became one of Tainy's favorites.

Tainy's story is similar to MAG's story of the creation of "Andrea." MAG was playing a song low in his headphones and didn't even intend for Bad Bunny to hear the song, but it resonated with Bad Bunny. These stories demonstrate the carefulness with which MAG and Tainy treat their art, and the esteem with which they hold Bad Bunny. Despite being such accomplished producers, MAG and Tainy are humble. They care what their artists think, and they might even have a little self doubt from time to time. This quality makes the bond between Bad Bunny and his producers make even more sense. Despite Bad Bunny's *Yo Hago Lo Que Me Da La Gana* stance, he constantly shows that he does care what other people think, and he cares about the impact his music is making, culturally and politically. That he keeps in his close company creatives who are equally careful and equally humble, despite their history of hitmaking, makes us believe that these qualities are a part of the key to Bad Bunny's success. One thing is clear: The signature sounds MAG and Tainy delivered on *Un Verano Sin Ti* helped make it a cultural juggernaut. With the album's astronomical popularity, a tour had to be coming.

Bad Bunny's World's Hottest Tour, which promoted *Un Verano Sin Ti*, began on August 5, 2022, in Orlando, Florida, and ended on December 10, 2022, in Mexico City. Not only did Bad Bunny travel across the Americas, but he also played some of the biggest and most prestigious venues, from Boston's Fenway Park to New York's Yankee Stadium to Mexico City's Estadio Azteca. Bad Bunny had ended his El Último Tour del Mundo just a few months earlier, on April 3, 2022, in Miami, Florida. Much like the two albums, their associated tours shared a parallel story. El Último Tour del Mundo included thirty-five sold out shows across the United States and Latin America, earning $116.8 million to become the highest-grossing tour by a Latin artist in history up to that point.[12] The World's Hottest

6.1 Bad Bunny performs with Li Saumet of Bomba Estéreo at his *Un Verano Sin Ti* concert in El Choli on July 28, 2022. Photo courtesy of Gabi Perez-Silver.

Tour, which included forty-three concerts, grossed $435.8 million, and became the highest-grossing tour ever recorded in a calendar year (to date).[13]

Just before the World's Hottest Tour began, however, Bad Bunny did something special for Puerto Rico: he performed three nights at El Choli (July 28, 29, and 30). Whereas tickets for the World's Hottest Tour ranged from hundreds to thousands of dollars,[14] tickets for the Puerto Rico shows ranged from $15 to $150, making the performances significantly more accessible.[15] Like the P FKN R concert the year before, the *Un Verano Sin Ti* shows were a major cultural event on the archipelago. The first of the three nights streamed live on Telemundo for those who couldn't go in person. Plazas all over Puerto Rico—from Santurce to Aguadilla, Ponce, and Fajardo—hosted viewing parties.[16] Across all three nights, several artists who were featured on the album joined Bad Bunny on stage. On the first night alone—attended by 18,749 people, breaking the previous attendance record that had been set by a Metallica concert in 2010—guests included Chencho Corleone, María Zardoya of The Marías, Tony Dize, Jhayco (formerly Jhay Cortez), Buscabulla, and Bomba Estéreo.[17] He also brought up other artists with whom he had previously collaborated, like Arcángel and Jowell y Randy as well as newer artists like Villano Antillano and Young Miko.[18]

For concertgoers, the event was a special experience. As MAG told us in an interview: "There was something in the air. And we were on stage with him. He invited all his friends and family, and his dancers. We were all on stage and he invited us to experience this with him. So during the concert, we were taking all of this in from his perspective."

And yet, it was not just those on stage with him who felt the power of the events. One fan, Alysa M. Alejandro Soto, told *Vox*, "It was just us and him. . . . I feel like that's something he wanted to achieve: a special, intimate moment with PR."[19] The Puerto Rican media covered the concert extensively, from the size of the crowds to the impact of the shows on the broader economy. The crowd was diverse, coming from all over the archipelago, sometimes in multigenerational groups. Sixty-seven-year-old Gladys Pacheco brought her thirteen-year-old nephew and her ninety-year-old mother to the show. She told *El Vocero*, "Bad Bunny represents a change in society. He is the person who dares to do something different and to influence our youth in a way that represents Puerto Rico around the world and that elevates our music."[20] Photos of the events in the plaza showed not only posters and T-shirts celebrating the artist but also materials that used the concert as an excuse to continue protesting against the crises impacting the archipelago. In one particularly poignant image, a man at one of the plazas held up a sign with the one-eyed heart that became the image associated with *Un Verano Sin Ti*. Written above it, the sign questioned, "Titi me preguntó, ¿Cuando sacamos a Pierluisi? ¡Pedimos la Justicia!" (Titi asked me, When will we kick out Pierluisi? We demand justice!), referring to the then-governor who at one time had been part of Rosselló's cabinet.[21] Indeed, many fans explained that even if they did not always agree with Bad Bunny, especially his use of vulgar language, they saw him as a great representative for Puerto Rico. For instance, Zaira de la Rosa from Toa Baja told *El Nuevo Día*, "This 41-year-old *doñita*, who could be your titi, is supporting him. He's given so much to Puerto Rico because thanks to him they know about us around the world. There are people who don't support him because he uses bad words, but I have kids his age and they're young and you have to support them."[22] Another mother, Ivelisse Fanatusi, brought her thirteen-year-old daughter to witness the event because even though "as a mother, there are things he says that I don't agree with," she felt that "Bad Bunny is art, a social movement," and she wanted her child to be part of the historic moment.[23]

Once again, Bad Bunny did not shy away from using his platform to articulate his own critiques of the situation in Puerto Rico. On the night of the first performance, with much of the archipelago watching in their homes, in the plazas, and at El Choli (not to mention diasporic Puerto Ricans like us, who watched illegal live streams online), Bad Bunny addressed the crowd: "We are facing so many obstacles. We are facing a government that is screwing us day after day, the worst electric system, and I will say it myself: Está cabrón [It's fucked] that I can do a worldwide tour and what I'm going to say now is not a joke. This is the only place where I perform and have to put up like fifteen generators because I cannot trust the electric system of Puerto Rico." He continued by criticizing the government along with the Canadian- and US-based private electric company called LUMA Energy that started operations in Puerto Rico in 2021. "Fuck LUMA!" Bad Bunny yelled as the crowd went wild. "And [Governor] Pierluisi and all the mamabichos who think they own this country.[24] This is our country, and *we* are the ones who have the power. *We* are the ones who need to take the power. I believe in this generation. I believe in this Puerto Rico. I want to live here forever with you guys. Thank you, Puerto Rico."[25] Though just a few minutes long, this speech was a pivotal moment in the concert that reverberated across Puerto Rico and its diaspora. More than simply venting his frustrations with LUMA, some interpreted Bad Bunny's words as an indictment on the colonial condition of Puerto Rico itself. Writer Carina del Valle Schorske told Vanessa of his concert speech: "I could have imagined him critiquing LUMA, but he was basically out here like '¡Puerto Rico Libre!' That's the most surprising thing to me—how explicitly and confrontationally political he is willing to be within a Puerto Rican context."[26]

After his impassioned speech, Bad Bunny closed out the first night of this historic concert series with his song "El Apagón," which literally means "the blackout." The song references the frequent blackouts that have plagued Puerto Rico due to the archipelago's failing electrical grid and infrastructure, and it makes the album's most impactful political statement. As MAG told us: "'El Apagón' became an anthem for Puerto Rico. So I think [Bad Bunny] strategically planned to close with this at home, in Puerto Rico." Just a few months later, Bad Bunny would utilize another major platform—music video—to present an even more virulent critique of LUMA and Pierluisi's administration.

On September 16, 2022, Bad Bunny, released the music video for "El Apagón," arguably his most explicitly political anthem to date. "El Apagón" celebrates Puerto Rican people and culture; however, it also expounds upon the critiques that Bad Bunny had leveled at LUMA and the government during his summer concerts. Bad Bunny's discussion of these seemingly conflicting truths is encapsulated in the opening line of the song: "Puerto Rico está bien cabrón." This phrase has two contradictory meanings: (1) Puerto Rico is screwed or messed up, and (2) Puerto Rico is amazing or badass. The phrase begins every verse, and then is repeated later at the bridge. Like the phrase P FKN R, "Puerto Rico está bien cabrón" reflects the simultaneous pride and frustration with Puerto Rican life. In fact, it is no accident that, before the beat even drops, the music video begins with the last few lines that Benicio del Toro states in the introductory video to the P FKN R concerts: "I am from P FKN R." These words are accompanied by aerial shots of that show's crowd and Bad Bunny's silhouette as he takes the stage.

The video was directed by acclaimed music video director Kacho López Mari. He had first worked with Bad Bunny on the music videos for "Callaíta" and "Volví," Bad Bunny's collaboration with bachata group Aventura. Kacho's music videos all have a distinct style and are grounded in the imagery and landscapes of the local communities where he films. By the time Kacho met Bad Bunny, he had already worked on a series of videos with many of Bad Bunny's biggest influences and reggaetón's most politically outspoken stars like Tego Calderón and Calle 13.

Sitting in his San Juan office, Kacho told us about the vision for "El Apagón" that was relayed to him by Bad Bunny's team. Bad Bunny had conveyed that he "wanted to make a video that is a party. It's going to start in Villa Palmeras, and the party will end on the beach,'" Kacho remembered. Villa Palmeras is a Puerto Rican community with a rich history as the home of many important cultural figures in Puerto Rico, including the beloved Puerto Rican composer and salsa singer Ismael "Maelo" Rivera whose 1969 song "Controversia" was sampled in "El Apagón." The percussive sample from "Controversia" opens the track and we hear Maelo's voice from a live performance—offering love to the audience—just before Bad Bunny's vocals kick in. "Maelo, dime," he utters before he begins to rap over the bare percussion. Bad Bunny wrote these lyrics inspired by the "Controversia" sample. MAG described Bad Bunny as "floating around" in the makeshift studio they put together in the living room of the house they rented as he was "writing these lyrics over this . . . sample from a song that he knows so well. But there were no vocals. It was just that beat so yeah. . . . He wrote all those lyrics." "El Apagón" expresses the P FKN R attitude, praising the beauty of beaches and expressing frustration with the Puerto Rican government, in particular (at one point Bad Bunny says he'll smack down Pipo, which is a nickname for then-Governor Pedro Pierluisi).

In several clips of the music video for "El Apagón," Bad Bunny sits on the porch of Maelo's small blue house, which is now a historic cultural landmark and museum. At other times, he perches on a white wall bordering the home with a tattered Puerto Rican flag hanging behind him. The camera cuts to residents of this historic neighborhood mouthing the lyrics to "El Apagón." Interspersed are images of iconic Puerto Ricans—rapper and reggaetón star Tego Calderón, actor Raúl Juliá, singer and dancer Iris Chacón, basketball player J. J. Barea, and independence leader Pedro Albizu Campos—alongside videos of Puerto Ricans protesting during the 2019 Verano Boricua (including Bad Bunny himself).

Then, midway through the song, the beat shifts from the percussion-based Ismael Rivera sample into a Latin house beat. As MAG described to us, "We decided to make it kind of like a freestyle house, a very Boricua, Latin house thing. Like the stuff I would hear in New York. And so I bumped up the tempo significantly, as soon as the sample cuts out, and then you hear the synth come in. The tempo of the song is rising fast. Because by the time the house drums come in, we're at a house tempo." The pressure builds and we hear the infamous DJ Joe line, "Me gusta la chocha de Puerto Rico" (I like pussy from Puerto Rico) on repeat until the crowd comes in, accompanying Bad Bunny as they sing "¡Puerto Rico está bien cabrón!"

The change in sound ushers in a new scene in the music video: a crew of motorcycles and ATVs rev their engines as they take off, driving at night through dark, pothole-ridden streets until they park next to some bushes. Their destination is El Túnel de Guajataca in Isabela, on the west coast of Puerto Rico, where Bad Bunny leads a massive party during a blackout. The party is lit only by flashlights. Perreando through the night, the crowd waves flags—pride flags, Puerto Rican flags, and the black and white Puerto Rican protest flags—until day breaks and we leave the tunnel, flying over the Puerto Rican coastline.[27]

All these visuals were intentional, selected to amplify the political message embedded in the song. While Kacho brought visual life to this anthem for Puerto Rico, MAG gave "El Apagón" its sound. MAG explained to

6.2 A still shot from the music video for "El Apagón" depicting the party scene in the historic beachside Túnel de Guajataca. The dancer striking a pose here is one of the performers from the ballroom house and organization Laboratoria Boricua de Vogue (or LaBoriVogue). The party scene is notable for its symbolism, as discussed in the main text, but also for its inclusivity and centering of the queer community and pride flag. The flashlights that light up the background were an important artistic and symbolic choice to build on the theme of the song, which is about blackouts in Puerto Rico. Video directed by Kacho López Mari.

us that, from the beginning, Bad Bunny wanted "El Apagón" to be an anthem for Puerto Rico appropriate for everyone. "That's the funny thing about this," MAG told us. "When we were making that song, Benito in our session, tells me, 'You know the last song for Puerto Rico that I made, which was 'P FKN R,' had so many curse words. I don't want this one to be that.' So we make it and, you know, it starts with the Ismael Rivera sample. . . . There's no cursing. Then halfway through us, working on this, we throw in, 'Me gusta la chocha de Puerto Rico.' We look at each other and we are like, 'Fuck! This is awesome. But we thought we were gonna make a clean, nonexplicit anthem!'"

The lyric was borrowed from the song "Vamos a Joder" (We're going to fuck) by DJ Joe and Great Kilo from DJ Joe's 2000 album *Fatal Fantassy*, but it was not sampled.[28] "A lot of people don't know that that's actually Benito's vocals. I told Benito, I'm like, 'Why don't you [sing it]?' He's so good at making voices. So I'm like, 'Why don't you try to sound like the sample? It'll be easier,'" MAG told us of the production of the song. Then

MAG pulled out his phone. "Let me see if I have it," he said, scrolling through his voice notes until he found the recording. He played for us the unmistakable line from an unmistakable voice. "So that's Benito's vocals. I had him do two takes on my phone on voice notes. I put it in Ableton and just made it sound like the sample. But that's actually an interpolation with Benito singing."[29]

DJ Joe was an early reggaetón and underground DJ known for his sexually explicit lyrics. This kind of line, let alone a song called "Vamos a Joder," was exactly the type of language that fueled the moral panic about the music's impact on youth during DJ Joe's heyday.[30] But for Bad Bunny, the song represented far more than a simple reference to a woman's anatomy. "For [Bad Bunny]," MAG explained to us, "la chocha is not a chocha. He is saying 'I like everything about Puerto Rico. I like the core of Puerto Rico. I like everything about my culture. Everything about Puerto Rico.' That's what *la chocha* means here." Bad Bunny himself spoke on this a bit in his interview with Chente. "Puerto Rican women make me feel weak . . . but there's a meaning that's beyond the literal *chocha*. The woman, the roots of Puerto Rico."[31]

This was also reflected in the music video's party scene in the Túnel de Guajataca. Kacho understood the deeper meaning of *chocha* in the song. He told us Bad Bunny "is talking about in some way a metaphor for the Puerto Rican body. And also, that is the chocha. It is the vagina. It is what we are born from. It is that portal that brings life. And in some way that tunnel also turned into that. That tunnel from which you emerge, and when you emerge, you are reborn."[32] Kacho decided that there was "no more perfect place than the Túnel de Guajataca to have this party. . . . Thinking that legendary parties have been held there in Puerto Rico, of electronic music and other things. But that's also where the train passes. The train passed through that tunnel, the one that went around Puerto Rico, distributing [sugar] cane and carrying passengers. It is also next to the beach."[33]

Once they settled on the historic beachside tunnel and prepared to shoot the video, Kacho explained that they decided, "We are going to bring 200 of us and we are going to bring the people from the perreo combativo, the people of LaBoriVogue." LaBoriVogue, or Laboratoria Boricua de Vogue, is a ballroom house and organization that provides a space for queer Puerto Rican performance as a tool for liberation and social justice.[34] In the context of the song's critique of the Puerto Rican government, the selection of queer performers is critical, referring back as Kacho notes to the perreo combativo that represented the resistance of queer and other marginalized communities against Ricky Rosselló's administration. Still, even when they hired professional performers, the party in the music video was what Kacho described to us as "a real party. The people are reacting to the fact that Bad Bunny is the one who invited them, and he is there. And Bad Bunny grabbed the microphone a couple of times and gave them a fucking show. The people who went to that video shoot had a Bad Bunny show in the Túnel de Guajataca . . . a mini Bad Bunny show."

Significantly, they used flashlights as the primary lighting for the scene in the tunnel. As Kacho explained, "Of course, the discussion at the beginning was, 'Well, in this country the power goes out—*el apagón*. What I came up with from day one and I presented it to him early on was, 'The power goes out, but we don't end the party, we are such *cabrones* that we power the party ourselves," he told us. "At first, we thought of using cell phones, but then we decided to use flashlights."

In fact, everything about the music video, even seemingly small details like whether to use cell phones or flashlights, were just as intentional as the sonic choices that MAG and Bad Bunny made while they were creating the song. For instance, one of the more iconic images of the video is Bad Bunny sitting atop a white wall in front of Maelo's house, a tattered Puerto Rican flag waving from the white bars over the windows. But this was not just any flag. Kacho told us that the flag came from the tomb of his uncle, Santiago Mari Pesquera, whose father (Kacho's grandfather) was Juan Mari Bras, pro-independence activist and leader of the Puerto Rican Socialist Party (1971–1983). Kacho recalled that his grandfather's politics got him "in trouble with the FBI. At that point, there was a lot of political persecution toward people that identified as socialist. My grandfather at that point was a candidate for governor in Puerto Rico for the Socialist Party, which was also persecuted. So at that point in [19]76 there was an order to kill my grandfather, to assassinate him, but instead of killing my grandfather, they killed my uncle."

Kacho's uncle is buried at Santa María Magdalena de Pazzis Cemetery where many prominent Puerto Ricans are buried, including pro-independence leader Pedro Albizu Campos. The cemetery is in La Perla, right against the city walls near El Morro on one side and the ocean on the other. As Kacho noted, "That's why the flag is all torn up . . . all the brutality of the sea in front of it, just hitting it, and the wind is really strong." Every year, Kacho's family replaces the Puerto Rican flag on Santiago's tomb with a new one, and one year Kacho decided to keep the tattered flag. He described his thinking when he chose to include the flag

6.3 Still shot from the video for "El Apagón," depicting Bad Bunny sitting alongside a wall that borders the historic home that used to belong to Puerto Rican salsa performer Ismael Rivera. Hanging on the side of the home is the tattered Puerto Rican flag that spent a year draped over the seaside tomb of Kacho López Mari's uncle, Santiago Mari Pesquera, who was assassinated because of his family's political activism. Video directed by Kacho López Mari.

in the music video: "When I was doing the technical scouts and locations [for the video], I went like hey, what if I bring my uncle's flag and put it behind [Bad Bunny]? And I think it's a metaphor for Puerto Rico. You know we're a little ripped. . . . We are proud. And when [Bad Bunny] says, 'Puerto Rico está bien cabrón.' . . . In Puerto Rico 'Bien cabrón' has two meanings. It's great, it's amazing. But also it's hard. And for me the flag is a symbol of pride for us Puerto Ricans, but a ripped flag is a message. It's a hidden message of the situation in Puerto Rico that he's talking about."[35] That the Puerto Rican flag would figure so prominently in the music video is not surprising given the political message of "El Apagón." However, the deliberate choice to use a flag that spent a year flying over the tomb of an assassinated independence leader's son, in a music video shot by that same independence leader's grandson, makes this message even more powerful.

After the party in the Guajataca tunnel, as the sun rises, the camera moves through the opening of the tunnel over the beach and travels along the coastline. The music shifts once more as the loud hard-hitting beat fades away to softer synth chords. We hear the voice of Gabriela Berlingeri, Bad Bunny's then-girlfriend, sing:

Yo no me quiero ir de aquí
Que se vayan ellos
Lo que me pertenece a mí
Se lo quedan ellos
Que se vayan ellos
Esta es mi playa
Este es mi sol
Esta es mi tierra
Esta soy yo.

I don't want to leave here
Let them leave
What belongs to me
They keep it for themselves
Let them leave
This is my beach
This is my sun
This is my land
This is me

Written by Bad Bunny, these lyrics are a direct reference to yet another crisis in Puerto Rico: the displacement of Puerto Ricans not only because of the failing infrastructure and lack of resources addressed in the first half of the song, but also because of the current gentrification caused by a massive influx of wealthy Americans from the US mainland into Puerto Rico. The haunting tone of Gabriela's voice heightens the emotions of the lyrics. MAG described to us, "My eyes got watery the first time I heard it, and even now . . . that part just hits home."

Kacho told us that he believes "El Apagón" is one of the best Puerto Rican protest songs in decades because it speaks to the urgent issues like gentrification facing Puerto Rico today. "The truth is that when I heard it for the first time, without having talked to them, without having the video or anything, I perceived it as a protest song," he told us. "That is, there is a call to action. Saying, this is my island, there is a reaffirmation of 'This is mine.'" Similarly, Bad Bunny told Chente:

It's a really special song for me. When I did ["El Apagón"], I was sitting on the beach with [friends and members of his team] Jan and Jomo. . . . I was at a little beach in Manatí listening to Ismael Rivera and I was writing in my notes: Wow. Puerto Rico is *bien cabrón*. Look at this landscape. There are people who pay thousands to come and visit here. And we have it. You have the most incredible sunsets, the most beautiful water, the most beautiful coasts at your disposal . . . and this is yours. They want to take it from us, but this is ours, it belongs to us. And that's what the song is about . . . a beautiful song about Puerto Rico, celebrating my people and patriotism. I feel proud of my island.[36]

MAG agreed. He told us that "El Apagón" is "the most meaningful song of my career for so many reasons. I have a lot of pride in that song. And it's still funny that we created this protest song that became a party song. We kind of tricked everybody. The song is an emotional roller coaster. . . . It's a roller coaster of an anthem for our people."

This trick—taking a party and turning it into a protest—is part of the use of music as resistance in Puerto Rico. "It is a party, but it is a protest," Kacho told us of the party scene in the video. "It is also a political expression, and that has always been our approach. This is still a form of resistance. We're here. We make the light for our party, and what are you going to do? And we're not going to stop being happy because we're in hardship. We are going to get our hands on it, we are going to fight it, we are going to win it, and we are going to party, and we are going to have fun and get as crazy as we please, right? And that's kind of the mentality coming from Benito." In this way, "El Apagón" reflects the very ethos of P FKN R, ending with, as Kacho described, a call to action and, ultimately, a message of hope.

On the surface, both the song and the music video for "El Apagón" are typical of the way that Bad Bunny uses his platform to promote Puerto Rico, even if the song is more overtly political than others. But this isn't just any music video. Just a few minutes into the music video, the song stops right before Bad Bunny sings, "Maldita sea, otro apagón" (Damn it, another blackout), and viewers see an explosion. Puerto Rican independent journalist Bianca Graulau explains how these kinds of regular explosions leave tens of thousands of residents without power, and that this particular explosion had left the entire island in darkness in April of that year (2022), including one of Puerto Rico's most important hospitals. The music video resumes, but this interruption is not a one off. After the end of the song, the camera moves over San Juan, where we see Graulau talking about gentrification with a small group, including Maricusa, a woman who explains how gentrification threatens her home. The group sits down to eat, and we hear the drum sample from "Controversia." So begins an almost twenty-minute documentary called *Aquí Vive Gente* (People live here). After delivering the completed music video to Bad Bunny, Kacho heard that Bad Bunny had a change of plans. "I get a call," Kacho said. "'Hey, Benito wants to do something [more] with this video. He wants to do like a fifteen- to twenty-minute documentary. And he wants to connect it to the video so that people go to watch the video and they see a documentary.' And my mind was blown once again."[37] Kacho was thrilled to be part of a project that would reach such a large audience given Bad Bunny's popularity and international superstar status.

At first Bad Bunny wanted a documentary about energy and the electrical grid since "El Apagón" is about blackouts. But then he wanted to expand the focus to include stories about displacement and gentrification. Kacho told us that Bad Bunny also decided he wanted to add content about "what is happening on the coasts," referring to the current controversies over development on Puerto Rico's public beaches.

Bad Bunny selected Bianca Graulau to do the reporting featured in the documentary. Graulau had amassed an impressive following on social media reporting on social and political issues in Puerto Rico and other places like Hawai'i and Mexico that are similarly struggling with the ongoing effects of colonialism, gentrification, and tourism. "Benito wanted to recognize her because of the work she had been doing and give her total freedom to say what she wanted to say from her point of view," Kacho explained.[38] Kacho then collaborated with Graulau, lending support in production and then eventually merging the two projects—the music video and the documentary—into one.

Overall, *Aquí Vive Gente* is a blistering critique of the ongoing economic crisis facing Puerto Rico. The film tackles gentrification and displacement, from increased housing prices to limited access to the beaches that inspired *Un Verano Sin Ti*. The documentary connects the current crisis to the larger history of colonialism in Puerto Rico. It also places gentrification in the context of the establishment of laws such as Act 60, which offers mainland Americans incentives to settle on the archipelago. The film shows the effects of these broader colonial histories and policies on the everyday lives of people who face evictions, an untenable cost of living, and the dangerous effects of climate change as a result.[39]

The first and most obvious issue that *Aquí Vive Gente* tackles is Puerto Rico's failing electrical grid. Graulau explains the transition of control of Puerto Rico's formerly public electrical company PREPA to the private American-Canadian company LUMA Energy. This transition took place with the promise of a more reliable electrical grid. PREPA (the Puerto Rico Electric Power Authority) was a public utility company created in 1941; it is generally considered to have contributed to the industrialization of Puerto Rico into the 1970s.[40] However, the financial crises in Puerto Rico over the past several decades took a toll on the archipelago's public utilities and infrastructure, and PREPA filed for bankruptcy in July 2017.[41] La Junta pushed Puerto Rico to sell off its assets, "but since PREPA couldn't be sold while undergoing debt restructuring, the government opted for a public-private partnership model in which it retained ownership of the assets—and the debt—while outsourcing operations."[42] When Hurricanes María and Irma destroyed the already failing electrical grid later that year, Governor Ricardo Rosselló presented this as an opportunity to achieve this long-held goal of privatizing the electric utility. As scholar Catalina de Onís argues, Rosselló called Puerto Rico a "blank canvas" for rebuilding and redevelopment, an attitude that journalist Naomi Klein has called "disaster capitalism."[43]

In the wake of the hurricanes, emergency contracts were signed with Oklahoma-based Cobra Acquisitions ($900 million) and Montana-based Whitefish Energy Holdings ($300 million) to improve the grid. The Whitefish Energy contract was canceled after one month of work, but the company's owner insisted that PREPA still owed them $130 million.[44] At the time Whitefish secured the contract, it had existed for only two years and had only two full-time employees. What's more, they charged Puerto Rico exorbitant prices.[45] As de Onís concludes, "These private contracts demonstrated a reliance on quick fixes and outside interventions that benefited US contractors. One journalist characterized the deals as a 'colonial-style plunder,' as the agreements prohibited any kind of company auditing and other accountability measures."[46]

Then, on June 1, 2021, LUMA Energy, a company based out of Canada and Houston, Texas, took over.[47] As Graulau notes in *Aquí Vive Gente*, although LUMA and the Puerto Rican government promised improvements, blackouts instead became more frequent and longer, with devastating consequences despite the steadily rising cost of electricity for residents.[48] Moreover, the Puerto Ricans who had previously worked at PREPA were offered jobs at LUMA with fewer benefits and reduced salaries, or they had to find other work.[49] Meanwhile, the executives of LUMA Energy were making salaries that far exceeded any amount ever paid at the public energy company that LUMA replaced.[50] Not only has Puerto Rico's electrical service worsened under LUMA while costing Puerto Rican residents more, but the company itself has been mired in scandal. Just five months after LUMA took over, a judge in Puerto Rico issued an order to detain Wayne Stensby, the company's chief executive, for failing to comply with a court order to provide documents about the company's finances to lawmakers who sought to understand just how it was that Puerto Ricans paid so much for electric service that often never materialized.[51] Still, then-Governor Pedro Pierluisi's administration doubled down on their support of LUMA, a moot point given that, at the end of the day, it is actually La Junta who determines whether or not LUMA's contract can be canceled.[52]

The consequences of Puerto Rico's degraded electrical grid are much worse than the mere inconvenience of being without power. Stories of Puerto Ricans on the archipelago suffering through the economic hardship as a result of the constant blackouts describe how "the rank smell of rotting food filled the stairs and hallways" of high rise apartment buildings where perishable food cannot be kept cold nor disposed of as residents are often trapped.[53] Harrowing stories of older adults who have not eaten as a result of these blackouts are sprinkled in the occasional news story about these everyday blackouts. As a *New York Times* article about one of these blackouts recounts: "A neighbor in her 80s, who lives alone on the 13th floor, cried when Ms. Rivera brought her a plate of hot food. 'I think she had not eaten in a while, because she started crying,' said Ms. Rivera as she stood in the middle of her dark and hot living room. 'I told her: 'Do not cry, stay calm. Tomorrow I'll bring you more.'"[54] LUMA has become a symbol of the many crises in Puerto Rico because not having reliable access to very basic needs like electricity is making the archipelago unlivable. This crisis of power and energy is about so much more than just electricity; ultimately, as de Onís argues, it is a crisis of Puerto Rico's ongoing colonial status that makes life in Puerto Rico difficult for many Puerto Ricans.[55]

This point relates to the second key theme in *Aquí Vive Gente*: displacement and gentrification. The documentary tells the story of Maricusa Hernández who has rented the same apartment in the San Juan neighborhood of Santurce for the last twenty-six years. The property was sold to a new owner, and the rent in her building skyrocketed so there was no way that she could afford to stay. Hernández subsequently received a thirty-day notice to vacate. Graulau explains that these heartbreaking scenarios are a result of laws implemented by the Puerto Rican government that lure in wealthy foreigners and corporations to Puerto Rico to take advantage of tax breaks, and how these policies trickle down to destroy the lives and livelihoods of locals.[56] "They're displacing Boricuas to become rich," Hernández explains in the documentary.[57]

Aquí Vive Gente also tells the story of residents of the historic working-class neighborhood Puerta de Tierra, located between Old San Juan and the wealthy, touristy neighborhood of Condado. Puerta de Tierra residents Jorge Luis González and Laura Mía González describe how their neighborhood has become unrecognizable, with schools and public housing being replaced by luxury condominiums to house primarily wealthy foreigners. Jorge Luis's comments echo the lyrics that close out "El Apagón." "It is not just to be displaced by economic interests," he says. "They want us to leave. No, no, if we were the ones who were born here, they are the ones who should leave." "Que se vayan ellos," he adds, directly quoting the lyrics from "El Apagón."

In between the stories of residents, Graulau explains in greater detail the various laws offering generous tax breaks to wealthy Americans that have ultimately wreaked havoc on Puerto Ricans. Former Governor Luis Fortuño, the very same governor responsible for billions of Puerto Rico's debt during his short tenure, passed Acts 20 and 22, claiming that they would spur investment in the archipelago's economy. Act 20 provides tax incentives for foreigners to establish and grow their export businesses in Puerto Rico, and it requires that they have five full-time Puerto Rican resident employees. Act 22 removed taxes on personal income for foreigners, including Americans from the US mainland, who received and maintained residency in Puerto Rico. In 2019, Governor Ricardo Rosselló combined the two laws into a singular piece of legislation called Act 60 that eliminated the requirement for a minimum number of employees (unless the business grosses over $3 million, in which case the tax beneficiary must hire *one* local resident).[58] It also offered these benefits to other types of investors like those in cryptocurrency, further enticing wealthy Americans to relocate to Puerto Rico.[59]

Proponents of Act 60 and its predecessors (Acts 20 and 22) argued that this legislation would attract investors to Puerto Rico whose presence would then improve the economy. But Puerto Ricans have not seen this benefit. Instead, as Graulau notes in the documentary, the relocation of investors to the archipelago has raised rent prices dramatically in recent years. Many Puerto Ricans are being displaced from apartments that they have lived in for decades. The increased influx of foreigners has made real estate property along the coast inaccessible for regular working-class Puerto Ricans.

Graulau reveals that the true beneficiaries of Act 60 are wealthy people who gobble up Puerto Rican real estate and displace Puerto Ricans. For example, she mentions that since 2018, eight foreigners have purchased at least twenty-eight properties in Puerta de Tierra, including what was once a public school that will be turned into luxury apartments with ocean views. Puerta de Tierra resident Laura refers to these predatory developers as "colonizing invaders because that's how they behave."

Graulau explains that much of the property purchased by Americans is used for tourism. She makes an explicit comparison between the tourist economy and Puerto Rico's historical plantation economies, pointing out that in both cases, it is the wealthy Americans who have become richer while the Puerto Rican laborers and residents remain impoverished and exploited. Graulau also addresses how Americans are striving to ensure that Puerto Ricans have increasingly less access to their nation's own natural resources. The last area of focus in *Aquí Vive Gente* is the informal privatization of Puerto Rican beaches. According to Puerto Rican law, the archipelago's beaches are entirely public property. However, this does not stop developers in their efforts to cut off public access to the beaches. One of the locations the film focuses on is the municipality of Dorado, on the north coast, about fifteen miles west of San Juan. The film teaches us that the beaches are required to have multiple entry points for public access. However, because Act 60 has motivated wealthy investors to move to Puerto Rico, owners and developers of waterfront mansions purposefully limit public access by closing off these entry points. In *Aquí Vive Gente*, Graulau introduces viewers to Rosa Rivera Martínez, who cleans homes in Dorado. The two women walk over one mile until they reach a bunch of jagged, slippery rocks and determine that the path is too dangerous to continue. This is the route any ordinary Puerto Rican resident must take if they want access the coveted West Beach, making the beach virtually impossible for anyone who cannot afford the multimillion-dollar homes that dot the coastline. This story mirrors the sentiment in the lyrics Bad Bunny penned for Berlingeri, "Esta es mi playa, esta es mi sol" (This is my beach, this is my sun).

Despite chronicling all these injustices, the documentary also highlights Puerto Rican resistance and triumph. The final story details a series of protests against the construction of a swimming pool on the beach in front of a private condominium complex in Rincón called Sol y Playa, where Pierluisi's cousin and former campaign director Walter Pierluisi owned a unit.[60]

This is not the only scenario where high-level politicians have been implicated in these conflicts. In 2023, Puerto Rico's former Governor Alejandro García Padilla joined the legal team defending a controversial coastal development in Aguadilla, after the developer's security guards shot protesters demonstrating against the development's proximity to the beach.[61] Protesters remain concerned not only about lawful access to public beaches but also about the serious environmental consequences of such construction. For example, the construction project in Rincón threatened the habitat of endangered sea turtles; in fact, one sea turtle, after laying 180 eggs in the sand, had become trapped inside the chain-link fence of the construction site. A judge eventually determined that the construction was unlawful and ordered demolition of all existing structures related to the pool. When the owners did not comply, protesters demolished the wall themselves. *Aquí Vive Gente* concludes with powerful imagery of the protesters taking matters into their own hands, demonstrating the collective and community-based anti-colonial struggle in which Puerto Ricans are constantly engaging.[62] As *Aquí Vive Gente* ends, one of the Puerta de Tierra residents says: "Resistance will last here until the very end." The final scenes of the documentary show aerial footage of protests, beaches, and iconic landmarks in Puerto Rico as we, again, hear Berlingeri sing the final lines of "El Apagón."

After Kacho completed "El Apagón" / *Aquí Vive Gente* in 2022, he learned that Bad Bunny and his team "didn't have a plan to release the video at any specific time." And then news surfaced that another storm, Hurricane Fiona, was barreling toward Puerto Rico. Kacho heard from Bad Bunny's team that now was the time to release the video because, as he recalled, they said, "If this hurricane hits, we're gonna have a real [blackout]. And that was exactly what happened. . . . The day after the video was released, we had a 100 percent blackout [in Puerto Rico]."[63] In a striking twist of fate, Fiona struck Puerto Rico on September 18, 2022, almost five years to the day after María devastated Puerto Rico on September 16, 2017. "Before [Hurricane] María, we'd never seen 100 percent of Puerto Rico without light," Kacho continued. "No electricity in 100 percent of the island. So yeah, that was that moment, you know. . . . That decision to release it at that point, and what happened right after was significant."

Not quite one week after Fiona hit, Puerto Ricans remained in darkness as they grappled with the aftermath of the hurricane. Once again,

Bad Bunny was on tour, performing two concerts in Las Vegas, Nevada, on September 23 and 24, 2022, for the World's Hottest Tour. On the first night of his two-night stint in Vegas, he gave an impassioned speech to his fans, again using his platform to shed light on an immediate issue facing Puerto Rico. He focused his comments on the meaning behind "El Apagón's" refrain, "Puerto Rico está bien cabrón." Bad Bunny began by claiming that Puerto Rico was bien cabrón because of its beauty, its culture, and its people. But then he noted the dual meaning of *cabrón* by explaining the ongoing problems facing Puerto Rico. "It is increasingly difficult to stay, and there are fewer and fewer resources for Puerto Ricans to live on the island and live in Puerto Rico," he told the audience. He criticized the government that "acts as an enemy, getting richer and richer each day and working for its own benefit, while putting the people last on its list of priorities." Next, he made a direct connection between Hurricanes Fiona and María. Bad Bunny told the audience that Puerto Rico lost electricity even before Fiona made landfall, and six days after the hurricane, most of the archipelago remained in a blackout. He then made a direct call to action: "Puerto Rico doesn't want pretty messages and messages like 'Puerto Rico Se Levanta.'[64] Puerto Rico wants action. Puerto Rico needs and deserves something better. . . . I love Puerto Rico more than anything else in the world. I feel proud of my flag, I feel proud of my country. The whole world knows Bad Bunny, and the whole world knows that Bad Bunny is from Puerto Rico and knows that Puerto Rico is bien cabrón."[65] This plea for help for his homeland immediately preceded Bad Bunny's performance of "El Apagón" that night. Bad Bunny's speech added context and depth to an already emotional and political song. This is an anthem for Puerto Ricans that leaves us simultaneously joyful, angry, elated, nostalgic, deeply sad, and prideful.

For Kacho, the ability to contribute to a project with such a powerful message was a highlight of his career. He was honored to work with an artist who was willing to use his platform to speak out about these causes for such a massive audience. Millions of people have watched the YouTube video. As Kacho described, they "started watching a Bad Bunny video and ended up learning and watching a documentary about gentrification and the Puerto Rican struggles."[66] As Juan Arroyo outlined in an article for *Rolling Stone*, Bad Bunny using this song and his platform to develop extensive educational content around ongoing crises in Puerto Rico was especially significant given the massive success of *Un Verano Sin Ti*. This video and documentary took advantage of an opportunity to "clue in fans who haven't been aware and rally support to push Puerto Rico toward a future he and its citizens have been envisioning. The song and music video are more than just a message—they're a call-to-action."[67]

On February 5, 2023, Bad Bunny brought his message to the biggest stage in music, the Grammy Awards, where he opened the award show with "El Apagón." Starting the 65th Annual Grammy Awards with his Puerto Rican protest song was a particularly significant cultural moment. Dressed informally in a white T-shirt, light blue jeans, white tennis shoes, and a backward black World Series baseball cap emblazoned with PR on the front, Bad Bunny entered the packed Los Angeles Crypto Arena with live drummers and horn players, Puerto Rican plena dancers in brightly colored skirts, and a troupe of Puerto Rican theater performers wearing cabezudos—giant papier-mâché heads that are a key feature of one of Puerto Rico's most important festivals, Las Fiestas de la Calle San Sebastián. The cabezudos, created for Bad Bunny's performance by the renown Puerto Rican theater group Agua, Sol y Sereno, represented a diverse array of figures in Puerto Rican history and culture, including some who are particularly relevant to "El Apagón," like Ismael Rivera and Tego Calderón. Other cabezudos included poet, abolitionist, and Puerto Rican independence fighter Lola Rodríguez de Tío, former San Juan mayor and the first woman to serve as mayor of any capital city in the Americas Felisa Rincón de Gautier (known more commonly in Puerto Rico as "Doña Fela"), poet Julia de Burgos, baseball legend and humanitarian activist Roberto Clemente, singer and songwriter of El Gran Combo de Puerto Rico Andy Montañez, and salsa composer Tite Curet Alonso.[68]

With this large crowd of performers accompanying him, Bad Bunny begins, "Puerto Rico está bien cabrón, está bien cabrón." But the audience only gets to hear him say "Puerto Rico está" before he lowers the mic and mouths, rather than sings, the remainder of the line. Since *cabrón* is technically a curse word, media outlets cannot broadcast it. Still, there is something satisfying about Bad Bunny silently mouthing cabrón—only those who know, will know. There are many parts of "El Apagón" that carry particular meaning to Puerto Ricans, including that line. Likewise, Bad Bunny could not say *chocha* on live television. Even without the lyric "me gusta la chocha de Puerto Rico" broadcast as part of the performance, the sentiment was still there. Referring to this part of the song, scholar and

6.4 Dancers and cabezudo performers from Bad Bunny's historic 2023 Grammy Awards performance gather around a Puerto Rican flag to memorialize the moment. The cabezudos include important Puerto Rican cultural figures such as Ismael Rivera, Roberto Clemente, Julia de Burgos, Andy Montañez, and Tego Calderón, among others. Photo courtesy of Jade Power-Sotoymayor.

dancer Jade Power-Sotomayor, who performed as a plena dancer along-side Bad Bunny at the 2023 Grammys, notes that this "rhythmic chant . . . invokes a motherland and a sexual entrega [dedication] to Puerto Rican pussies, but it also names the kinds of extraction brought by investors and gentrifiers that see Puerto Rico as a port opening to exploitable riches." Thus, there was immense power in opening the show with "El Apagón"—a song that calls out Puerto Rican colonialism for what it is.[69]

After performing a snippet of "El Apagón," Bad Bunny's performance transitioned into "Después de la Playa." Dahian El Apechao and his band appeared on stage, as did dozens of other dancers, including some from the World's Hottest Tour.[70] Throughout the performance Bad Bunny appeared alongside an extremely diverse array of Caribbean artists and dancers with different body types and sizes, skin tones, and gender expressions. Dancers were grooving alone, switching partners, and engaging with the audience, while the cabezudos roamed around and invite more people to get up and

6.5 This image is from Bad Bunny's performance of "Después de la Playa" at the 2023 Grammys. The song exemplifies the Caribbean party culture. JC Olivera/ WireImage via Getty Images.

dance. As Power-Sotomayor explains, Bad Bunny's staging at the Grammys, like in his World's Hottest Tour, replicated the highly communal nature of Caribbean dance party culture in which both the music itself and the joy of moving and releasing in community is key to resistance.[71]

The five-minute party that Bad Bunny put on at the Grammys was a small taste of the protest party Kacho described while filming "El Apagón" in the Túnel de Guajataca. The Grammy performance was an act of music as resistance that instilled pride in Puerto Ricans the world over. His bold move to open with the Puerto Rican anthem and protest song "El Apagón" further cemented his authenticity as someone dedicated to his homeland, and willing to use his platform to speak out in ways that counter what we might expect of celebrities who many see as more inclined to avoid political stances, not embrace them. Furthermore, to do so at the most prestigious music awards show in the United States suggested that he had perhaps done the impossible—completed a global mainstream crossover while singing in Spanish about Puerto Rican issues. And yet, despite his place at the center of the zeitgeist of popular music today, he is in some ways still treated as outside mainstream culture.

7

SINGING IN NON-ENGLISH: BAD BUNNY LOST IN TRANSLATION

On August 28, 2022, Bad Bunny made MTV Video Music Award history as the first Latin music artist to win the award for Artist of the Year. In his acceptance speech, which was entirely in Spanish, he said: "From my heart, I don't have words to describe what I feel, the pride I feel being tonight at Yankee Stadium, and receiving this award. I have been saying I always believed from the beginning that I could become a huge artist, that I could become one of the biggest stars in the world without having to change my culture, my language, my slang. I am Benito Antonio Martínez Ocasio, from Puerto Rico to the entire world."[1] Bad Bunny's determination to perform in Puerto Rican Spanish, with Puerto Rican slang, has been central to his career. It has endeared him to fans as an authentic performer without compromising his ability to conquer the US mainstream.

Despite his unprecedented success as a Spanish-language reggaetón artist, though, the media industry and institutions that offer him these recognitions continue to signal Bad Bunny's otherness. For example, when Bad Bunny opened the Grammy Awards with a Spanish-language performance of "El Apagón" and "Después de la Playa" in 2023, viewers at home saw closed captions with the text "singing in non-English" instead of his Spanish lyrics or their English translations. Later the subtitles said that Bad Bunny was "speaking in non-English" when he accepted his award for Best Música Urbana Album. Fans on social media, outlets from the *New York Times* to the *Today Show*, and even Congressman Robert Garcia (CA-42) promptly criticized CBS for furthering the perception of Spanish as foreign and unintelligible.[2] In contrast, Bad Bunny posted screenshots of these "subtitles" to his Instagram account, suggesting he was proud of "speaking in non-English."[3]

It was a moment that brought his success and the industry's bafflement over it into sharp relief. It recalled another major Grammy moment, Ricky Martin's bilingual 1999 Grammy performance of his hit "La Copa De La Vida," which is often discussed as a watershed for Latin music that ushered in the so-called Latin boom. The Latin boom of the late 1990s and early 2000s refers to a particular moment in pop culture when Martin and several other Spanish-language music stars crossed over into the US mainstream market by releasing new albums in English. Even as they gained market success, these artists were portrayed as overly sexed and exotic others; they were given airtime only if they embodied Latin lover stereotypes; and they were rewarded for using Spanish in ways that often reinforced the problematic, racist stereotypes of their foreignness.[4] During Martin's 1999 performance, the Puerto Rican heartthrob swiveled his hips in tight leather pants in front of generic Latin sights and rhythms, such as a conga line and carnivalesque dancers. In performing these stereotypes, Latin boom artists like Martin satisfied the desires and expectations of a mainstream American audience. In contrast, Bad Bunny's becoming number one despite his refusal to accommodate the English-dominant US market broke new ground.[5]

Several months later, in October 2023, Bad Bunny openly mocked CBS's failure to accommodate a Spanish-language performance, when he hosted the sketch comedy show *Saturday Night Live*. He was the first Spanish-language artist to perform on the show.[6] During his opening monologue, Bad Bunny said in English, "People are wondering if I can host this show since English is not my first language. . . . I do whatever I want. . . . I can host this show in English, I can order McDonald's in English, I can have sex in English, but I prefer sex in Spanish because it's just better. I just prefer Spanish. You know what—" Then he switched to Spanish. "Vamos a aprender eso aquí un momento. Primero que todo, quiero mandar un saludo a todos los Latinos del mundo entero. En especial los que me están viendo live en Puerto Rico."[7]

The bottom of the screen flashed: "[SPEAKING IN NON-ENGLISH]." Bad Bunny continued, "Not again, please. Cámbiame eso, cámbiame eso.[8] Excuse me, can we change that, can we do it right?" The captions changed to: "[SPEAKING A SEXIER LANGUAGE]." The crowd cheered and Bad Bunny gave a thumbs up.

While the monologue poked fun at CBS's botched translation of his words at the 2023 Grammys, it reinforced the dissonance between Bad Bunny's status as a worldwide musical icon and how US media (mis) understood him both literally and figuratively. The jokes throughout his monologue centered on these types of misunderstandings. At one point Bad Bunny abandoned the subtitles altogether and invited Chilean American actor Pedro Pascal to come translate. But even then, Pascal playfully mistranslated Bad Bunny's comments as part of the joke, one time limiting what Bad Bunny said to a more basic point, and another refusing to translate correctly in favor of proclaiming himself Bad Bunny's favorite actor. In some ways, the joke was on the US media itself, showing that the US mainstream simply couldn't handle a Spanish-speaking Latino.

But the monologue was also troubling for its reliance on long-standing stereotypes of the hypersexualized Latin lover. The monologue frequently referenced Bad Bunny's sexual prowess. At one point, Pascal advised Bad Bunny to make fun of himself by showing an embarrassing picture. A photo in which the singer was sunbathing naked flashed across the screen. "How is that embarrassing?" Pascal asked, suggesting that there was certainly nothing embarrassing about the star's body. "Because I forgot to put on clothes!" Bad Bunny exclaimed. With this emphasis on Bad Bunny's sexuality, *Saturday Night Live* reverted back to old stereotypes even if his hosting gig broke new ground.

As experts in Latin music and media representation, we are frequently called on by journalists working on stories about related topics, during which we are often asked how and why Bad Bunny has obtained such a massive level of fame globally. Why Bad Bunny? Why now? We've been asked if his US mainstream success indicates that the United States is so evolved culturally that speaking Spanish and being Latino are no longer barriers to popularity among English-speaking music fans. In this vein journalists ask if it means that the United States is "finally ready" for a Spanish-speaking Latino star. However, reproducing old stereotypes of Latinos as foreign, unassimilable, Latin lovers suggests that institutions like *Saturday Night Live* are not ready, not any more than CBS was equipped with Spanish-speaking closed-captioning staff.

Certainly, the success of Spanish-language artists in the United States is cause for celebration. However, the very authenticity that has made Bad Bunny a star often gets overlooked when US media outlets cover his success. They misinterpret or even outright miss the Puerto Rican cultural and political references that Bad Bunny makes in his artistry and interviews. And some outlets remain resistant to covering him despite his impressive chart metrics and the numerous records he has broken. From journalists to paparazzi, media workers we know have told us how difficult it is to convince their editors to publish pieces about Bad Bunny because these media outlets perceive him as too niche or too unrecognizable to mainstream audiences. While there has been a slight shift of this perception since his unprecedented global success in 2022, Bad Bunny's status as a Latin artist who both speaks and performs in Spanish remains a barrier to his full acceptance into the US mainstream.

The winter of 2022–23 was one of the coldest and longest winters in Los Angeles's history. By March, Angelenos are usually expecting warm days and spring weather, but it was frigid and rainy. Bad Bunny had taken up residence in an $8.8 million dollar home right off the iconic Sunset Strip in the Hollywood Hills in January 2023. At a time when fans were wondering what the move would mean for his artistry and how it would impact his homegrown appeal, Bad Bunny was photographed with reality television star-turned-model Kendall Jenner.

Gossip had suggested the two were a couple. Jenner is a member of the Kardashian family that has built an empire based on their television show *Keeping Up with the Kardashians* and its many spin-offs, beauty products, and what some critics have argued is a hefty dose of cultural appropriation of Black and Latino culture.[9] One of Vanessa's frequent collaborators in her research on celebrity media, paparazzi photographer Jeff, captured the first images of the couple.[10] Jeff is unequivocally known as a talented photographer among his peers, though, like all paparazzi he is not respected by the staff at the media outlets that rely on his labor.[11] In this case, his photo captures Bad Bunny, Jenner, and Jenner's sister Kylie exiting a famous but low-key sushi spot tucked away in the second floor of a shopping plaza in Hollywood, shortly after the gossip social media account Deuxmoi reported the two had been spotted kissing at a club.[12] Three days later, Jeff told Vanessa that his photo agency had made tens of thousands of dollars from the photos from online outlets alone. "The blogs are all forking over five, six, seven, eight thousand dollars," he said. Jeff anticipated that print media outlet purchases would increase the amounts. While he only earns a small percentage of the sales of the images, since the photo agencies that sell paparazzi photographs keep the lion's share of the profits, it had been a significant payday for him and one he hoped to repeat.[13]

On March 10, 2023—the night of Bad Bunny's twenty-ninth birthday—Vanessa joined Jeff as he sought more shots of the couple. The weather was in the fifties and rainy, very cold by Los Angeles standards. They met up near Bad Bunny's Hollywood Hills home. That Jeff knew where Bad Bunny lived is not surprising; part of the manufacturing of celebrity entails most celebrities having folks inside their own teams who actively feed tips to the paparazzi even as they revile these same paparazzi in public.[14] Within the entertainment industry, the Kardashian-Jenner family's cooperative relationship with paparazzi is common knowledge, and throughout the growth of the Kardashian-Jenner empire, they have been known to receive compensation from photo agencies for allowing select paparazzi to exclusively shoot family vacations and other occasions.[15]

While Vanessa and Jeff waited for any sign of the couple, they discussed how Jeff ended up getting the first few sets of photos of Bad Bunny with Kendall Jenner. Jeff underscored that it was Jenner's presence that made it worthwhile to shoot Bad Bunny, in terms of the potential interest in and value of the photos for major US media outlets. "Even with [Bad Bunny's] status, the story is Kendall. That's the hook. Bad Bunny on his own, we don't really care. I'm not going to be pissed if I miss Bad Bunny alone," Jeff explained. Bad Bunny was the most popular musician in the world. Yet celebrities of color are actively devalued in the celebrity photo market, particularly in comparison to white celebrities, whose images tend to be the most coveted photos, and thus the most lucrative for the photographer.[16] Even as the biggest music star in the world, it is not enough when the star is a Spanish-speaking Puerto Rican. Mainstream US media is generally not interested unless the artist is tethered to a white family, *the* white American family.[17] Indeed, Jeff noted that photos of Bad Bunny and his former girlfriend, Puerto Rican jewelry designer Gabriela Berlingeri, did not sell well.

The US mainstream media constantly reminds us who is and who is not American, or at least who is American enough. Early American newspapers and magazines were often used as tools for racist propaganda. Some of the most iconic historical American cartoons are of Uncle Sam ridiculing his inferior colonial subjects, including Puerto Ricans, who are depicted as racist caricatures.[18] Hollywood media has been no better. In anthropologist Hortense Powdermaker's groundbreaking book *Hollywood, the Dream Factory*, she writes, "Hollywood people live more or less normal family lives, and it is the current studio policy to do everything possible to publicize this. Publicity and fan magazines have been concentrating on pictures of 'normal' family life."[19] Note the emphasis on the word *normal*, which, when combined with *family life*, tends to reference the status quo white American nuclear family. Latinos have always been written out of narratives of Americanness, a point that is reinforced each and every time a Latino makes it in the mainstream music industry. Bad Bunny is no different.

As a love interest of a true American reality-star sweetheart like Jenner, Bad Bunny was of interest because of his new proximity to whiteness and how he contributed to celebrity media's focus on heteronormative love. In the 1950s, *I Love Lucy* made Desi Arnaz the first Latino television star and the first person to speak Spanish on television; it also made Arnaz and Lucille Ball the first interracial couple on television (among many other firsts). There is no doubt that Arnaz's acceptance and popularity was due in large part to his relationship to a beloved white American actress and that the show relied on extremely racist tropes about Latinos.[20] All these decades later, Jeff's job was to photograph Jenner in hopes of getting images of her with her new Latino boyfriend.

As Jeff and Vanessa stood outside in the misty cold, hoping for Bad Bunny's SUV to pull around the corner, Jeff described how he had discovered that Kylie and Kendall Jenner were out for sushi before he had any idea that Bad Bunny might be joining them. The first clue was Kylie's bodyguard, who knew who Jeff was. "I give the guy a peace sign because we recognize each other," Jeff explained. "Then I think, 'Shit, should I have done that?' Maybe he wouldn't have noticed me." Jeff waited for the group to head upstairs to the restaurant knowing that there was no other way for them to enter the establishment from the underground parking structure. Then, he recalled, "Kylie pulls up in her Navigator, and it's like a stretch Navigator. It's one of one. There are no others in Hollywood, so it's obvious."

As the ostentatious Navigator suggests, celebrities often make choices that make themselves more visible. They know that flashy, easily identifiable vehicles (such as Justin Bieber's rare, brightly colored sports cars) make them more obvious to paparazzi and, thus, easier to follow, but they still perform irritation when caught on camera. Such choices serve to amplify their brand by ensuring that their images remain in circulation. In spite of a popular perception that celebrities object to how paparazzi invade their personal space and privacy, celebrities often cooperate with paparazzi; these celebrities seem to care more about the monetization of their images than about people taking their photos.[21] The Kardashian-Jenner family began in precisely this way. Initially, interest in the family developed in the wake of the 2007 release of Kim Kardashian's sex tape with her ex-boyfriend, singer Ray J. What's more, the popularity of *Keeping Up with the Kardashians* hinges upon the reality show's claim that viewers get full access to every angle of the family's private lives.[22] Still, at any given moment they might prioritize signaling that they care about their privacy; as a result, Jeff considered the possibility that it would have been better if Kylie's bodyguard had not noticed him. Even a family that has built an empire from relinquishing their private lives occasionally decides to revoke the informal agreement that gives paparazzi access.

Jeff told Vanessa how he had waited outside the restaurant to see who would show up. He was excited to see Kendall arrive first because, according to Jeff, "Kylie's always good [to shoot], but with Kendall, it's got a little more buzz." After heading to his car to grab his camera, Jeff saw Bad Bunny's Escalade turn into the underground parking lot. In that moment, Jeff realized that he could be the one to confirm rumors of a relationship between Jenner and Bad Bunny. He saw Bad Bunny enter the restaurant with a bandana over his face, and waited for the group to come out at the end of their meal so he could get a picture of Jenner and Bad Bunny together. "Chances are slim," he recalled. "It ultimately boils down to [Bad Bunny] because Kylie and Kendall are all about the media coverage. He is a little more private . . . it doesn't seem like he's really interested in media attention." To Jeff's surprise, the couple emerged from the restaurant together and went down to their cars. "They positioned the cars in a way that they're so close to the wall, he could have hopped in and you couldn't see. But I ran into the parking area and I ran behind the cars, and that's when I got the pics."

Despite the fact that Bad Bunny was of interest only because he was out with the Jenner sisters and because he was dating one of them, the paparazzi asserted that it was really up to Bad Bunny whether the photographer could get the shot. Bad Bunny himself has made it clear that he fiercely protects his personal life. He told Chente Ydrach in 2018, "There are many people who dream of being an artist. There are many people who dream of being famous. I didn't dream of being famous. I dreamed of being an artist. And those are two different things. The artist is the one who makes art, the one that does something that people appreciate. The celebrity is a guy the whole world recognizes."[23] This brings up interesting distinctions between the brand of celebrity the Kardashian-Jenners maintain versus the brand of celebrity Bad Bunny maintains, and it also underscores the difference between their respective relationships to media. Despite the fact that Bad Bunny's level of fame has grown exponentially since his 2018 interview with Chente, Bad Bunny continues to emphasize to reporters that he remains focused on his art, and he still keeps his personal life as private as possible.[24] While he moved to Los Angeles—the center of the media machine—Bad Bunny told *Rolling Stone*'s Julyssa Lopez that, for him, it was actually easier to stay "under the radar" in Los Angeles than in Puerto Rico. This may be surprising given LA's status as a hub of entertainment, the massive number of celebrities who live there, and the ubiquitous celebrity media culture in the city. But Julyssa explained to us that Puerto Rico is "just smaller, and so word travels faster. Like people know where he's at, and it just becomes like a circus." In LA, Bad Bunny said that he can "go eat at a restaurant calmly, go see a movie, relax, go for a walk."[25] It is hard to ignore the possibility that his status as a Spanish-language, Puerto Rican performer whose image is literally not worth as much as his white counterparts plays a role in this maintenance of privacy.

Just as Jeff noted that few paparazzi actually seek out Bad Bunny alone, he was the only photographer covering Bad Bunny on the night Vanessa joined him for the ride-along. It comes down to simple math, simple economics: which photos, which faces and bodies, will make them money? Photos of celebrities of color have proven to earn the paparazzi less money than photos of white celebrities. Actors of color are noticeably underrepresented in Hollywood films and television, and this correlates directly with their value to magazines and other news media.[26] If they are not cast, they do not receive symbolic or economic capital through promotion via media like celebrity magazines and other news outlets that most often purchase paparazzi photos. This all contributes to a broader economy of celebrity bodies in which white bodies are systematically attributed greater value. The racial hierarchies built into the various realms of the entertainment industry reinforce the racism that is at its core. And this extends even to the ways in which celebrity couples are marketed and valued, and the ways in which even their children are valued. For example, *People* paid $14 million for photographs of the twins born to Brad Pitt and Angelina Jolie but only $6 million for photographs of the twins born to Jennifer Lopez and Marc Anthony.[27]

It was unsurprising that the lucrative sale of Bad Bunny paparazzi shots depended on the presence of Kendall Jenner. As media scholar Alice Leppert notes, the Kardashian-Jenner family has reaped profits by promoting their romantic relationships; they are invested in the circulation of intimacy.[28] The combined couple name "Kimye" (referring to Kim Kardashian and Kanye West) was the only name used in the tabloids that included a Black person; unusually, in this case it was the woman's name (Kim) that preceded the man's.[29] The discrepancy in representation of couples of color (and LGBTQ+ couples) has nothing to do with the aesthetics of the potential combined name or the level of fame of the individuals. Rather, it reflects conservative decisions made by celebrity media producers (reporters and editors alike) based on what they think will sell to the imagined consumer, whom they generally presume to be middle-class, white, English speakers, or the so-called mainstream.[30] Jeff's observations about the different values of Kendall Jenner and Bad Bunny to him as a paparazzi and on gossip blogs—both literally, in terms of money, and figuratively—extends to other aspects of the US media machine.

In the summer of 2023, Bad Bunny graced the cover of *Rolling Stone*'s "Future of Music" summer double issue in which new music is introduced. The production costs for this cover were among the highest in *Rolling Stone*'s history, and Bad Bunny told *Rolling Stone* senior editor Julyssa Lopez that he was thrilled to get the true superstar treatment. Not only did *Rolling Stone* fly in Lady Gaga's stylist from Europe but, at Bad Bunny's request, they hired jewelry designers Avi Davidov and Ofir Ben-Shimon to create custom-made replicas of the diamond-encrusted chains of his greatest reggaetón influences for the shoot.[31] Julyssa mentioned in an interview with us that it was not only notable that a Spanish-language artist was the cover of the magazine's most important issue of the year. It was also a rare honor for Bad Bunny to appear on the cover only three years after his previous cover. As Julyssa and Petra sifted through the past years' covers at *Rolling Stone*'s Manhattan office during the summer of 2023, Julyssa pointed out that most artists—whether they perform in Spanish or not—do not get a second cover so quickly after their first; most artists had to wait at least five years.

Bad Bunny's first appearance on a *Rolling Stone* cover in 2020 was also an outlier. It marked the culmination of a process of slow change that began when Suzy Exposito, a young Latina reporter, joined *Rolling Stone* full time in 2015. She began lobbying for the magazine to cover Latin music, citing its mushrooming popularity across the globe. In a 2023 presentation at Hunter College's Center for Puerto Rican Studies, Suzy explained how hard it was to make change: "I think what was so challenging was like constantly having to really push and explain why these artists mattered. You know, just because they're not Daddy Yankee or Shakira, or like JLo, doesn't mean that they don't have something interesting to say. You know, I feel like there's a lot of interesting music happening. And so it was just kind of like a Groundhog Day where, every time we had a pitch meeting, I'd be like, 'Reggaetón is having a renaissance right now, I think we should cover it.'"[32] Suzy persisted, and she eventually was able to convince magazine editors to give her the opportunity to cover Latin music on their digital platforms. She became the founding editor of their Latin music section in 2018.

The cover story featuring Bad Bunny in January 2020 was the first in the magazine's history written by a Latina and the first with photos shot by a Latina (photos were by Bad Bunny's then-girlfriend Gabriela Berlingeri). It was also the first cover story featuring a reggaetón artist. One might assume that both Bad Bunny's success on the charts and Suzy's expanding *Rolling Stone*'s reach might make his historic 2020 cover a shoo-in. But that was not the case. During a fireside chat with Vanessa at Loyola Marymount University in March 2023, Suzy described the process of making the historic cover story happen. In a packed university theater, students crammed in to hear Suzy talk about the global icon she helped bring into the mainstream. She said, "It took a lot of convincing my editors to even put him on the cover. At first . . . I pitched putting him and J Balvin on the cover when they released *Oasis* the year before [in 2019] and that fell through. I couldn't get them to listen. It was like, 'Oh no, we gotta give Harry Styles another cover.' . . . I was like, [Bad Bunny's] gonna blow up. He's gonna be a huge deal. It's better that we do this like ASAP before . . . any other major publication does."[33]

The timing for a Bad Bunny cover seemed right when buzz about his second studio album *YHLQMDLG*, set to release in February 2020, began. Suzy worked with Bad Bunny's publicist, Sujeylee Solá. "I was like, why don't you just bring him to the office? He will just pop in. Why doesn't he play a song [from *YHLQMDLG*] for us? I'll ask my bosses to go."[34] As

Sujeylee described on social media, Bad Bunny at first hesitated to share his music prior to its release with anyone who was not in his inner circle, but his manager Noah Assad convinced him.[35] Suzy described Bad Bunny playing his album from the head of the table in a conference room, as a crowd of people from the office started trickling in, sitting on the floor and spilling out into the hallway hoping to hear the new music and meet the star. His popularity was clear to her editors. Suzy remembered, "It was funny 'cause it was originally supposed to be like only eight people in the office, and then it suddenly ballooned into over fifty people trying to crowd in." She went on:

> There were these glass windows and there were people sitting on the ground outside because we couldn't fit any more people in the conference room. It was literally like . . . a bunch of my coworkers, [and] people I didn't even work with who were doing marketing and reception and stuff. They were like, "Oh my God, it's Bad Bunny." And so then finally my bosses were like, "'I guess we should stop by and see what's going on because all these girls are screaming." . . . So we played a few songs and by the end of it, [music editor Christian Hoard] was like, "All right, we want him on the cover."[36]

The cover story was successful in terms of sales and clicks. Yet Suzy's account of how difficult it was to get Bad Bunny on the cover is commonplace; the US music industry continues to marginalize Latin music and Latin artists in general, especially those who perform in Spanish. Latin artists are constantly treated as foreign others within the context of the US music industry, regardless of their citizenship status or where they were born, and regardless of how well they chart and what their streaming numbers look like.[37]

Journalists we interviewed who have done major stories on Bad Bunny since the 2020 *Rolling Stone* cover describe only a little less of a struggle to get their higher-ups to agree to a news story. Andrew Chow and Mariah Espada worked for years to get *Time* magazine to greenlight a cover story about Bad Bunny. "At first, [Bad Bunny] was like really a dream of like [*Time*] would never [put him on the cover]! They would never agree. It didn't register that we could actually make a Bad Bunny cover happen," Andrew told us. In addition to their own lobbying efforts, Andrew and Mariah credited Bad Bunny's "enormous year" in 2022, with his back-to-back record-breaking tours and the astronomical success of *Un Verano Sin Ti*, for making the *Time* cover story possible.

Bad Bunny's rise in the early 2020s took place against the backdrop of Latin music's increasing popularity more generally. Much of this had to do with the advent of streaming, which has forced the music industry to acknowledge the significance of Latin music in a way that traditional charts based primarily on sales did not. Latin music divisions have consistently received smaller promotional budgets and less support than mainstream pop divisions.[38] However, the real-time nature of streaming statistics and the more expansive audience that streaming captures has forced the music industry to look at the consumption of Latin music more closely.

Many people we spoke to, from folks like Jerry Pullés at Apple Music, Jesús Triviño at TIDAL, and Angie Romero, formerly of Amazon Music and Spotify, to music producers like Tainy and MAG, and artists like Jowell y Randy, credited streaming with helping to propel the contemporary rise of Latin music around the globe. Given that streaming now accounts for 89 percent of total music industry revenue,[39] streaming services have had to respond to a growing global demand for Latin music. Eddie Santiago, former head of US Latin artist partnerships for Spotify, was always willing to invest in promoting Latin music and Latin artists "because the data was there." While Latin music streaming in the United States and its territories like Puerto Rico was increasing, Eddie said that Spotify's Latin American team was "developing the market and making the service more widely distributed."

Former Global Content Programming Lead at Amazon Music and former Senior Editor at Spotify Angie Romero explained that SoundScan, which had been the source of music chart data for *Billboard* since the 1990s, failed to accurately capture Latin music listeners. It relied on barcode scanners at large record stores in the United States and thus missed many of the smaller local stores popular in the US Latino community as well as all record sales throughout Latin America.[40] She also suggested that streaming had replaced piracy, which had been a major mode of distribution in Latin American and Latino communities and which operated outside of the SoundScan apparatus. Angie said that streaming made the music industry "see the increasing power of Latin America" because the numbers were more visible.

Streaming can reproduce many of the same inequities that plague the music industry overall, but it has undeniably made a huge impact in the consumption of Latin music.[41] Over and over again, we heard from journalists, artists, and music industry executives that streaming has created a more accurate picture of the numbers of people who actually consume Latin music and has enabled a more expansive look at where they live. As a result, global territories like Latin America that were not previously counted in charts can now be part of the overall ecosystem of Latin music consumption. Moreover, as Angie told us, "Latinos over-index on streaming," meaning that US Latino consumers utilize streaming more than many other groups. At the same time, *Time*'s Andrew Chow points out that it's not just US Latinos who are driving the Latin music market. Streaming has amplified the impact of music listeners "everywhere around the world. So we're seeing these huge explosions in India, and the Philippines, and in Mexico and all over South America." Latin music, and reggaetón in particular, is a central part of the global mainstream trends, regardless of the ongoing divisions in the music industry.

Andrew also notes, "Obviously Bunny has been really central to this Latino boom." Getting Bad Bunny on the cover of *Rolling Stone* in 2023 was a much easier lift for editor and cover-story author Julyssa Lopez than it had been for Suzy back in 2020. Julyssa told us that Suzy's 2020 cover story "was huge, like it performed traffic-wise, which tends to be a big metric that decides how many magazines put people on the cover." The growth of Bad Bunny's star power also changed things. Julyssa recalled that the "conversation to get him on that cover was much, much easier," even if some were hesitant about whether or not he could "carry a double issue." Although it took some convincing, "it was never the way that it happened with Suzy." Bad Bunny's name was "in the mix" from the beginning. According to Julyssa, "Suzy had broken that barrier, and that foundation was already there." Add in Bad Bunny's "undeniable" success and the cover seemed even more obvious. "What were they gonna say? He's not big enough? There's no argument," Julyssa told us of the decision. Bad Bunny's global success thus made it much easier for Julyssa to convince higher-ups at *Rolling Stone* to put him on the cover in 2023. And yet the US media market has not changed fundamentally, as the many misinterpretations, mistranslations, and continued stereotyping that appear in its content reflect.

It was Bad Bunny's idea to include the chains worn by reggaetón artists who came before him in the photographs of his 2023 *Rolling Stone* cover story. As Julyssa wrote in her profile, "Bad Bunny had been toying with the idea for a long time, thinking he would wear the necklaces to pay homage to the reggaetón greats at a major concert or public performance. 'When the opportunity to shoot with *Rolling Stone* came along, I was like, "Damn, that would be perfect."'[42] The first page of the article shows a black-and-white photograph of Bad Bunny, shirtless, staring defiantly at the camera. In his right arm, he holds up the custom replicas of chains worn by reggaetón pioneers like Tego Calderón, Don Omar, and Daddy Yankee. His physique is lean and chiseled—this was the time when he was actively rehearsing for Coachella and dabbling in professional wrestling. It is a striking image.

In this image, those in the know can recognize the significance of these chains. The diamond-encrusted cursive DY refers to Daddy Yankee, and the blinged out portrait of a Black man with an Afro is one of Bad Bunny's biggest influences Tego Calderón. The photograph places Bad Bunny in the center but pays tribute to all the reggaetoneros who paved the way for him but never received the same level of US mainstream recognition.

The *Rolling Stone* cover image, by contrast, features a close-up of Bad Bunny's face. He wears a thick chain-link necklace, and a pair of sunglasses with frames also covered in chains. For Julyssa, this cover was a missed opportunity. She explained to us:

> I think what was frustrating was that I thought the photo with him, shirtless with the chains, like that to me should have been the cover. It was so beautiful. It would have been such a statement, I think, to have that on the cover, and it meant a lot to him. . . . But I don't decide what image goes [on the cover]. . . . They showed it to me later, and it was the one of him in the sunglasses which is fine. I think in their heads they were like "He looks like such a rock star, that's such a celebrity look."

Even if the star and the reporter who wrote his profile thought that the photo of the chains would be meaningful, *Rolling Stone* decided instead to put a much more typical photo devoid of any Puerto Rican markers on the cover.

This is but one example of a time when the press did not fully honor Bad Bunny's self-presentation and ideological commitments. The consequences were greater when *Time* magazine published its cover story about him, first online on March 28, 2023, and then in print on April 10, 2023.

Reporters Andrew Chow and Mariah Espada were sensitive to some of the complications of covering Bad Bunny due to their linguistic differences from the artist. It was *Time*'s first ever cover in Spanish. Many journalists have told us that Bad Bunny does not particularly enjoy interviews and

7.1 This photograph appeared inside the 2023 *Rolling Stone* feature profile of Bad Bunny. He holds replicas of chains of reggaetón artists who inspired him such as Don Omar, Daddy Yankee, and Tego Calderón. Photo by Daniel Sannwald for *Rolling Stone.*

7.2 Cover of the Future of Music *Rolling Stone* issue from July/August 2023. The magazine's editors preferred this photograph because of the "rock star" image they believed it portrayed. Photo by Daniel Sannwald for *Rolling Stone.*

that interviews go much better when he is comfortable with the interviewer. In fact, this is why in 2019 Petra was asked to meet him early at Harvard University to have time to build rapport, so he would be more at ease during their public conversation. In the case of the *Time* interview, it was the reporters who made the decision to ensure he was comfortable. Andrew and Mariah were very intentional about conducting the interview in Spanish so that Bad Bunny could "voice his whole self and all his thoughts," Andrew told us. This understanding of Bad Bunny's feelings about language aligns with what others have told us, and Bad Bunny recently told *Vogue*, "I like speaking English in private, not on camera or somewhere else."[43]

The *Time* magazine cover showed Bad Bunny, with the words "El Mundo de Bad Bunny" in all caps, and a quote "No voy a hacer otra cosa para que a tí te guste" (I am not going to do something else so that you like it). "We felt that would be like a small, if powerful symbolic gesture to have the cover be in Spanish," Andrew told us in an interview he did along with Mariah. "We felt strongly that the cover should be in Spanish, especially because one of the primary ideas of the story was that he does not sing in English and [he] doesn't need to."

Time also published the full Spanish-language Q&A with Bad Bunny online, although the main story both online and in print was in English. Mariah told us that "85 percent of the conversation was in Spanish with a few questions here and there in English." Mariah explained that her Nuyorican background helped her with the Spanish conversation, while Andrew recalled that he "was able to understand a lot" of the Spanish conversation. Mariah added that after the interview ended, they contracted someone from Puerto Rico who "really gets the slang, and we were able to kind of get into the nitty gritty" to help with the transcription and translation.

Mariah and Andrew worked hard to make sure Bad Bunny was comfortable with the interview. Nevertheless, the published article ultimately contained a lot of mistranslations that would cause problems for Bad Bunny, particularly in the context of fans' dissatisfaction with his relationship with Kendall Jenner, which many saw as evidence of his diminished authenticity since moving to Los Angeles. As Andrew notes, there were many "tweets and screen grabs from the article of his quotes, which stirred up a decent amount of controversy—which we were expecting, because we asked him about some thorny topics, so we were not surprised to see the level of discourse to be pretty high after that."

One particularly "thorny topic" was the issue of race and colorism in the music industry. The article states: "When Benito is asked whether he believes race and colorism play a role in the success of a reggaeton artist, he responds, 'Because I haven't seen it or lived it, I can't say. It'd be irresponsible of me to say yes. They asked me about if [2000s reggaetón superstar] Tego Calderón would've been bigger if he wasn't Black. But in my eyes, Tego Calderón is the biggest singer in the industry.'" The comment ignited fierce backlash online. A subsequent *Los Angeles Times* article quoted fans who tweeted statements like "I ain't going to lie Bad Bunny really broke my heart after he admitted that he doesn't believe in colorism," and "Bad Bunny speaking up about colorism is sooooooooo disappointing and not what I expected from him."[44] A few weeks later, Petra met a young woman in line at the merch tent at Coachella who said that she had been excited to see Bad Bunny, but his comments on colorism had soured her on the artist and she considered skipping his performance.

To be sure, these comments are incredibly disappointing. But the Spanish-language Q&A that *Time* published online provides much more nuance about his views as well as about how his thinking may have changed since a 2020 interview in the *New York Times Magazine*.[45] In response to a question about whether he thinks race and skin color play a role in the success of reggaetón artists in general, Bad Bunny told Andrew and Mariah:

Me han preguntado eso antes . . . ha pasado mucho tiempo desde que tuve una pregunta como esa. Dentro de mi ignorancia no lo entendía. Dije que eso no puede ser. No podía imaginarlo. No puedo decir que sí o que no porque no lo he vivido. Tampoco he visto con mis propios ojos que sí, esta persona no se volvió más exitosa debido a su piel, no lo he visto. Sería irresponsable de mi parte decir que sí. Por ejemplo, me preguntaron si Tego Calderón, si hubiera sido más grande si no fuera negro. Pero a mis ojos, Tego Calderón es el cantante más grande de la industria. ¿Tú entiendes? No entendía cosas sobre la industria que tal vez sean ciertas. Quizás las puertas se cerraron por su piel, quizás algún promotor prefirió a un artista más blanco que él. Pero esas cosas no las sé, no las he vivido. Cuando me preguntaron dije: "¿Qué? Para mí Tego Calderón es el cantante más grande del género, también es uno de mis ídolos. ¿Qué quieres decir con no tan grande? ¿Quién es más grande que él?"[46]

This answer includes past and conditional tenses that indicate that Bad Bunny has, in fact, reflected on questions of racism and colorism, even if his answers are not wholly satisfying for many of his fans. He begins by answering that it has been a while since someone asked him about these issues, and that when he was asked in the past, "In my ignorance, I didn't understand [racism and colorism]. I said, 'This can't be. I can't imagine it.'" He then goes on to say that he has not seen racism with his own eyes, and he does not know whether or not an artist like Tego Calderón could have had a more successful career if he were not Black. After declaring that, from his perspective, Tego Calderón is "the biggest artist in the industry," Bad Bunny explains, "I didn't understand things about this industry that might be true. Maybe doors were closed in [Tego's] face, or maybe a promoter preferred a white artist over him." Although Bad Bunny says he is unsure because he hasn't "lived" these experiences, he certainly shows that he has an understanding of the possibility of anti-Black racism within the music industry.

Anti-Black racism is endemic throughout the Latin music industry, and it always has been.[47] There is no doubt that Afro-Latino artists face significantly more barriers to success than their non-Black counterparts, and they remain profoundly underrepresented in the music industry (and all media industries) both in the United States and throughout Latin America. Bad Bunny has not experienced this himself because he is not perceived as Black in either a US or Puerto Rican context. This is made all the more complex given that the US and Puerto Rico ascribe to different systems of racial classification. The US has consistently depicted Latinidad and Blackness as fundamentally distinct.[48] By contrast, Puerto Rican racial discourses are more in line with other places in Latin America that recognize various degrees of race mixture.[49] However, both the United States and Puerto Rico (along with the rest of the Americas) ultimately value whiteness over Blackness.[50] This is reflected in the systemic anti-Blackness of the Latin music industry that tends to promote artists who embody the so-called Latin look of lighter skin, wavy hair, and Eurocentric features. Regardless of the ambiguity around Bad Bunny's racial identity, the reality is that he embodies many of the qualities of this Latin look. In this context, Bad Bunny's apparent dismissal of racism in the Latin music industry appeared particularly insensitive to many people who argued that Bad Bunny, in fact, benefited from white privilege within the music industry.[51] Reacting to Bad Bunny's comments, cultural critic Katelina "La Gata" Eccleston told *Time* that Bad Bunny "still does not understand his positionality."[52] Critics are right to object to him seeming to imply that racism does not occur in the Latin music industry. However, the full Spanish-language quote presents a more complicated picture of Bad Bunny's perceptions of racism in the music industry. He recognizes that Tego Calderón may well have experienced anti-Black racism. Bad Bunny notes that he is learning, that his ignorance prevented him from having more nuanced answers in the past, and that his understanding of how the industry works is shifting. This is not the translation the English-speaking audience received, and it was consequential.

Fans were also disappointed in Bad Bunny's statements that appeared in the *Time* article about his political anthem "El Apagón." The article noted that "El Apagón" exemplifies the political nature of Bad Bunny's work, and that in the song's lyrics he "even dismiss[ed] the non-Latinos who want to participate in reggaeton culture or take advantage of Puerto Rican land as lacking *sazón* (flavor)." But, it says, "he says he feels less strongly about the *sazón* lyric than when he wrote it.[53] 'I was upset,' he says. 'But now that feeling has passed me. Our culture and music impacts people in other places. They want to try and feel it. So why am I going to be bothered by that, if they do it with respect?'" In her *Rolling Stone* article, Julyssa quoted a tweet that accused Bad Bunny as having been "sadly consumed by the gringo market. . . . How does he regret writing one of the most iconic lines in 'El Apagón'?" Another person criticizing Bad Bunny's statements in a video on TikTok put it down to "a fully colonized mind."[54] Social media commentary from fans demonstrated a deep sense of betrayal due to their perception that the artist they championed for writing one of the most important Puerto Rican protest songs of our time was now blasé about the sentiments expressed in the song's lyrics.

Mariah said that she and Andrew "were very intentional and careful" in their article. They had not meant to expose the singer to criticism. But of course "once you send [the story] off to the world, we are absolutely not in control." As is typical when soundbites are pulled, she thinks the controversy "became larger and a little bit more removed from what was actually written in the piece." Andrew also noted that the publication online was just weeks after the publication of Jeff's photographs showing Bad Bunny with Kendall Jenner. "It was like a lot of these discussions were already being had on Twitter, and all Twitter needed was like some more fuel to the fire," Andrew told us. Concerns were already high that the Puerto Rican star might be abandoning his commitment to the archipelago because of his move to LA and his new white American girlfriend. In this context, Bad Bunny's comments took on a life of their own.

The second *Rolling Stone* cover story about Bad Bunny in June 2023 gave the singer the opportunity to respond to his critics. It was clear from the story that the artist with the motto *Yo Hago Lo Que Me Da La Gana* (I do what I want), and who sings about not caring what others think, actually does care. Deeply. In his interview with Julyssa, Bad Bunny expressed frustration with the misunderstanding of his perspective on racism. Julyssa wrote that Bad Bunny told her that he had said what he said in the *Time* article because "he didn't want to speak over the experiences of people who have suffered racism." Bad Bunny told her, "I'm Latino, Caribbean, my skin is white. I have felt *rejection* in the U.S., maybe in some places because of being Latino. I've felt rejected in a world where there's a lot of rich people and you could have $100 million in your bank, and to them, you're [looked down on] for being Latino. It's obvious that racism [and] colorism exist in all parts of the world, in all industries."[55] Clearly he has an awareness of his own complex positioning within racial hierarchies— he is "Latino" but has "white skin." He also clearly knows that racism exists everywhere, including in the Latin music industry. In fact, in our conversation with her, Julyssa recalled that when she asked Bad Bunny about race, he actually criticized her and the larger media industries:

He said something like, "I don't understand why journalists are always asking white artists these questions." And I was worried that that was going to be taken like, "Oh, I shouldn't have to answer these questions." But that's not what he was saying. He was saying . . . he didn't understand why journalists aren't putting Black artists on the cover, or doing these in-depth interviews with Black artists. And why, instead, it's being filtered through an artist like him. And I think he understood when I said to him, "Yeah, but . . . there's like a certain level that you've reached globally." I think he understood that, but what I got was that it was strange to him that those questions are being asked of people who haven't lived those experiences. He did say very directly . . . journalists should be talking to Black people.

Julyssa's recollection of this conversation shows that Bad Bunny also has a critical understanding of racism in the media. Our point here is not that Bad Bunny is above reproach; certainly, one should engage critically with his comments. However, the discrepancy between his discussions of race in *Rolling Stone* and in *Time* suggests that editorial decisions can have a significant impact on how someone's words are recorded and interpreted, fueling misunderstandings that can reverberate over time.

Bad Bunny also spoke frankly about his frustration with being criticized for his comments about "El Apagón." Julyssa quoted Bad Bunny in her article:

> "When I saw [people saying] that I had regretted writing 'El Apagón,' it shocked me, like when did I ever say that in the interview? I would never say that in my fucking life," he continues. [Being misunderstood] frustrated him because of what the song meant. "It was a whole journey, like the process that began with something patriotic, and then the party and the messing around, and later the sentimental part, the conscience in it. I always say that's the life of people in Puerto Rico: We're proud of being Puerto Rican, we love to celebrate and act like nothing matters, and then we clash against a reality that is often very painful."[56]

In talking to us, Julyssa reflected on the conversation with Bad Bunny: "He was trying to strike a balance between explaining that [what others say] affects him, and I think annoys him and frustrates him, while also trying to be like, 'But I don't care, and I still want to do what I want.' And like trying to . . . negotiate that idea that he's always been this artist who does whatever he wants." This aspect of Bad Bunny's style and narrative is central to his image as an artist. But, Julyssa said, "I actually do think he's kind of a sensitive guy. . . . I don't think that he's somebody who can just turn it off and go live a rock star life. . . . [M]y impression, being there in the room, wasn't at all that he was dismissive. I felt like he really wanted to talk about how frustrated he was with how that came across."

Ultimately, the incongruity between Bad Bunny's quotes in *Time* and in *Rolling Stone* reveal the structural inequities that can arise when a Spanish-speaking artist like Bad Bunny enters the mainstream market. First, editorial decisions are often made in relation to what is most relevant or legible to white US audiences, as was the case with the decision on which photograph to use on the *Rolling Stone* cover. This is even more obvious knowing that the magazine invested a tremendous amount of effort and money to produce those chains, yet still thought they were not important enough to include on a cover. Bad Bunny may be breaking musical barriers with his Spanish-language songs, and the trajectory in which it has become progressively easier for reporters to convince their editors to run stories about him is suggestive of increasing cultural acceptance. But the misinterpretations that ensue in interviews show that there is still a long way to go for full acceptance of Spanish-speakers in the United States.

Bad Bunny is at once mainstream and marginalized. He is one of the biggest celebrities in the world and, yet, he is still undervalued and sometimes outright dismissed in the US mainstream celebrity and entertainment world. When he is included, Bad Bunny is often framed within the same stereotypes that have always dictated representations of Latinos in the United States, or his words are subject to misinterpretation. Skeptics might argue that this is always true of celebrities—interviews are always filtered through the eyes of journalists and editors, pictures are photoshopped and changed. One never knows the extent of an artist's actual level of control over their image. Bad Bunny is one artist who frequently claims to have complete control over his work. And, in fact, music producers, music video directors, and others who know him have all told us that he takes a seriously hands-on approach to determining how a song sounds, how a video looks, or how a performance takes shape.

But in the US mainstream, he is represented in ways that are the most legible to white American audiences. For instance, most Americans have no idea that Puerto Ricans on the archipelago are US citizens, but many know the pop culture juggernaut that is the Kardashians.[57] In this context, it makes sense that some would care more about whether Jenner and Bad Bunny kissed after their dinner date than about the latest apagón in Puerto Rico. Media outlets are driven by what sells or what attracts the most clicks. Because they assume that consumers are overwhelmingly white and suburban, they prioritize celebrities that they think those consumers know over others they might not know. This is why journalists have to work so hard to get coverage for Bad Bunny despite his being one of the biggest musical stars in the world. And even then, the lack of resources for anything Latin within the media world makes mishaps perhaps more likely.

The bottom line is that Latino celebrities, like Latino communities, are devalued and dismissed by the US media regardless of their status in the Spanish-speaking world. And even if Bad Bunny has broken language barriers, he remains limited by the same tropes that have always governed Latino representation. Media representations of Latinos have always underscored that they are perpetually foreign, oversexed, lawless others who will never be American (regardless of their citizenship). They are presented as not deserving the respect or even the attention of the American public.[58]

Still, despite online criticism that Bad Bunny has lost his way, he remains deeply committed to representing and advocating for Latinos, and especially Puerto Rico, in his music and performances. Julyssa commented that Bad Bunny "really feels like it's his work that speaks to . . . his political depth, or what he thinks about certain issues. He wishes the value of his work was what mattered more than the words that get pulled out of him or taken out of context." And he was about to represent Puerto Rico on perhaps one of the most prestigious mainstream stages of all: Coachella.

8

"NUNCA ANTES HUBO UNO COMO YO": BAD BUNNY, COACHELLA, AND LATINO BELONGING IN THE UNITED STATES

In February of 2023, Petra was hanging out in her living room when she got a call from music video director Kacho López Mari. He wanted some help on a new project. "You know Bad Bunny and how he's doing Coachella?" Kacho asked. "We need your help."

The Coachella Valley Music and Arts Festival is one of the biggest and most prestigious music festivals in the world. It began in 1999 in the Empire Polo Club in Indio, California, as a two-day rock festival headlined by Tool, Beck, and Rage Against the Machine. Since then, Coachella has become widely recognized as a trendsetter in music and fashion. Pop music heavyweights like Madonna, Red Hot Chili Peppers, Jay-Z, Lady Gaga, Prince, Paul McCartney, Drake, the Cure, and Beyoncé have performed

there. The festival grosses millions of dollars in revenue and features partnerships with major corporations. The festival is now offered on two separate weekends, each with three days of festivities. When Bad Bunny performed in 2023, a general admission ticket for just one weekend would set
you back $549 *before fees*. Goldenvoice, the company that puts on Coach-
ella, earns an estimated $115 million annually on the event.[1] Coachella not
only makes big money, it sets big trends.

Kacho explained Bad Bunny's vision for Coachella 2023. Bad Bunny
would be the first Spanish-speaking artist and solo Latino to headline
Coachella. Adding to the prestige, the organizers had granted him a blackout set, meaning that no other stages had acts during his performance.
He was the only 2023 headliner to have a blackout set, joining the ranks
of pop royalty like Beyoncé, who had a blackout set in 2018. Bad Bunny
wanted to take advantage of this opportunity to highlight the history and
contributions of Puerto Rican musicians to US popular music with a series of videos.

The project was ambitious in scope. Bad Bunny was adamant that his
videos provide information that was accurate and thorough. Petra's task
was to put together an outline of major events in reggaetón's development
from its early years in the 1980s and 1990s, all the way up to Coachella
in 2023. It would have names of artists and links to clips and visuals that
could be incorporated into the videos. And it had to be done fast. Coachella was only two months away, and Kacho's team would need to gather
archival footage, create a script, record voice-overs, and film new footage
in both Puerto Rico and the California desert.

Petra spent the next few days assembling the ten-page outline that
would form the basis of two of the videos that would be projected as part
of Bad Bunny's historic set. Kacho and his team then took Petra's outline and worked with acclaimed Puerto Rican journalist Hermes Ayala
to create a script that conveyed the information in an accessible way, all
subject to Bad Bunny's ultimate approval. In the end, with the historical
research provided by Petra and other scholars, they produced four different videos—one on the impact of Latinos in popular music, one on the
history of salsa (working with salsa historian César Colón-Montijo), and
two based on Petra's outlines about the history of reggaetón. All four were
presented in English, in line with the dominance of English-speakers at
the event. Two videos were shown during the first weekend of Coachella,
and two videos were shown during the second weekend's set. The reggaetón videos directly preceded Bad Bunny's performance with reggaetón

pioneers Jowell y Randy, and Ñengo Flow of the underground-inspired track "Safaera."

The research, development, and execution of the videos reflect Bad Bunny's dedication to telling these histories and his broader commitment to using his platform to highlight Puerto Rican culture and history. This project could have been done in a much simpler way—perhaps a quick montage of popular music video images from the mid-2000s would have sufficed. The fact that he and his team hired historical consultants indicated how seriously Bad Bunny took accuracy and thoroughness. He took one of music's biggest stages and used it to deliver a minicourse in Latin music's historical, social, and political importance in the United States.

We both joined 125,000 other fans in Indio, California, to see the finished product and witness the audience's response. Finding that Coachella's relatively young audience made the bar areas a bit less crowded, we were able to snag a spot at the front of the 12 Peaks Bar, just to the left of the main stage. Resting against the white gate that separated us from the VIP section, we waited. Fellow Puerto Ricans shouted out "Boricua!" at Vanessa as they passed because she had the Puerto Rican flag draped over her back.

Now middle-aged moms, we were unaccustomed to the late-night concert starts of our youth. But despite being in the hot sun all day and staying up way past our bedtime, we were too excited to be tired when, right at 11:00 p.m., the bright lights that illuminated the field where we stood suddenly went dark. Bad Bunny was right on time. In true Bad Bunny fashion, the two-hour set was an incredible display of special effects, impeccable vocals, and infectious summer party vibes. As Kacho had told us that day, every aspect of the performance came from Bad Bunny's own mind and his vision. Nothing was coincidental. In an interview with Apple Music, Bad Bunny said his favorite part of the Coachella show "was when I showed the salsa story and [the] reggaetón and Caribbean music story. When I performed with [the música Mexicana band] Grupo Frontera and talked about all these Latino music legends. . . . I brought the real sound of Puerto Rico, I brought the real sound of Latino music. . . . I was really proud. That definitely was the best part of Coachella for me."[2] Bad Bunny made a statement about the role of Puerto Ricans and Latinos in shaping US popular music on one of the biggest stages a musician can have. By bringing this "real sound," Bad Bunny utilized his set, his guest stars, and his videos to stake a claim for Latino belonging in the United States.

As soon as the lights went out, the first video showed the sunrise over the mountains surrounding the Coachella Valley with a line of palm trees in the foreground. These images came from the design of Coachella's famous line-up posters that the festival has utilized since its inception. The horizon brightened with new daylight, and we heard Bad Bunny begin his Spanish narration: "For more than twenty years, the sun and stars over the Coachella Valley have witnessed the most epic events, the happiest days, the most magical nights." Bad Bunny's voice echoed across the crowd as he talked about how Coachella is a site of inspiration for many artists who would be introducing themselves to the world for the first time at the festival. He asked us to think back to the first time we kissed, we loved, we saw our favorite artist. Images of former headliners like The Weeknd, Billie Eilish, Childish Gambino, and Kendrick Lamar flashed across the screen. Even these stars, he said, had a first time performing at Coachella. Posters from previous years consistently scrolled across the screen and Bad Bunny said, "It is incredible to see the list of so many legends who for more than twenty years appeared here. But even more incredible is that among all of these, there has never been one like me before." His famous performances like his MTV VMA performance at Yankee Stadium and important moments like when he accepted a Grammy were interspersed with the other images. And then, the softer electronic sounds shifted to a piercing anthem with trumpets and bass created by Tainy. Images of Bad Bunny over the course of his career danced across the screen. In the distance, Bad Bunny's silhouette at last appeared on stage, surveying the crowd. Massive letters spelled out Bad Bunny, and then the stage went black.

With this video, Bad Bunny placed himself within an elite group of extremely popular English-language artists, the crème de la crème of pop who, like Bad Bunny, had started on smaller stages and had then become headliners. It was also a statement of belonging that made a critical intervention into the positioning of Latin music in the US pop scene. By situating himself in relation to stars like Billie Eilish and The Weeknd, Bad Bunny put himself within the larger history of English-language pop. Thus, he rejected the ubiquitous narrative of Latin music as foreign and exotic. In the weeks leading up to Coachella 2023, many on online forums like Reddit ridiculed the festival for having "unknown" headliners like Bad Bunny and the K-pop girl group BLACKPINK. The announcement of the headliners (the third being African American artist Frank Ocean) stirred up lively debate online, in which some claimed that Bad Bunny wouldn't be able to deliver enough fans to sell out the festival because no one knew who he was. Despite the fact that, at the time, Bad Bunny had already broken record after record for ticket sales and global streams, some online commenters nonetheless claimed that he would not be able to deliver as many fans as his predecessors.

Such perceptions reflect a pattern in US media portrayals of Latin music—and Latinos as a whole—as perpetually foreign, recent arrivals, even though Latin music and Latinos have a long history in the United States. Scholars Wilson Valentín-Escobar and María Elena Cepeda term this phenomenon the "Columbus effect," whereby successful Spanish-language artists are repackaged as new discoveries for US mainstream markets.[3] Such was the case in the 1990s Latin boom, when established Latin megastars like Ricky Martin and Shakira released English-language albums that many US media outlets treated as "debuts" or "introductions," reflecting the assumption that the US English-language mainstream audience is the only audience that matters for music success. Similarly, when tejana music icon Selena was tragically murdered in 1995, US media outlets lamented her passing before fully achieving her potential since she died just before the release of her crossover English album. Selena's tremendous success and groundbreaking musical contributions to música Mexicana and the Latin music industry were ignored.[4] And even when Spanish-language hits make it into the US mainstream, they are still framed as if they are subordinate to artists who have always recorded in English. The media's presentation of Canadian English-language pop star Justin Bieber's appearance on the remix of Luis Fonsi and Daddy Yankee's hit "Despacito" illustrates this. Bieber requested to be on the remix after hearing the song while traveling in Colombia. And yet, many reports claimed that it was Fonsi who contacted Bieber for help and credited Bieber for making the song successful. In a bizarre incident, Spotify crowned Bieber a "Latin king" for his contribution, although the company eventually apologized after criticism from Latin music fans.[5] The original song had dominated the Latin charts prior to the remix's crossover success (in fact, Luis Fonsi has stated that he never intended for the song to be a crossover hit). US coverage reflects an assumption that success with English-speaking, middle class, white Americans is the pinnacle of popular music and global success.[6]

Bad Bunny's tremendous global success has never involved pandering to this US mainstream audience. Instead, as we have shown throughout this book, he has succeeded in part by doubling down on representing his culture, his island, and his language. But, as his insistence on giving a history lesson at Coachella suggests, Bad Bunny is also keenly aware of those who came before him and who paved the way for his success. As he told Julyssa Lopez of *Rolling Stone*, "There were a lot of people way before me who did huge things. Sometimes people forget or, who knows, maybe gringos weren't paying as much attention. But now that the focus is on us [Latinos], I wanted to make it clear there's been a long road before me."[7]

While Bad Bunny expresses pride in Latino and Puerto Rican identity, he deliberately undermines the erroneous assumption by fans and critics alike that Latin musicians all perform a style that is easily legible as "Latin." As we have shown throughout the book, Bad Bunny's genre-blending work in albums like *El Último Tour del Mundo* and *Un Verano Sin Ti* directly contradict the idea that Latin music maps neatly onto different national identities (e.g., mariachi with Mexico, son with Cuba). His work also shows that influences from US pop and rock have long played a role in Latin music's development and vice versa, as is evident in Bad Bunny's collaborations with MAG.

Bad Bunny knows this history, and he foregrounded it in one of the videos he showed during weekend two of Coachella. It began with sounds of the classic mambo and narrator Ayala declaring, "Latin music has conquered the world, and we know that we own this."

The soundtrack to the video shifts with the narration, drawing from a host of hit Latin songs, from pop to rock to salsa. Similarly, the visuals present a dizzying array of Latin American and Latino artists including mambo legends Machito y sus Afrocubanos, Mexican stars Vicente Fernández and Juan Gabriel, "Caribbean queens" like Celia Cruz and La Lupe, famous singer-songwriters like Juan Luis Guerra and Mercedes Sosa, salsa legends the Fania All-Stars, and Latin pop stars like Thalia and Ricky Martin. The video foregrounds some of the artists who crossed over as part of the 1990s Latin boom, including Martin, Enrique Iglesias, and Shakira, as well as pop stars like Gloria Estefan and Jennifer Lopez, who have infused their pop with Latin sounds. It also includes Latino artists from the United States who rarely, if ever, sing Latin music, such as Mariah Carey and Christina Aguilera.

Together, all these references showcase the diversity and innovation of Latino musicians over the decades. The video dismisses the notion that Latin music is a stereotypical, tropical sound by calling attention to the diverse genres and styles encompassed in the label "Latin music." "Even though it sounds like pop, you're grooving to the soul of Latin America," says narrator Ayala. With this line, the video underscores that Latin music is not foreign, but instead an integral part of the US popular music land-scape in much the same way that Bad Bunny's introductory video represents him as equally worthy of headlining Coachella as all the English-language stars who did so before him.

The video also emphasizes that Latin music is not new—the voice-over comments, "This is not an arrival. We have always been here." After the video concluded, we were reminded of this point when the live performance began again. Bad Bunny entered on a fake palm tree that floated across the crowd, something he had done during his stadium con-certs for World's Hottest Tour, and then landed on a long runway stage that stretched into the middle of the audience. An older man holding an acoustic guitar waited for him. We saw the man's silhouette against the smoky haze wafting from the fog machine below. We noticed the distinc-tive hairdo—teased up a bit at the top, wispy behind the ears, not quite shoulder length. Petra yelled, "I think it is José Feliciano!" Those around us didn't seem as overcome, and we wondered if anyone else in the audi-ence knew who Feliciano was. For us the significance of the moment was overwhelming.

José Feliciano is a Puerto Rican musical icon. But he is also arguably the most potent reminder Bad Bunny could have provided that "we have always been here." Born in Lares, Puerto Rico, in 1945, Feliciano moved as a young child to New York City, where he learned to play the guitar begin-ning with the Puerto Rican cuatro. He became a guitar virtuoso drawing inspiration from Puerto Rican music, soul, rock, classical, and jazz. Feli-ciano made a name for himself as a young man singing in the cafés around Greenwich Village. In 1968, he released the groundbreaking album *Feli-ciano!* The album blended his Latin jazz–inspired guitar and soulful vocals in covers of famous hits like the Mamas & the Papas' "California Drea-min'" and the Beatles' "And I Love Her." The crown jewel of the record was Feliciano's recording of the Doors' song "Light My Fire." Feliciano's version reached number three on the Billboard charts and earned him the Grammy Award for Best New Artist. Later that year, the Detroit Tigers invited Feliciano to sing the national anthem for game five of the World Series. He did so in classic Feliciano fashion, blending Latin jazz sounds with a folksy singing style. This proved extremely controversial. Critics admonished Feliciano for changing the national anthem and interpreted his version as a protest against the Vietnam War that was raging at the time. Whereas Feliciano defended his performance as expressing his love for the United States, others saw it as unpatriotic and even called for his deportation (displaying their ignorance that people born in Puerto Rico are US citizens).[8] As a result, Feliciano was essentially blacklisted by many in the music industry for about two years; he explained to NPR in 2017, "They stopped playing me. Like I had the plague or something."[9]

Things changed in 1970, when Feliciano released his first Christmas album, which included the original composition "Feliz Navidad." Feliciano wrote the song because he felt nostalgic for Puerto Rico, but he never expected it to be able to compete with established Christmas standards.[10] The song incorporated English and Spanish to increase radio play since English-language stations generally did not play Spanish-language songs at the time. According to music critic Leila Cobo, "Feliz Navidad" was a "revolutionary and prescient" hit that paved the way for future bilingual songs like "Despacito" to make it on the charts.[11] Bad Bunny chose to include Feliciano precisely for this reason. Bad Bunny explained in *Rolling Stone*, "It struck me that I think a lot of younger people don't know how big [Feliciano] was. People are like 'Oh Bad Bunny is breaking ground with gringos!' No papi—José Feliciano was breaking ground with gringos since the seventies, you hear me? He was doing worldwide tours, he was in London, singing in English, singing to Anglophone audiences."[12]

At Coachella, Feliciano accompanied Bad Bunny on the songs "La Canción" and "Yonaguni." He also offered Bad Bunny some love advice as well as information on the provenance of his guitars. Despite the significance to both of us of Feliciano's inclusion and prominence in the performance, we realized that not everyone in the audience recognized the historical connections that Bad Bunny had described in *Rolling Stone*. The next day, Petra met a young Latina server at a brunch spot. Seeing Petra's Coachella wristband (what you wear to gain access into the festival), the server shared that she had attended Bad Bunny's performance the night before but had resold her bracelet for Saturday's events to avid BLACKPINK fans. They talked about the program, and Petra mentioned that her favorite part was seeing Feliciano and Bad Bunny perform together. The server explained that she had to search the internet after the show because she didn't know who had joined Bad Bunny on stage. After learning it was Feliciano, she remembered that her parents used to play his music.

In the moment, we knew that most of the people around us at Coachella were not sure who Feliciano was. But in some ways, we imagined, that was the point. Bad Bunny highlighted José Feliciano for a new audience who might otherwise not have recognized him, even if they almost certainly were familiar with his work, particularly "Feliz Navidad." Journalist Julyssa Lopez told us that in her conversations with Bad Bunny, he mentioned that he had done so in part because he felt that Feliciano "would have been a headliner" if Coachella had existed when he was younger. As Julyssa elaborated in our conversation, "In the context of what Coachella is . . . young people taking photos on Instagram and all these influencers, it's kind of a bold move to bring this [seventy-seven]-year-old. . . . I like the Post Malone thing [referencing Bad Bunny's guest during weekend one of Coachella], I think it makes a lot of sense for what the audience is. But [Bad Bunny] was like, 'Actually let's do something different for the second weekend and bring out this guy who probably not a lot of people are going to recognize.'" Including Feliciano was an intentional move on Bad Bunny's part to directly connect his success to the paths blazed by people before him. Along with the videos he showed, this decision emphasized not only the historic nature of Bad Bunny's performance but also his ongoing investment in highlighting the histories of Latino icons before him.

While Bad Bunny's set staked a claim for all Latinos' influence in popular music, he still represented Puerto Rico as he always does. Most of the videos he used during the performance showcased Puerto Rico's contributions to popular Latin genres, especially salsa and reggaetón. For example, weekend one featured a video that explained the history of salsa. "This is the music that made us," says narrator Ayala. The video begins by explicitly connecting Cuba and Puerto Rico to African drums from Nigeria and Congo. It mentions the various genres, rhythms, and instruments from Cuba and Puerto Rico that all influenced contemporary salsa, beginning with Afro–Puerto Rican bomba and Afro-Cuban rumba that Ayala describes as the "music of resistance." Not only does this highlight the African diasporic origins of this music but it also situates salsa and its precursors as music grounded in the pride and resistance of Puerto Ricans. The video highlights the various Puerto Rican and Cuban musicians from the 1920s through the 1960s who shaped salsa with their mambo, boleros, tríos, música jíbara, son cubano, and more. Ayala declares "in the '60s, la clave became the way, from the sound of these two Antillas all the way to New York City, baby!" The video showcases a host of Puerto Ricans who helped develop the genre in New York including Nuyoricans like Eddie Palmieri, Tito Puente, Willie Colón, and Héctor Lavoe. The video also mentions others like Dominican flutist Johnny Pacheco and Cuban singers Celia Cruz and La Lupe. It ends with a montage of later stars, like La India and Marc Anthony, as Ayala declares, "There is a long way to go because the music that made us will never end."

An extensive dance performance followed the video. Golden light shone from the stage as smoke swirled around two of Bad Bunny's dancers dressed in tight shiny silver pants and crop tops. They performed a routine to Ismael Rivera's 1975 hit "Las Tumbas" from his album *Soy Feliz*.

A second couple arrived after the first one left the stage as Héctor Lavoe's classic intro to "Aguanile" began. The drums sounded in anticipation until the couple moved into a rapid routine to the chorus. Like Rivera, Lavoe is a Puerto Rican salsa legend. Born in Ponce, Puerto Rico, in 1946, Lavoe migrated as a teenager to New York, where he connected with Willie Colón. Together, the two blended Colón's street savvy and musical chops with Lavoe's jíbaro vocal style, characterized by a high, tense, and dramatic vocal delivery, to create the sound of Fania Records—the most important salsa record label of the twentieth century.

The music in the dance performance on stage shifted once again to Rafael Ithier's distinct piano riff on El Gran Combo's hit, "Brujería." Formed in the 1960s and still performing today, El Gran Combo is one of the most iconic bands in Puerto Rican history, continuing to uplift its Afro-Caribbean roots and approaching social commentary with humorous lyrics and innovative styles. Once "Brujería's" chorus began, the rest of the dancers appeared on stage. Their synchronized choreography was suggestive of the slick moves of El Gran Combo's three singers who always dance in unison during the band's performances. Bad Bunny's dancers also incorporated moves that tie directly to Afro-Puerto Rican bomba dancing, paying homage to both El Gran Combo's roots and that of the archipelago's Black communities. In fact, toward the end of the segment, one dancer performed as the others gathered in a semicircle to urge her on, staging the classic bomba batey format that emphasized the communal nature of the music and dance.

But then the song stopped and the dancers froze. The bluesy piano melody under the first verse of Pete Rodríguez's 1967 boogaloo classic "I Like It (I Like It Like That)" started. Bad Bunny emerged from behind the dancers just as the audience heard Rodríguez unmistakable chorus intro, "Yeaaaah baby." As soon as the chorus responds "I like it like that!," the beat dropped for the Tainy-produced hit "I Like It," recorded by Bad Bunny, Cardi B, and J Balvin. Like Rodríguez's original, "I Like It" has bilingual lyrics with

Cardi B rapping in English and Bad Bunny and J Balvin in Spanish. To date, the song is Bad Bunny's only number one hit on the Billboard Hot 100 charts, and it introduced him to many English-speaking listeners. For Tainy, "I Like It" was a "game changer" for reggaetón. He was having dinner with Colombian reggaetón singer J Balvin, when the two learned that the song was climbing up the Billboard Hot 100 chart and that it was projected to become number one in the next week. Tainy told us, "That was really shocking to me, because it's like a place where [Latin musicians] are not supposed to be. For me [it showed] the potential that Latin music had as well." However, the mainstream success of "I Like It" did not require that Tainy, Bad Bunny, or J Balvin change their style to make it more palatable to a new audience. Instead, the mainstream came to them. As Tainy explained, "In terms of my music, people, not only Latinos, but also people and artists from [the English-language US] market, are now wanting to understand who worked on that song. So now thanks to that song, [Latin producers] can work with [English-language pop singers] Selena Gomez or Justin Bieber or Dua Lipa or Shawn Mendes." Like with Feliciano, "I Like It" demonstrates the critical contributions that Latin music has made to the US pop scene. At the same time, introducing "I Like It" at Coachella immediately after a lengthy performance and video about the history of salsa identified the song as a particularly Puerto Rican one and one rooted in Black diasporic communities and traditions.

Bad Bunny's Coachella appearance continued in this vein with two additional videos about the history of reggaetón. Weekend two's video dealt with the genre's global domination, a point consistent with the overall theme of the evening on the tremendous success and impact of Latin music worldwide. Weekend one's video traced the origins of reggaetón from Panamanian reggae en español to the 2004 release of Daddy Yankee's "Gasolina." Based on Petra's book *Remixing Reggaetón*, it framed reggaetón—much like salsa—as music of resistance that came from low-income and predominantly Black communities to "challenge authority and become the voice of the voiceless." The video included a brief mention of Puerto Rico's Mano Dura Contra el Crimen (Iron Fist Against Crime), the 1990s anti-crime initiative spearheaded by then-Governor Pedro Rosselló that unjustly targeted the urban poor, caseríos, and reggaetón's predecessor underground music. As part of this initiative, the US National Guard was called in to help Puerto Rican police target caseríos thought to be the epicenters of the drug trade. They staged military-style invasions of the caseríos complete with helicopters and tanks. The initiative involved arresting suspected drug traffickers and was followed by continued police presence in the caseríos, the construction of gates and guard towers enclosing them, and ongoing militarized police action. Despite officials' claims that the campaign was a complete success, the reality was that Mano Dura did not accomplish all it set out to do. In fact, homicide rates actually increased as a result of the raids, in part because the moving of drug points to different areas ignited new turf wars and waves of violence.[13] Scholars like Marisol LeBrón, Zaire Dinzey-Flores, and Petra have demonstrated that the real result of Mano Dura was to further concentrate violence in poor urban neighborhoods and, perhaps more insidiously, to reinforce racist and classist stereotypes that painted poor, Black, and young urban residents (especially men) as violent delinquents.[14]

Proponents of Mano Dura pointed to underground music as evidence of this delinquency. Whereas artists argued that their lyrics reflected what happened in the streets, critics assumed that underground promoted violence, drugs, and sex. To be sure, underground lyrics were very explicit, but this did not mean that they actually fomented violence. Instead, would-be censors targeted underground because of the music's associations with the very same urban, poor, and Black populations that Mano Dura targeted. As cultural critic and sociologist Raquel Z. Rivera writes, "Policing and restricting underground could, therefore, be easily portrayed by government authorities as a logical extension of anti-crime state policies."[15]

Eventually, criticism of underground turned into outright censorship when, in 1995, police raided record stores and confiscated underground records. In an effort to stymie the popularity of the music, authorities charged store owners, distributors, and even sometimes DJs themselves with violating obscenity laws. For fans like Tainy's manager Pablo Batista, these efforts seemed misplaced. Pablo recalled to us that during this time, "You would literally see dead people on the front page of the newspaper every day. So why are you going after kids who are doing music instead of going after los narcos?" However, censoring underground was much easier than actually dealing with the systemic inequalities that created the conditions for violence that flourished in Puerto Rico. Furthermore, it was no accident that these initiatives targeted underground once the music began leaving the caseríos and entering other segments of Puerto Rican society. The moral panic around underground's spread revealed the profound racism and classism that motivated the initiative since it was only when the music reached middle-class youth that it was seen as especially concerning.[16]

The marginalization of underground continues to reverberate in the music industry's treatment of reggaetón despite the success of Bad Bunny and others. Tainy has observed these criticisms over the course of his own career. He described, "We were making this genre of music that was always, like, kind of marginalized and kind of scorned within Latin music." At Coachella, Bad Bunny underscored this history of marginalization within Puerto Rico, making a case not only about the impact of Latinos and Latin music on the US mainstream but also about the importance of reggaetón, specifically, within the Latin music realm.

After highlighting pioneers like Renato, Vico C, El General, DJ Playero, DJ Negro, and Daddy Yankee, the Coachella video calls out the urban areas where reggaetón developed, declaring, "The sound of Carolina and Santurce [both referring to Puerto Rican urban areas] has become the legacy of Latin America." As with the salsa video, the video on the history of reggaetón highlights the Afro-Caribbean roots of the genre and the multiple communities that helped create it while simultaneously foregrounding the role and impact of Puerto Ricans on the music's development and global success.

Both of the videos about reggaetón were couched within a longer vignette about a fictional Puerto Rican youth named Giovanni who comes to the US mainland to visit his uncle in the Coachella Valley. It begins with Giovanni packing his things as he prepares to go to the airport. At his mother's behest, he runs inside to his room to get his ID, but instead he opens a box of reggaetón CDs and other keepsakes. The film shows Daddy Yankee's *Barrio Fino* (2004) tucked slightly underneath Tego Calderón's *El Abayarde* (2002), two albums that played a critical role in the globalization of reggaetón in the mid-2000s. Yankee's *Barrio Fino* included the hit "Gasolina," a landmark moment in reggaetón's history that placed the genre squarely within the global mainstream. If many have argued that Daddy Yankee brought reggaetón to the global marketplace, it was Calderón's *El Abayarde* that made it big in Puerto Rico. Even some of reggaetón's staunchest critics in Puerto Rico praised *El Abayarde*.[17] Calderón is also known for his overt stance on Puerto Rican politics, especially in relation to racial justice. Songs like "Loíza" from *El Abayarde* directly call out the ongoing systemic anti-Black racism in Puerto Rico. Many critics have considered Calderón to be the modern heir to Ismael Rivera.[18] Bad Bunny listed Calderón as one of his major influences, telling the *New York Times* that Tego is his "favorito full," or his absolute favorite.[19] Thus, the decision to make Calderón's album the "protagonist of that moment" in the video, as Kacho told us, was a deliberate way to position Bad Bunny within this "Tego school" of reggaetón. After Giovanni opens the chest with the CDs in it, Calderón's record begins to glow as the video shifts from the scene in Giovanni's house to the history of reggaetón. Foregrounding Calderón as a godfather-like figure for reggaetón underscores the genre's Afro-Caribbean roots and connections to Puerto Rican politics.

Giovanni's movement between Puerto Rico and the US mainland also signals an acknowledgment of the Puerto Rican diaspora. After the educational portions of the video end, we see him arrive at the airport in California, where his uncle picks him up. Giovanni's uncle secures the suitcase to the top of the car with a pair of orange bungee cords because it cannot fit in the car's trunk, which is housing an enormous sound system (the kind typically used in underground parties). The two take off for Coachella along the dusty roads of the California desert, surrounded by shrubs and Joshua trees, as a medley of past reggaetón and underground hits blasts out of the trunk. Those in the Coachella crowd familiar with old-school reggaetón by the likes of Plan B and Don Omar could sing along. The images of the car's enormous sound system, the suitcase on top, and the Puerto Rican flag that hangs from the rear view mirror would all be familiar to a Caribbean crowd. Thus, showcasing these images against the backdrop of the Coachella Valley inserts Puerto Ricanness into the California desert. Eventually, Giovanni and his uncle make it to the Coachella festival where a security guard asks for ID. This is the first time that we hear the uncle speak in fluent, unaccented English, a moment that situates him within the larger Puerto Rican diaspora. After getting their security clearance, Giovanni and his uncle drive onto the Coachella grounds as the lights of the sound system's speakers glow bright red in the background.

In addition to showcasing the histories of these Puerto Rican musical traditions, Bad Bunny included references that would be legible to his fans familiar with his work in Puerto Rico as well. At the very beginning of both weekends at Coachella, Bad Bunny appeared on top of what looked like a gas station, on a platform covered in a blue and orange design. A large spinning sign of his rabbit logo rotated on the left. His dancers performed below. This set design referenced the ninety-minute concert he gave with his friend and mentor Arcángel atop a Gulf gas station on Calle Loíza in San Juan in December 2022 as part of filming the music video for the song "La Jumpa." Thousands of fans gathered in the street to watch the filming of the video, which was widely celebrated in the media and especially by TikTokkers and fans in Puerto Rico.

8.1 Bad Bunny performs at Coachella on April 14, 2023. The set design is reminiscent of the gas station on Calle Loíza in San Juan where he and Arcángel filmed their music video for "La Jumpa," during which they performed an impromptu concert. Christopher Polk/Variety via Getty Images.

As literary and cultural studies scholar Jossianna Arroyo argues, the location of the Gulf Station in Calle Loíza carried significance for those who associate the area with Dominican immigrants and the urban poor, many of whom have been displaced by the gentrification of San Juan. Arroyo noted that the gas station's location was accessible from different neighborhoods, and thus brought together tourists, residents of the nearby caseríos, and more upper-class Puerto Ricans. For Arroyo, the location is a reminder of the crises wrought by tourism and gentrification alongside the bringing together of a wide swath of Puerto Rican society.[20] Only fans familiar with the earlier concert would completely grasp the significance of incorporating the gas station into his Coachella set design, thus signaling a special connection to these fans.

Further clinching the connection, on weekend two, Arcángel joined Bad Bunny to perform "La Jumpa" live on top of his makeshift gas station. One of the Coachella festival's allures is the illustrious roster of surprise guests who join the show. Puerto Rican artists Jhayco, Jowell y Randy, and Ñengo Flow all performed during weekend one. However, multiple tech problems had derailed the participation of Post Malone, who would have played the guitar accompaniment during Bad Bunny's acoustic set. The fact that Post Malone was the only US English-language artist to participate in Bad Bunny's set (and that he had been unable to do so) upped the ante for weekend two. Rumors swirled that someone "big" like Cardi B or Drake might show up on weekend two to make up for that mishap. Along with the aforementioned Puerto Rican artists from the previous weekend, Bad Bunny gave them two "big" people in Arcángel and José Feliciano, fellow Puerto Rican artists, people who are hardly household names in mainstream US pop even though they are big in the Latin scene. With this group, Bad Bunny emphasized Puerto Rican musicians who came before him (save for Jhayco, who released his first single in 2017), who paved the way either by helping innovate reggaetón style in the 2000s and 2010s, like Arcángel and Jowell y Randy did, or breaking ground in the US mainstream with Puerto Rican music, like Feliciano did decades before.

Bad Bunny frequently talks about how artists like Jowell y Randy and Arcángel have been critical to his own musical development. In 2018, he told Puerto Rican podcasters Molusco and Chente Ydrach, "When I was 13 or 14, my memories are of perreo from Jowell y Randy, Arcángel, De La Ghetto. I have respect for them and I want to share that."[21] When Vanessa sat down with Jowell y Randy in their backstage trailer at the 2024 Latin music festival Sueños, the duo spoke about the magnitude of performing with Bad Bunny on the 2023 Coachella stage. Like their contemporary De La Ghetto told us, Jowell y Randy appreciated the homage that Bad Bunny always pays to those who came before him. Randy said, "For us it is an honor that many of these kids of the new generation have us as references."

Not only were they honored by the invitation to share the stage, but they also felt like they had never experienced anything like performing at Coachella before. Randy explained, "Jowell and I have been on thousands of stages, thousands of stages. I think this is the most monstrous stage and the energy is very different." Jowell added that it was "a dream" to be at Coachella and that they "never imagined" they would grace that stage. "When you add up the two weekends together, you realize the numbers. More than half a million people saw us there live. Then you must adjust the show, at least in our case as performers.... We have ... ten cameras on top of us, we must do what [the director] tells us and how we're supposed to act. In a way, we must get into our heads that we are not in the club!" Randy added, "The energy was *duro*"—hard, intense, bad ass. He noted that Coachella has historically been more known for rock acts, but that

Bad Bunny's headlining set showed how "they are bringing in the Latinos, little by little." It was clear that the Coachella set was as historically significant for the individual performers as it was for the genre of reggaetón and for Puerto Rican music more broadly.

Taken together, the educational videos, choreography, set design, and special guests all foregrounded the role of Puerto Rican music and musicians in the development of reggaetón and Latin music more generally. It was a show for everyone, but there were particular cues for Puerto Rican fans and reggaetón fans that people unfamiliar with Puerto Rican culture might have missed. Thus, Bad Bunny insisted on recognition for Puerto Rico as a site of musical innovation and development, but he also insisted on full belonging for Puerto Ricans on their own terms.

Bad Bunny represented Puerto Rico at Coachella like he always does, inviting audiences into his world and showcasing the critical impact of Puerto Ricans on popular music. But he also took the opportunity to express solidarity with other Latino groups. For example, he established Latino musicians' contributions to US popular music in the documentary components of the films he showed, referencing artists from a wide range of countries (Argentina, Mexico, Colombia, and the Dominican Republic, among others). He also actualized moments of collaboration across Latino groups with the participation of Grupo Frontera, a música Mexicana group from Texas's Rio Grande Valley, during weekend two.

Bad Bunny and Grupo Frontera released a surprise single, "un x100to," between the two Coachella weekends. The song quickly rose to the top of the charts with its blend of Grupo Frontera's cumbia and Bad Bunny's urban sound. Grupo Frontera is composed of five members: Juan Javier Cantú on accordion, Julián Peña Jr. on percussion, Carlos Guerrero on drums, Alberto "Beto" Acosta on bajo quinto, Brian Ortega on bass, and Adelaido "Payo" Solís on vocals. They hail from the border city of McAllen, Texas. They began as an ancillary to Acosta's business taking photographs for weddings and quinceñeras, a band he formed to perform as part of his event packages. He connected with Cantú, who had previously played with Guerrero. The group got together and started performing to local crowds.

In April of 2022, Grupo Frontera posted a YouTube video of their cover of Colombian pop group Morat's "No Se Va." The video features the band in jeans, light blue button ups, and cowboy hats singing the song in a funky new norteño-style. Cantú credits the integration of Peña's congas as key to their distinct sound: "It doesn't sound like your typical norteño song; in fact, it sounds like something fresh with that reggaetón vibe."[22] The video garnered millions of views, and their cover climbed the Latin charts, peaking at number three on the Hot Latin Songs chart, and even breaking into Billboard's Hot 100 chart (a rare feat for a música Mexicana song).[23]

Eventually, the group caught the attention of Mexican American producer Edgar Barrera, who also was raised near McAllen. Like many kids on the border, Barrera grew up regularly traveling across it, in his case between Roma, Texas, and Ciudad Miguel Alemán in Tamaulipas, Mexico.[24] He began his career in 2010 at just twenty years of age when he got an internship with songwriter Andrés Castro in Miami.[25] By the time he met Grupo Frontera in 2022, he had won eighteen Latin Grammys, one Grammy, and numerous other awards. He has written and produced songs across an incredible range of genres and styles, from reggaetón to música Mexicana to salsa to pop. He has written for a diverse set of artists, including Maluma, Camilo, Reik, Christian Nodal, Shakira, Marc Anthony, Daddy Yankee, Peso Pluma, Ed Sheeran, Ariana Grande, and Madonna.

Barrera played "un x100to" for the members of Grupo Frontera in 2023. It had been in his back pocket for a while, but no one had picked it up. Grupo Frontera loved the song, and they recorded an initial version of it. Meanwhile, Bad Bunny and his team were hard at work on a trap album with no plans to do any música Mexicana songs at the time. Producer MAG told us how this unexpected collaboration came from a simple conversation at an awards show where he ran into Edgar. MAG asked Edgar to share any ideas or demos with him that could be the basis of a Bad Bunny and Grupo Frontera collaboration.

At this point, MAG recalled, he was just "thinking out loud." He had never broached the subject of a potential Grupo Frontera collaboration with Bad Bunny. Instead, just like he had with songs like "WHERE SHE GOES," MAG started thinking about a new, different sound that he would encourage Bad Bunny to pursue. The following day, Edgar Barrera sent MAG the demo for "un x100to," with a caveat saying it was not mixed and that he would be willing to offer something else or even start from scratch on a new project. MAG loved the demo and decided to bring it to Bad Bunny, who, after first listen, agreed that they should collaborate with Grupo Frontera even though, as MAG recalled, it "didn't fall in line with anything we were working on." MAG and Bad Bunny wanted to change some aspects of the song to reflect Bad Bunny's sound. After Frontera's singer Payo performed the first verse with the band, MAG added some synthesizer chords that marked the transition to Bad Bunny's verse on the song. MAG explained to us that this was an unusual approach to música Mexicana that doesn't usually have "electronic elements [that] just come in and cut off the song." But this approach worked, and the song debuted at number three on the Hot Latin Songs chart and even broke into the top five songs of the Billboard Hot 100 in its first week.[26]

MAG told us that the whole process took only three or four weeks. At the time, Bad Bunny was rehearsing for Coachella in Las Vegas. Bad Bunny wanted to release the song in the week between his weekend performances at Coachella. Grupo Frontera arrived at a site in Nevada to film the music video. While on set, they learned Bad Bunny had recorded the song and met Bad Bunny for the very first time.[27]

They released the music video on Monday, April 17, 2023. On weekend two, just about one year after their "No Se Va" video was released on YouTube, Grupo Frontera found themselves performing at Coachella. They took the stage just after the video about the rich history of Latin music. Bad Bunny truly shared his historic platform, sacrificing time to sing his songs to offer Grupo Frontera the opportunity to perform their songs "No Se Va" and "Bebe Dame" before he joined them for "un x100to." The group performed before an image of a rundown desert house similar to the one used in the music video, and as soon as the beat dropped and the first verse began, a Mexican flag and a Puerto Rican flag unfurled from the top of the porch. It was a statement of Latino solidarity, of belonging and cross-cultural appreciation.[28]

Obviously this moment aligned with the overall show's emphasis on staking a claim for Latinos and Latin music in the mainstream pop culture space of Coachella. The substantial space Bad Bunny offered Grupo Frontera also reflects how he continuously shares the spotlight with up and coming groups that he supports, often from marginalized communities. In this case, you can trace Grupo Frontera's success directly to the history of Mexican laborers in the United States. Grupo Frontera primarily performs cumbia, a genre that originally developed in Colombia but gained traction and spread throughout Mexican and Mexican American communities in the mid-twentieth century.[29] In Texas, many accordion-based groups began integrating cumbia into their repertoires such that by the 1970s it became a necessary staple of any successful música Mexicana

8.2 Bad Bunny performs "x100to" with Grupo Frontera at Coachella on April 21, 2023. The set design, especially the house, reflects the western theme of their music video. The two flags hanging on the porch express Mexican and Puerto Rican solidarity. Still from Coachella videographer Mickey Pierre-Louis.

group in the state.[30] By the 1990s, tejana superstar Selena broke open the Latin market with her updated cumbias. In the United States, Mexican migrants also listened to cumbia. Other musical groups that catered to migrant communities played música Norteña, which, though different from the música Tejana of Selena, also incorporated cumbia.[31]

For Bad Bunny to share the Coachella stage with a group from the Texas-Mexico border, one that is steeped in the musical traditions of Mexican migrant workers, is significant. The Coachella festival takes place in Indio, California, a working-class town populated primarily by Mexican and Mexican American agricultural workers. The Coachella Valley has a long history of hiring immigrant laborers, including Japanese, Filipinos, and especially Mexican laborers. It is for this reason that the Coachella Valley became a central location for the United Farm Workers organizing efforts, led by Dolores Huerta and Cesar Chavez. Mexican immigrant workers in the Coachella Valley have long faced poverty, dangerous work conditions, and the constant threat of deportation. Currently, most Mexican farmworkers in the Coachella Valley make less than $20,000 annually, and the vast majority are undocumented.[32] The reality for many residents of the Coachella Valley is a stark contrast to the opulence of the Coachella music festival. In fact, the Coachella Music Festival has received repeated criticism for creating an elite and exclusive venue rife with displays of wealth and consumption without acknowledging social inequalities and economic hardships facing the surrounding area.[33] In this context, Grupo Frontera's performance takes on even greater significance.

With Grupo Frontera, Bad Bunny not only highlighted música Mexicana but also presented a moment of Latino solidarity. Their musical fusion brought together two genres that emerged from the history of migration and working-class life between Latin America and the United States. With the Mexican and Puerto Rican flags waving behind them, Grupo Frontera and Bad Bunny both honored their distinct homelands while also foregrounding their similarities as two groups who have contributed to US life, history, and culture despite facing racism, classism, and (neo) colonialism.

Bad Bunny's historic Coachella performance highlighted the impact of Latin music in Spanish on US popular culture, but it also did much more than that. With this performance, Bad Bunny continued to represent Puerto Rico to the fullest. Bad Bunny was aware that his Coachella audience was a mix of fans and newcomers to his world. This was clear in the introductory video, and it was also part of his motivation for integrating into his performance the educational videos about the history of these genres and the history of Latinos in the United States. The debates about what "counts" as Latin music and where Latin music fits in the US music market are not just about sales and trends. These debates also say something about how Latino people are understood in the United States. Their dark underside is what Leo Chavez has termed the "Latino threat narrative"—that is, the assumption that Latino immigrants, and Mexicans in particular, will "take over" the United States with profound cultural and demographic changes.[34] In this context, Bad Bunny's Coachella performance was more than an incredible concert. It was also a proud call for belonging for Puerto Ricans and Latino people more generally in ways that counter the dominant narratives that have been used to further the systemic marginalization of these communities. We have always been here.

9

"PRENDE UNA VELITA": CONTINUED HOPE, CONTINUED RESISTANCE

Just one month after Coachella, on May 18, 2023, Bad Bunny released the lead single "WHERE SHE GOES" from his upcoming album *Nadie Sabe Lo Que Va a Pasar Mañana* (commonly referred to as *Nadie Sabe*). He had filmed the video in the Lucerne Valley in California just five days after wrapping up his performance at Coachella.[1] The video begins with Bad Bunny driving through the desert in an old Rolls Royce (the same one that he would subsequently use at the listening party for the album in San Juan). He then raps from atop a single flowered tree, in a nighttime scene surrounded by roosters and at a party at a giant bonfire. Images of a woman with angel wings and, especially, several scenes of horses running through the desert appear throughout the video.

Speculation circulated online that "WHERE SHE GOES" is about his rumored girlfriend at the time, Kendall Jenner. *Teen Vogue* speculated whether the image of the woman with angel wings referred back to Jenner's modeling career and if the scorpion pictured in the video was because Scorpio is her astrological sign. But the biggest clue was the horses. "There are also horses in the video. Random . . . until you remember that Jenner is a documented horse girl, to the extent that she took Benito on a horseback riding date," journalist Aamina Inayit Khan surmised.[2] Fans also thought that the horses were for Kendall; one wrote on Twitter/X, "In the video, there are horses all the time, and Kendall loves horses."[3]

Others speculated that the horses signaled a desire to dabble in música Mexicana, which dominated the Latin charts at the time. Bad Bunny had just collaborated with Grupo Frontera. Although MAG told us this collaboration resulted from MAG's coincidental meeting with Edgar Barrera, some fans speculated that the collaboration was simply Bad Bunny following a trend (despite the fact that Bad Bunny had already collaborated on one of the earliest corridos tumbados back in 2019 when he joined Natanael Canó's "Soy El Diablo [Remix]").[4] This was also a time when country music was starting to dominate streaming in the United States, and things like cowboy hats and cowboy boots were in style (thanks also to pop stars like Beyoncé who started wearing cowboy hats as part of her *Renaissance* album in 2022).[5] In their *Rolling Stone* review of *Nadie Sabe*, Jon Dolan and Vita Dadoo claim that the album's cover art featuring Bad Bunny in a fringed blue outfit riding a bronco was "a nod to the renaissance and durability of the cowboy figure, . . . salutes the prominence of música Mexicana . . . and it's a sign of his ability to lock into what's popular."[6] In other words, if the horse was not about Kendall Jenner, then maybe it was about Bad Bunny jumping on the country or música Mexicana bandwagons—a move that could be interpreted as just as inauthentic.

From the fallout over the *Time* magazine cover story about him to Kendall Jenner's presence at Coachella, Bad Bunny faced a tremendous amount of backlash as a result of his personal choices and explosive professional success (and the expectation of responsibility that comes with that success). At the core of these critiques was a sentiment that Bad Bunny's actions demonstrated that he no longer cared about Puerto Rico or Latinos. He was living in Los Angeles and dating a gringa. What did he stand for? At least this was the sentiment expressed largely by US Latinas.[7] Even our students who had considered themselves fans became increasingly disillusioned. As professors who teach courses about Bad Bunny's work and its cultural and political significance, we understood why fans were asking critical questions. For many of his fans, Bad Bunny's work felt culturally and politically consequential, while Jenner and her family were known largely for being rich, frivolous, and for engaging regularly in cultural appropriation.[8] Thus, the content of Bad Bunny's interviews and his choice of romantic partner seemed incongruent with what fans perceived to be his morals and priorities.

In many ways, *Nadie Sabe* reflected the changes in Bad Bunny's life since he had achieved such massive levels of global stardom. The album responded to critiques of his resettling in Los Angeles and dating Kendall Jenner. Reviewers of the album commented on his constant reference to grappling with the problems of fame and money, and some seemed to lament that this was a far cry from the sounds and themes of *Un Verano Sin Ti*.[9] *Nadie Sabe Lo Que Va a Pasar Mañana* was marketed as an album for Bad Bunny's "real fans" who had stuck with him since his early trap days—a return to his roots. But for some reviewers, the question remained whether his fans would be able to understand him and whether he had grown more distant with fame. As one review in *Variety* noted, "Though most listeners probably can't relate to selling their Bugatti because it didn't go fast enough, Bunny proclaims he hasn't changed since achieving stardom."[10] This skepticism combined with disapproval of his rumored relationship with Jenner made it seem that Bad Bunny's entrance into the global media machine had fundamentally altered his authenticity.

But back in Puerto Rico, we heard a different interpretation. While meeting fans who were waiting in line to buy tickets for the *Nadie Sabe* listening party in San Juan in October of 2023, the overwhelming sentiment we heard was that Puerto Rican fans continued to view Bad Bunny as committed to Puerto Rico above all else. We heard multiple times how proud people felt about having such a top artist come from Puerto Rico and speak about Puerto Rican issues. We also heard from fans who saw Bad Bunny's listening party, where Puerto Ricans could hear his album hours before the rest of the world, as evidence of his ongoing focus on Puerto Ricans and Puerto Rico *despite* his status as a global star. One thing we did not hear much about was Kendall Jenner. "There's a lot of haters out there because of all that stuff with Kendall," one fan said, "but that doesn't really matter."

In fact, these Puerto Rican fans were right to assume that Puerto Rico was front and center in Bad Bunny's new album, and not only because it harkened back to his roots in Latin trap. The whole concept of the album itself was about Puerto Rico. The horse became the image of the album, featured on the cover, in the music video, and in the visualizers. But the horse was not about Kendall Jenner, nor was it about being trendy. We learned from producer MAG that the entire inspiration from the album was grounded in the legacy of Vuelve Candy B, "the most famous Puerto Rican [race] horse." Vuelve Candy B won several critical races in the 1990s to become the only Puerto Rican thoroughbred to win over one million

9.1 The cowboy theme of *Nadie Sabe Lo Que Va a Pasar Mañana* was inspired by the Puerto Rican racehorse Vuelve Candy B, for which one of the album's songs is named. Many fans and media outlets speculated about the true meaning of the album's theme, and the actual significance was lost on many in mainstream American media. Album cover design by Matt McCormick.

dollars. MAG emphasized to us that there are many cultural references in the song "VUELVE CANDY B" that speak directly to a Puerto Rican audience, and that only one familiar with Puerto Rican culture and history might understand. The whole concept of the song "VUELVE CANDY B" as well as the album itself was to celebrate Puerto Rico as a land of "champions," just like the real Vuelve Candy B.[11]

Another anthem for Puerto Rico on the album was "ACHO PR," the old-school inspired Latin trap song featuring De La Ghetto, Arcángel, and Ñengo Flow. De La Ghetto told us that when he arrived in the New York City studio to record, he did not know what kind of song they were making.

"I thought it was going to be something more clubby, more ratchet, you know," he explained to us. But then Bad Bunny started telling them the goal of the song. De La Ghetto recalled:

> It was something pa' la calle pero pa' la *gente* [for the street, but for the people]. For the underdogs.... So they could feel proud of being Puerto Rican, so they could feel proud of being Latino, so they could feel proud of being from the barrio, from the *island*. We represent this pride. Not only us, all the Miss Universes, Héctor Lavoe, Tito Trinidad, Macho Camacho, Benicio del Toro, entiende'. It's one of those songs that makes you feel good to be from the island, to be Puerto Rican so I understood his message. And he was saying, "Listen, I want you to write about what you went through, what were you feeling. We want to motivate our people from the island," he told me.

De La Ghetto's recollection of how Bad Bunny described "ACHO PR" as a song of pride and motivation for Puerto Ricans reflects the broader ethos of *Nadie Sabe Lo Que Va a Pasar Mañana*. Despite the speculation that Bad Bunny did not care anymore about Puerto Rico or Latinos, Bad Bunny actually doubled down on his dedication to the archipelago with the deep cultural references to Puerto Rico that the mainstream had obviously missed. Missing these references speaks to the ongoing devaluation of Puerto Rican culture and Bad Bunny's work by the US mainstream. At the same time, *Nadie Sabe* speaks to Bad Bunny's continued advocacy for Puerto Rico. And he was just getting started.

Bad Bunny ended his Most Wanted Tour for *Nadie Sabe Lo Que Va a Pasar Mañana* in Puerto Rico with three sold out nights in a row at El Choli from June 7 to June 9, 2024. In a video that opened the show, narrated by Bad Bunny himself, he declared: "Si has visto a Bad Bunny cantar en vivo, pero no lo has hecho en Puerto Rico, realmente no lo has visto" (If you have seen Bad Bunny perform live, but not in Puerto Rico, you really haven't seen him).[12] Beyond both the artist's and the audiences' over-the-top emotion and energy for the shows in his homeland, Bad Bunny concerts in Puerto Rico always have components that stateside audiences do not get. The closing of his Most Wanted Tour was no exception. His Puerto Rico shows opened with an orchestra playing the melody for "La

Borinqueña," Puerto Rico's official national anthem. The crowd instantly erupted in chorus.[13]

While the list of guests varied slightly each day, many artists featured on the album made cameos over the course of the three days, including Young Miko, Bryant Myers, Mora, YOVNGCHIMI, Luar la L, De La Ghetto, Arcángel, and Ñengo Flow. Bad Bunny's second show also included Colombian reggaetón star Feid, and his third show featured fellow Puerto Rican trap star Eladio Carrión.[14]

At the Puerto Rico shows for *Nadie Sabe*, all the artists on the song "ACHO PR" came together to perform the song live for the first time. De La Ghetto described the experience to us, "We felt like gladiators live in the Coliseum of Rome when we came out to sing that song. It was another chapter in my career and his career, and everybody's career. Era histórico, me entiende'? It was historic. It felt super super because when I was on the stage and I looked at the audience, I would see kids nine or ten [years old] to grown-ups in their fifties and sixties. It was what united us, our genre unites people." During one performance of the song, Bad Bunny was moved to tears, covering his face with the Puerto Rican flag.[15]

Unlike the rest of his tour dates, where he closed his shows with an encore performance of "WHERE SHE GOES," the grand finale of the Puerto Rican shows was "El Apagón." Cabezudos donning masks and outfits based on Bad Bunny's *Nadie Sabe* ensemble danced on stage while he performed.[16] MAG, who was at the Puerto Rico concerts, told us that Bad Bunny's closing of "El Apagón" was "like a party! But the lyrics are so beautiful . . . and this chapter closing with 'El Apagón' and seeing our people singing it, it's hard to put into words [what it meant] . . . because it's home. It's on the island. It's a song for Puerto Rico! So I think he strategically planned to close at home in Puerto Rico, but also to close with 'El Apagón,' which became this anthem for Puerto Rico." Despite his massive global fame and the fact that the majority of his fans all over the world are not Puerto Rican, these shows demonstrated that he has a very intentional approach to his shows in his homeland, and a different cultural relationship and dedication to his fans in Puerto Rico.

For those Puerto Ricans in the archipelago who could not make it to El Choli, Bad Bunny broadcast his show live into movie theaters across Puerto Rico. What's more, he took advantage of this offer to encourage his fans, especially young people, to vote in the 2024 gubernatorial elections in Puerto Rico. With the support of his record label Rimas, he offered tickets to see the Most Wanted Tour at theaters "two for the price of one," but only if you showed your voter registration identification card.[17] This was a particularly significant move, considering that Puerto Rico generally has low voter registration *and* low voter turnout rates, and 2024 data showed that 75 percent of eighteen- to twenty-one-year-olds were not registered to vote at the time.[18]

In the summer of 2024, Bad Bunny had not actually endorsed any particular candidate in the gubernatorial race, even if he was invested in getting out the vote. Pablo Batista told us that part of the reason that Bad Bunny is so effective as someone who engages people politically is because he is not heavy-handed, obvious, or coming from a particular political party. Bad Bunny's openness and refusal to be boxed in creates possibilities for a growing audience of people who similarly don't know where they fit politically, but who know that they don't agree with the corrupt nature of the government that was revealed leading up to the protests during 2019's Verano Boricua in Puerto Rico. Bad Bunny marching and producing protest anthems alongside Residente during the Verano Boricua showed the public where he stood without his having to declare allegiance to anything aside from Puerto Rico itself.

Although the struggle for justice in Puerto Rico continues, the hopefulness of imagining a new future remains. Puerto Ricans continue to contest gentrification, the privatization of public services, the inadequate infrastructure, and environmental racism. In more formal electoral politics, 2023 saw the formation of the electoral alliance La Alianza de País (La Alianza, for short), a coalition of the Puerto Rican Independence Party (PIP) and Movimiento Victoria Ciudadana (MVC). The parties joined forces to promote pro-independence activist and politician Juan Dalmau for governor, and Afro–Puerto Rican lawyer and feminist activist Ana Irma Rivera Lassén for resident commissioner (the nonvoting representative of Puerto Rico to the US Congress). La Alianza advocates for a more inclusive Puerto Rico that prioritizes the needs of Puerto Ricans rather than the interests of US investors or the US government. La Alianza has pushed the conversation about the failures of pro-statehood and pro-commonwealth policies into the open.[19] For the first time, it seemed that the dominance of the PNP and PPD in Puerto Rico could break and that a pro-independence advocate could actually have a shot at becoming the governor, making 2024 a historic election for Puerto Rico.

Bad Bunny has actively used his social media platform to outright criticize the pro-statehood and pro-commonwealth parties. In an interview on the local Puerto Rican YouTube podcast *El Tony Pregunta* on September 2, 2024, Bad Bunny was moved to tears talking about his worries for the future of Puerto Rico, and he encouraged young people to vote. Although he said he preferred to stay out of politics, he discussed his approach to addressing politics in his work, noting that he doesn't like to be dogmatic about it. He said he would not want to release a political song in which he might call PNP candidate Jenniffer González-Colón a liar and wish death to the statehood party.[20] He improvised:

Jenniffer Mentirosa
No seas embustera
Muerte al PNP
A to' lo' corruptos
Puerto Rico se merece algo mejor[21]

Jenniffer's a liar
Don't be deceitful
Death to the PNP
To all the corrupt ones
Puerto Rico deserves something better

Online content creators quickly put Bad Bunny's vocals over an old-school hip-hop beat.[22] The song went viral. T-shirts with "Jenniffer mentirosa, no seas embustera" emblazoned on the front began selling online. In an Instagram conversation with La Alianza/PIP gubernatorial candidate Juan Dalmau, artist Residente wore one of the shirts.[23] Even images of American pop stars like Sabrina Carpenter wearing the shirt surfaced online.[24]

González-Colón was not amused. As the song became increasingly popular, González-Colón responded by stating that Bad Bunny would not have the freedom to say such things if he lived in Venezuela; this was her effort to alarm voters and make them think Bad Bunny preferred a socialist dictatorship to a democracy.[25] In so doing, González-Colón recycled the age-old PNP tactic of promoting fear among Puerto Ricans that independence would have catastrophic consequences. Other members of the PNP fueled the fire of the false discourse, with Thomas Rivera Schatz, president of the Senate in Puerto Rico, referring to La Alianza as "La Alianza Comunista" (The Communist Alliance).[26]

Although Bad Bunny told El Tony that he preferred to stay out of politics, he found himself in a political maelstrom and the target of PNP ire. Rebuttals to González-Colón emerged across social media accounts, including from independent journalists like Bianca Graulau, outlining this nonsensical and decontextualized communist fearmongering from the PNP.[27] These responses demonstrated that not only did Bad Bunny have the support of journalists, influencers, and his fans, but that many people were paying attention and heeding his call to get involved.

Prior to 2024, Bad Bunny had stayed relatively quiet about his own political affiliations. During the 2024 elections, a video and an article from 2020 surfaced in which Bad Bunny explained he would not vote for either the PNP or PPD in that year's elections, and that he "would never want to see Puerto Rico as a state."[28] Although lyrics to songs like "El Apagón" might make some listeners assume things about his political position, the 2024 elections became a political turning point for Bad Bunny. Leading up to the elections, he used his platform more clearly and forcefully than ever to advocate for a better future for his homeland through his support of La Alianza.

Just a few weeks after the El Tony / "Jenniffer mentirosa" debacle, Bad Bunny made his next political move. He paid for a series of billboards across Puerto Rico that critiqued the PNP. Each billboard had a message printed in white on a black background. The first read, "Quien vota PNP no ama a Puerto Rico" (Those who vote for PNP don't love Puerto Rico). Additional billboards said, "Votar PNP es votar por la corrupción" (To vote for the PNP is to vote for corruption), and "Votar por PNP es votar por LUMA" (To vote for PNP is to vote for LUMA). The billboards became a source of great controversy in Puerto Rico. Rumors swirled that they were Bad Bunny's billboards, and the PNP filed a complaint with the electoral comptroller, taking issue with the fact that the billboards did not initially-include legally required information regarding who paid for them.[29] And this is when the world got confirmation that, in fact, it was Bad Bunny who had paid for them. On September 24, 2024, a line was added to the bottom of the billboards that said: "Ad paid for by Benito A. Martínez, yoamoapr@gmail.com. It was not authorized by any contender, candidate or political party."[30] Bad Bunny also posted images of the billboards on his social media accounts, along with the confirmation that he had paid for them, and that he was "un puertorriqueño que ama a Puerto Rico" (a Puerto Rican who loves Puerto Rico).[31]

9.2 On September 24, 2024, Bad Bunny posted on X (formerly Twitter) multiple images of political billboards in Puerto Rico that he had sponsored. The text on this billboard translates to: "Those who vote for the PNP do not love Puerto Rico." Bad Bunny's tweet confirmed that he had, indeed, paid for these billboards, and he asserted that he is a Puerto Rican who *does* love Puerto Rico. Photo from X @sanbenito.

9.3 This is another Bad Bunny–sponsored billboard that the artist posted to his social media on September 24, 2024. This billboard translates to: "A vote for the PNP is a vote for corruption." These billboards created tremendous controversy across Puerto Rico and helped lay the foundation for the political efforts Bad Bunny would make in advance of the 2024 gubernatorial election in Puerto Rico. Photo from X @sanbenito.

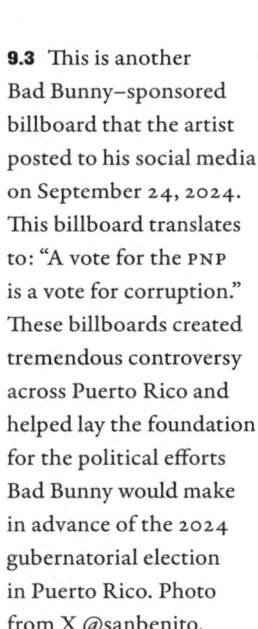

The day after Bad Bunny claimed responsibility for the billboards, a new billboard attacking Bad Bunny appeared in Puerto Rico. This one prominently declared that Senator Rivera Schatz's campaign paid for it, and it included the PNP logo, a dark blue rectangle with a white palm tree in the middle.[32] The billboard said: "El 5 de noviembre, ¡barremos!" (Let's sweep on November 5!) It continued, Para que Benito _ame!" Without the space in front of *ame*, the phrase would read "So that Benito can love it!" However, the blank space in front of _*ame* made clear that the word was actually meant to be *mame*, making the phrase, "So that Benito can suck it!" (referring to fellatio). Puerto Rican media outlets harped on the vulgarity of the billboard.[33] Given the history of the government targeting reggaetón music for its vulgarity, Rivera Schatz's move seemed especially hypocritical.[34]

Rivera Schatz did an interview with the Puerto Rican radio station Magic 93.7 FM on the day his billboard went up. The radio show hosts questioned him about its vulgarity. At first, Rivera Schatz owned up to it, stating, "I invite people to come to their own conclusions. The message is clear." He went on to justify this vulgar message by stating that "these people" (meaning Bad Bunny, and reggaetón artists more generally) "use strong language against" the PNP and the governor, and "in their own lyrics, they use strong language against women." Thus, Rivera Schatz claimed he was merely "giving them a taste of their own medicine" to make "a statement that we are going to win."[35] Later in the interview, when one of the hosts said plainly that *mame* was the intended word, Rivera Schatz snapped, "Do not put words in my mouth!" Instead, he questioned whether anyone who might be offended by his billboard "was offended when Benito used words against the governor, against Jenniffer . . . when he used derogatory words against women in his lyrics."[36] Rivera Schatz reiterated old stereotypes of reggaetón and tired arguments about its vulgarity to make a moral claim about the PNP, whose members were clearly threatened by the fact that the most popular artist in Puerto Rico, and one of the most popular in the world, was calling out their hypocrisy and corruption.

But this was not the end of the billboards attacking Bad Bunny. Within about a week, additional billboards appeared alongside Puerto Rico's Highway 22, which runs along the north coast of Puerto Rico and through Bad Bunny's hometown of Vega Baja. The first said, "Benito vive en Los Ángeles y su novia es gringa. ¿Así amas a Puerto Rico?" (Benito lives in Los Angeles and has a white girlfriend. That's how you love Puerto Rico?). The other suggested that Bad Bunny benefited from the tax incentives of Puerto Rico's Act 60, followed by "#Hipocresía."[37] Rivera Schatz had peddled this falsehood earlier during the aforementioned radio interview. He said: "There are some people here who do not live in Puerto Rico who criticize Act 60 but benefit from it. . . . They are hypocrites." Yet most Puerto Ricans from the archipelago are not eligible for these tax breaks since, to claim the benefit, one has to have been a resident outside of Puerto Rico for at least ten years before settling back on the archipelago.[38] Bad Bunny never stopped being a resident of Puerto Rico. The longest time he has ever been away from Puerto Rico is seven months.[39] Bad Bunny's tax status had previously been debated publicly when Act 60 beneficiary and US YouTube personality Logan Paul became upset after he was called out in the "El Apagón" / *Aquí Vive Gente* music video and documentary. In response, Paul erroneously accused Bad Bunny of enjoying the same tax breaks he critiqued in the film.[40] That these false accusations were being regurgitated by the PNP proved Bad Bunny's point—that they are mentirosos.

In comments on social media, many Puerto Ricans noted the ridiculousness of the PNP's hyperfocus on Bad Bunny as an individual. A Facebook user with the username Assilem Maldonado said: "BB [Bad Bunny] is not even running as a politician, and he is already in the attacks of the PNP. [Puerto Rico] is a joke to the PNP, and they talk about a dictatorship, but they live for attacking those who think differently than them, how poorly things are going for us. Why so much focus on BB?"[41] Another Facebook user, Kariana Ashley Feliciano, said: "As if Bad Bunny were a candidate."[42]

The Highway 22 billboards did not get the same amount of media attention as the earlier ones from Bad Bunny and Rivera Schatz. As a Facebook post made by the Puerto Rican local news show *Directo y Sin Filtro* on ABC-5 underscored, these billboards had none of the legally required information regarding who paid for them.[43] Another Facebook user Raúl Cabán Pérez made the accusation, "Since the attack isn't against the PNP, they don't care who paid for it."[44] No news emerged regarding who did pay for them, but the information on the billboards was clearly in defense of the PNP and echoed the lies that Rivera Schatz spewed in his radio interview.

Just a few days later, Bad Bunny sponsored additional billboards targeting both the PNP and PPD. One said "Cada vez que se te vaya la luz, recuerda que es culpa del PNP y PPD" (Every time your electricity goes out, remember that it's the PNP and PPD's fault). Another stated, "El PNP no es estadidad. El PNP es corrupción" (The PNP is not statehood. The PNP is corruption).[45] A third said, "No olvides lo que dijeron en el chat. El PNP quiere un Puerto Rico sin Puertorriqueños. ¡Que se vayan ellos!"

(Don't forget what they said in the chat. The PNP wants a Puerto Rico without Puerto Ricans. They should leave!)[46] In that final billboard, Bad Bunny referenced disgraced former Governor Ricardo Rosselló's remark in the infamous 2019 "Chatgate" chats that said: "I saw the future. It's so wonderful, there are no Puerto Ricans."[47] He also referenced the end of his own song "El Apagón," when Gabriela Berlingeri sings, "Que se vayan ellos, que se vayan ellos." Despite criticism from Rivera Schatz and other PNP supporters, Bad Bunny remained resolute.

On October 29, 2024, a pointed video ad discussing the crisis of education in Puerto Rico made its rounds on social media and Puerto Rican television. Bad Bunny teamed up again with director Kacho López Mari for the ad. According to Kacho, Bad Bunny wrote the script, and Kacho directed and edited the clip. The poignant advertisement highlights how Puerto Rican youth have suffered as a result of cuts to education in Puerto Rico. With striking imagery of damaged schools and discouraged, yet hopeful, young faces, the ad underscores the harsh reality that more than six hundred schools in Puerto Rico have closed in the last decade. "I don't want to leave Puerto Rico," one child says. "They rob our present and our future," another says. "The same two parties have robbed all the money," the video declares. It ends with "We need a change," before it identifies Benito A. Martínez Ocasio as the person who paid for the ads (with small text and sped-up audio).

Between the "Jenniffer mentirosa" song, the billboards, and this new commercial, Bad Bunny caused a hullabaloo across Puerto Rico. So, he decided to make a public statement. On November 1, 2024, he took out a full-page ad called "Muerte al PNP" in the Puerto Rican daily newspaper *El Nuevo Día*. It consisted of a letter that Bad Bunny addressed to PNP/statehood supporters, "and not to the politicians who take advantage of them." The letter took up one full page of the paper despite its very small print, and appeared on the first page of that day's issue. In it, Bad Bunny once again made clear that his concern was the well-being of Puerto Rico and its people, not an alliance with any specific political party.[48]

Bad Bunny also clarified his differentiation between those who support the PNP and those who support statehood. "To be pro-statehood is to want Puerto Rico to be another state of the United States, but to be a 'penepe' [PNP] today is to support and be complicit in THE CORRUPTION OF THAT PARTY" (capitalization in the original). Furthermore, since people like González-Colón and Rivera Schatz had both accused him of actually wishing death upon people, Bad Bunny explained:

"DEATH TO PNP" is not the death of a human, "DEATH TO PNP" is the death of the party that has failed the people, that has stolen from the people, that has lied to the people, that has disrespected the people, and when I say "the people" I include you, too, because you are part of the people, too. You also lose power every day while they charge you more every time. You also got your pension money stolen. You also have to go to hospitals that are in shambles without specialists or medicines. Your children and grandchildren have also had their schools closed and they have had to watch a loved one leave the country wanting to stay and it is all because the INCOMPETENT AND CORRUPT PNP GOVERNMENT affects everyone equally (obviously, except their little friend$).

Bad Bunny told his fellow Puerto Ricans who are PNP supporters that the PNP doesn't "even respect you, their most faithful followers, or did they perhaps forget that phrase worse than mine in Ricky's famous chat: 'WE EVEN FOOL OUR OWN PEOPLE'? That phrase was for you, not for anyone else, and it didn't come from me, it came from them."[49] Here, Bad Bunny once again called out the hypocrisy of the PNP that criticized him for using offensive language when it was really the PNP that offended and took advantage of Puerto Rico. Throughout the letter, Bad Bunny emphasized that, for him, the elections were not about political parties but about ending the well-documented corruption that Puerto Rico faced (and continues to face) under the PNP leadership.

On November 3, 2024, at least 50,000 people attended the closing campaign event for La Alianza aptly called Festival de la Esperanza, or Festival of Hope.[50] The event was produced by Tristana Robles, with Kacho as the creative director.[51] Representatives from both PIP and MVC spoke at the festival, but there was also a tremendous soundtrack. Artists like Residente, Jowell y Randy, iLe, Kany García, Rafa Pabön, Chuwi, Fabiola Méndez, and others performed throughout the day-long event. Many expected Bad Bunny to appear. Nearly six hours into the event, he took the stage.

Bad Bunny began with a thirty-minute speech that brought together the various pieces of the political messaging he had been communicating throughout the fall with his billboards, interviews, ads, and his own music. During the speech, he spoke of his hopes for a better future for Puerto Rico. "I dream of a Puerto Rico where the education of our children is a priority and not a dirty system of corruption," he declared. "I dream of a Puerto Rico where young people don't have to leave to fulfill their dreams. I dream of a functional and accessible healthcare system.... I dream of roads where I don't blow a tire every time I go out. I dream of something as basic as the power not going out every day in my country. I dream of an awakened people who recognize the strength we have, that here the people are in charge, that here you are in charge, we are in charge—not political parties."[52]

After recounting that he voted for PNP candidate Luis Fortuño the first time he was eligible to vote (he noted it was the only time he voted PNP), he expressed how he has changed since that first vote. Bad Bunny also acknowledged the new generations of Puerto Ricans, many of them his fans, who had been supporting this movement for Puerto Rico. He said, "It fills me with pride that it's the young people, the youth, the heart of this movement demanding change." He pointed out that the election could be a turning point in Puerto Rico, where the two political parties, PNP and PPD, who for "over five decades, have deceived, lied, and profited from the people, who've disrespected Puerto Ricans," might finally be ousted from power so a new Puerto Rico could emerge.[53] With this speech, Bad Bunny firmly situated himself as part of the "Yo No Me Dejo" generation, that is, the young people who "won't let you" (meaning the government) continue damaging Puerto Rico.[54] Political scientist José Laguarta Ramírez sees a direct through line between Bad Bunny and his generation, and earlier activists and political mobilizations against both the US colonialism and Puerto Rican government corruption and austerity measures.[55]

In this vein, Bad Bunny reaffirmed his deep devotion to his homeland: "I'm here because I love my country as much as I love my mother, and I'd give my life for her." He made clear that his number one allegiance was to the people of Puerto Rico who, he said, had "given a powerful, real endorsement.... It's you, who have inspired me once again, you, the people of Puerto Rico, who've told me that this November 5, we should vote for Juan Dalmau and La Alianza de País."[56] Kacho explained to us that this historic event, which was a culmination of the growing acceptance and popularity of the independence movement in Puerto Rico, was both vindicating and emotional for him and his independentista family. For Kacho, it was especially moving to hear one of Puerto Rico's biggest stars speak about independence: "Tears were shed. Seeing Benito standing there, this mega star who has the whole world looking at him, saying, 'This is what has to be done!' To see this country standing up saying, 'We are Puerto Ricans. This is our flag. This is who we are.' That's resistance. And it is so significant."

As Bad Bunny finished his speech, he teased the themes of the song he would perform as well as the reality that the forecast for election day was heavy rain. "In two days, rain, thunder, lightning, nothing will stop us from making history!" he exclaimed. He reminded the audience of the disregard, corruption, and ineptitude that the people of Puerto Rico faced under PNP leadership in the wake of Hurricane María. "I will never forget how those people abandoned us during the hurricane," he said. In contrast, he warned that, "This Tuesday, November 5, we will be the storm, and nothing will save them from us."[57]

This line referenced a lyric in his song "Una Velita": "Por ahí viene tormenta, ¿quién nos va a salvar?" (A storm is coming, who will save us?) It was fitting that the year Bad Bunny came out most explicitly and forcefully in Puerto Rican political discourse, he created yet another moving anthem, "Una Velita." Tainy produced the track, which was released on September 19, 2024, the seventh anniversary of Hurricane María. "Una Velita," which translates to "A Little Candle," recounts the ubiquitous anxiety many Puerto Ricans feel about a coming hurricane after the trauma of Hurricane María, a feeling that Bad Bunny said inspired the song.[58]

At the same time, "Una Velita" presents a storm as a metaphor for the coming election. Not only was the song released on the anniversary of Hurricane María, but it was also released just a few days prior to the Puerto Rican voter registration deadline of September 21. In the song, Bad Bunny directly criticizes the PNP, noting that they do not do anything for the people and actively take from them. At one point, he raps, "La palma en la que quieren ahorcar el país, un día de estos la vamos a tumbar" (The palm tree they want to use to hang the country, one of these days we'll tear it down). Here, he not only argues that the PNP is actively harming Puerto Rico, he also asserts that the Puerto Rican people will demolish the PNP, as symbolized by the palm tree.

"Una Velita" also incorporated direct references to Puerto Rican independence. In one especially powerful line, Bad Bunny states "La señal ya se dio y no la quieren ver / Falta que el boricua quiera despertar" (The signal has already been given, but they don't want to see it / We just need Puerto Ricans to wake up). This line references the poem "La Borinqueña," also referred to as the "Himno Revolucionario" (Revolutionary anthem) by Lola Rodríguez de Tió, a nineteenth century poet and activist for abolition, women's rights, and Puerto Rican independence. Now, however, there are multiple versions of lyrics to the anthem "La Borinqueña." Rodríguez de Tió's poem was originally sung over a traditional Puerto Rican danza composition from the early 1860s. While the music of "La Boriqueña" has remained, the lyrics have shifted over time. The words to the current official national anthem "La Borinqueña," written by Manuel Fernández Juncos in 1903, celebrate the beauty of Puerto Rico. However, the words from Rodríguez de Tió's original "La Borinqueña" were inspired by the Grito de Lares in 1868, a revolt organized by independence activists to oust Spain from Puerto Rico and to abolish slavery. The Spanish military responded swiftly and aggressively, arresting hundreds. Despite the fact that the revolution did not succeed, it remains a major symbol of Puerto Rican nationalism and pro-independence movements.[59] Rodríguez de Tió's version begins, "¡Diespierta Borinqueño / Que han dado la señal!" (Wake up, Boricua / They have given us the signal). Despite being adopted initially as the lyrics of the danza composition, these words were eventually considered too controversial, and were thus replaced with those penned by Fernández Juncos.[60] Since then, this line has served as a call for Puerto Rican independence. Bad Bunny's rephrasing of Rodríguez de Tió's line directly ties "Una Velita" to this broader revolutionary history.

Tainy's production on the song mirrors the intensity and haunting qualities of Bad Bunny's lyrics and delivery. The song begins with some minor synth chords and winds swirling in the background as a youthful chorus sings. Then, bomba drums come in, providing the rhythmic base for the track. Bad Bunny hums dramatically between his verses in a pitch that fluctuates throughout the track. In its lower pitch, it sounds like the deep moan of someone in pain. As the pitch gets higher, it turns into an erratic cry—perhaps the cry of the wind approaching with the storm, unpredictable and bringing trouble. The ending of "Una Velita" sees a mood change. The song moves from the intense energy of simultaneous fear and fearlessness to a softer, more melodic tone. A high-pitched voice sings that the sun will come out again. Nothing, not even immense uncertainty and change, is scary with loved ones by your side, the song suggests. Thus, the song ends on a note of love and hope—esperanza.

Bad Bunny performed "Una Velita" live for the first time at the Festival de la Esperanza. The performance began with nearly one minute of intense drumming on the barril—the signature drum of Puerto Rican bomba music. Then, a team of backup singers began with the first few lines of Lola Rodríguez de Tió's "La Borinqueña": "Despierta Borinqueño / Que

9.4 Bad Bunny performed his song "Una Velita" at La Alianza's closing campaign event, the Festival de la Esperanza, November 3, 2024. Photo courtesy of Thais Llorca.

han dado la señal." The stage is almost pitch black save for the candles in the singers' hands. It mimics a blackout and conjures up the darkness of the coming storm. Suddenly, the chords begin and the chorus sings the opening lines to "Una Velita." The drummers accompany Bad Bunny throughout the entire song, and the all-women chorus perform the dynamic humming. On the streamed recording of the concert, Bad Bunny moves across the stage, occasionally standing to the side so as not to block the view of the other musicians, while the foreground shows a sea of more than 50,000 Puerto Ricans waving Puerto Rican flags and green and white Independence Party flags. The imagery is moving. It is emotional. It feels like we are witnessing the beginning of yet another revolution, another push for major change. Like the proverbial "palma" that Bad Bunny references in the song is going to get taken down. In polls leading up to the election, Dalmau was neck in neck with González-Colón. At the end of the performance, as the lyrics explain that he is waiting for the sun to come back out, the imagery of a sun rising is projected on the stage. There is hope.

The day before the elections, there was uproar particularly from La Alianza after a district court in Puerto Rico gave the PNP permission to count early votes outside of the normal process; typically, representatives from each party would participate in the vote count, but in this instance, Judge Raúl Candelario López ruled that the PNP could begin counting votes alone.[61] Bad Bunny posted to social media: "It's messed up that those who have spent thousands on a fear campaign with dictatorship and communism are the same ones who have screwed up democracy and the electoral process in Puerto Rico. They are the same ones who have been doing a thousand tricks and juggling with the people's vote. The PNP is trying to steal the elections!"[62]

On election day, when a journalist asked what he would recommend to those who haven't decided who they're voting for, Bad Bunny implored, "Listen to your heart. . . . The Puerto Rican people are not stupid. Puerto Ricans are intelligent. And I'm sure that they know what the best decision is for Puerto Rico. I would say think about your children, think about your grandchildren, think about your future, think about yourselves, those who have left and want to return, that they listen to their hearts."[63]

In the end, despite controversy over the election outcomes, the PNP prevailed. But Puerto Ricans are not discouraged. This election completely reconfigured Puerto Rican politics, making La Alianza (and the parties they represent) central players in the Puerto Rican political system. Puerto Rico's two party system dominated by PNP and PPD has been broken. While Dalmau's highly contested loss may seem like another hit to Puerto Rican resistance, even his supporters feel moved and motivated. In an interview the day after the elections, November 6, 2024, Residente said, "This is a great triumph. . . . We got more than 30 percent [of the vote]. [The PNP and PPD] are scared, not because Puerto Rico is doing worse, but because they're doing worse."[64] That same day, Bad Bunny wrote a lengthy post on social media, explaining his pride, sympathizing with those who feel frustrated, but also underscoring the hope he feels "because more and more people are waking up and joining those who dream and fight for a better Puerto Rico. We are still here, we are not giving up." With more encouraging words, his post continues:

My people, nothing was in vain. We educate with love and patience. Here we will continue to raise our voice and defend our land. Whoever governs, I have always been and will always be available and ready to contribute to my country as I have always done. Whoever governs, we will be vigilant, monitoring, and ensuring that things are done right and we will not wait four years to confront anyone who does things wrong. It is up to the people to defend what is ours. The people have changed and you can feel it. . . . I LOVE YOU Puerto Rico. We are still here, we are not leaving.[65]

Though he constantly reiterates that he is not interested in running for office, Bad Bunny has demonstrated his ability to be a leader and an agent for change. We will never be able to calculate exactly how much Bad Bunny's involvement impacted the Puerto Rican elections. However, we cannot ignore that this historic election occurred while Bad Bunny was shaping political discourse through billboards, social media, and ad campaigns focused on key issues like education in Puerto Rico. What is clear is that major changes are happening in Puerto Rico, and Bad Bunny has been central to those conversations.

Just as the Grito de Lares did not succeed in ousting Spain, the hard work of organizers for La Alianza and the creative efforts of Bad Bunny, Kacho López Mari, Residente, and other artists who came out in support of the independence candidate did not succeed in tumbando la palma, as Bad Bunny sings about in "Una Velita." But, like the revolutionaries who led the Grito de Lares succeeded in winning "a decisive symbolic battle,"[66] so too did independence candidate Juan Dalmau and those who supported him. The process of cutting down the palm tree will be a long one. It has grown out of corruption. It has grown out of false claims about what the possibility of statehood can bring Puerto Rico. But the colonial realities have never been clearer. Statehood is not an option. The current US government has explicitly said that they will not admit Puerto Rico as a state, and no plebiscite has ever shown any movement toward statehood.[67] "Una Velita" uses the very words from Rodríguez de Tió's "La Borinqueña" to motivate Puerto Ricans today. This lyrical link demonstrates that resistance has never stopped. It has only evolved.

CONCLUSION

"SEGUIMOS AQUÍ"

Without Puerto Rico, I wouldn't have made it. That's why I always include you in my dreams, why I always share my achievements with you, and why I'll always, always be here for you. You've supported me, loved me, believed in me, defended me, and most importantly, you've inspired me. You've inspired me. That's why I'll always represent you. I represent you, and I'll always represent you with the purest pride, wherever I go.

BAD BUNNY, SPEECH AT FESTIVAL DE LA ESPERANZA

On January 5, 2025—the eve of the important Puerto Rican holiday Día de los Reyes (Three Kings Day)—Bad Bunny dropped his seventh solo studio album *DeBÍ TiRAR MáS FOTòS (DTMF)*.[1] Fans already had a series of hints about the album's themes, from the traditional Christmas aguinaldo in his second single "PIToRRO DE COCO," to a Google Map/ Spotify scavenger hunt leading fans around Puerto Rico to find titles of songs, to a short film starring legendary Puerto Rican actor and director Jacobo Morales, to Apple Music's release of intimate behind-the-scenes photos of Bad Bunny and his team in the Puerto Rican countryside working on the album. As Marissa Lopez of Apple Music told us, "We [Apple Music] went to him and said, 'We would love to tease the album. . . . It will give a premonition of what's coming. Send us photos that you took while you were creating the album.'" On December 24, 2024, just two weeks before the album dropped, a post on Apple Music's Instagram feed featured several intimate photos from the production of *DTMF*. In one, Bad Bunny shaves in the mirror. In another, MAG and Tainy are sitting at a table, hard

C.I This image was posted to Apple Music's Instagram account on December 24, 2024. This was part of the plan to drop hints about the imminent release of Bad Bunny's album *DeBÍ TiRAR MáS FOToS*. Here, Bad Bunny's two main producers, MAG and Tainy, are working together on the album. Photo from Instagram @applemusic.

at work on their computers. Fans even get a glimpse of the working environment, with a photo of a computer on a table on a covered patio with the Puerto Rican mountains in the background. Marissa told us, "Benito took a lot of them. It caused a huge rage, and the fans were like, 'Oh, my God! Something's coming.' It went viral. And then he dropped the album, of course, which was massive. And the album did everything that we knew it was going to do."

DTMF quickly became number one on every streaming platform and received critical acclaim from numerous prestigious publications and music critics. As with his 2022 album *Un Verano Sin Ti*, many reviews referred to *DTMF* as a love letter to Puerto Rico.[2] But labeling this album a love letter massively oversimplified what Bad Bunny was doing. In *DTMF*, Bad Bunny's commitment to Puerto Rico was clearer than ever before—the album's songs celebrate Puerto Rico as the most beautiful, wonderful place on the earth, but they also warn that everything that makes it special is at risk.

This was perhaps best exemplified by the symbol of the sapo concho, the endangered crested toad native to Puerto Rico. The sapo concho appeared in many of the teasers for *DTMF*, including the short film that Bad Bunny released just days before the album. Invasive foreign toad species and the destruction of the crested toad's natural habitat due to land development has pushed the sapo concho to the brink of extinction. In the short film, actor Jacobo Morales digs up a box of photographs out of the ground in the Puerto Rican countryside—a direct link to the end of the music video for the album's first single "EL CLúB," when Bad Bunny buries the box (an image of this moment was among the photos posted by Apple Music to tease the album). Playing the role of an aging Bad Bunny, Morales brings the box back to his home, where he goes through the photos with his friend Concho, the crested toad. The pair are hungry, and Morales decides to stop by a local bakery to grab a snack. He walks past homes occupied by Americans playing loud rock and country (as opposed to the reggaetón he used to hear) to buy food for himself and Concho at a local bakery. There, Morales encounters an English-speaking American cashier who offers him strange versions of Puerto Rican food, most notably a traditional quesito (cheese-filled puff pastry) *without* the cheese. In a poignant moment, a young Puerto Rican man pays for Morales, who does not have a phone to use at the newly cashless bakery. "*Seguimos aquí*," he tells Morales. We're still here. Just like the endangered sapo concho, the video's message makes clear that what is at stake is the loss not just of Puerto Rican culture but of Puerto Rico as a whole. Puerto Ricans must continue to fight for their culture and their community.

The songs included on the album continue in this vein. As MAG explained to us, the album is a "loop" that begins in New York with the song "NUEVAYoL," goes back to Puerto Rico with the second track "VOY A LLeVARTE PA PR" (I'm going to take you to PR) and continues until the final track "LA MuDANZA" (The move) starts the loop of migration via music again. MAG explained that from the very beginning, the concept of the album was to "tak[e] you on a journey through the sounds of Puerto Rico." This includes the sounds of Puerto Rico that took shape in (or were heavily influenced by) the diaspora. The unique blends of plena, salsa, bomba, and música jíbara with the reggaetón, dembow, and

C.2 This still shot from the short film *DeBÍ TiRAR MáS FOToS* depicts actor Jacobo Morales (playing an older Bad Bunny) complaining that the bakery had cheeseless quesitos and that they should not be allowed to be called quesitos if they don't have cheese. His friend, Concho—an endangered sapo concho, or crested toad—listens as he munches on a cheese-filled quesito. Morales sips from a small green plastic cup made from an old margarine container; these plastic cups are another Puerto Rican cultural reference given that they are (or were) ubiquitous in Puerto Rican households. These visual cues contribute to the film's overall warning that gentrification threatens Puerto Rican ways of life. The short film was posted to YouTube on January 3, 2025, three days before Bad Bunny's album by the same name was released. Film directed by Bad Bunny and Arí Maniel Cruz Suárez, produced by Rimas Entertainment.

trap sounds that fans have grown accustomed to hearing from Bad Bunny clearly illustrate this sonic concept. Bad Bunny was not the first person to do this; for instance, his idol Tego Calderón's debut record *El Abayarde* was celebrated for its fusions of salsa and bomba with reggaetón. Whereas Calderón's work brought reggaetón into the mainstream in Puerto Rico, DTMF used this same strategy to bring these traditional Puerto Rican sounds to the global mainstream pop market. As Jerry Pullés of Apple Music explained to us, "Those types of rhythms are really important to different groups of people, but it's not the stuff that you usually see hit the mainstream, and I just hope that the legacy of this album is that he helped, you know, make those very traditional, folkloric sounds something that's accepted in the mainstream."

More than the sounds, the songs themselves bring listeners on a journey through Puerto Rico. Some songs are typical party songs. Rather than outliers, they are couched between songs with more explicit political content, suggesting that joy and celebration continue to be part of the protest. The album's final song, "LA MuDANZA," is a fast-paced salsa song that ends with the joyous and triumphant refrain, "Yo soy de P FKN R." Even with the party vibes of the song, Bad Bunny inserts overt political messaging into his lyrics. For instance, in the second verse Bad Bunny sings: "Si mañana muero, yo espero que nunca olviden mi rostro / Y pongan un tema mío el día que traigan a Hostos / En la caja la bandera azul clarito" (If I die tomorrow, I hope they never forget my face / And that they play one of my songs on the day they bring back Hostos / With the light-blue flag on the coffin). Hostos is Eugenio María de Hostos, a Puerto Rican intellectual and independence activist from the nineteenth century. Hostos died in 1903. He is interred in the Dominican Republic, where he said he wanted his remains to stay until Puerto Rico became independent.[3] The line about the pro-independence Puerto Rican flag with the light-blue triangle being draped over a coffin directly links the two men since it is unclear if the coffin is Bad Bunny's or that of Hostos. The overlap between the two suggests that they could be one and the same, and it directly aligns Bad Bunny with one of the most important figures in Puerto Rican independence.

While virtually every song on DTMF addresses some aspect of Puerto Rican politics, perhaps none does so as forcefully as "LO QUE LE PASÓ A HAWAii," which translates to "What happened to Hawai'i." The slow, haunting song warns Puerto Ricans that their land, their culture, their very existence might disappear. Like Puerto Rico, the United States declared Hawai'i an American territory in 1898. Although it became a state in 1959, Hawai'i faces many of the same issues as Puerto Rico, from wealthy Americans taking over Indigenous Hawaiian lands (often illegally) to the decimation of Hawaiian culture.[4] In his song, Bad Bunny warns:

Quieren quitarme el río
Y también la playa
Quieren el barrio mío
Y que mi abuelita se vaya
No, no suelta la bandera

No olvide el lelolai
Porque no quiero que pase contigo
Lo que le pasó a Hawai'i

They want to take my river
And also the beach
They want my neighborhood
And for my grandmother to leave
Don't let go of the flag
Don't forget the lelolai
Because I don't want what happened to Hawai'i
To happen to you

Bad Bunny explicitly warns about the displacement and erasure of Puerto Ricans and Puerto Rican culture, directly calling out the beaches and barrios that make Puerto Rico home but that are also in danger of being bought up and destroyed by foreign-backed development. For instance, *lelolai* is a Puerto Rican phrase included in many traditional songs on the archipelago. He combines this with the image of an elderly grandmother remaining in Puerto Rico, as if the last vestiges of Puerto Rican life were hanging on. More than a call to hold onto Puerto Rican culture, though, this song also makes a direct comment on US imperialism and its ongoing effects, linking together Hawai'i and Puerto Rico as island territories of the United States.

The music videos for many of the songs of DTMF similarly address these themes. The very first single from the album, "EL CLúB," was released on December 5, 2024. The music video depicts Bad Bunny ruminating over the end of his relationship. It ends with Bad Bunny wandering through the Puerto Rican countryside carrying a box of photos. Four jíbaros follow behind him. The idealized image of the jíbaro depicts a man, often imagined as a white Puerto Rican, who lives in the rural interior of Puerto Rico and maintains an authentically Puerto Rican way of life unsullied by the influence of Americanization in particular. He is typically pictured wearing a straw hat known as a pava, a white guayabera, and slacks. Some scholars have critiqued the jíbaro figure for homogenizing the rural Puerto Rican experience and marginalizing Blackness and Afro–Puerto Rican history.[5] Nevertheless, the jíbaro has remained the embodiment of Puerto Rican national culture. In "EL CLúB," the four jíbaros who follow Bad Bunny through the campo are faceless, suggesting that they are ghosts who linger on the land. At the end of the video, he buries his box of photos and plants a small Puerto Rican independence flag at the site.

We might also interpret the ghostly jíbaros as a nod to the overarching theme of displacement that pervades DTMF. This is evident in other music videos for the album, too. The music video for "PIToRRO DE COCO" features Bad Bunny drinking pitorro (Puerto Rican moonshine) with his elders. A homemade sign stating "Aquí te espero, Boricua" (I'm waiting for you here, Boricua) is secured onto the overhang covering the patio where they are sitting. The song itself laments the end of a relationship. But more than waiting for a former lover, the sign suggests that the community is waiting for the return of those Puerto Ricans who have had to leave for the United States mainland. The music video for "TURiSTA" similarly addresses displacement. In that music video, Bad Bunny plays the role of a house cleaner who must clean up after tourists who have trashed their vacation rental. The simple video carries a deep message that shows the consequences of the displacement of Puerto Ricans as a result of gentrification, much of which has been driven by the boom in private short-term rentals from digital platforms like Airbnb.[6]

The music video for "LA MuDANZA" similarly foregrounds this protest against displacement, with the words "No Me Quiero Ir De Aquí"—which translates to "I don't want to leave here" and references the iconic phrase from his song "El Apagón"—plastered in white over a black background. Just like the song's lyrics, the music video includes imagery that references Puerto Rican independence, most notably in an extensive scene of Bad Bunny sprinting through the countryside carrying a large Puerto Rican flag. A group of officials dressed in all black chase him until he escapes behind a group of young Puerto Ricans in light-blue jumpsuits pointing sticks shaped like rifles at the law enforcement officers. This scene, along with the lyric "aquí mataron gente por sacar la bandera" (here they killed people for showing the flag) references La Ley de la Mordaza (also known as the Gag Law), which was passed in 1948 and remained in effect until 1957. Not only did the Gag Law prohibit any discussion of independence (even in private), it also made it a felony to display the Puerto Rican flag (even in one's home). After escaping the authorities, Bad Bunny makes his way past the black sign and approaches a large crowd where a woman places a Puerto Rican pava on his head. The crowd is composed of musicians and dancers who are as much celebrating as they are protesting—again making that connection between music, resistance, and joy—until, at the end, a drone shot shows the crowd spelling out P FKN R

C.3 Still from the music video "La MuDANZA," released on March 10, 2025. This scene features Bad Bunny running through the countryside holding a Puerto Rican flag with the light blue triangle which is associated with Puerto Rican independence. A group of unidentified officials chase him. This scene, along with the song's lyrics, reference the Ley de La Mordaza, or Gag Law, that from 1948 to 1957 prohibited anyone from displaying the Puerto Rican flag. Video directed by Janthony Oliveras.

with their bodies. These music videos thus amplify the message of *DTMF* as a whole, which, like P FKN R, is both a call to action and a celebration of Puerto Rican life and culture.

Just a week after the release of *DTMF*, Bad Bunny announced a residency at El Choli in Puerto Rico, which later took place every weekend between July 11 and September 14, 2025. The name of his residency, "No Me Quiero Ir De Aquí," references what Bad Bunny expressed in the announcement: his desire to stay home.[7] Only residents of Puerto Rico could purchase tickets to the first nine shows of the summer residency, with the rest of the dates available for anyone who could get their hands on tickets. But the residency's massive popularity, with more than 2.5 million people registering for access to be able to purchase only a few hundred thousand tickets, led to the residency expanding from its original twenty-one dates to thirty. For the resident-only shows, tickets were exclusively sold in person. People literally camped out for days in nine different towns throughout Puerto Rico waiting to get a card with a QR code that would enable them to purchase tickets.[8] Tickets sold out the first day they went on sale.

The remaining shows, available to anyone in the world, sold out in under four hours.[9] This made Bad Bunny's residency historic not only

C.4 This photograph was posted to MAG's Instagram account to celebrate the release of *DeBÍ TiRAR MáS FOToS* (January 2025). It depicts Bad Bunny seated at a makeshift production studio, with the mountains of central Puerto Rico in the background. This part of Puerto Rico is often associated with the jíbaro, the rural and traditional farmer who has come to represent traditional Puerto Rican culture; the album itself pays homage to Puerto Rican culture. Bad Bunny and his production team, including MAG, stayed together in the Puerto Rican countryside to finish the album. Photo from Instagram @itz_mag.

because it was the first formal residency by any singer at El Choli but also because they were the fastest-selling tickets in the history of the venue.[10] On September 15, the day after the residency had supposedly ended, an additional residents-only show was added. On September 20, Bad Bunny's residency finale was livestreamed around the world via Amazon Music. It was the most-watched solo artist show in the app's history. Because the residency took place during hurricane season, which is typically low season for tourism in Puerto Rico, the residency made an even bigger impact on the Puerto Rican economy than it would have at other times of the year.[11] Others have pointed out that it naturally increased Airbnb rentals, which can have a detrimental impact on Puerto Rican locals.[12] Still, Bad Bunny's bold move to create a residency at this iconic venue in his homeland, as opposed to opting for something like a residency in Las Vegas as so many other artists have done, emphasizes his determination to contribute to Puerto Rico. After the backlash he faced for moving to Los Angeles during *Nadie Sabe*, everything about the residency—from its location in Puerto Rico, to reserving tickets specifically for Puerto Rican residents, to the residency's name that directly contests the displacement of Puerto Ricans—underscores that Bad Bunny remains committed to Puerto Rico.

In *DTMF*, Bad Bunny lyrically links all the crises and struggles of Puerto Rico that we have addressed throughout this book. Bad Bunny has shown us his dedication to his homeland and to his generation. He has demonstrated his determination to pay homage to those who came before him. He has musically led his generation through tremendously uncertain and difficult times, offering hope and joy, two things that make it possible for resistance movements to continue growing. He has contributed to a shifting political and cultural landscape in Puerto Rico. While he is not an organizer and he does not attempt to take credit for the mass anti-colonial movement in Puerto Rico, he does help build its soundtrack. He is a key part of the contemporary face of resistance in Puerto Rico. And regardless of whatever else he may do as an artist, in just a decade of music-making, political advocacy, and social engagement, he has left his mark on Puerto Rican politics and on global culture.

ACKNOWLEDGMENTS

This book evolved out of a short Zoom call we had in the summer of 2022. Petra had created her Bad Bunny class at Wellesley, and Vanessa reached out while preparing her own Bad Bunny class. That conversation led to the creation of a website called the Bad Bunny Syllabus, which provides educational resources to help contextualize Bad Bunny's work. After teaching our classes for a few semesters and seeing our website grow, we decided to write a book that would build from this work. We write this book for our children so that they can know their histories, and for our fathers, who taught us to love and be proud of all things Puerto Rican.

Many people made this book possible. First, we thank everyone who generously gave their time and insights during the interviews we conducted for this project: Pablo Batista, Eduardo Cabra, Andrew Chow, De La Ghetto (Rafael Castillo Torres), Krystina De Luna, Carina del Valle Schorske, Mariah Espada, Alejandro García Padilla, iLe (Ileana Cabra Joglar), Jowell (Joel Muñoz Martínez), Gustavo Lopez, Julyssa Lopez, Marissa Lopez, Kacho López Mari, MAG (Marcos Borrero), Emilio Morales, Jerry Pullés, Randy (Randy Ortiz Acevedo), Angie Romero, Eddie Santiago, Tainy (Marco Efraín Masís Fernández), and Jesús Triviño.

We could never have completed this book without the support and guidance of several people who did more than just answer our questions: They gave us advice about navigating the music industry, and they really believed in this project. A huge thank you to Julyssa Lopez of *Rolling Stone*, who supported this project when it was just an idea, and who helped us figure out where to go to tell this story. We want to express deep gratitude to Leila Cobo of *Billboard* for her guidance, encouragement, and support of our work. Thank you to Jerry Pullés, Marissa Lopez, and Krystina De Luna at Apple Music, who have enthusiastically supported us along the way. Thanks to Jason Pascal, whose enthusiasm for this project from our very first meeting helped keep us motivated. Thanks also to Elina Adut, Joel Albelo, Lizbeth Alvarez, Cat Bartosevich, Paul Dryden, Suzy Exposito, Jesús González, Emilio Morales, Mayna Nevarez, Jesús Polanco, Carolina Quixano, Jesús Rodríguez, Anthony Rosa, Colleen Thais, and Richard Vega.

Thank you to Pablo Batista for generously giving his time, for honestly answering our questions, and for trusting us to tell the important history of reggaetón. This is just the beginning!

Thank you to Tainy for talking with us for so long, and for sharing your musical genius with us and the world. We are incredibly grateful for your willingness to be a part of this book. We hope this book will help Akira understand how important your legacy is.

A huge thank you to MAG. We are so grateful to have your support, guidance, and trust in this project. We are so happy that this book connected us, and we are honored to now call you our friend. We know how much you care about documenting this musical history for Zaia Luna and future generations. We hope that we have done your work justice. Thank you for everything.

Mil gracias to Kacho López Mari, who first reached out to Petra to consult on the history of reggaetón videos that he created for Bad Bunny's Coachella set. Who knew that that one phone call would morph into this. We admire your work, artistic vision, and dedication to making the world a better place. It has been a huge honor to have you be a part of this project, and we hope it makes you proud. ¡Viva Puerto Rico libre!

We are so grateful to the scholars who have encouraged us to pursue this project and whose work informed our arguments in this book: Yarimar Bonilla, María Elena Cepeda, Yomaira Figueroa, Marisol LeBrón, Jorell Meléndez-Badillo, Jade Power-Sotomayor, and Jonathan Rosa. Thank you to our colleagues at the Puerto Rico Syllabus for inviting us to collaborate and for creating such an incredible resource. We want to extend a special thank you to Yarimar Bonilla, Cristel Jusino Díaz, Centro, and all the scholars and journalists who participated in Centro's 2023 Bad Bunny Symposium. Thank you to Inés Casillas (UC Santa Barbara) and Angelina Tallaj-García (Fordham University) for inviting us to give talks, which carved out time and space for us to think through this project with other inquiring minds. Thank you to Kate Epstein for your careful reading and editing of our work.

The enthusiasm our editor (and Duke University Press's editorial director) Gisela Fosado had from our first conversation about the book remains unmatched. We could not have done this without your support and encouragement. Thank you also to Ale Mejía at Duke for all your support.

Thank you to all our student research assistants, past and present, who have contributed to the Bad Bunny Syllabus and who offered support as we completed this book. At Loyola Marymount University (LMU): Dennis Marciuska, Mateo-Luis Planas, Carolina Acosta, Natalie Acevedo-Colón, Mani Angeles, Bianca Valentín, Luis Rodríguez, Ivanna Clemesha, Mia Cornelison, Valerie Hernández-Nieblas, Ricardo Bras Nevares, and Sofía Valle Menendez. At Wellesley College: Daniela Findlay, Thandiwe Birchwood, Anna Vorhaben, Cecilia Rao, and Yahana Streeter. We're grateful to all our students who have taken our Bad Bunny courses and to our departments (the American Studies Department at Wellesley and the Chicana/o and Latina/o Studies Department at LMU) for supporting the courses.

We are grateful for the generous funding we have each received to support the research this project required. At Wellesley College, Petra would like to thank the Provost's Office, the Suzy Newhouse Center for the Humanities, the Knapp Social Science Center, the Project on Public Leadership and Action, the Transforming Stories, Spaces, Lives Mellon Grant team, and the Lulu Chow Wang '69 Center for Career Education. At LMU, Vanessa would like to thank Media Arts and a Just Society, the Provost's Office, Global-Local Affairs, the LMU Global Policy Institute, the Bellarmine College of Liberal Arts (BCLA) Dean's Office, BCLA Fellowships Committee, and the BCLA Rains Research Assistant program. Vanessa would also like to thank LMU MarComm for their various forms of support for this work.

PETRA'S PERSONAL ACKNOWLEDGMENTS: Thanks always to Ryan for supporting me through this crazy journey. I appreciate and love you always. Thanks to my children, Adrian and Rafael, for everything always and forever. Thanks to Mom and Dad for always being in my corner and for always supporting me. Thanks to Carmen for introducing me to Bad Bunny many moons ago (I think that "Tú No Vive Así" was the first song you ever played me) and for always keeping me grounded. Thanks to my niece Nalini, this book is for you, too. Thanks to Nico, Brenda, Kevin, Ashley, Titi Cookie, and the rest of the family. I love you all so so so so so much. Special thanks to Susan, Genevieve, and Sabriya for the beers, bundts, and bochinche. Thanks to Irene for always modeling for me and everyone else what it is to be a great teacher-scholar. Thanks to Paul, Yoon, Elena, and Michael for always supporting my work. Thanks to Charisse,

Danielle, Melanie, Tianna, Jenn, Carla, and Maryclaire. (I know I'm forgetting people and I'm sorry!) And the number one thanks to Vanessa—I literally never would have done this without you. I can't even express what this project means to me, and I am eternally grateful that we had the opportunity to come together and make it happen.

VANESSA'S PERSONAL ACKNOWLEDGMENTS: Thank you to my mother, Jeannie, who is the most fearless warrior I know. You kept my siblings and me connected to Puerto Rico and to Puertoricanness when our father could not. To my dad, I wish you were here to read this book and see how we are carrying on your legacy of resistance for Puerto Rico's liberation. You physically left my life far too early, but you gave me the greatest gift— you made me Puerto Rican. To my siblings Woody, Larissa, and Angie: I hope this book makes you proud. To my children, Anacaona and Clemente, may you carry on the legacy of your namesakes, and may this book always remind you that Puerto Rico también es su casa, donde nació su abuelo. To my partner, Ben, thank you for your fierce support of my wildest ideas, for your brilliance, and for your appreciation for Puerto Rico and its music. To Alex, thank you for being a part of this work and for being one of my anchors to Puerto Rico. I'm so grateful for all my chosen family, especially Bridget, Joey, Alana, Liz, Naomi, Jill, and Loren. And, finally, a note of gratitude to my coauthor extraordinaire, Petra: Working with you is so powerful. Our work together embodies the Puerto Rican spirit of resistance that this book is about. For me, our work is a part of an intellectual revolution I hope we continue to see grow. Since our first conversation about our courses, our collaboration has always been grounded in respect and the understanding that we are stronger when we come together. This project exists because we were open to intellectual and creative growth and change, and because we do not subscribe to the competitive and siloed tendencies of our profession. May we continue to document our history, our culture, our resistance, our joy.

NOTES

Epigraph: The front matter epigraph is from the booklet that was distributed to attendees of Bad Bunny's October 12, 2023, listening party for his album *Nadie Sabe Lo Que Va a Pasar Mañana* as they entered the event's venue—the Coliseo de Puerto Rico José Miguel Agrelot (or "El Choli"). Both Petra and Vanessa attended this event.

INTRODUCTION

Note: The chapter title references the following song: Bad Bunny, "¿Quién Tú Eres?," *X 100PRE* (Rimas Entertainment, 2018).

1 Traditionally, pitorro is a homemade Puerto Rican moonshine.

2 Throughout this book we refer to the artist Bad Bunny, whose real name is Benito Martínez Ocasio, by his artist name, unless direct quotes from interviews refer to him otherwise. Several quotes included in this section appear in Vanessa Díaz, "Bad Bunny Took Plena and Salsa Songs to Number One. Here's Why That Matters," *Rolling Stone*, January 20, 2025, https://www.rollingstone.com/music/music-latin/bad-bunny-baile-inolvidabe-dtmf-salsa-plena-1235239752/.

3 Gary Trust, "Bad Bunny's 'DtMF' Dominates Billboard's Global 200 Chart," *Billboard*, January 21, 2025, https://www.billboard.com/music/chart-beat/bad-bunny-dtmf-global-200-chart-number-one-1235879525/.

4 Keith Caulfield, "Bad Bunny's 'El Último Tour del Mundo' Debuts at No. 1 on Billboard 200 Chart, Is First All-Spanish No. 1 Album," *Billboard*, December 6, 2020, https://www.billboard.com/pro/bad-bunny-el-ultimo-tour-del-mundo-billboard-200-number-one/.

5 Billboard's website contains a full overview of Bad Bunny's chart history. See "Bad Bunny," *Billboard*, accessed May 15, 2025, https://www.billboard.com/artist/bad-bunny/chart-history/hsi/.

6 Althea Legaspi, "Bad Bunny Is the Most Streamed Artist on Spotify for Third Consecutive Year," *Rolling Stone*, November 30,

2022, https://www.rollingstone.com/music/music-latin/bad
-bunny-spotify-most-streamed-artists-2022-1234638759/.

7   See the Latin Grammy Awards website for a list of nominations and
    wins: https://www.latingrammy.com/en/artists/bad-bunny/35119-01.

8   Griselda Flores, "Bad Bunny's 'Un Verano Sin Ti' Is Now the Most
    Streamed Album in Spotify History," *Billboard*, July 10, 2023,
    https://www.billboard.com/music/latin/bad-bunny-un-verano
    -sin-ti-most-streamed-album-spotify-history-1235368920
    /; "The 250 Greatest Albums of the 21st Century So Far," *Roll-
    ing Stone*, January 10, 2025, https://www.rollingstone.com
    /music/music-lists/best-albums-21st-century-1235177256
    /ghostface-killah-supreme-clientele-2-1235187823/.

9   Eric Frankenberg, "Bad Bunny Closes Out 2022 with Record-
    Breaking $435 Million in Tour Grosses," *Billboard*, Decem-
    ber 13, 2022, https://www.billboard.com/pro/bad-bunny
    -2022-concerts-earn-record-breaking-435-million/.

10 While it is known colloquially as "Coachella," the full name of this
    event is the Coachella Valley Music and Arts Festival. It is an annual
    festival that takes place in Indio, California, and it is widely recog-
    nized as among the most important music festivals in the world.

11 Robert Lang, "The 10 Biggest Music Tours of 2024," *Deadline*,
    December 13, 2024, https://deadline.com/gallery/top-10-music
    -tours-2024/.

12 Jon Pareles, "Bad Bunny Looks Back and Hunkers Down," *New York
    Times*, October 16, 2023, https://www.nytimes.com/2023/10/16/arts
    /music/bad-bunny-nadie-sabe-lo-que-va-a-pasar-manana-review.html.

13 Vanessa Etienne, "Kendall Jenner Faces Accusations of Cultural Ap-
    propriation in New 818 Tequila Ad," *People*, May 21, 2021, https://
    people.com/food/kendall-jenner-faces-accusations-of-cultural
    -appropriation-new-818-tequila-ad. All the Kardashian and Jen-
    ner sisters have faced extensive scrutiny for appropriating Black
    culture as well as that of other minoritized groups. For example,
    see Cady Lang, "*Keeping Up with the Kardashians* Is Ending. But
    Their Exploitation of Black Women's Aesthetics Continues," *Time*,
    June 10, 2021, https://time.com/6072750/kardashians-blackfishing
    -appropriation/; Eve Buckland, "Moana Was a Person of Colour!
    Kourtney Kardashian Is Accused of 'Cultural Appropriation' for
    Likening Herself to Polynesian Disney Character in Snaps from Kim's
    Controversial 40th Island Birthday," *Daily Mail*, October 29, 2020,
    https://www.dailymail.co.uk/tvshowbiz/article-8892821/Kourtney
    -Kardashian-accused-cultural-appropriation-likening-Moana.html.

14 *Nadie Sabe Lo Que Va a Pasar Mañana* did, in fact, contain many
    references to Puerto Rico and Puerto Rican culture, even if they
    were lost on fans. We discuss this in more detail later in the book.

15   For example, see Maria Sherman, "Music Review: Bad Bunny's
        'Debí Tirar Más Fotos' Is a Love Letter to Puerto Rico," *AP News*,
        January 5, 2025, https://apnews.com/article/bad-bunny-debi
        -tirar-mas-fotos-review-856f8e4f89e48e6ab104a491ae3dbcde.

16   Vanessa Díaz and Petra Rivera-Rideau, "Bad Bunny's New Album Is So
        Much More Than a Love Letter to Puerto Rico," *Latina*, January 15, 2025,
        https://latina.com/bad-bunny-debi-tirar-mas-fotos-album-review/.

17   *YHLQMDLG* is an acronym for "Yo Hago Lo Que Me Da
        La Gana," which translates to "I do what I want."

18   Rosa, "Bad Bunny, Good PR," at 00:24:00–00:27:25; the expletive
        infixation is specifically mentioned at 0:26:13.

19   Meléndez-Badillo, *Puerto Rico*, 1.

20   Meléndez-Badillo, *Puerto Rico*, 4.

21   La Ley de la Mordaza, also known as the Gag Law, prohibited Puerto
        Ricans from displaying the Puerto Rican flag, even in private spaces,
        from 1948 to 1957.

22   Isabelia Herrera, "Bad Bunny Pens Statement Criticizing Puerto
        Rico's Failing Education System," *Remezcla*, October 22, 2018,
        https://remezcla.com/music/bad-bunny-education-puerto-rico/.

23   Jan Figueroa Roqué, "Atraídos por el 'fenónmeno,'" *El Vocero*,
        July 29, 2022, 24.

24   We discuss this at greater length in chapter 4, but for more information
        about the censorship campaign, see Rivera-Rideau, *Remixing Reggaetón*.

25   For instance, see Rivera-Servera, "Reggaetón's Crossings."

26   Feil, *Fearless Vulgarity*.

27   For example, Marisol LeBrón points out how the policing of Puerto
        Rican underground in the 1990s occurred simultaneously with the
        policing of queer nightclubs and spaces. She writes that the two were
        connected because "a general concern with policing bodily autonomy,
        particularly displays of nonnormative sexuality in the public sphere,
        played an important . . . role in designating certain populations for
        surveillance and control." See LeBrón, *Policing Life and Death*, 103.

28   For more analyses of reggaetón and queerness in Puerto Rico, see
        Rivera-Servera, "Reggaetón's Crossings."

29   Herrera, "Bad Bunny Pens Statement."

30   Herrera, "Bad Bunny Pens Statement."

31   Metro PR, "Bad Bunny le contesta a maestra frustrada," *Metro
        PR*, October 19, 2018, https://www.metro.pr/pr/entretenimiento
        /2018/10/19/bad-bunny-le-contesta-maestra-frustrada.html.

32   El Tony PR, "Yo Quiero que mi gente viva feliz en Puerto Rico" Benito
        (Bad Bunny), interview by El Tony, posted September 2, 2024, You-
        Tube, 01:14:43, https://www.youtube.com/watch?v=zw7bLZOnou4.

33   Leila Cobo, "The Bunny King," Bad Bunny special edition issue, *Billboard*,
        December 2022.

34   El Tony PR, "Bad Bunny le contesta," around 1:14:43.

35   See Damaris Suárez, Víctor Rodruíguez Velázquez, and Omaya Sosa Pascual, "A Nightmare for Puerto Ricans to Find a Home, While Others Accumulate Properties," *Centro de Periodismo Investigativo*, December 19, 2022, https://periodismoinvestigativo.com/2022/12/a-nightmare-for-puerto-ricans-to-find-a-home-while-others-accumulate-properties/; Bianca Graulau (@biancagraulau), "Rich people are moving to Puerto Rico and some Puerto Ricans are not happy about it. #boricua #gentrification #doradopuertorico," TikTok, April 15, 2021, https://www.tiktok.com/@biancagraulau/video/6951534168668916997?lang=en.

36   Bad Bunny declined an interview request for this book. All his quotes in this book come from publicly available interviews. His record label, Rimas Entertainment, is not affiliated with this project.

37   The popularity of visualizers has grown in recent years, at the same time as YouTube streams began getting counted in *Billboard*'s data for the Hot 100 charts. For more about YouTube's influence on music distribution and data, see Molanphy, *Old Town Road*, 74–79.

38   You can see Bad Bunny's visualizers on YouTube at "BAD BUNNY—DeBÍ TiRAR MáS FOToS," accessed May 15, 2025, https://www.youtube.com/playlist?list=PLRW7iEDD9RDT_19SQk3uKFkJUCA_uGr7Y. For more on Jorell Meléndez-Badillo's involvement with the project, see Andrea Flores, "Bad Bunny's 'Debí Tirar Más Fotos' Is a Love Letter to Puerto Rico. This Professor Helped Him Tell the Island's History," *De Los/Los Angeles Times*, January 7, 2025, https://www.latimes.com/delos/story/2025-01-07/bad-bunnys-debi-tirar-mas-fotos-puerto-rico-jorell-melendez-badillo-visualizers.

39   Ayala and Bernabe, *Puerto Rico in the American Century*, 1.

40   For an overview of these debates see Erman, *Almost Citizens*; Duany, *Puerto Rican Nation on the Move*; Ramírez, "Indians and Negroes in Spite of Themselves."

41   For more on the Insular Cases, see Fusté, "Repeating Islands of Debt"; Erman, *Almost Citizens*; Burnett and Marshall, *Foreign in a Domestic Sense*.

42   For more details about the limits of Puerto Rican citizenship, see Meléndez-Badillo, *Puerto Rico*, 84; Torruella, "To Be or Not to Be"; and Valle, "Race and the Empire-State."

43   Erman, *Almost Citizens*.

44   Ayala and Bernabe, *Puerto Rico in the American Century*, 171–73.

45   Meléndez-Badillo, *Puerto Rico*, 112.

46   Meléndez-Badillo, *Puerto Rico*, 112. More recently, in 2016, the US Supreme Court issued a ruling in *Puerto Rico v. Sánchez Valle* that only strengthened this arrangement. The court case centered on two men who had been convicted on gun charges by both the US federal government and by Puerto Rican law. The

Supreme Court ruled that they could be prosecuted *only* by the
US federal government. Meléndez-Badillo, *Puerto Rico*, 173.

47　For more information, see Meléndez-Badillo, *Puerto Rico*; Ayala
and Bernabe, *Puerto Rico in the American Century*;
and Powers, "Seeing the U.S. Empire."

48　For an overview of these movements, see Ayala and Bernabe,
Puerto Rico in the American Century, 229–46.

CHAPTER 1. LAS COSAS ESTÁN EMPEORANDO

Note: The chapter title references the early Bad Bunny hit, "Soy Peor"
(Hear This Music, 2016).

1　Bad Bunny, "Bad Bunny ft. Arcángel, De La Ghetto, Ñengo Flow—
ACHO PR (Video Oficial)," March 10, 2024, YouTube, 00:11:21,
https://www.youtube.com/watch?v=ssdN7ZfavHs.

2　Morales, *Fantasy Island*, 68–73.

3　Meléndez-Badillo, *Puerto Rico*, 164.

4　Lucas Vila, "WATCH: Bad Bunny Gives Impassioned Speech in Puerto
Rico Ahead of Elections," *Remezcla*, November 4, 2024, https://
remezcla.com/culture/watch-bad-bunny-gives-speech-puerto-rico/.

5　Ayala and Bernabe, *Puerto Rico in the American Century*,
268; Meléndez-Badillo, *Puerto Rico*, 150.

6　For more on the impact of the international oil crisis on the Puerto
Rican economy, see Ayala and Bernabe, *Puerto Ricoin the American
Century*, 192–93, 245–46.

7　Cabán, "PROMESA," 166; Ayala and Bernabe, *Puerto Rico in the
American Century*, 246; Meléndez- Badillo, *Puerto Rico*.

8　Ayala and Bernabe, *Puerto Rico in the American Century*, 269;
Cabán, "PROMESA," 173; Morales, *Fantasy Island*, 65–67.

9　For more background on these policies, see Fusté, "Repeating Islands of
Debt"; Dick, "US Tax Imperialism in Puerto Rico"; Cabán, "PROMESA."

10　Meléndez-Badillo, *Puerto Rico*, 150; Morales, *Fantasy Island*.

11　Cabán, "PROMESA," 26.

12　García Padilla explained that this was because all states have to
conform to the uniformity clause of the US Constitution such that
"no state can have privileges that another state does not have. The
federal taxes you pay in New York, you pay them in California, you pay
them in Georgia, you pay them in Nebraska. Everyone pays them."

13　Morales, *Fantasy Island*, 68–73.

14　Meléndez-Badillo, *Puerto Rico*, 171–72.

15　For a critique of the stereotype of Puerto Rico as a "welfare island,"
see Rebollo-Gil, *Writing Puerto Rico*, 39–45; Morales, *Fantasy
Island*; Dávila Ellis, "'¿Dónde están las yales?'"

16   Meléndez-Badillo, *Puerto Rico*, 167–71.

17   Laguarta Ramírez, "¡Yo no me dejé!," 14.

18   Stefanie Fernández, "A Day in the Life of Bad Bunny, Introverted Superstar," *Pitchfork*, March 5, 2020, https://pitchfork.com/features /interview/bad-bunny-yhlqmdlg-interview/. For more on Law 7, see Morales, *Fantasy Island*, 96–97; Laguarte Ramírez, "¡Yo no me dejé!," 14.

19   In 2019, Acts 20 and 22 were consolidated into Act 60.

20   Morales, *Fantasy Island*, 244.

21   Morales, *Fantasy Island*, 108.

22   Meléndez-Badillo, *Puerto Rico*, 171.

23   Danica Coto, "Puerto Rico OKs Airport Privatization amid Protests," *Associated Press*, March 1, 2013, https://www .usatoday.com/story/todayinthesky/2013/03/01/puerto -rico-airport-privatization-deal-lifts-off/1956407/.

24   Meléndez-Badillo, *Puerto Rico*, 171.

25   Morales, *Fantasy Island*, 119.

26   Michael Corkery and Mary Williams Walsh, "Puerto Rico's Governor Says Island's Debts Are 'Not Payable," *New York Times*, June 28, 2015, https://www.nytimes.com/2015/06/29/business/dealbook /puerto-ricos-governor-says-islands-debts-are-not-payable.html.

27   Morales, *Fantasy Island*, 149.

28   Cabán, "PROMESA," 162.

29   "What Is PROMESA? Frequently Asked Questions," Financial Oversight and Management Board for Puerto Rico, accessed October 4, 2024, https://oversightboard.pr.gov/faq/.

30   Meléndez-Badillo, *Puerto Rico*, 174.

31   Prados-Rodriguez, "Puerto Rico's Fight for a Citizen Debt Audit."

32   For an overview of the impact of PROMESA, see Cabán, "PROMESA"; Meléndez-Badillo, *Puerto Rico*; Morales, *Fantasy Island*.

33   For more about PROMESA's impact on public education in Puerto Rico, see Brisa and Godreau, "Dismantling Public Education in Puerto Rico."

34   Laguarta Ramírez, "¡Yo no me dejé!"

35   Resdiente, "El Influence[R]—Residente & Bad Bunny," posted August 8, 2019, YouTube, 00:38:18, https:// www.youtube.com/watch?v=VCNyJIUnejk.

36   The space outside the bodega in La Perla called La Placita is not to be confused with the popular market La Placita de Santurce.

37   Some argue that Panamanian reggae en español was the original reggaetón. To be sure, reggae en español was a critical ingredient in reggaetón, but reggaetón as we know it now differs in some significant ways from the Panamanian genre. These distinctions were created by Puerto Rican DJs in the underground scene. For more about Panamanian reggae en español, see R. Rivera, Marshall, and Pacini Hernandez, *Reggaeton*, 79–108; Watson, "Reading National Identity"; and Rivera-Rideau, *Remixing Reggaetón*, 29–33.

38 The full history of reggaetón is beyond the scope of this chapter. For more information, see Rivera-Rideau, *Remixing Reggaetón*; Marshall, "From Música Negra to Reggaeton Latino"; R. Rivera, "Policing Morality, *Mano Dura Stylee*"; LeBrón, *Policing Life and Death*, 83–113.

39 For more about the roles of "Bailando" and "Despacito" in creating reggaetón pop fusions, see Rivera-Rideau, "Reinventing Enrique Iglesias"; and Rivera-Rideau and Torres-Leschnik, "Colors and Flavors of My Puerto Rico."

40 For more on the rise of Colombian reggaetón, see Eduardo Cepeda, "Tu Pum Pum: The Rise of Colombian Reggaetón and Perreo's Pop Transformation," *Remezcla*, April 9, 2019, https://remezcla.com/features/music/tu-pum-pum-colombian -reggaeton/; and Cepeda, "'A Cartel Built for Love.'"

41 For a broader analysis of shifts in reggaetón's sounds and lyrical content, see Rivera-Rideau, "Race, Latinidad, and Latin Pop"; and Solis Miranda, "*Bienaventurando.*"

42 April Salud, "Ozuna, Bad Bunny, De La Ghetto, Farruko and Messiah Narrate a Brief History of Latin Trap," *Billboard*, August 17, 2017, https://www.billboard.com/music/latin/latin-trap -brief-history-ozuna-bad-bunny-de-la-ghetto-7933904/.

43 Salud, "Ozuna, Bad Bunny, De La Ghetto."

44 While Latin trap developed in Puerto Rico, there was another scene developing in New York City with artists like Messiah and Tali. De La Ghetto recalls that Messiah, who is Dominican-American, would make popular Spanish versions of English-language trap songs and perform them in New York's nightclubs. He argued that some of Messiah's songs became popular in the Dominican-owned hookah lounges in San Juan in the mid-2010s. While De Le Ghetto sees synergy between the New York scene and Puerto Rico, he maintains that Puerto Rico is where Latin trap really began and flourished.

45 Drott, *Streaming Music, Streaming Capital*, 1.

46 *Up Next: Sky's the Limit/Up Next: Bad Bunny*, Apple Music, 00:05:00, March 9, 2018, https://music.apple.com/us/episode/up-next- skys-the-limit/1353682414.

47 Carina del Valle Schorske, "The World According to Bad Bunny," *New York Times Magazine*, October 11, 2020, https://www.nytimes .com/interactive/2020/10/07/magazine/bad-bunny.html.

48 Exposito, "Fireside Chat on 'Bad Bunny and Resistance in Puerto Rico.'"

49 Fruity Loops was rebranded FL Studio in 2003. But in Puerto Rico the name Fruity Loops carried meaning; and as Tainy told us, some people were very attached to particular versions of the older software, opting not to update operating systems just to keep older versions of Fruity Loops working. We acknowledge the brand change, but continue to call it Fruity Loops, since that is how it is referred to by artists in Puerto Rico.

Also, the rebrand to FL Studio was done only in response to challenges in obtaining a US trademark due to Kellog's Fruit Loops cereal.

50   Del Valle Schorske, "The World According to Bad Bunny."

51   Rivera-Figueroa, "Bad Bunny's Transgressive Gender Performativity," 93.

52   Exposito, "Fireside Chat on 'Bad Bunny and Resistance in Puerto Rico.'"

53   Leila Cobo, "Noah Assad: CEO, Rimas Entertainment," *Billboard*, April 25, 2020, Gale OneFile: Pop Culture Studies, accessed June 30, 2025.

54   Cobo, "Noah Assad."

55   For more information about how Rimas Entertainment has utilized different partnerships, including YouTube, to give their artists greater access to global markets, see Rivera-Figueroa, "Bad Bunny on the Global Stage."

56   Leila Cobo, "Latin Newcomers Take On Big Labels," *Billboard*, February 14, 2019, https://www.billboard.com/pro/bad-bunny-latin-artists-no-longer-need-record-deals/.

57   *Bad Bunny Live in Miami*, Apple Music, 00:29:00, May 24, 2018, https://music.apple.com/us/episode/bad-bunny-live-in-miami/1380483765.

58   Chente Ydrach Clips, "Bad Bunny Cuenta Su Amistad Con Janthony," May 12, 2022, YouTube, 00:02:28, https://www.youtube.com/watch?v=cEPR5tQnpDo.

59   Julyssa Lopez, "Bad Bunny Conquered the World. Now What?," *Rolling Stone*, June 21, 2023, https://www.rollingstone.com/music/music-features/bad-bunny-coachella-el-apagon-controversy-future-interview-1234770225/.

60   Kyle Denis, "Bad Bunny Celebrates 1 Billion Spotify Streams for 'Tití Me Preguntó': 'Nothing I Say in That Song Is a Lie,'" *Billboard*, August 30, 2023, https://www.billboard.com/music/latin/bad-bunny-billion-spotify-streams-titi-me-pregunto-billions-club-1235403722/. See the video here: https://www.tiktok.com/@todaystophits/video/7271281880874388778.

CHAPTER 2. ¿"ESTAMOS BIEN"?

Note: This chapter's title references the following song: Bad Bunny, "Estamos Bien," *X 100PRE* (Rimas Entertainment, 2018).

1   "Bad Bunny: Estamos Bien (TV Debut)," television clip, posted by the *Tonight Show with Jimmy Fallon*, September 27, 2018, YouTube, 00:04:25, https://www.youtube.com/watch?v=SIQXI0UuX8M.

2   Kishore et al., "Mortality in Puerto Rico after Hurricane Maria."

3   Bonilla and LeBrón, *Aftershocks of Disaster*.

4   Hostetler-Díaz, "Calles de La Resistencia"; Meléndez-Badillo, *Puerto Rico*, 189.

5 For details on the destruction, see "David Begnaud Talks About His Documentary 'Puerto Rico: The Exodus After Hurricane Maria,'" CBS *News*, September 21, 2018, https://www.cbsnews.com/newyork/news/david-begnaud-hurricane-maria-documentary/. For more on rainfall, see Victor Daniel, "Five Years Later, Fiona Brings Back Painful Memories of Maria," *New York Times*, September 20, 2022, https://www.nytimes.com/2022/09/19/us/hurricane-maria-anniversary-puerto-rico.html.

6 For more on Vieques see, Camille Padilla Dalmau, "Why Does the Puerto Rican Island of Vieques Not Have a Hospital 6 Years After Hurricane María?," USC Center for Health Journalism, November 7, 2023, https://centerforhealthjournalism.org/our-work/insights/why-does-puerto-rican-island-vieques-not-have-hospital-6-years-after-hurricane.

7 Frances Robles and Luis Ferré-Sadurní, "Puerto Rico's Agriculture and Farmers Decimated by Maria," *New York Times*, September 24, 2017, https://www.nytimes.com/2017/09/24/us/puerto-rico-hurricane-maria-agriculture-.html, 2017.

8 Cabán, "Puerto Rico's Forever Exodus"; Pedro Cabán and David Smiley, "Florida Politicians Are Courting Displaced Puerto Ricans. But What Are Their Motives?," *Miami Herald*, January 11, 2018, https://www.miamiherald.com/news/politics-government/state-politics/article194045294.html.

9 It is difficult to determine the precise number of people who left Puerto Rico due to Hurricane María; moreover, since many of the initial reports, some Puerto Ricans have returned to the archipelago. However, overall, researchers agree that there has been a massive net loss in the Puerto Rican population as a result of the storm. For more information, see Duany, "'May God Take Me to Orlando.'"

10 Just a few days after Hurricane María destroyed Puerto Rico, President Trump began posting angry tweets condemning NFL players for kneeling during the National Anthem at games in protest of police brutality against Black people. This was commented on extensively in the media. For example, a CNN piece read: "Instead of rallying the country behind the 3.4 million American citizens who live in Puerto Rico, Trump has instead sent more than a dozen tweets about the NFL and the alleged lack of patriotism demonstrated by players who kneel or sit during the National Anthem." Chris Cillizza, "Trump's NFL and Puerto Rico Tweets Prove His Goal Is to Divide, Not Unite the Country," CNN, September 26, 2017, https://www.cnn.com/2017/09/26/politics/trump-nfl-tweets/index.html.

11 Vanessa Díaz (@Vanessa Díaz), "If you want to know what's really happening in #PuertoRico and what the PR people are experiencing, read what my best friend Alexander reported to me from

the metro area yesterday," Facebook, September 26, 2017, https://www.facebook.com/vanessadiaz/posts/10106828665596209.

12 Nicole Acevedo, "Judge Gives End Date for Puerto Rican Hurricane Evacuees in FEMA Temporary Housing," *NBC News*, August 30, 2018, https://www.nbcnews.com/storyline/puerto-rico-crisis/judge-gives -end-date-puerto-rican-hurricane-evacuees-fema-temporary-n905111.

13 This was on top of Puerto Rico's desperate financial situation, exacerbated by PROMESA and the austerity measures of La Junta. It was no surprise, then, that this story also addressed the eruption of protests among Puerto Ricans in response to these increasing austerity measures, which included slashing budgets for public education and pensions, and the selling of the publicly owned electric grid. Laura Sullivan, "How FEMA Failed to Help Victims of Hurricanes in Puerto Rico Recover," NPR, May 1, 2018, https://www.npr.org/2018/05/01/607483473/how-fema-failed -to-help-victims-of-hurricanes-in-puerto-rico-recover.

14 Molinari, "Authenticating Loss and Contesting Recovery," 218.

15 Dánica Coto, "Thousands in Puerto Rico Still Without Housing Since Maria," *AP News*, July 24, 2020, https://apnews.com/article/ ap-top-news-puerto-rico-latin-america-caribbean-hurricanes- a2cf35e2f8893592ec4b59d90baae1ac.

16 Kevin Lui, "'FEMA Chief Slammed for Calling Puerto Rico Relief Efforts the 'Most Logistically Challenging Event,'" *Time*, October 2, 2017, https://time.com/4964574/hurricane-maria-fema- brock-long-puerto-rico-logistics/.

17 Vanessa Díaz (@Vanessa Díaz), "If you want to know what's really happening in #PuertoRico."

18 Meléndez-Badillo, *Puerto Rico*, 186; Negrón-Muntaner, "Our Fellow Americans," 97–98.

19 Nicole Einbinder, "How the Response to Hurricane Maria Compared to Harvey and Irma," PBS, May 1, 2018, https://www.pbs.org/ wgbh/frontline/article/how-the-response-to-hurricane-maria- compared-to-harvey-and-irma/.

20 Kate McCormick and Emma Schwartz, "After Maria, Thousands on Puerto Rico Waited Months for a Plastic Roof," PBS, May 2, 2018, https://www.pbs.org/wgbh/frontline/article/after-maria-thousands- on-puerto-rico-waited-months-for-a-plastic-roof/.

21 Daniella Silva, "Trump Defends Throwing Paper Towels to Hurricane Survivors in Puerto Rico," NBC, October 7, 2018, https://www.nbcnews. com/politics/politics-news/trump-defends-throwing-paper-towels- hurricane-survivors-puerto-rico-n808861.

22 "Puerto Rico: Trump Paper Towel-Throwing 'Abominable,'" BBC, October 4, 2017, https://www.bbc.com/news/world-us-canada -41504165; Jenna Johnson and Ashley Parker, "Trump Hails 'Incredible' Response in 'Lovely' Trip to Storm-Torn Puerto Rico," *Washington*

Post, October 3, 2017, https://www.washingtonpost.com/politics
/trump-praises-himself-for-administrations-great-job-in-puerto-rico
/2017/10/03/fdb5eeb4-a83a-11e7-8ed2-c7114e6ac460_story.html.

23 "Trump Says Puerto Rico in Trouble After Hurricane, Suffering
from 'Broken Infrastructure' and 'Massive Debt,'" CNBC, September 25, 2017, https://www.cnbc.com/2017/09/25/trump-says-puerto
-rico-in-trouble-after-hurricane-debt-must-be-dealt-with.html.

24 Gabriela Meléndez Olivera, "President Trump's Response to Hurricane Maria in Puerto Rico Confirms Second-Class Citizenship,"
ACLU, October 3, 2017, https://www.aclu.org/news/human-rights
/president-trumps-response-hurricane-maria-puerto-rico-confirms
-second-class. For more on Trump's Twitter tirades about Puerto
Rico, see Yarimar Bonilla, "Trump's False Claims About Puerto Rico
Are Insulting. But They Reveal a Deeper Truth," *Washington Post*,
September 14, 2018, https://www.washingtonpost.com/outlook
/2018/09/14/trumps-false-claims-about-puerto-rico-are-insulting
-they-reveal-deeper-truth/. For more information about depictions
of Puerto Ricans in the early twentieth century, see Duany, *Puerto
Rican Nation on the Move*, 39–58; and Erman, *Almost Citizens*.

25 Molinari, "Authenticating Loss," 219–20.

26 Lloréns, "US Media Depictions of Climate Migrants."

27 Scholars have rightly compared the failed governmental response to
María to the failures of the response to Hurricane Katrina in 2005,
when the predominantly African American victims suffered tremendous neglect, inadequate housing and healthcare, and forced
migration. Several scholars have argued that anti-Black racism
colored how the federal government responded to Katrina, much in
the same way that racist stereotypes served as alleged justification
for the neglect of Puerto Ricans after María. For more see, Fussell et al., "Race, Socioeconomic Status, and Return Migration."

28 Vanessa Díaz (@Vanessa Díaz), "If you want to know what's really
happening in #PuertoRico."

29 For examples see Bonilla, "Coloniality of Disaster"; Massol-Deyá,
"Energy Uprising"; Roberto, "Community Kitchens."

30 Laura Sullivan, "FEMA Blamed Delays in Puerto Rico on Maria;
Agency Records Tell Another Story," NPR, June 14, 2018, https://
www.npr.org/2018/06/14/608588161/fema-blamed-delays-in
-puerto-rico-on-maria-agency-records-tell-another-story.

31 Bonilla and Klein, "Trauma Doctrine."

32 Torres Gotay, "'I'm Quite Comfortable.'"

33 Yarimar Bonilla, "Why Must Puerto Ricans Always Be Resilient?," *New York Times*, October 10, 2022, https://www.nytimes
.com/2022/10/10/opinion/fema-fiona-puerto-rico.html.

34 Meléndez-Badillo, *Puerto Rico*, 188–89.

35 Meléndez-Badillo, *Puerto Rico*, 188.

36   Following María, the number of Puerto Ricans suffering from depression, anxiety, and post-traumatic stress disorder (PTSD) exploded. Among adults, suicides increased by 18 percent in the first nine months after the hurricane. For more information, see Abrams, "Puerto Rico, Two Years After Maria."

37   This quote is from personal communication.

38   John D. Sutter, Leyla Santiago, and Khushbu Shah, "We Surveyed 112 Puerto Rican Funeral Homes to Check the Accuracy of the Hurricane Death Toll. This Is What We Found," CNN, November 20, 2017, https://www.cnn.com/2017/11/20/health/hurricane-maria-uncounted-deaths-invs/index.html.

39   Kishore et al., "Mortality in Puerto Rico After Hurricane Maria."

40   Adrian Florido, "An Impromptu Memorial to Demand That Puerto Rico's Hurricane Dead Be Counted," NPR, June 1, 2018, https://www.npr.org/2018/06/01/616216225/an-impromptu-memorial-to-demand-puerto-ricos-hurricane-dead-be-counted#.

41   Benito Martínez Ocasio (@sanbenito), "wow! por muchos años cada vez que me salían las distintas fotos de este día me quedaba mirando un rato a ver si encontraba el par mío que dejé allí. Nunca grabé, ni tiré foto, ni publiqué nada," X, September 20, 2024, https://x.com/sanbenito/status/1837192098514149752?s=46.

42   Vanessa Díaz (@Vanessa Díaz), "I know so many of us are in the same position right now, but if anyone here has any way of getting in contact with anyone in Rincón or Mayaguez, PR, please let me know. My grandfather was at the Bella Vista hospital in Mayaguez when the hurricane hit. My Titi Sandra was at our house in Rincón, right off 413. We have not heard from either since last Tuesday. We have tried every person we know with any connection, every number possible, and we can't get any information. Please, if you know anyone who can help, let me know. I'm happy that our other loved ones on the island are ok (though struggling just to get enough water to survive), but we are scared and waiting for news of my grandfather and aunt. #puertorico #hurricanemaria #help #rincon #mayaguez," Facebook, September 25, 2017, https://www.facebook.com/vanessadiaz/posts/10106824805965939.

43   Royal Caribbean offered stranded people in Puerto Rico, Saint Thomas, and Saint Croix free passage to the United States, and brought "900,000 cases of water, medical supplies and other relief supplies" to Puerto Rico just days after the hurricane. Chabeli Herrera, "Cruise Ship Carries Thousands of Hurricane Evacuees to Fort Lauderdale," *Tampa Bay Times*, October 3, 2017, https://www.tampabay.com/florida-politics/2017/10/03/cruise-ship-carries-thousands-of-hurricane-evacuees-to-fort-lauderdale/.

44   A screen shot of this Instagram post is available at genius.com, https://genius.com/Bad-bunny-mi-puerto-rico-lyrics (accessed July 18, 2025).

45 "Concierto de Bad Bunny Completo 2020–Uforia Live," posted by LM Cleans, January 1, 2021, YouTube, 00:53:46, https://www.youtube.com/watch?v=T6CajLXgmlg.

46 Shortly after the song went viral, Bad Bunny uploaded it onto streaming platforms, like Apple Music and Spotify. Because Bad Bunny frequently deletes everything from his social media accounts, the only remaining version of the original Instagram video we could find was an excerpt included in Apple Music's Up Next video featuring Bad Bunny from early 2018. *Up Next: Sky's the Limit/Up Next: Bad Bunny*, Apple Music, 00:05:00, March 9, 2018, https://music.apple.com/us/episode/up-next-skys-the-limit/1353682414.

47 "Mi Puerto Rico" (lyrics), *Genius*, September 26, 2017, https://genius.com/Bad-bunny-mi-puerto-rico-lyrics.

48 Bonilla, "Postdisaster Futures," 157.

49 Elias Leight, "'Te Boté': How Nio García, Casper Mágico and Darell's Reggaeton Hit Took America,'" *Rolling Stone*, September 22, 2018, https://www.rollingstone.com/music/music-latin/te-bote-nio-garcia-casper-magico-darell-722826/.

50 Pamela Bustios, "Producer Young Martino Says 'Te Boté' All Started with Hurricane Maria," *Billboard*, March 21, 2019, https://www.billboard.com/pro/young-martino-producer-te-bote-interview/.

51 How It Went Down Billboard (@HowItWentDown), "'Nio Garcia and Casper Mágico chat about the creation of their song 'Te Bote,'" Facebook, August 14, 2018, https://www.facebook.com/watch/?v=846154122245397.

52 "Young Martino," Our Artists and Writers, Universal Music Publishing Group, https://www.umusicpub.com/latin/Artists/Y/Young-Martino.aspx.

53 Herrera, "Cruise Ship Carries Thousands of Hurricane Evacuees." For analysis of "Despacito" in the wake of María, see Rivera-Rideau and Torres-Leschnik, "'The Colors and Flavors of My Puerto Rico.'"

54 "'Data Loading' Tainy (Recap)," uploaded by Neon 16, YouTube, January 17, 2024, 00:01:09, https://www.youtube.com/watch?v=RrDDrk_T478.

55 This is Tainy's age at the time of the book's publication.

56 Suzy Exposito, "Bad Bunny Makes Powerful TV Debut on 'Fallon,' Dedicates 'Estamos Bien' to Hurricane Maria Victims," *Rolling Stone*, September 27, 2018, https://www.rollingstone.com/music/music-latin/bad-bunny-fallon-estamos-bien-hurricane-maria-729857/.

57 Bad Bunny has removed much of his Instagram content, but some of his Instagram live videos have been reposted to YouTube by fans, including the material referenced in this paragraph. Alberto Ruiz, "Bad Bunny Canta en Directo de Instagram YHLQMDLG Parte 1," uploaded May 3, 2020, YouTube, 00:51:51, https://www.youtube.com/watch?v=zCEZ9BSS2Jc.

58 Chente Ydrach, "La Única Entrevista que Bad Bunny Va a Dar -Masacote," uploaded December 24, 2018, YouTube, 01:28:46, at 47:00, https://www.youtube.com/watch?v=6obyXYrr_gQ.

59 Ydrach, "La Única Entrevista," at 44:30.

60 See "Bad Bunny, Instagram (ig) Live, *X100PRE* Album part 1 #BadBunny," posted by Estrella R, December 26, 2018, YouTube, 28:29, https://www.youtube.com/watch?v=Bq8XNKFhXjo.

61 Both this quote and the previous sentence about Hear This Music not permitting Bad Bunny to have a studio album were from Bad Bunny's Instagram Live about his album *X 100PRE*, now reposted on YouTube. See "Bad Bunny, Instagram (ig) Live, X 100PRE Album part 1 #BadBunny."

62 Ruiz, "Bad Bunny Canta."

63 The Jones Act (section 27 of the Merchant Marine Act of 1920) is a US federal statute that makes it extremely difficult and costly to ship goods to Puerto Rico while simultaneously generating massive amounts of revenue for the United States. For more, see Teresa Carey, "The Jones Act, Explained (and What Waiving It Means for Puerto Rico)," PBS, September 29, 2017, https://www.pbs.org/newshour/nation/jones-act -explained-waiving-means-puerto-rico; Meléndez-Badillo, *Puerto Rico.*

64 Bonilla, "Why Must Puerto Ricans Always Be Resilient?"

CHAPTER 3. "EL PUEBLO NO AGUANTA MÁS INJUSTICIA"

Note: The title of this chapter is a quote from one of Bad Bunny's verses in the song "Afilando Los Cuchillos," a song released on YouTube during the height of the 2019 mass protests in Puerto Rico against then-Governor Ricardo Rosselló. Residente, iLe, and Bad Bunny, "Afilando Los Cuchillos," posted by Residente, July 17, 2019, YouTube, 05:19, https://www.youtube.com/watch?v=RSh7HIH2pvg.

1 LeBrón, *Against Muerto Rico,* 29.

2 Luis J. Valentín Ortiz and Carla Minet, "Las 889 páginas de Telegram entre Rosselló Nevares y sus allegados," *Centro de Periodismo Investigativo,* July 13, 2019, https://periodismoinvestigativo.com/2019/07/las -889-paginas-de-telegram-entre-rossello-nevares-y-sus-allegados/.

3 LeBrón, "Protests in Puerto Rico Are About Life and Death."

4 "Bad Bunny deja temporalmente la música para unirse a las protestas contra el Gobierno de Puerto Rico," *La Sexta,* July 20, 2019, https://www.lasexta.com/noticias/cultura/bad-bunny -deja-temportalmente-musica-unirse-protestas-gobierno-puerto -rico-video_201907205d338b2focf2c80663da1abf.html.

5 As with many of the other social media posts in this chapter, this quote has been translated from Spanish by the authors. Capitalizations for these quotes were in the original versions.

Salvatore Maicki, "Bad Bunny Is Breaking from His European Tour to Protest Governor Ricardo Rosselló in Puerto Rico," *The Fader*, July 16, 2019, https://www.thefader.com/2019/07/16/bad-bunny-puerto-rico-protests-governor-ricardo-rossello.

6   Quoted in "Bad Bunny se retira temporalmente para protestar en Puerto Rico," *Milenio*, July 16, 2019, https://www.milenio.com/espectaculos/famosos/bad-bunny-pausa-carrera-protestar-ricardo-rossello.

7   Quoted in "Bad Bunny se retira temporalmente."

8   David Renshaw and Patty Shaw Ramirez, "Bad Bunny, Ricky Martin, and More Puerto Rican Artists Celebrate Ricardo Rosselló's Resignation," *Fader*, July 25, 2019, https://www.thefader.com/2019/07/25/bad-bunny-ricky-martin-ricardo-rossello-resignation.

9   *Boricua* is an Indigenous term that means Puerto Rican, and it is significant in the context of decolonial struggle.

10   Frances Robles and Patricia Mazzei, "Puerto Rico's Deposed Governor Describes His Family's Panicked Flight from the Island," *New York Times*, January 14, 2021, https://www.nytimes.com/2021/01/13/us/ricardo-rossello-puerto-rico.html.

11   Robles and Mazzei, "Puerto Rico's Deposed Governor."

12   Zambrana, "Black Feminist Tactics." See also LeBrón, *Against Muerto Rico*, 33; Fernando Tormos-Aponte, "The Politics of Survival," *Jacobin*, April 2, 2018, https://jacobin.com/2018/04/puerto-rico-left-hurricane-maria-colonialism-independence. Another Black feminist organization that had already been organizing prior to the protests and who took an active role in them was Colectivo iLe; for more on their work see Abadía-Rexach "Summer 2019."

13   LeBrón, *Against Muerto Rico*, 29.

14   Isabelia Herrera, "For This Feminist Collective in Puerto Rico, the Mass Protests Were a Long Time Coming," *New York Times*, July 25, 2019, https://www.nytimes.com/2019/07/25/style/feminist-collective-puerto-rico-protests.html.

15   Aidan Gardiner, "Late Ambulances, Leaking Roofs: Puerto Ricans on Why They Rose Up," *New York Times*, July 25, 2019, https://www.nytimes.com/2019/07/25/reader-center/puerto-rico-economic-struggles.html.

16   Throughout the protests, police used excessive force against nonviolent protesters, including launching tear gas and beating protesters. See also, LeBrón, *Against Muerto Rico*, 43–48; Evan Hill and Ainara Tiefenthäler, "Did Puerto Rican Police Go Too Far During Protests? What the Video Shows," *New York Times*, July 27, 2019, https://www.nytimes.com/2019/07/27/us/puerto-rico-violence-protests.html.

17   LeBrón, *Against Muerto Rico*, 30–31.

18   Quoted in Cecilia Aldarondo, dir., *Landfall* (Blackscrackle Film, 2020), at 00:01:40.

19   LeBrón, *Against Muerto Rico*, 30–31.

20   Frances Robles, "'Sharpening the Knives': Musicians Join the Pro-
        tests in Puerto Rico,'" *New York Times*, July 19, 2019, https://www
        .nytimes.com/2019/07/19/us/puerto-rico-residente-ile-afilando
        -los-cuchillos.html. For an analysis of the ways that the protests cut
        across race and gender lines, see Abadía-Rexach, "Summer 2019."

21   Ricky Martin (@Ricky_Martin), "#PuertoRico nos vemos mañana en
        el la marcha a ls 5 P.M. frente al Capitolio," Twitter (now X), July 16,
        2019, https://twitter.com/ricky_martin/status/1151319129455906816.

22   Trap Music (@Trapmusictv), "#BadBunny hace un llamado a
        la población de puerto rico, para que renuncie el gobernador
        #RickyRosello/#RickyRenucia," Twitter (now X), July 16, 2019,
        https://x.com/Trapmusictv_/status/1151126760970321921.

23   Nuria Net, "Why Bad Bunny Wants Puerto Rican Youth to Take the
        Streets," *Rolling Stone*, July 17, 2019, https://www.rollingstone.
        com/music/music-latin/bad-bunny-residente-puerto-rico-
        protest-governor-rossello-859419/.

24   AP Archive, "Ricky Martin, Bad Bunny Join Thousands of Protestors in
        Puerto Rico Demanding Governor Resignation," YouTube, July 23,
        2019, https://youtu.be/wVsDeH9YERs.

25   Robles, "'Sharpening the Knives.'"

26   Net, "Why Bad Bunny Wants Puerto Rican Youth to Take the Streets."

27   LeBrón, *Against Muerto Rico*, 43.

28   LeBrón, *Against Muerto Rico*, 45.

29   For more analysis of the arguments leveled against perreo, see Rivera-
        Rideau, *Remixing Reggaetón*; and Rivera-Servera, "Reggaetón's Crossings."

30   Rivera-Servera, "Reggaetón's Crossings," 99.

31   Los Cocos Restaurant (@LosCocosRestaurant), "¡Si no podemos
        perrear, no es nuestra revolución 2!," Facebook, December 22,
        2018, https://www.facebook.com/events/375846082989687/.

32   See for example El Hangar en Santurce, https://www.facebook.com
        /Elhangarensanturce/. See also Verónica Dávila Ellis and Marisol
        LeBrón, "How Music Took Down Puerto Rico's Governor," *Washing-
        ton Post*, August 1, 2019, https://www.washingtonpost.com/outlook
        /2019/08/01/how-music-took-down-puerto-ricos-governor/.

33   Karla Claudio-Betancourt, *Perreo Combativo*, July 25,
        2019, 00:01:00, https://vimeo.com/350139441.

34   Zambrana, *Colonial Debts*, 134–38.

35   There were also popular slogans at the protest that did not have
        to do with reggaetón, such as "Somos más y no tenemos miedo"
        (There are more of us, and we're not scared) and "Ricky Renuncia,
        y llévate a la junta" (Ricky, Resign and take la junta with you).

36   Dávila Ellis and LeBrón, "How Music Took Down Puerto Rico's
        Governor."

37   Grace (@marie01_31), "YO QUIERO LA COMBI COMPLETA, ¿QUÉ?
        Ricky!!! Renuncia!!! PUÑETA!!! #RickyVeteYa #RickyRenuncia

"#PuertoRicoMarcha," Twitter (now X), July 17, 2019, https://twitter.com/marie01_31/status/1151688037736341506?s=20.

38   Aldarondo, *Landfall*, at 00:02:00.

39   Aldarondo, *Landfall*, at 00:02:00.

40   Dávila Ellis and LeBrón, "How Music Took Down Puerto Rico's Governor."

41   Cintrón-Moscoso and Díaz, "Photo Essay: The Power of Popular Protest."

42   Meléndez-Badillo, *Puerto Rico*, 161–62.

43   Residente, "Residente & Bad Bunny," *El Influence[R]*, August 8, 2019, YouTube, 38:18, https://www.youtube.com/watch?v=VCNyJIUnejk.

44   Residente, "Residente y Bad Bunny," at 00:04:24.

45   Residente, "Residente y Bad Bunny," at 00:04:24.

46   Robles, "'Sharpening the Knives.'"

47   Alexia Fernández, "Calle 13's Residente on His New Collaboration with Bad Bunny and Taylor Swift's Masters Dilemma," *People*, July 15, 2019, https://people.com/music/residente-talks-new-collaboration-bad-bunny/.

48   Suzy Exposito, "Inside Residente, Bad Bunny's Conscious Summer Jam 'Bellacoso,'" *Rolling Stone*, July 26, 2019, https://www.rollingstone.com/music/music-latin/residente-bad-bunny-bellacoso-video-interview-857951/.

49   Residente, "Residente y Bad Bunny," at 00:02:00.

50   Residente, "Residente y Bad Bunny," at 00:21:40.

51   Residente, "Residente y Bad Bunny," at 00:20:30.

52   Vogue, "73 Questions with Bad Bunny," interview by Joe Sabia, April 29, 2024, YouTube, 00:20:44, https://www.youtube.com/watch?v=KYuBLoSE-5I.

53   Chente Ydrach, "La Única Entrevista que Bad Bunny Va a Dar—Masacote," uploaded December 24, 2018, YouTube, 01:28:46, https://www.youtube.com/watch?v=6obyXYrr_gQ.

54   Hot97, "Residente on Frustration w/ Grammys, Bad Bunny, + 'This Is Not America,'" posted April 19, 2022, YouTube, 00:33:33, https://www.youtube.com/watch?v=veF6oFAHv14.

55   The song was recorded and released via the internet within a few days of Ojeda Ríos's killing. For more about Ojeda Ríos's death and its significance in Puerto Rico, see Meléndez-Badillo, *Puerto Rico*, 163.

56   Rachel Lee Harris, "Puerto Rico Cancels Calle 13 Concert," *New York Times*, October 18, 2009, https://www.nytimes.com/2009/10/19/arts/music/19arts-PUERTORICOCA_BRF.html.

57   "A la web, histórico concierto de Calle 13," *Telemundo 47*, August 17, 2014, https://www.telemundo47.com/entretenimiento/internet-historico-concierto-calle-13/1957015/.

58   For more on Tego Calderón's music and politics, see Rivera-
      Rideau, *Remixing Reggaetón*; Rivera-Rideau, "'If I Were You'";
      Rivera-Rideau, "'Cocolos Modernos'"; Calderón, "Black Pride."

59   For more about state repression of independence movement see
      Melendez-Badillo, *Puerto Rico*; LeBrón, "Puerto Rico and Colo-
      nial Circuits of Policing"; Power, "Seeing the U.S. Empire."

60   Negrón-Muntaner, "Poetry of Filth."

61   Lloréns, "Brothels, Hell, and Puerto Rican Bodies."

62   Anne Hoffman, "New Calle 13 Video 'Muerte En Hawaii' Pushes
      the Limit," NPR, July 12, 2011, https://www.npr.org/sections/altlatino/
      2011/07/13/137773941/new-calle-13-video-muerte-en-hawaii-pushes
      -the-limit.

CHAPTER 4. "¿POR QUÉ NO PUEDO SER ASÍ?"

Note: This chapter's title is a lyric from the following song: Bad
Bunny, "Caro," *X 100PRE* (Rimas Entertainment, 2018).

1   Nieves Moreno, "A Man Lives Here"; Rivera-Figueroa,
     "Bad Bunny's Transgressive Gender Performativity."

2   Isabelia Herrera, "Bad Bunny Says He Was Refused Service at
     a Nail Salon for Being a Man," *Remezcla*, July 18, 2018, https://
     remezcla.com/music/bad-bunny-nail-salon-service/.

3   Patricia Tortolani, "Bad Bunny Is Here at the Right Time,"
     Allure, November 2021, https://www.allure.com/story
     /bad-bunny-cover-interview-november-2021

4   Gabriela Cavanagh, "Bad Bunny Explains the Inspiration
     Behind His Met Gala Look," *Vogue*, May 4, 2022, https://www
     .vogue.com/video/watch/getting-ready-with-bad-bunny.

5   For critiques specific to Bad Bunny, see Dávila Ellis, "Doing Reggaeton
     However He Wants"; Frances Solá-Santiago, "The Classist History
     Behind Bad Bunny's 'Bichiyal,' *Code Switch*, NPR, March 17, 2020,
     https://www.npr.org/sections/codeswitch/2020/03/17/816479053
     /the-classist-history-behind-bad-bunnys-bichiyal. For broader critiques
     of misogyny in reggaetón see Báez, "En Mi Imperio"; Dávila Ellis,
     "'¿Dónde están las yales?'"; Jiménez, "(W)rapped in Foil"; Rivera-
     Rideau, *Remixing Reggaetón*; Solis Miranda, "*Bienaventurado*." It is
     worth mentioning that, while reggaetón's gender representations do
     often reproduce sexist representations of women, this is not unique to
     the genre; in fact, music scholar Noel Allende Goitía offers an over-
     view of the history of similar song lyrics across a variety of Puerto
     Rican music genres, including plena, bolero, and música jíbara, to
     show how "Bad Bunny and the host of other reggaetoneros are not
     deviant or abnormal in Puerto Rican musical culture. They belong . . .

to a long tradition of unwholesome and vulgar language usage" (40). See Allende Goitía, "The Profane, the Lewd, and the Misogynistic."

6 Josefina Pieres, "'Bad Bunny Rewatches His Music Videos, From 'Callaíta' to 'Yo Perreo Sola,'" *Vanity Fair*, September 12, 2023, YouTube, 00:08:36, https://www.youtube.com/watch?v=gm6MkN73EHQ&t =516s.

7 Suzy Exposito, "Bad Bunny Drops Surprise New Song, 'Callaíta': Listen," *Rolling Stone*, May 31, 2019, https://www.rollingstone. com/music/music-latin/bad-bunny-drops-new-song-callaita-tainy-841942/.

8 For analysis of this trope, see Rivera-Rideau, "Race, Latinidad, and Latin Pop."

9 For more detailed analysis of the Anti-Pornography Campaign, see Rivera-Rideau, *Remixing Reggaetón*, 52–80.

10 Rivera-Rideau, *Remixing Reggaetón*, 68–70.

11 This representation aligns with Ramón Rivera-Servera's arguments that perreo could be a site for women to reclaim their sexuality and agency; see Rivera-Servera, "Reggaetón's Crossings."

12 Bad Bunny, "Callaíta," posted May 31, 2019, YouTube, 00:04:11, https://www.youtube.com/watch?v=acEOASYioGY.

13 Pieres, "Bad Bunny Rewatches His Music Videos," at 00:09:49.

14 Bad Bunny, "LA DIFICIL YHLQMDLG," posted February 28, 2020, YouTube, 00:03:12, https://www.youtube.com/watch?v=fEYUoBgYKzw.

15 Rivera-Rideau, *Remixing Reggaetón*, 71–77.

16 For more about conflicting perceptions of women's agency in reggaetón, see Báez, "'En Mi Imperio.'"

17 Bad Bunny, "Solo de Mí," posted December 15, 2018, YouTube, 00:03:19, https://www.youtube.com/watch?v=7rbprAR_Reg.

18 Valdez, "Vivir sin miedo," 237.

19 Valdez, "Vivir sin miedo," 238.

20 A despecho is a song about heartbreak.

21 Chente Ydrach, "La Única Entrevista que Bad Bunny Va a Dar— Masacote," uploaded December 24, 2018, YouTube, 01:28:46, at 0:26:43, https://www.youtube.com/watch?v=6obyXYrr_gQ.

22 Aramburu and Carrasquillo Hernández, "From Victimization to Feminist Revolution," 17.

23 For an example of this critique by providers, see Sanabria Leon and Torres, "Colonial Necropolitics."

24 Ríos Ruíz, "Estado de emergencia," 128–29.

25 See Ríos Ruíz, "Estado de emergencia"; Sanabría León and Torres, "Colonial Necropolitics."

26 Aramburu and Carrasquillo Hernández, "From Victimization to Feminist Revolution," 10.

27 Jhoni Jackson, "Weekend-Long Protest Against Domestic Violence in Puerto Rico End with Police Pepper Spraying Activists,"

Remezcla, November 26, 2018, https://remezcla.com/features /culture/police-pepper-spray-activists-puerto-rico/.

28   Valdez, "Vivir sin miedo," 238.

29   Quoted in Suzy Exposito, "Inside Residente and Bad Bunny's Meeting with Puerto Rico Governor Rosselló," *Rolling Stone*, January 16, 2019, https://www.rollingstone.com/music/music -latin/residente-bad-bunny-meet-governor-rossello-puerto-rico -778809/. It is worth noting that the reporting on this particular incident is inconsistent; some accounts claim that they met at 2 a.m., others at 5 a.m. Either way, the point is that the three men had a meeting in the middle of the night about the issue.

30   Exposito, "Inside Residente and Bad Bunny's Meeting"; Isabelia Herrera, "Bad Bunny and Residente Paid the Puerto Rican Governor a Visit at 2 a.m.," *Remezcla*, January 11, 2019, https://remezcla .com/music/bad-bunny-residente-ricardo-rossello-meeting/.

31   Quoted in Herrera, "Bad Bunny and Residente Paid the Puerto Rican Governor a Visit at 2 a.m."

32   Rosselló eventually did meet with La Colectiva Feminista en Construcción but only after talking to Bad Bunny and Residente; see Valdez, "Vivir sin miedo," 228.

33   Jaclyn Diaz, "How #NiUnaMenos Grew from the Streets of Argentina into a Regional Women's Movement," NPR, October 14, 2021, https:// www.npr.org/2021/10/15/1043908435/how-niunamenos-grew-from -the-streets-of-argentina-into-a-regional-womens-movemen.

34   Harmeet Kaur and Rafi Rivera, "A Transgender Woman's Murder Has Shocked Puerto Rico and Renewed a Conversation About Transphobia," CNN, February 29, 2020, https://www.cnn.com/2020 /02/29/us/alexa-puerto-rico-transgender-killing/index.html.

35   Amanda Holpuch, "2 Men Plead Guilty in Attack on Transgender Woman Who Was Later Found Dead," *New York Times*, September 26, 2023, https://www.nytimes.com/2023/09/26/us/puerto-rico-hate -crime-alexa-transgender-killing.html. To date no one has been charged with Alexa's death, although two men were charged with assaulting her.

36   Ríos Ruíz, "Estado de emergencia."

37   Rodríguez-Madera et al., "Experiencias of Violence."

38   Ríos Ruíz, "Estado de emergencia," 128.

39   Benji Hart, "For Trans Puerto Ricans, Passing Laws Is Only Part of the Battle for Liberation," *Autostraddle*, March 31, 2021, https://www. autostraddle.com/for-trans-puerto-ricans-passing-laws-is-only-part- of-the-battle-for-liberation/.

40   Gary Suarez, "Bad Bunny and Sech Land Their First Hot 100 Together," *Forbes*, February 25, 2020, https://www.forbes.com/sites/garysuarez /2020/02/25/bad-bunny-and-sech-land-their-first-hot-100-hit-together/.

41   The frequency with which people are misgendered in the media and by state officials is not surprising considering the extensive, difficult

legal battles trans activists have waged in Puerto Rico for recognition of their gender identities. Finally, in 2018, the Puerto Rican courts upheld the right of trans Puerto Ricans to change their gender identities on all official documents. See Castro Pérez "La lucha por derecho a ser."

42 Karla Montavlán, "Bad Bunny's New Song 'Andrea' Sends Powerful Message on Femicide," *People*, May 11, 2020, https://peopleenespanol .com/chica/bad-bunny-andrea-gender-based-violence-femicide/.

43 Nicole Acevedo, "Puerto Rico's New Tipping Point: Horrific Femicides Reignite Fight Against Gender Violence," NBC *News*, May 16, 2021, https://www.nbcnews.com/news/latino/puerto-rico-s-new -tipping-point-horrific-femicides-reignite-fight-n1267354.

44 See Acevedo, "Puerto Rico's New Tipping Point."

45 Luis Alfredo Del Valle, "What It Means for Pop Music to Raise Awareness About Intimate Partner Violence," interview by Isabella Gomez Sarmiento, May 28, 2022, NPR, transcript, https://www.npr.org /transcripts/1101921360.

46 Karla Montavlán, "'Bad Bunny Spills the Deets on the True Meaning Behind His Song 'Andrea,'" *People*, May 19, 2022, https:// peopleenespanol.com/chica/bad-bunny-andrea-song-true-meaning/.

47 Nieves Moreno, "A Man Lives Here."

48 For more about Ricky Martin's race and class positioning as a blanquito within Puerto Rico, see Negrón-Muntaner, *Boricua Pop*, 247–72.

49 Martin, *Me*.

50 Rodríguez, "Getting F****d in Puerto Rico."

51 La Fountain-Stokes, "Recent Developments."

52 La Fountain-Stokes, "Recent Developments," 511.

53 Chamberlain, "From Father to Humanitarian," 100.

54 Brittany Spanos, "Ricky Martin Presents Bad Bunny with 2023 GLAAD Vanguard Award," *Rolling Stone*, March 31, 2023, https:// www.rollingstone.com/music/music-news/bad-bunny-ricky -martin-glaad-award-1234707135/. GLAAD is an LGBTQ+ advocacy group focused on media representations of the community.

55 Kelly Clarkson, "Ricky Martin Praises Bad Bunny for LGBTQ+ Allyship," *The Kelly Clarkson Show*, March 28, 2024, YouTube, 1:08, https://www.youtube.com/watch?v=P6bMh7mvIvc&t=1s.

56 Suzy Exposito, "Bad Bunny in Captivity," *Rolling Stone*, May 14, 2020, https://www.rollingstone.com/music/music-features/bad -bunny-cover-story-lockdown-puerto-rico-new-albums-996871/.

57 Kate Linthicum, "How Bad Bunny Broke Every Rule of Latin Pop— and Became Its Biggest and Brightest Star," *Los Angeles Times*, February 28, 2020.

58 Linthicum, "How Bad Bunny Broke Every Rule."

59 André Wheeler, "'Bad Bunny: Does a Straight Man Deserve to be Called a 'Queer Icon,'" *The Guardian*, May 19, 2020, https://www

.theguardian.com/music/2020/may/19/bad-bunny-queer-icon-rapper-ricky-martin.

60   Dávila Ellis, "Doing Reggaetón However He Wants."

61   Pippa Raga, "'Trap Queen' Nesi Is a Huge Reason 'Yo Perreo Sola' Is Such a Big Success,'" *Distractify*, October 16, 2020, https://www.distractify.com/p/nesi-reggaeton-explainer.

62   Dávila Ellis, "Doing Reggaetón However He Wants." Dávila Ellis's comment references the work of artists like Glory and Jenny la Sexy Voz, who often sing the catchy, famous hooks on reggaetón songs without receiving artist credits. For more, see Jiménez, "(W) rapped in Foil"; and Isabelia Herrera, "Jenny La Sexy Voz is the Woman Behind Reggaeton's Biggest Hooks," *Remezcla*, May 16, 2016, https://remezcla.com/features/music/jenny-la-sexy-voz-profile/.

63   Miguel Ángel Escudero, "Ex novia de Bad Bunny vence al cantante en los tribunales por el uso de su voz," *El Diario*, May 11, 2024, https://eldiariony.com/2024/05/11/ex-novia-de-bad-bunny -vence-al-cantante-en-los-tribunales-por-el-uso-de-su-voz/.

64   It should also be noted that this trend of not crediting women vocalists has a long history across various musical genres and was perhaps made most known after the success of the documentary *20 Feet from Stardom*, about women background vocalists. Morgan Neville, dir., *20 Feet from Stardom* (Anchor Bay Entertainment, 2014).

65   Jiménez, "(W)rapped in Foil."

66   Herrera, "Jenny La Sexy Voz."

67   Herrera, "Jenny La Sexy Voz."

68   Julio Capó Jr., "Counter-Editorial: Bad Bunny Is Queer to Me," *Abusable Past*, May 27, 2020, https://abusablepast.org/counter -editorial-bad-bunny-is-queer-to-me/.

69   Bernardo Sim, "Bad Bunny Isn't Queerbaiting and Those Claims Are Missing the Point," *Out Magazine*, August 29, 2022, https://www. out.com/commentary/2022/8/29/bad-bunny-isnt-queerbaiting-those-claims-are-missing-point.

70   Isabella Gomez Sarmiento, "For Puerto Rico's Villano Antillano, Femininity Is a Shield—and a Superpower," NPR, March 13, 2023, https://www.npr.org/2023/03/13/1158426326/villano-antillano-la-sustancia-x-interview.

71   Carlos Nogueras, "Villano Antillano Shows Us We Can Have Our Cake and Eat It Too. In Her Case, Make-Out with It," *Al Día*, August 30, 2022.

72   For more about Kevin Fret and his cultural impact, see La Fountain-Stokes, *Translocas*.

73   Julia Rocha, "Villano Antillano and Ana Macho Dream of Queer and Trans Futures," *Latino USA*, March 17, 2023, 00:32:43, at 00:08:30, https://www.latinousa.org/2023/03/17/anaandvillana/.

74   Verónica Bayetti Flores, "Villlano Antillano Knows Her Magic," *Rolling Stone*, June 26, 2023, https://www.rollingstone.com/music

/music-features/villano-antillano-interview-
bizarrap-bad-bunny-1234770907/.

75 "Young Miko le agredece a bad bunny," posted by karriri_, TikTok, June 9,
2023, https://www.tiktok.com/@karrirri_/video/7378654132237815070.

76 Pieres, "Bad Bunny Rewatches His Music Videos."

77 Solá-Santiago, "The Classist History Behind Bad Bunny's 'Bichiyal'";
Mariana Viera, "Bad Bunny's Embrace of Femininity Comes with
a Caveat," *Vice*, October 3, 2018, https://www.vice.com/en/article
/vbky9x/bad-bunnys-embrace-of-femininity-comes-with-a-caveat.

78 Viera, "Bad Bunny's Embrace of Femininity"; Dávila Ellis, "Doing
Reggaetón However He Wants."

CHAPTER 5. "EL MUNDO ES MÍO"

Note: The title of this chapter references the following song:
Bad Bunny, "EL MUNDO ES MÍO," *El Último Tour del Mundo*
(Rimas Entertainment, 2020).

1 Suzy Exposito, "Bad Bunny in Captivity," *Rolling Stone*, May 14,
2020, https://www.rollingstone.com/music/music-features/bad
-bunny-cover-story-lockdown-puerto-rico-new-albums-996871/.

2 Exposito, "Bad Bunny in Captivity."

3 Keith Caulfeld, "Bad Bunny's 'El Último Tour del Mundo' Debuts at No. 1 on Billboard 200 Chart, Is First All-Spanish
No. 1 Album," *Billboard*, December 6, 2020, https://www
.billboard.com/pro/bad-bunny-el-ultimo-tour-del-mundo
-billboard-200-number-one/. The Billboard 200 chart
measures all albums across genres and platforms.

4 Chente Ydrach, "La Última Entrevista de Bad Bunny del Mundo,"
posted November 27, 2020, YouTube, 01:19:36, at 00:00:21,
https://www.youtube.com/watch?v=WFvceJB9-B8&t=3757s.

5 Gary Trust, "Bad Bunny and Jhay Cortez's 'Dakiti' Holds at
No. 1 on Billboard Global Charts," *Billboard*, November 23,
2020, https://www.billboard.com/pro/bad-bunny-jhay
-cortez-dakiti-billie-eilish-therefore-i-am-global-charts/.

6 Gary Suarez, "'Bad Bunny's 'Las Que No Iban a Salir,'" *Rolling
Stone*, May 12, 2020, https://www.rollingstone.com/music/music
-album-reviews/bad-bunny-las-que-no-iban-a-salir-2-998311/.

7 Exposito, "Bad Bunny in Captivity."

8 Leila Cobo, "Bad Bunny Talks Surprise New Album 'El Último
Tour del Mundo' and Rosalía Collab," *Rolling Stone*, November 27,
2020, https://www.billboard.com/music/latin/bad-bunny-surprise
-album-interview-el-ultimo-tour-del-mundo-rosalia-9490254/.

9 Julyssa Lopez, "Bad Bunny Release Wonders 'Where She Goes'
Over a Jersey Club Beat," *Rolling Stone*, May 18, 2023, https://

www.rollingstone.com/music/music-features/bad-bunny
-where-she-does-new-song-jersey-club-1234737998/.

10   Amber Corrine and Regina Cho, "The Most Influential and Essential Jersey Club Records, from 1999 to Today," *Vibe*, June 5, 2024, https://www.vibe.com/lists/best-jersey-club-records
-1999-to-2024/not-like-us-jersey-club-remix-sjayy/.

11   Gary Trust, "Bad Bunny's 'Where She Goes' Blasts In at No. 1 on Billboard Global 200 Chart," *Billboard*, May 30, 2023, https://
www.billboard.com/music/chart-beat/bad-bunny-where
-she-goes-number-one-global-200-chart-1235342428/.

12   For more about the importance of El Gran Combo in Puerto Rican musical history, see Berríos-Miranda and Dudley, "El Gran Combo."

13   Gary Trust, "Max Martin Breaks Record for Most Hot 100 No. 1s Among Producers as Ariana Grande's 'Yes, And?' Debuts," *Billboard*, January 22, 2024, https://www.billboard.com/lists/max-martin-most-
hot-100-number-1s-producers/.

14   For critique of this see Rivera-Rideau, *Fitness Fiesta!*; Pacini Hernandez, *Oye Como Va!*

15   Ramos, *Unbelonging*; Corona, "Cultural Locations of US Latin/o Rock"; Pacini Hernandez, *Oye Como Va!*

16   Exposito, "Bad Bunny in Captivity."

17   R. Rivera, "Will the Real Puerto Rican Culture Please Stand Up"; Flores, *The Diaspora Strikes Back*.

18   Jiménez Román, "Boricua vs. Nuyoricans—Indeed!"

19   Flores, *Diaspora Strikes Back*, 5; see also Findlay, "Slipping and Sliding."

20   For more about Operation Bootstrap, see Findlay, *We Are Left Without a Father Here*; and Meléndez, *Sponsored Migrations*.

21   For more information and critique of the narrative of overpopulation in Puerto Rico, see Meléndez-Badillo, *Puerto Rico*, 121–22; Whalen, "Colonialism, Citizenship."

22   This was not the first state-sponsored migration of Puerto Rican laborers. In 1900, US companies began recruiting Puerto Ricans to work on plantations in Hawaiʻi, at the time also a newly acquired US territory with significant US investment. These laborers endured terrible travel conditions, traveling first by boat to Louisiana, then by train to California, and then by another boat to Hawaiʻi. Many fled, choosing to remain in California rather than continue the journey. Still, others went to Hawaiʻi where they endured harsh working conditions alongside Japanese, Filipino, Portuguese, and other workers. They established a critical community in the Puerto Rican diaspora. For more about labor recruitment and Puerto Ricans in Hawaiʻi, see Guevarra, *Aloha, Compadre*, 65–101; and Poblete, *Islanders in the Empire*.

23   For more information about S. G. Friedman's recruitment efforts to Lorain, Ohio, see E. Rivera, "La Colonia de Lorain, Ohio."

24   Whalen, "Colonialism, Citizenship," 29.

25   Flores, *Diaspora Strikes Back*.

26   Duany, *Puerto Rican Nation on the Move*.

27   Venator-Santiago and Gupan, "Puerto Rican Population Change."

28   Hinojosa, "Puerto Rican Exodus."

29   LM Cleans, "Concierto de Bad Bunny Completo 2020—Uforia Live," posted January 1, 2001, YouTube, 01:51:05, at 00:54:17, https://www.youtube.com/watch?v=T6CajLXgmlg.

30   Duany, *Puerto Rican Nation on the Move*.

31   "Ten Years of Rimas Entertainment: Billboard Latin Music Week 2024," interview by Leila Cobo with Noah Assad, Jonathan Miranda, Junior Carabaño, and Raymond Acosta, *Billboard*, October 15, 2024.

32   LM Cleans, "Concierto de Bad Bunny Completo 2020," at 00:05:04.

33   Bergad, *Dominican Population of the New York Metropolitan Region*.

34   LM Cleans, "Concierto de Bad Bunny Completo 2020," at 00:01:42.

35   In the 2010s, Florida became the state with the largest Puerto Rican population, and it is now one of the centers of the current Puerto Rican migration. For more information see Duany, "'May God Take Me to Orlando.'"

36   For more on this see Findlay, *We Are Left Without a Father Here*, 93–97; Thomas, *Puerto Rican Citizen*, 39–146.

37   Office of the New York State Comptroller, Thomas P. DiNapoli, *Recent Trends and Impact of COVID-19 in the Bronx*, June 2021, https://www.osc.ny.gov/reports/osdc/recent-trends-and-impact-covid-19-bronx#:~:text=The%20Bronx%20had%20the%20City's, experienced%20significantly%20higher%20unemployment%20rates; Kimiko de Freytas-Tamura, Winnie Hu, and Lindsey Rogers Cook, "'It's the Death Towers': How the Bronx Became New York's Virus Hot Spot," *New York Times*, May 26, 2020, https://www.nytimes.com/2020/05/26/nyregion/bronx-coronavirus-outbreak.html.

38   *Tonight Show Starring Jimmy Fallon*, "Bad Bunny on His Record-Breaking Album, Working with Al Pacino, and Saturday Night Live (Extended)," posted October 20, 2023, YouTube, 00:08:48, at 00:06:30, https://www.youtube.com/watch?v=Dwg_45e5OX4.

39   Jennifer Drysdale, "Bad Bunny on How His 'Dark' New Album Helped His Mental Health During Quarantine (Exclusive)," *ET*, November 26, 2020, https://www.etonline.com/bad-bunny-on-how-his-dark-new-album-helped-his-mental-health-during-quarantine-exclusive-156966.

40   Rebecah Jacobs, "Bad Bunny Instantly Sells Out Special 'P FKN R' Concert in Puerto Rico," *Hola*, August 21, 2021, https://www.hola.com/us/entertainment/20210820g1lom3qujk/bad-bunny-instantly-sells-out-puerto-rico-concert/.

41   Chente Ydrach, "'BAD BUNNY: 'no es fácil ser yo,'" posted May 11, 2022, YouTube, 02:36:14, at 00:01:07, https://www.youtube.com/watch?v=3i5afhwxiUc&t=1516s.

42   Ydrach, "'BAD BUNNY: 'no es fácil ser yo,'" at 00:01:11.

43   Frances Robles, "Puerto Rico Faces Staggering Covid Case Explosion," *New York Times*, January 2, 2022, https://www.nytimes.com/2022/01/02/us/coronavirus-puerto-rico.html; Nicole Narea, "Why One of the Most Vaccinated Places in America Couldn't Avoid Omicron," *Vice*, January 9, 2022, https://www.vox.com/22870713/puerto-rico-omicron-covid-vaccine-travel-restrictions; Jhoni Jackson, "4-Hour Delay to Catch Bad Bunny's Landmark 'P FKN R' Event," *Rolling Stone*, December 11, 2021, https://www.rollingstone.com/music/music-live-reviews/bad-bunny-p-fkn-r-concert-live-review-1270509/; Jessica Roiz, "Inside Badchella: Highlights From Bad Bunny's 'P FKN R' Concert in Puerto Rico," *Billboard*, December 11, 2021, https://www.billboard.com/music/latin/bad-bunny-p-fkn-r-concert-puerto-rico-highlights-1235008384/.

44   Ydrach, "BAD BUNNY: 'no es fácil ser yo.'"

45   Ydrach, "BAD BUNNY: 'no es fácil ser yo,'" at 00:01:11.

46   Jackson, "4-Hour Delay."

47   Ydrach, "BAD BUNNY: 'no es fácil ser yo,'" at 00:01:12.

48   Robles, "Puerto Rico Faces Staggering Covid Case Explosion."

49   Robles, "Puerto Rico Faces Staggering Covid Case Explosion"; Narea, "Why One of the Most Vaccinated Places in America Couldn't Avoid Omicron."

50   Jessica Roiz, "Everything We Know About Bad Bunny's Two-Day 'P FKN R' Concert in Puerto Rico," *Billboard*, December 10, 2021, https://www.billboard.com/music/latin/what-to-know-bad-bunny-p-fkn-r-concert-1235008055/; Rosalina Marrero Rodríguez, "Afinan detalles del Concierto," *El Nuevo Día*, December 9, 2021, *ProQuest* database.

51   Quoted in Roiz, "Everything We Know." See also Marrero Rodríguez, "Afinan detalles."

52   Shakira Vargas Rodríguez, "Noah Assad, sus tropiezos y cantazos de camino al éxito" *El Nuevo Día*, November 20, 2023, https://www.elnuevodia.com/entretenimiento/musica/notas/noah-assad-sus-tropiezos-y-cantazos-de-camino-al-exito/.

53   "Entrarán Solo Los Vacunados," *El Nuevo Día*, August 19, 2021. *ProQuest* database.

54   A load-in is the process of bringing in equipment and creating the set for a concert or other stage production.

55   Debi Moen, "Bad Bunny Fills a Stadium in Tribute to Puerto Rico," *Production, Lights, and Staging News*, February 4, 2022, https://plsn.com/articles/designer-insights/bad-bunny-fills-a-stadium-in-tribute-to-puerto-rico.

56   Moen, "Bad Bunny Fills a Stadium in Tribute to Puerto Rico."

57   Roiz, "Inside Badchella."

58   Ydrach, "BAD BUNNY: 'no es fácil ser yo.'"

59   Jackson, "4-Hour Delay"; see also Roiz, "Inside Badchella."

60   Jackson, "4-Hour Delay."

61   Roiz, "Inside Badchella."

62   Chente Ydrach, "BAD BUNNY: UN JANGUEO DE PROPORCIO-
      NES BÍBLICAS," posted December 14, 2021, YouTube, 00:36:44,
      https://www.youtube.com/watch?v=mFMWZqZ1q2Y.

63   Marrero Rodríguez, "Afinan detalles."

64   Ydrach, "BAD BUNNY: 'no es fácil ser yo,'" at 00:01:10.

65   While there are several species of coquí, most of them are
      endemic to Puerto Rico. While they have been taken else-
      where, often transported accidentally via plants exported
      from Puerto Rico, they are uniquely matched to be in the
      Puerto Rican ecosystem, which is why they have developed a
      bad reputation as highly invasive in other spaces where they
      have been forcibly placed (e.g., the Hawaiian Islands).

66   Pedro Albizu Campos is one of the most important figures in the
      Puerto Rican movement for independence. After attending Har-
      vard University and Harvard Law School, Albizu Campos returned
      to Puerto Rico and in 1930 became the president of the pro-
      independence Puerto Rican Nationalist Party, a position he held until
      his death in 1965. Albizu Campos spent the majority of his years as
      the party's president in prison due to his advocacy for Puerto Rican
      independence. Blanca Canales led an insurrection against the United
      States in Jayuya, Puerto Rico, in 1950. Lolita Lebrón was another
      pro-independence activist. In 1954, she and four men entered the
      US Capitol where they fired shots and wounded five congressmen
      after shouting "¡Viva Puerto Rico!" They each spent twenty-five
      years in federal prison. For more information about these and other
      actions of the Puerto Rican independence movement, see Meléndez-
      Badillo, *Puerto Rico*; and Power, "Seeing the U.S. Empire Through
      the Eyes of the Puerto Rican Nationalists Who Opposed It."

67   The video was officially screened only at the P FKN R concerts,
      although unofficial versions existed on YouTube. Bad Bunny then
      posted it on his official Instagram account on October 29, 2024,
      in response to comedian Tony Hinchcliffe's calling Puerto Rico
      a "floating island of garbage" at a rally for Donald Trump's presi-
      dential campaign. See Benito Antonio (@badbunnypr), "garbage,"
      Instagram, October 29, 2024, https://www.instagram.com/p
      /DBtmbHquuhb/. See also Isabela Raygoza, "Bad Bunny Hits
      Back at Tony Hinchcliffe's 'Garbage' Comment with a Passionate
      Tribute to Puerto Rico," *Billboard*, October 29, 2024, https://www
      .billboard.com/music/latin/bad-bunny-tony-hinchcliffe-puerto
      -rico-comment-video-response-1235814039/; Joe Coscarelli,
      "Bad Bunny Responds to Racist Remarks at Trump Rally with a
      Message of Puerto Rican Pride," *New York Times*, October 29,
      2024, https://www.nytimes.com/2024/10/29/us/politics
      /bad-bunny-trump-harris-puerto-rico.html.

68   For more about the term *roncar* as it pertains to reggaetón, see Rivera-Rideau, *Remixing Reggaetón*, 125.

69   Alberto Ruiz, "BAD BUNNY CANTA EN DIRECTO DE INSTAGRAM
YHLQMDLG PARTE 2," posted May 3, 2020, YouTube, 00:53:47, at
00:09:34, https://www.youtube.com/watch?v=6rcpIQEBIn0&t=2s.

70   Ydrach, "BAD BUNNY: UN JANGUEO DE PROPORCIONES BÍBLICAS,"
at 00:20:00.

CHAPTER 6. "PUERTO RICO ESTÁ BIEN CABRÓN"

Note: This chapter title's quote is from the following song: Bad
Bunny. "El Apagón." *Un Verano Sin Ti* (Rimas Entertainment, 2022).

1   Sandwiched between the release of his first studio album
X 100PRE in 2018 and his second solo studio album YHLQM-
DLG in 2020, Bad Bunny also recorded his collaborative album
Oasis with Colombian reggaetón star J Balvin in 2019.

2   While the song "Tití Me Preguntó" includes an acute accent
on the second *i*, typical spelling of the word is unaccented.

3   For more about the impact of Dominicans on the development of
reggaetón, see Pacini Hernandez, "Dominicans in the Mix." It is
worth noting that there is also a large Dominican community in
Puerto Rico. For more on the Dominicans in Puerto Rico see Duany,
"Dominican Migration to Puerto Rico"; and Martínez-San Miguel,
"De ilegales e indocumentados." For more about the cultural con-
nections between Dominicans and Puerto Ricans, see Reyes-Santos,
Our Caribbean Kin; and Rivera-Rideau, "If I Were You . . ."

4   Moises Mendez II, "Bad Bunny's 'Un Verano Sin Ti' Is Already Breaking Many Records," *Remezcla*, May 9, 2022, https://remezcla.com
/music/bad-bunny-un-verano-sin-ti-breaking-records-spotify/.

5   The only other album to spend thirteen weeks at the top of the list was
Drake's *Views* in 2016. Keith Caulfield, "Bad Bunny's 'Un Verano Sin Ti'
Is Luminate's Top Album of 2022 in U.S.," *Billboard*, January 11, 2023,
https://www.billboard.com/music/chart-beat/2022-us-year-end-music
-report-luminate-top-album-bad-bunny-un-verano-sin-ti-1235196736/.

6   Caulfield, "Bad Bunny's 'Un Verano Sin Ti' Is Luminate's Top Album
of 2022 in U.S."

7   Keith Caulfield, "Bad Bunny's 'Un Verano Sin Ti' Debuts at No. 1 on
Billboard 200 Albums Chart," *Billboard*, May 15, 2022, https://www.
billboard.com/music/chart-beat/bad-bunny-un-verano-sin-ti-
billboard-200-chart-debut-1235071183/.

8   Griselda Flores, "Bad Bunny's 'Un Verano Sin Ti' Is Now the Most
Streamed Album in Spotify History," *Billboard*, July 10, 2023,
https://www.billboard.com/music/latin/bad-bunny-un-verano
-sin-ti-most-streamed-album-spotify-history-1235368920/.

9   Flores, "Bad Bunny's 'Un Verano Sin Ti' Is Now the Most Streamed
        Album in Spotify History."

10   Stefanie Fernández, "Bad Bunny's 'Un Verano Sin Ti' Is a Caribbean
        Love Letter to Puerto Rico," NPR, May 14, 2022, https://www.npr
        .org/2022/05/14/1098222737/bad-bunnys-un-verano-sin-ti-review.

11   Exposito, "Fireside Chat on 'Bad Bunny and Resistance in Puerto Rico.'"

12   Jeanette Hernandez, "Bad Bunny's 'El Último Tour Del Mundo' Is the
        Highest Grossing Tour by a Latine Artist," *Remezcla*, April 6, 2022,
        https://remezcla.com/remezcla/bad-bunny-el-ultimo-tour-del-mundo
        -highest-grossing-tour-by-a-latin-artist/; Kai Grady, "Bad Bunny Just
        Broke a Record with His El Último Tour del Mundo," *Los Angeles Times*,
        April 7, 2022, https://www.latimes.com/entertainment-arts/music
        /story/2022-04-07/bad-bunny-highest-grossing-tour-latinx-artist.

13   Mandy Dalugdug, "Bad Bunny Grosses $435M from 81-Date
        Tour in 2022, Setting New All-Time Calendar Year Record,"
        Music Business Worldwide, December 13, 2022, https://www
        .musicbusinessworldwide.com/bad-bunny-grosses-435m-worlds
        -hottest-tour-in-2022-setting-new-all-time-touring-record-report/.

14   Jeanette Hernandez, "Bad Bunny's World's Hottest Tour Tick-
        ets Are Now on Sale—& the Internet Is Freaking Out," *Remezcla*,
        January 28, 2022, https://remezcla.com/music/bad-bunny-worlds
        -hottest-tour-tickets-now-on-sale-internet-is-freaking-out/.

15   Rimas (@rimas), "Un Verano Sin Ti 🎙 Diagrama de asientos y
        detalles de venta en el @coliseopr de Puerto Rico," Instagram,
        July 7, 2022, https://www.instagram.com/p/Cftlm1_Lxem/
        ?utm_source=ig_embed&ig_rid=39a7d8de-0b3a-4aab-bda6–
        3a898ac1153a; Griselda Flores, "Planning to Go to Bad Bunny's
        Puerto Rico Shows? Here's What You Need to Know," *Billboard*,
        July 7, 2022, https://www.billboard.com/music/latin/bad-bunny
        -puerto-rico-shows-un-verano-sin-ti-tickets-1235111838/.

16   "Bad Bunny ofreció histórico concierto en su natal Puerto Rico: Así
        fue su show," *Telemundo*, July 29, 2022, https://www.telemundo
        .com/entretenimiento/latinx-now-espanol/musica/bad-bunny
        -ofrecio-historico-concierto-en-puerto-rico-asi-fue-su-show-e
        -rcna40694; Izzie Ramirez, "Bad Bunny Threw the Party of the
        Year for Puerto Ricans—and Didn't Skip the Politics," *Vox*, Au-
        gust 5, 2022, https://www.vox.com/culture/23292674/bad
        -bunny-el-choli-concert-puerto-rico-politics-luma-gentrification;
        "Bad Bunny ahora es que es," *Primera Hora*, July 28, 2022, 33.

17   Lucas Villa, "Here Are All the Special Guests at Bad Bunny's 'Un
        Verano Sin Ti' Show," *Remezcla*, July 29, 2022, https://remezcla.com/
        music/here-are-all-the-special-guests-at-bad
        -bunnys-un-verano-sin-ti-show/.

18   Ramirez, "Bad Bunny Threw the Party of the Year for Puerto Ricans."

19   Ramirez, "Bad Bunny Threw the Party of the Year for Puerto Ricans."

20 Jan Figueroa Roqué, "Atraídos por el 'fenómeno,'" *El Vocero*, July 29, 2022, 24.

21 Carlos González, "Se apodera de la isla," *El Nuevo Día*, July 30, 2022, 27.

22 Figueroa Roque, "Atraídos por el 'fenómeno.'"

23 Figueroa Roqué, "Atraídos por el 'fenómeno.'"

24 *Mamabichos* translates to "cocksuckers."

25 Univision, "Primer cacerolazo en casa del gobernador: Exigen en Puerto Rico la renuncia de Pedro Pierluisi y salida de LUMA," *Univision Puerto Rico*, August 22, 2022, https://www.univision .com/local/puerto-rico-wlii/puerto-rico-luma-energy-renuncia -gobernador-pedro-pierluisi-cacerolazo-bad-bunny.

26 Carina del Valle Schorske, "Bad Bunny and Resistance in Puerto Rico" (virtual visit to Vanessa Díaz's class), Loyola Marymount University, Los Angeles, CA, March 8, 2023.

27 Much of this paragraph is from our written contributions to the El Apagón Syllabus, which is a collaborative project between our BadBunnySyllabus.com and PuertoRicoSyllabus, https:// www.badbunnysyllabus.com/apag%C3%B3n-syllabus.

28 DJ Joe, "Vamos a Joder," by Joselly Adrian Rosario, track 15 on *Fatal Fantassy* (Fantasy Records, 2000), CD.

29 Ableton Live, commonly referred to simply as Ableton, is a popular digital audio workstation (DAW) software used for music production. It is used widely in the music industry.

30 For more about this moral panic, see R. Rivera, "Policing Morality, *Mano Dura Stylee.*"

31 Chente Ydrach, "BAD BUNNY: 'no es fácil ser yo,'" posted May 11, 2022, YouTube, 02:36:14, https://www.youtube.com/ watch?v=3i5afhwxiUc&t=1516s.

32 Kacho López Mari, "Bad Bunny Syllabus and Puerto Rico Syllabus Present: El Apagón Micro-Syllabus" September 21, 2023, virtual event via Zoom.

33 López Mari, "Bad Bunny Syllabus and Puerto Rico Syllabus Present."

34 For more on LaBoriVogue, see Rivera Velázquez, "Caribbean Kiki"; and González Cedeño and Costales del Toro, "Ballrooms and the Sacred Runway."

35 Kacho López Mari, "Bad Bunny and Resistance in Puerto Rico" (virtual visit to Vanessa Díaz's class), Loyola Marymount University, Los Angeles, CA, February 7, 2024.

36 Ydrach, "BAD BUNNY: 'no es fácil ser yo.'"

37 López Mari, "Bad Bunny and Resistance in Puerto Rico."

38 López Mari, "Bad Bunny Syllabus and Puerto Rico Syllabus Present."

39 López Mari, "Bad Bunny Syllabus and Puerto Rico Syllabus Present."

40 Israel Meléndez Ayala, "Betrayal and Blackouts in Puerto Rico," *New York Times*, September 23, 2022, https://www.nytimes.com /2022/09/22/opinion/puerto-rico-fiona-power-luma.html.

41   Lauren Hirsch and Nick Brown, "Puerto Rican Power Utility Files for Bankruptcy," Reuters, July 2, 2017, https://www.reuters.com/article/business/puerto-rican-power-utility-files-for-bankruptcy-idUSKBN19O02E/.

42   Yarimar Bonilla, "Puerto Rico Should Not Be the Land of Blackouts," *New York Times*, June 25, 2024, A22.

43   De Onís, *Energy Islands*, 86; Klein, *Battle for Paradise*.

44   De Onís, *Energy Islands*, 84.

45   Laurel Wamsley, "Here's What's in That $300 Million Whitefish Contract," NPR, October 27, 2017, https://www.npr.org/sections/thetwo-way/2017/10/27/560422492/heres-what-s-in-that-300-million-whitefish-contract.

46   De Onís, *Energy Islands*, 85.

47   Meléndez Ayala, "Betrayal and Blackouts in Puerto Rico."

48   In July 2024, customers were subject to a nearly 5 percent increase in electricity rates, making their rates 41 percent higher than the average US electricity rate. For more information, see Coral Murphy Marcos, "Puerto Rico Approves Electricity Rate Increase Weeks After Massive Blackout," *AP News*, July 1, 2024, https://apnews.com/article/puerto-rico-electricity-rates-blackout-53f96091f59738b79af3be515b8e6915.

49   Bonilla, "Puerto Rico Should Not Be the Land of Blackouts."

50   Patricia Mazzei, "'Why Don't We Have Electricity?': Outages Plague Puerto Rico," *New York Times*, October 19, 2021, https://www.nytimes.com/2021/10/19/us/puerto-rico-electricity-protest.html.

51   Patricia Mazzei, "Arrest Is Sought for Executive of Energy Firm in Puerto Rico," *New York Times*, November 11, 2021, A12.

52   Mazzei. "Arrest Is Sought for Executive"; Bonilla, "Puerto Rico Should Not Be the Land of Blackouts."

53   Laura N. Pérez Sánchez, "'I'm So Tired': Puerto Ricans Stuck in Dark Fear Extended Blackout," *New York Times*, September 25, 2022, A29.

54   Pérez Sánchez, "'I'm So Tired.'"

55   De Onís, *Energy Islands*.

56   Juan J. Arroyo, "Bad Bunny's Video for 'El Apagón' Is a Blistering Call to Action That Everyone Needs to See," *Rolling Stone*, September 16, 2022, https://www.rollingstone.com/music/music-latin/bad-bunny-releases-documentary-for-el-apagon-1234594915/.

57   Arroyo, "Bad Bunny's Video for 'El Apagón.'"

58   If a business turns $3 million or less in profits, they do not have to hire any local employees. If the business has more than $3 million in profits, they have to employ only one person in Puerto Rico. See Puerto Rico Incentives Code, Act 60 (July 2019), § 45041, Section 1030.01, Job Creation (13 L.P.R.A. § 45022), https://bvirtualogp.pr.gov/ogp/Bvirtual/leyesreferencia/PDF/2-ingles/60-2019.pdf.

59   For more about the impact of crypto business investors on Puerto Rican gentrification see Meléndez-Badillo, *Puerto Rico*, 204–7; Klein, *Battle for Paradise*.

60   Pierluisi denied that his cousin's owning property in Sol y Playa
      had any impact on his approval of the project, although the his-
      tory of Puerto Rican corruption made this hard to believe. In
      fact, just a few years later, in 2023, Walter and his brother Edu-
      ardo pled guilty to embezzling $3.7 million in federal funds that
      were supposed to have been used for public housing in Puerto
      Rico. See Javier Colón Dávila, "Puerto Rico Governor's 2 Cous-
      ins Guilty in Embezzlement Case," *AP News*, April 13, 2023,
      https://apnews.com/article/puerto-rico-governor-pierluisi
      -cousins-embezzled-c7ee4693c4f5112f205c3fc797f77f58.

61   Manuel Guillama Capella, "Exgobernador Alejandro García Padilla
      será abogado de los desarrolladores de condo hotel en Aguadilla," *El
      Nuevo Día*, March 3, 2023, https://www.elnuevodia.com/noticias
      /locales/notas/exgobernador-alejandro-garcia-padilla-sera-abogado
      -de-los-desarrolladores-de-condohotel-en-aguadilla/; "Man Shot
      During Land Privatization Protests in Puerto Rico," *NBC News*,
      February 2, 2023, https://www.nbcnews.com/now/video/man-shot
      -during-land-privatization-protests-in-puerto-rico-162515525992.

62   For more details see Alexander C. Kaufman and Hermes Ayala
      Guzmán, "The Battle over the Last Piece of Puerto Rico
      That Wasn't for Sale," *Huff Post*, October 14, 2021,
      https://www.huffpost.com/entry/puerto-rico-beaches
      -privatization_n_6160a321e4b0cc44c50c93e3.

63   López Mari, "Bad Bunny and Resistance in Puerto Rico." For more de-
      tails on the blackout, see "Hurricane Knocks Out Power in Puerto Rico;
      Warnings of Mudslides," *New York Times*, September 19, 2022, A15.

64   Here Bad Bunny is referencing the phrase that was commonly used and
      promoted in Puerto Rico after Hurricane María, saying "Puerto Rico
      will rise," or "Puerto Rico stand up." It was supposed to be motivational
      but was received as a call to action by folks who were down, who were
      dying, and who were suffering. We discuss this in chapter 3 as well.

65   Benito A. Martínez Ocasio, Speech at Allegiant Stadium, Las
      Vegas, NV, Instagram, September 23, 2022, https://www.instagram
      .com/reel/Ci48jnFgidT/?igsh=MzRlODBiNWFlZA==.

66   López Mari, "Bad Bunny Syllabus and Puerto Rico Syllabus Present."

67   Arroyo, "Bad Bunny's Video for 'El Apagón.'"

68   Lucas Villa, "Here's Who Bad Bunny Honored with the Cab-
      ezudos from His Grammy Performance," *Remezcla*, February 6,
      2023, https://remezcla.com/music/this-is-the-team-behind
      -the-cabezudos-from-bad-bunnys-grammy-performance/.

69   Power-Sotomayor, "Dancing in Non-English at the Grammys."

70   Jeanette Hernandez, "Is Dahian El Apechao Joining Bad Bunny for
      Grammys Performance?" *Remezcla*, February 2, 2023,
      https://remezcla.com/music/is-dahian-el-apechao-joining-bad-bunny-
      for-grammys-performance/.

71   Power-Sotomayor, "Dancing in Non-English at the Grammys."

CHAPTER 7. SINGING IN NON-ENGLISH

Note: This chapter title references the 2023 Grammy Awards show controversy during which Bad Bunny's performance was broadcast with the closed captions "singing in non-English," as opposed to translations. His speech, also delivered in Spanish, similarly received closed captions that read "speaking in non-English." We expand on this controversy further in this chapter.

1   Video Music Awards (@videomusicawards), "Bad Bunny Wins Artist of the Year | 2022 Video Music Awards," Facebook, August 28, 2022, https://www.facebook.com/watch/?v=403949604994036.

2   Anthony Robledo, "This Member of Congress Called Out the Grammys' Bad Bunny Snafu as Lacking 'Respect,'" *BuzzFeed News*, February 9, 2023, https://www.buzzfeednews.com/article/anthonyrobledo/robert-garcia-grammys-statement-bad-bunny; Liz Calavario, "Rapper 50 Cent Slams Grammys for Not Having Spanish Subtitles for Bad Bunny Performance, Speech," *Today*, February 9, 2023, https://www.today.com/popculture/music/rapper-50-cent-slams-grammys-not-spanish-subtitles-bad-bunny-performan-rcna70008; Yarimar Bonilla, "Bad Bunny Is [Winning in Non-English]," *New York Times*, February 11, 2023, https://www.nytimes.com/2023/02/11/opinion/bad-bunny-non-english-grammys.html?searchResultPosition=1.

3   Bad Bunny posted the iconic image of him performing at the 2023 Grammy Awards, with the closed captions "[SPEAKING IN NON-ENGLISH] / [SINGING IN NON-ENGLISH]," to his Instagram account on February 6, 2023. The post has since been removed.

4   Cepeda, *Musical ImagiNation*, 35–60; Fiol-Matta, "Pop Latinidad"; Rivera-Rideau and Torres-Leschnik, "'The Colors and Flavors of My Puerto Rico.'"

5   It is important to note that Bad Bunny uses many words in English in his song titles and lyrics, and when he is speaking Spanish in interviews. This is reflective of the colonial relationship between the United States and Puerto Rico, which has heavily influenced Puerto Rican Spanish. Shortly after taking colonial control of Puerto Rico, the United States declared Puerto Rico bilingual, despite virtually nobody in the archipelago speaking English, and it forced Puerto Rican schools to switch to fully English instruction, which led to a near collapse of Puerto Rico's educational system. These draconian policies did not end until 1949. Thus, as linguistic anthropologist Jonathan Rosa has illuminated, Puerto Ricans experience English and Spanish as intimately intertwined as a result of the colonial violence

that Puerto Ricans have experienced at the hands of the United States. While we focus on Bad Bunny as a Spanish-language artist, it is also important to acknowledge the significant place of English within his Spanish—Puerto Rican Spanish. For more on US language policy toward Puerto Rico, see J. González *Harvest of Empire*, 274–75. For more on Bad Bunny's usage of English, see Rosa, "Bad Bunny, Good PR"; and Pérez, "More Than Spanish to English Code-Switching."

6   Cuban-born actor and singer Desi Arnaz hosted and performed on SNL on February 21, 1976. In 2001 and 2010, Jennifer Lopez also hosted and performed on SNL. While both of these Latin music artists had songs in Spanish, Lopez performed in English and Arnaz performed one English and one Spanish song. Both songs Bad Bunny performed were entirely in Spanish. Critics celebrated the episode for featuring some of the only fully Spanish or mostly Spanish skits in SNL history. For more, see Esther Zuckerman, "SNL Didn't Need Subtitles," *The Atlantic*, October 22, 2023, https://www.theatlantic.com/culture/archive/2023/10/bad-bunny-saturday-night-live-snl/675731/.

7   Translation: "Ok, we're going to learn this for a moment. Before anything else, I want to send greetings to all of the Latinos across the world, especially those who are watching me live in Puerto Rico."

8   Translation: "Change that for me, change that for me."

9   Cady Lang, "*Keeping Up with the Kardashians* Is Ending. But Their Exploitation of Black Women's Aesthetics Continues," *Time*, June 10, 2021, https://time.com/6072750/kardashians-blackfishing-appropriation/; Teen Vogue, "Kendall and Kylie Jenner Accused of Cultural Appropriating Chola Culture," *Teen Vogue*, August 29, 2017, https://www.teenvogue.com/story/kendall-kylie-jenner-cultural-appropriation-chola-culture-plaid-shirt; Andrea Arterbery, "Why the Kardashian-Jenner's Hairstyles Are Cultural Appropriation," *Teen Vogue*, August 11, 2016, https://www.teenvogue.com/story/kardashian-jenners-cultural-appropriation-hair; Sam Reeds, "Kendall Jenner's Tequila Brand Actually Is Problematic," *InStyle*, September 2, 2022, https://www.instyle.com/celebrity/kendall-jenner-818-tequila-problematic-explained; Naomi Larsson, "Kendall Jenner Defends Her Tequila Brand After Calls of Cultural Appropriation," *Elle*, September 17, 2021, https://www.elle.com/uk/life-and-culture/a37629528/kendall-jenner-defends-818-tequila-brand-cultural-appropriation-mexico/.

10   At the request of the photographer, we are using Jeff as a pseudonym.

11   As Vanessa's book *Manufacturing Celebrity* recounts, from 2002 to 2008, the demographics of the Los Angeles paparazzi transitioned from a labor force of predominantly white men to one of predominantly Latino men, many of whom are immigrants. This demographic transition also correlated with increasing

antipaparazzi legislation in California and antipaparazzi sentiment in the entertainment industry that has built upon broader
anti-immigrant discourse. See Díaz, *Manufacturing Celebrity*.

12 The original post is no longer available but is referenced in multiple
articles, including Carrie Wittmer, "Kendall Jenner and Bad Bunny
Were Photographed Getting 'Very Cozy' at Coachella," *Glamour*,
April 17, 2023, https://www.glamour.com/story/kendall-jenner-and
-bad-bunny-were-photographed-getting-very-cozy-at-coachella.

13 For more on the system of sales for paparazzi photos, see Díaz,
Manufacturing Celebrity, 80–86.

14 In her own work as a reporter, Vanessa was often given tips as to where
A-list celebrities would be dining so that Vanessa could go to a specific
restaurant to "report" on that celebrity, who they were dining with, and
so on. Paparazzi were often waiting outside these same restaurants, as
they were also tipped off about the celebrity by people in the celebrity's camp. Celebrities often use paparazzi strategically, calling on
them to photograph moments that might help quell rumors of marital
issues, and so on. See Díaz, *Manufacturing Celebrity*, 106–7, 165–66.

15 You can read more about these arrangements and see some
photo examples of this in Díaz, *Manufacturing Celebrity*,
82–83. See also Kyndall Cunningham, "Meet the Photo Agency
That Turns Celeb Watchers into Conspiracy Theorists," *Vox*,
June 4, 2024, https://www.vox.com/culture/352715/backgrid
-explained-paparazzi-photo-agency-celeb-couple-sightings.

16 Díaz, *Manufacturing Celebrity*.

17 To further complicate things, Kendall Jenner is not a Kardashian
(Kendall and Kylie Jenner's parents are Kris Jenner and Caitlyn Jenner;
the Kardashian siblings' parents are Kris Jenner and the late Robert
Kardashian; thus the Jenner and Kardashian siblings share the same
mother, who is white). Since the Jenners and Kardashians are siblings,
they are often conflated. However, the racial identity of the Kardashians
is often under scrutiny. The culturally appropriative practices of members of the combined Kardashian-Jenner family are also regularly under
scrutiny. For more on the racial identity of the Kardashians, see Tehranian, "Is Kim Kardashian White (and Why Does It Matter Anyway)?"

18 For more information about depictions of Puerto Ricans in the early
twentieth century see Duany, *Puerto Rican Nation on the Move*,
39–86, and Erman, *Almost Citizens*.

19 Powdermaker, *Hollywood, the Dream Factory*.

20 Sandoval-Sánchez, *José, Can You See?*, 21–61.

21 Díaz, *Manufacturing Celebrity*, 102–18.

22 Of course, Kim Kardashian's father, Robert Kardashian, rose to prominence as an attorney in the O. J. Simpson trial. However, the family as a
whole did not become the center of constant media attention until the

release of the sex tape. As a celebrity reporter, prior to the release of the tape, Vanessa was often asked personally by Paris Hilton to interview Kim Kardashian when Paris brought Kim to red carpet events. Episodes of the first season of *Keeping Up with the Kardashians* focused on the release of the sex tape, suggesting its release may have been strategic.

23 Chente Ydrach, "La Única Entrevista que Bad Bunny Va a Dar—Masacote," uploaded December 24, 2018, YouTube, 1:28:36, at 00:16:20, https://www.youtube.com/watch?v=6obyXYrr_gQ.

24 See Michelle Ruiz, "Bad Bunny's Year . . . of Rest and Relaxation," *Vanity Fair*, October 2023, https://archive.vanityfair.com /article/2023/10/bad-bunnys-yearof-rest-and-relaxation.

25 Julyssa Lopez, "Bad Bunny Conquered the World. Now What?," *Rolling Stone*, June 21, 2023, https://www.rollingstone .com/music/music-features/bad-bunny-coachella-el -apagon-controversy-future-interview-1234770225/.

26 Smith et al., "Inequality in 1,600 Popular Films," 3–4.

27 Díaz, *Manufacturing Celebrity*, 90, 232–33, 238.

28 Leppert, "Momager of the Brides."

29 Díaz, *Manufacturing Celebrity*, 238.

30 Díaz, *Manufacturing Celebrity*, 236–40. For more about the broader definition of mainstream audiences, see Cepeda, *Musical ImagiNation*; Coddington, *How Hip Hop Became Hit Pop*; and Rivera-Rideau and Torres-Leschnik, "'Colors and Flavors of My Puerto Rico.'"

31 Davidov and Ben-Shimon have designed jewelry for many well-known musicians from Cardi B to Justin Bieber. Their work has been displayed in the American Museum of Natural History. Janae Pierre, "This NYC Jeweler Iced Out Some of Hip-Hop's Biggest Names. Now His Work Is at AMNH," Gothamist, June 20, 2024, https://gothamist.com/arts-entertainment/this-nyc-jeweler-iced -out-some-of-hip-hops-biggest-names-now-his-work-is-at-amnh.

32 Exposito, "Mediating Bad Bunny," at 00:21:20.

33 Exposito, "Fireside Chat on 'Bad Bunny and Resistance in Puerto Rico.'"

34 Exposito, "Fireside Chat on 'Bad Bunny and Resistance in Puerto Rico.'"

35 Sujeylee Solá (@sujeylee), "Bad Bunny's first *Rolling Stone* cover! This is still a little surreal for me to finally see it. I'm so incredibly proud of this one. I started the talk with my amazing contacts at Rolling Stone October of last year and continued emailing monthly. We received an insane amount of online support but still no cover. We finally had plans to go to NY before the album release and I asked Noah if we can take Beno to the *Rolling Stone* office and do an exclusive album listening session for everyone. There was serious hesitation because Bad Bunny does not show his music to anyone that's not his inner circle and team. Thank God Noah said 'I'll talk to him and we'll make it happen. Let's do it.' To make this story kind of short taking him to that office sealed the deal, everyone there was able to witness why

BAD BUNNY deserved to be on the cover of *Rolling Stone*. His huge supporter and writer for the cover story Suzy built up the excitement to her co-workers after each song kept playing and it was just epic watching all of this happen. The meeting ended with a hand shake and an offer to be on the cover. Then quarantine happened and I got scared this cover won't be able to happen anymore because of course we are facing one of the toughest moments in our lives and this one was no longer important. BUT here it is music keeps us alive and why not do an at home photoshoot during quarantine with Bad Bunny (great idea @catrionaniaolain), he's constantly breaking all the rules on how things are done and this is no exception. Thank you everyone that worked so incredibly hard in making this the cover story and feature what it is. @badbunnypr is the first latin urban male artist to appear on the cover of @rollingstone and we have the first Latin journalist to write a cover story for RS @brujacore and the first Latina photographer to shoot a RS cover, @gabriela-berlingeri I'm so proud of you," Instagram, May 14, 2020, https://www.instagram.com/sujeylee/p/CALB6fVHYoi/?img_index=3.

36   All quotes from Suzy Exposito in this paragraph are from "Fire-side Chat on 'Bad Bunny and Resistance in Puerto Rico.'"

37   For instance, mainstream US media coverage of the smash hit "Despacito" frequently framed Puerto Ricans Daddy Yankee and Luis Fonsi, both US citizens, as foreign others, while assuming that the white pop star Justin Bieber, who is a Canadian citizen, was not foreign. For more see Rivera-Rideau and Torres-Leschnik, "'Colors and Flavors of My Puerto Rico,'" 104.

38   For an overview of the uneven distribution of resources to Latin music, see Negus, *Music Genres and Corporate Cultures*. Negus wrote about salsa music in the 1990s; however, many of his observations were reiterated by the Latin music executives we have interviewed who frequently told us about the difficulties they had promoting their artists within an English-dominant industry.

39   Ana Durrani, "Top Streaming Statistics In 2024," *Forbes*, August 15, 2024, https://www.forbes.com/home-improvement/internet/streaming-stats/.

40   For more on Soundscan's impact on the charts, see Molanphy, *Old Town Road*, 44–46.

41   For critiques of streaming see Drott, *Streaming Music, Streaming Capital*.

42   Lopez, "Bad Bunny Conquered the World."

43   Joe Sabia, "73 Questions with Bad Bunny," *Vogue*, April 29, 2024, YouTube, 00:20:44, at 00:06:19, https://www.youtube.com/watch?v=KYuBLoSE-5I.

44   Shaadi Devereaux, "Latinx Files: Reggaeton Has a Color Blindness Problem," *Los Angeles Times*, April 6, 2023, https://www.latimes.com/world-nation/newsletter/2023-04-06/latinx-files-bad-bunny-colorism-tego-calderon-racism-time-interview-latinx-files.

45   The nuances in Bad Bunny's answers were lost elsewhere in the interview, as well. For more, see Mariana Alessandra (@marianalessandra), "Bad Bunny's TIME Interview: Spanish vs. English," TikTok, March 20, 2023, https://www.tiktok.com/@marianalessandra/video/7216066739832966443.

46   Andrew R. Chow and Mariah Espada, "'Hago Música Como Si Fuera la Única Persona en el Mundo.' Bad Bunny sobre Coachella, Hollywood y Superándose a sí Mismo," *Time*, March 28, 2023, https://time.com/6266396/bad-bunny-entrevista-coachella/.

47   For more information about anti-Blackness in the Latin music industry, see Abreu, *Rhythms of Race*; Rivera-Rideau, "Reinventing Enrique Iglesias"; and Rivera-Rideau, "Race, Latinidad, and Latin Pop."

48   For more see Jiménez Román and Flores, *Afro-Latin@ Reader*.

49   For more about racial ideologies in Puerto Rico, see Jiménez Román, "Hombre (Negro) del Pueblo"; Godreau, *Scripts of Blackness*; Rivera-Rideau, *Remixing Reggaetón*.

50   For an excellent overview of the commonalities between US and Latin American racial ideologies, see Hernández, "Envisioning the United States in the Latin American Myth."

51   For an example of arguments that Bad Bunny benefits from the preference for whiteness in Latin media industries, see Eduardo Cepeda, "Bad Bunny's Silence Speaks Volumes," *Remezcla*, June 12, 2020, https://remezcla.com/features/music/bad-bunny-silence-speaks-volumes/.

52   Quoted in Andrew Chow and Mariah Espada, "Bad Bunny's Next Move," *Time*, March 28, 2023, https://time.com/6266349/bad-bunny-cover-story/.

53   In this song, he says: "Ahora todos quieren ser latino / Pero les falta sazón / Batería y reggaetón" (Now everyone wants to be Latino / But they don't have the flavor / Rhythm and reggaetón).

54   Lopez, "Bad Bunny Conquered the World."

55   Quoted in Lopez, "Bad Bunny Conquered the World."

56   Quoted in Lopez, "Bad Bunny Conquered the World."

57   Frances Negrón-Muntaner cites one poll from 2017 that revealed that only 54 percent of Americans know that Puerto Ricans are US citizens. See Negrón-Muntaner, "Our Fellow Americans."

58   Picker and Sun, *Latinos Beyond Reel*.

CHAPTER 8. "NUNCA ANTES HUBO UNO COMO YO"

Note: This chapter title is a direct quote from one of the videos that was projected as part of the opening of Bad Bunny's 2023 Coachella set. Part of this speech, including this quote, are translated later in this chapter.

1   This statistic comes from reporting in 2023. Jordan Darville, "Report: Coachella Spent Millions on Frank Ocean's Ice Rink, Still Trying

to Figure Out How to Use It," *Fader*, April 21, 2023, https://www
.thefader.com/2023/04/21/report-coachella-spent-millions-on
-frank-oceans-ice-rink-still-trying-to-figure-out-how-to-use-it.

2   Apple Music, "Bad Bunny: 'WHERE SHE GOES,' Coachella & Wrestling," posted May 19, 2023, YouTube, 00:13:14, at 00:03:54,
https://www.youtube.com/watch?v=YzHtDRpsS8U.

3   Cepeda, *Musical ImagiNation*.

4   For more about Selena and her impact, see Paredez, *Selenidad*.

5   Rivera-Rideau and Torres-Leschnik, "'The Colors and Flavors
of My Puerto Rico.'"

6   Rivera-Rideau and Torres-Leschnik, "'The Colors and Flavors of My
Puerto Rico'"; Cepeda, *Musical ImagiNation*; Coddington, *How Hip
Hop Became Hit Pop*.

7   Julyssa Lopez, "Bad Bunny Conquered the World. Now
What?," *Rolling Stone*, June 21, 2023, https://www.rollingstone
.com/music/music-features/bad-bunny-coachella-el
-apagon-controversy-future-interview-1234770225/.

8   Karen Grigby Bates, "A Different National Anthem, Before the
Nation Was Ready for It," *CodeSwitch*, NPR, November 2, 2017,
https://www.npr.org/sections/codeswitch/2017/11/02/560948130
/a-different-national-anthem-before-the-nation-was-ready-for
-it; Vazquez "Toward an Ethics of Knowing Nothing," 35–37.

9   Bates, "A Different National Anthem"

10   Cobo, *Decoding "Despacito,"* 12.

11   Cobo, *Decoding "Despacito,"* 12.

12   Lopez, "Bad Bunny Conquered the World."

13   LeBrón, *Policing Life and Death*, 44–46.

14   Dinzey-Flores, *Locked In, Locked Out*; LeBrón, *Policing Life and Death*;
Rivera-Rideau, *Remixing Reggaetón*.

15   R. Rivera, "Policing Morality, *Mano Dura Stylee*," 122. See also LeBrón, *Policing Life and Death*, 83–113; and Rivera-Rideau, *Remixing Reggaetón*, 21–51.

16   R. Rivera, "Policing Morality, *Mano Dura Stylee*."

17   Rivera-Rideau, *Remixing Reggaetón*.

18   Rivera-Rideau, "'Cocolos Modernos.'"

19   Carina del Valle Schorske, "The World According to Bad Bunny,"
New York Times Magazine, October 11, 2020, https://www.nytimes
.com/interactive/2020/10/07/magazine/bad-bunny.html.

20   Arroyo, "Bad Bunny Caribeño."

21   Chente Ydrach, "La Única Entrevista que Bad Bunny Va a Dar," posted
December 24, 2018, YouTube, 01:28:36, https://www.youtube.com
/watch?v=6obyXYrr_gQ.

22   Quoted in Jessica Roiz, "Latin Artist on the Rise: How Grupo Frontera Went from a Local Band to the Billboard Charts," *Billboard*,
December 22, 2022, https://www.billboard.com/music/latin
/grupo-frontera-interview-latin-artist-on-the-rise-1235190705/.

23 Roiz, "Latin Artist on the Rise."

24 Suzy Exposito, "Edgar Barrera Talks About Writing Hits for Peso Pluma, Grupo Frontera and Bad Bunny, Shakira, Karol G—and Madonna, Too," *GQ*, February 2, 2024, https://www.gq.com/story /edgar-barrera-talks-about-writing-hits-for-peso-pluma-grupo -frontera-and-bad-bunny-shakira-karol-g-and-even-madonna.

25 Leila Cobo, "Why Edgar Barrera's New Era in Latin Music Is His Biggest Yet—And How He's Crossing Over to the Mainstream," *Billboard*, February 28, 2022, https://www.billboard.com/music/latin/edgar -barrera-edge-songwriter-producer-latin-airplay-interview-1235036339/.

26 Pamela Bustios, "Grupo Frontera Secures Career High Debut on Hot Latin Songs Chart with Bad Bunny Collab 'Un x100to,'" *Billboard*, April 25, 2023, https://www.billboard.com/music/chart-beat/grupo -frontera-bad-bunny-un-x100to-hot-latin-songs-chart-1235315339 /; Griselda Flores, Jason Lipshutz, Isabela Raygoza, Jessica Roiz, and Andrew Unterberger, "Is Grupo Frontera and Bad Bunny's 'Un x100to' Going to Be One of the Songs of the Summer?," *Billboard*, May 2, 2023, https://www.billboard.com/music/chart-beat/grupo -frontera-bad-bunny-un-x100to-hot-100-success-1235320076/.

27 Lucas Villa, "Grupo Frontera Reveals How Their Bad Bunny Collaboration Came Together," *Remezcla*, April 18, 2023, https://remezcla.com/music/grupo-frontera-reveals-how -their-bad-bunny-collaboration-came-together/.

28 In her analysis of a 2011 performance by música Mexicana group Los Tigres del Norte and reggaetón artist Residente, María Elena Cepeda notes that these cross-cultural collaborations can conform to transnational Latin marketing trends that collapse ethnoracial distinctions within Latinidad. However, Cepeda notes that this is a contradictory process. She shows how young fans both acknowledge the distinctions between Puerto Ricans and Mexicans while also seeing commonalities between the two groups' ethnoracialization as Latinos. See Cepeda, "Marketing, Performing, and Interpreting Multiple Latinidades."

29 Pacini Hernandez, *Oye Como Va!*, 119–21.

30 Pacini Hernandez, *Oye Como Va!*, 123.

31 For more about the link between música norteña and Mexican migrant workers, see Ragland, *Música Norteña.*

32 Paíz, "Essential Only as Labor."

33 For example, see Gustavo Arellano, "Coachella Makes Millions, but the Festival's Impoverished Mexican Neighbors See Very Little of It," *Los Angeles Times*, April 18, 2018, https://www.latimes .com/opinion/op-ed/la-oe-arellano-coachella-valley-20180418 -story.html; Rachel Treisman, "Coachella Began as a Typo. Here's What Happened Next," NPR, April 16, 2025, https://www.npr.org /2025/04/16/nx-s1–5365781/coachella-festival-valley-history.

34 Chavez, *Latino Threat.*

CHAPTER 9. "PRENDE UNA VELITA"

Note: This chapter title is a lyric from the following song: Bad Bunny, "Una Velita" (Rimas Entertainment, 2024).

1   Julyssa Lopez, "Bad Bunny Conquered the World. Now What?," *Rolling Stone*, June 21, 2023, https://www.rollingstone .com/music/music-features/bad-bunny-coachella-el -apagon-controversy-future-interview-1234770225/.

2   Aamina Inayit Khan, "Did Bad Bunny Hide Kendall Jenner References in the 'Where She Goes' Video?," *Teen Vogue*, May 19, 2023, https://www.teenvogue.com/story/bad-bunny -kendall-jenner-references-where-she-goes-music-video.

3   Quoted in Angie Orellana Hernandez, "Fans Think Bad Bunny Planted These Kendall Jenner Easter Eggs in New Music Video 'Where She Goes,'" *E! News*, May 18, 2023, https://www.eonline .com/news/1374888/fans-think-bad-bunny-planted-these-kendall -jenner-easter-eggs-in-new-music-video-where-she-goes.

4   Corridos tumbados are a subgenre of Mexican corridos known for blending Mexican musical traditions with hip-hop and reggaetón, and often address themes common in narcocorridos. For more information, see Elda Cantú, "Everyone Loves Corridos Tumbados. In Mexico, It's Complicated," *New York Times*, December 12, 2023, https://www.nytimes.com /2023/12/05/arts/music/corridos-tumbados-peso-pluma-mexico.html.

5   For more on country music's inroads in the music industry in 2023, see Ethan Millman, "Country Music's Summer of Streaming Domination," *Rolling Stone*, September 5, 2023, https://www.rollingstone.com/music /music-features/country-music-streaming-surge-morgan-wallen-zach -bryan-1234817052/; Conor Murray, "Country Dominates Spotify, Apple Year-End Charts—But Right-Wing Anthems by Jason Aldean, Oliver Anthony Aren't Near the Top," *Forbes*, November 29, 2023, https://www.forbes.com/sites/conormurray/2023/11/29/country -dominates-spotify-apple-year-end-charts-but-right-wing-anthems -from-jason-aldean-oliver-anthony-arent-near-the-top/; Xander Zellner, "Every Country Music Record Broken on the Hot 100 in 2023: From Morgan Wallen to Oliver Anthony Music and More," *Billboard*, September 5, 2023, https://www.billboard.com/lists/country -music-records-hot-100-morgan-wallen-oliver-anthony/most -country-songs-in-the-top-50-of-the-hot-100-in-a-single-week/.

6   Jon Dolan and Vita Dadoo, "Bad Bunny Is Paranoid, Petty, Bored, Brilliant on 'Nadie sabe lo que va a pasar mañana," *Rolling Stone*, October 16, 2023, https://www.rollingstone.com/music/music-album-reviews /bad-bunny-nadie-sabe-lo-que-va-a-pasar-manana-1234855236/.

7   Jillian Hernandez, "Bad Bunny Fans Are Upset—and Not Just About the Kendall Jenner Dating Rumors," *Refinery29*, last up-

dated April 11, 2023, https://www.refinery29.com/en-us/2023
/04/11353281/bad-bunny-fans-reaction-kendall-jenner-race.

8   Hernandez, "Bad Bunny Fans Are Upset."

9   For example, see Thania Garcia, "Bad Bunny Grapples with Fame
in 'Nadie Sabe Lo Que Va a Pasar Mañana,' a Trap-Infused Diary
Entry: Album Review," *Variety*, October 16, 2023, https://variety
.com/2023/music/news/bad-bunny-nadie-sabe-lo-que-va-a-pasar
-manana-album-review-1235757265/; Dolan and Dadoo, "Bad
Bunny Is Paranoid, Petty, Bored, Brilliant"; Jon Pareles, "Bad Bunny
Looks Back and Hunkers Down," *New York Times*, October 16,
2023, https://www.nytimes.com/2023/10/16/arts/music/bad
-bunny-nadie-sabe-lo-que-va-a-pasar-manana-review.html.

10   Garcia, "Bad Bunny Grapples with Fame."

11   It is also worth noting that Latinos have a long history of participat-
ing in and dominating horse racing in the United States. Historian
José Alamillo notes that Latinos were so dominant in horse racing in the 1960s that "*Sports Illustrated* declared a 'Latin invasion'
on major U.S. horse tracks." Alamillo also reports that since 2000,
about half of all professional jockeys in the US are Latino, including Puerto Ricans. Alamillo, "History of Latino/as and Sports."

12   Marina Ortiz Cortés, "El divertido (e incómodo) momento en el que
Bad Bunny se queda enganchado a una bailarina," *El Independiente*,
October 6, 2024, https://www.elindependiente.com/gente/2024
/06/10/bad-bunny-enganchado-bailarina-posicion-incomoda/.

13   Puerto Rico Vive (@prvive), "Entrada del concierto de Bad Bunny.
Orquesta de PR tocando el himno de Puerto Rico ✊ 🎺 ❤ ORGULLO
BORICUAAAAAA❤ 📍 Puerto Rico ✊ 💼 @jlpromotionspr 👥 Face-
book: PRviveOfficial 📱 Instagram: @PRvive ♻ NO DEJEN BASURA,
CUIDEMOS LO NUESTRO," Instagram, June 7, 2024, https://www
.instagram.com/reel/C78RoA8t_vP/?igsh=MzRlODBiNWFlZA==.

14   Jeanette Hernandez, "Here Are All the Special Guests at Bad Bunny's Most Wanted Tour Shows in Puerto Rico," *Remezcla*, June 10,
2024, https://remezcla.com/music/here-are-all-the-special-guests
-at-bad-bunnys-most-wanted-tour-shows-in-puerto-rico/.

15   Mariana Garibay, "VIDEO | Bad Bunny llora en pleno concierto y
usuarios temen que podría retirarse de la música," *La Razón*, September 6, 2024, https://www.razon.com.mx/entretenimiento
/2024/06/10/video-bad-bunny-llora-en-pleno-concierto
-y-usuarios-temen-que-podria-retirarse-de-la-musica/.

16   Juan Arroyo, "Bad Bunny Ends 'Most Wanted' Tour with a Historic
Three-Night Run in Puerto Rico," *Rolling Stone*, June 10, 2024,
https://www.rollingstone.com/music/music-news/bad-bunny-most
-wanted-puerto-rico-el-choli-surprise-guests-feid-1235037045/.

17   EFE, "Bad Bunny anuncia venta de boletos 2×1 en Puerto Rico
para impulsar electores a votar" *El Diario*, June 6, 2024, https://

eldiariony.com/2024/06/06/bad-bunny-anuncia-oferta-de-venta
-de-boletos-2x1-en-puerto-rico-para-impulsar-electores-a-votar/.

18 Nicole Acevedo, "Bad Bunny Spoke Out Against Voter Apathy in Puerto Rico and It's Having an Effect," NBC News, September 5, 2024, https://www.nbcnews.com/news/latino/bad-bunny-puerto-rico-voting-2024-election-rcna169739.

19 Abraham, "Puerto Rico's New Leftist Alliance Poses a Threat."

20 El Tony PR, "'Yo quiero que mi gente viva feliz en Puerto Rico' Benito (Bad Bunny)," posted September 2, 2024, YouTube, 01:28:21, https://www.youtube.com/watch?v=zw7bLZOnou4.

21 Wapa Digital, "La Alianza compone canción con expresiones de Bad Bunny contra el PNP y JGo," Wapa PR, September 10, 2024, https://wapa.tv/noticias/entretenimiento/la-alianza-compone-canci-n-con-expresiones-de-bad-bunny-contra-el-pnp-y-jgo/article_fb6a52b0-6a1d-11ef-b9af-cb559e7d1d31.html.

22 JPTG, "Bad Bunny—Jeniffer Mentirosa (clip)," posted September 5, 2024, YouTube, 00:00:30, https://www.youtube.com/watch?app=desktop&v=holgxIow15s.

23 Telemundo PR, "¿Ya lo endosó? Residente sube una foto a las redes con Juan Dalmau," Telemundo PR, September 22, 2024, https://www.telemundopr.com/noticias/puerto-rico/ya-lo-endoso-residente-sube-una-foto-a-las-redes-con-juan-dalmau/2647313/.

24 TALKESHI (@talkeshipod), "buenos días," Instagram, October 4, 2024, https://www.instagram.com/p/DAuSb1iyCbD/?igsh=MzRlODBiNWFlZA==.

25 Jugando Pelota Dura, "Jenniffer González reacciona a expresiones de Bad Bunny sobre el PNP," posted September 5, 2024, YouTube, 00:10:00, at 00:02:55, https://www.youtube.com/watch?v=DmO9-cIsvRA.

26 Magic TV, "Primicia—El senador PNP, Thomas Rivera Schatz validó los billboards en contraataque a Bad Bunny," posted September 25, 2024, YouTube, 00:06:33, quote at 00:04:25, https://youtu.be/PL7KQXkPKbw?si=vGIpc4SMszB4ke-J.

27 Bianca Graulau (@biancagraulau), "Esta es la razón por la cual yo empecé a cubrir otros países. Tenemos que mirar al mundo, aprender y exigir más," Instagram, September 4, 2024, https://www.instagram.com/reel/C_gtEPNuTAW/?igsh=MzRlODBiNWFlZA==. See also Con(Sentimientos) (@con.sentimientospr), Instagram, September 17, 2024, https://www.instagram.com/reel/DACQJlgOVQI/?igsh=MzRlODBiNWFlZA==.

28 Amanda Mars, "Bad Bunny: 'Hay que romper eso de que los gringos son dioses . . . No, papi,'" El País Semanal, January 3, 2021, https://elpais.com/elpais/2020/12/30/eps/1609327975_051296.html; Patria Nueva Cuenta Oficial (@patrianuevapr) and Juan Dalmau Ramírez (@juandalmaupr), Instagram, June 6,

2024, https://www.instagram.com/reel/C75IsHhPGLh/?igsh
=MzRlODBiNWFlZA==; El Vocero, "Bad Bunny votará en las
elecciones generales,"*El Vocero*, August 20, 2020, https://www
.elvocero.com/escenario/bad-bunny-votar-en-las-elecciones
-generales/article_b5838e86-e31e-11ea-8faf-df2c68c2bf3d.html.

29 Telemundo PR, "Aparecen nuevos 'billboards' de Bad Bunny
contra el PNP y PPD," *Telemundo PR*, October 7, 2024, https://
www.telemundopr.com/noticias/puerto-rico/aparecen-nuevos
-billboards-de-bad-bunny-contra-el-pnp-y-ppd/2651396/.

30 Star Staff, "Electoral Comptroller: Bad Bunny Could Be Fined
over Political Signs," *San Juan Daily Star*, September 26,
2024, https://www.sanjuandailystar.com/post/electoral
-comptroller-bad-bunny-could-be-fined-over-political-signs.

31 Jessica Roiz, "Bad Bunny Slams Puerto Rico's New Progres-
sive Party in Billboards He Paid For," *Billboard*, September 26,
2024, https://www.billboard.com/music/latin/bad-bunny-slams
-puerto-rico-new-progressive-party-billboards-1235785480/.

32 This logo sometimes appears with the reverse color scheme.

33 Wapa Digital, "Thomas Rivera Schatz le responde a Bad
Bunny con 'billboard' para que '_ame.'" *Wapa PR*, November 1, 2024, https://wapa.tv/noticias/politica/thomas-rivera
-schatz-le-responde-a-bad-bunny-con-billboard-para-que-ame
/article_812a4044-7b45-11ef-9d79-fbad70be20b8.html.

34 And yet, in the 2024 general assembly meeting for the PNP, they
hired legendary reggaetón artist DJ Playero, to DJ the event. During his set, the phrase "Todo el mundo bellakeando" (Everyone
is fooling around sexually) flashed on the screen, projected to the
entire event. Ultimately DJ Playero took responsibility for pro-
jecting the phrase, but the irony is clear. El Vocero, "DJ Playero
aclara controversial estribillo durante asamblea del PNP," *El Vocero*, September 23, 2024, https://www.elvocero.com/escenario
/dj-playero-aclara-controversial-estribillo-durante-asamblea-del
-pnp/article_35cdbf8a-7a01-11ef-abb8-3b71a1bbf79e.html.

35 Magic TV, "Primicia—El senador PNP, Thomas Rivera Schatz,"
at 00:01:40.

36 Magic TV, "Primicia—El senador PNP, Thomas Rivera Schatz,"
at 00:04:55.

37 Directo y Sin Filtro por ABC Puerto Rico (@Directo y Sin Filtro por ABC Puerto Rico), "⬛ **¡Sigue la guerra de los billboards!** ⬛ Así amaneció hoy el expreso PR-22, en direc-
ción de San Juan a Arecibo, cerca del peaje de Toa Baja, con
un nuevo anuncio que ha llamado la atención de todos. 😱

Esta vez, el mensaje va en contra de @badbunnypr, pero
lo más curioso es que el anuncio **no está firmado** ni in-
cluye la información legal que identifica quién lo paga.

¿Qué te parece? ¿Quién crees que está detrás de este polémico billboard? 🙄," Facebook, October 3, 2024, https://www.facebook.com/directoysinfiltroabc/posts/987138256547838.

38 Puerto Rico Incentives Code, Act 60 (July 2019), § 45041, https://bvirtualogp.pr.gov/ogp/Bvirtual/leyesreferencia/PDF/2-ingles/60-2019.pdf.

39 Partido Independentista Puertorriqueño, "Festival de la Esperanza," live streamed on November 3, 2024, YouTube, 08:23:36, at 05:45:37, https://youtu.be/DHkVsRV-Xzw?t=20737.

40 Jamie Burton, "Logan Paul Slammed for Accusing Bad Bunny of 'Tax Fraud' in Puerto Rico," *Newsweek*, October 6, 2022, https://www.newsweek.com/logan-paul-slammed-accusing-bad-bunny-puerto-rico-act-22-tax-fraud-exploitation-1749337.

41 Assilem Maldonado, "BB ni está corriendo político y ya lo tienen en los ataques del PNP. PR es un chiste para el PNP y hablan de dictadura y viven atacando a quienes piensan diferentes a ellos, que mal nos va. PQ tanto enfoque en BB?," reply to Directo y Sin Filtro por ABC Puerto Rico, Facebook, October 3, 2024, https://www.facebook.com/directoysinfiltroabc/posts/987138256547838.

42 Karina Ashley Feliciano, "Como si BB fuera candidato," reply to Directo y Sin Filtro por ABC Puerto Rico, October 3, 2024, https://www.facebook.com/directoysinfiltroabc/posts/987138256547838.

43 Directo y Sin Filtro por ABC Puerto Rico, "¡Sigue la guerra del billboards!

44 Raúl Cabán Pérez, "Como Ataque No Es PNP ellos no importa Quien Pago," reply to Directo y Sin Filtro por ABC Puerto Rico, Facebook, October 3, 2024, https://www.facebook.com/directoysinfiltroabc/posts/987138256547838.

45 Telemundo PR, "Aparecen nuevos 'billboards' de Bad Bunny contra el PNP y PPD."

46 Jay Fonseca, "🎶 Bad Bunny publicó esta tarde nuevos billboards en los que critica también al Partido Popular Democrático (PPD). 📱 Las imágenes fueron tomadas por el analista político Néstor Duprey en su cuenta de la red social "X." 🙄 Una de las vallas publicitarias dice: "Cada vez que se te vaya la luz recuerda que es culpa del PNP y el PPD."🙄 Además, un segundo billboard dice: "No olvides lo que dijeron en el chat . . . El PNP quiere un Puerto Rico sin puertorriqueños. ¡Qué se vayan ellos!." ¿Y tú ya decidiste por quién votar?," Facebook, October 7, 2024, https://www.facebook.com/photo.php?fbid=1107835054034227&set=a.267813968036344&type=3.

47 Ortiz and Minet, "Las 889 páginas de Telegram."

48 Benito A. Martínez Ocasio, "Muerte al PNP," *El Nuevo Día*, November 1, 2024, 2.

49 Valeria María Torres Nieves, "'No me arrepiento de ninguna de mis expresiones': Bad Bunny dirige carta abierta a los estadistas,"

El Nuevo Día, November 1, 2024, https://www.elnuevodia.com
/noticias/politica/notas/no-me-arrepiento-de-ninguna-de-mis
-expresiones-bad-bunny-dirige-carta-abierta-a-los-estadistas/.

50 Ramón "Tonito" Zayas, "Estos fueron algunos de los artistas que se
presentaron en el 'Festival de la Esperanza' de la Alianza de País,"
El Nuevo Día, November 3, 2024, https://www.elnuevodia.com/
entretenimiento/farandula/fotogalerias/estos-fueron-algunos-
de-los-artistas-que-se-presentaron-en-el-festival
-de-la-esperanza-de-la-alianza-de-pais/.

51 Kacho and Tristana are the cofounders of production company Filmes
Zapateros.

52 Partido Independentista Puertorriqueño, "Festival de la Esperanza,"
at 05:51:41.

53 Partido Independentista Puertorriqueño, "Festival de la Esperanza,"
at 05:58:03.

54 For a longer description of this generation and phrase, see Laguarta
Ramírez, "¡Yo no me dejé!"

55 Laguarta Ramírez, "¡Yo no me dejé!"

56 Partido Independentista Puertorriqueño, "Festival de la Esperanza,"
at 06:01:05.

57 Partido Independentista Puertorriqueño, "Festival de la Esperanza,"
at 06:02:50.

58 Bad Bunny (@badbunnypr), "huracán," Instagram, September 23,
2024, https://www.instagram.com/p/DARbzcPSqDM/.

59 Meléndez-Badillo, *Puerto Rico*, 42, 48.

60 For more details about the complex history of "La Borinqueña,"
see Joanna McKee, "Puerto Rico's National Anthem 'La
Borinqueña': The Story Behind the Song," Kennedy Center,
June 19, 2024, https://www.kennedy-center.org/education
/resources-for-educators/classroom-resources/media-and
-interactives/media/music/story-behind-the-song/the
-story-behind-the-song/la-borinquena---english/.

61 Metro Puerto Rico, "Bad Bunny: '¡El PNP se está tratando de
robar las elecciones!," *Metro*, November 4, 2024, https://
www.metro.pr/entretenimiento/2024/11/04/bad-bunny
-el-pnp-se-esta-tratando-de-robar-las-elecciones/.

62 Benito Antonio (@sanbenito), "Está cabrón que los que han
gastado miles en campaña de miedo con dictadura y comu-
nismo son los mismos que han jodido la democracia y el proceso
electoral en Puerto Rico. Son los mismos que llevan haciendo
mil trucos y malabares con el voto del pueblo. ¡EL PNP SE ESTÁ
TRATANDO DE ROBAR LAS ELECCIONES!," X, November 4,
2024, https://x.com/sanbenito/status/1853516159246913781.

63 PUERTO RICO 🏴 (@puertoricogram), "🗽 🏴 Bad Bunny Llega
Al Colegio De Votaciones A Ejercer Su Derecho Al Voto," In-

stagram, November 5, 2024, https://www.instagram.com
/reel/DB_nPShxJ_p/?igsh=MzRlODBiNWFlZA==.

64 JuventudDeIzquierda 🐙 (@juventudizquierdista), "Residente: 📧 Después de 55 años el partido La Alianza se con-
solida como segunda fuerza política en puerto rico 🍂🏝️" Instagram, November 6, 2024, https://www.instagram.com
/reel/DCCKB4_x_yb/?igsh=MzRlODBiNWFlZA==.

65 Benito Antonio (@sanbenito) "Hoy más que nunca me siento
orgulloso de quien soy, de mis acciones y del amor que le tengo
a mi tierra. Se vale estar triste, se vale sentirse desanimado pues
entiendo la frustración que sentimos muchos. A mi también me
preocupa el futuro de PUERTO RICO y a los daños que se pudiera
enfrentar en los próximos años, por eso me expreso y no dejaré de
hacerlo. Pero yo aun sigo con esperanza porque cada vez son más
los que despiertan y se unen a quienes sueñan y luchan por un mejor
Puerto Rico. Aquí seguimos, no nos quitamos," X, November 6,
2024, https://x.com/sanbenito/status/1854198311944851773?s=48.

66 Meléndez-Badillo, *Puerto Rico*, 48.

67 In a postelection interview in 2024, Mitch McConnell, as the leader
of the incoming majority party, stated that the Republican-led
government would not admit any states to the union that would not
benefit the Republican Party in terms of governmental representation. This was the day after the hypothetical question regarding
choice for US president asked on the Puerto Rican election ballot
resulted in a landslide of Puerto Ricans favoring Democrat Ka-
mala Harris over Donald Trump. For more on McConnell's statement, see José Delgado, "'There Won't Be Any New States Admitted,' says Mitch McConnell, Senate Republican Leader," *El Nuevo
Día*, November 7, 2024, https://www.elnuevodia.com/english
/news/story/there-wont-be-any-new-states-admitted-says-mitch
-mcconnell-senate-republican-leader/. For more on plebiscites, see,
for example, Cristina Corujo, "Puerto Rico Votes in Favor of Statehood. But What Does It Mean for the Island?," *ABC News*, November 8, 2020, https://abcnews.go.com/US/puerto-rico-votes-favor
-statehood-island/story?id=74055630; CNBC Television, "Senate
Minority Leader Mitch McConnell Speaks After Trump's election
victory—11/6/2024," live streamed November 6, 2024, YouTube,
00:17:15, at 00:04:23, https://youtu.be/DMpIn_6oOzE?t=261.

CONCLUSION

Note: This chapter title references a phrase used by Puerto Ricans asserting their place within Puerto Rico as gentrification and
displacement worsens; it also references a quote from the short

film *DeBÍ TiRAR MáS FOToS* that was released in advance of Bad Bunny's album of the same name. Benito A. Martínez Ocasio and Arí Maniel Cruz Suárez, dir., *DeBÍ TiRAR MáS FOToS* (Rimas Entertainment, 2025), posted by Bad Bunny, January 3, 2025, YouTube, 00:12:58, https://www.youtube.com/watch?v=gLSzEYVDads.

1 Many of the arguments in this conclusion are borrowed from the album review we coauthored for *Latina*. See Vanessa Díaz and Petra Rivera-Rideau, "Bad Bunny's Album Is So Much More Than a Love Letter to Puerto Rico," *Latina*, January 15, 2025, https://latina.com/bad-bunny-debi-tirar-mas-fotos-album-review/.

2 For example, see Lola Méndez, "Bad Bunny's New Album Is a Love Letter to Puerto Rico—and These Are the Most Important Details," *Architectural Digest*, January 15, 2025, https://www.architecturaldigest.com/story/bad-bunnys-new-album-is-a-love-letter-to-puerto-rico-and-these-are-the-most-important-details; Maria Sherman, "Bad Bunny's 'Debí Tirar Más Fotos' Is a Love Letter to Puerto Rico," *AP News*, January 5, 2025, https://apnews.com/article/bad-bunny-debi-tirar-mas-fotos-review-856f8e4f89e48e6ab104a491ae3dbcde.

3 Meléndez-Badillo, *Puerto Rico*, 71–72.

4 Although the United States formally annexed Hawai'i in 1898, it did not acquire the islands through the Treaty of Paris as it did Puerto Rico. Instead, this annexation came on the heels of several decades of military and economic intervention, including the overthrow of the Hawaiian monarchy by successful American businessmen. For more about Hawai'i see Aikau and Vicuña Gonzalez, *Detours*.

5 For an overview of these critiques, see Godreau, *Scripts of Blackness*, 83–92.

6 For more information about the impact of short-term rentals on the San Juan Metro area, in particular, see Santiago-Bartolomei, "In Two Caribbean Cities, Digital Platforms Drive Gentrification."

7 Nicole Acevedo, "Bad Bunny to Launch First-Ever Residency in Puerto Rico," *NBC News*, January 13, 2025, https://www.nbcnews.com/news/latino/bad-bunny-first-residency-puerto-rico-rcna187433.

8 Telemundo Puerto Rico, "Vale la pena: Termina larga espera para fanáticos de Bad Bunny," posted January 15, 2025, YouTube, 00:02:25, https://www.youtube.com/watch?v=CJ5Fxr_T7p0.

9 Thania Garcia, "Bad Bunny Sells Out Puerto Rico Residency," *Variety*, January 17, 2025, https://variety.com/2025/music/news/bad-bunny-sells-out-puerto-rico-residency-1236277639/.

10 Jessica Roiz, "Bad Bunny's Puerto Rico Residency Aims to Boost Local Economy," *Billboard*, January 15, 2025, https://www.billboard.com/pro/bad-bunny-puerto-rico-residency-help-local-economy/.

11 Roiz, "Bad Bunny's Puerto Rico Residency Aims to Boost Local Economy"; see also Jhoni Jackson, "What Bad Bunny's Residency

Means for Puerto Rico's Economy," *Yahoo News*, January 15, 2025, https://www.yahoo.com/news/bad-bunny-residency-means -puerto-130000613.html; Yamili Habib, "Bad Bunny's Residency in Puerto Rico Is Sparking an Economic and Cultural Revival," *Mitú*, July 15, 2025, https://wearemitu.com/wearemitu /culture/bad-bunnys-residency-in-puerto-rico-impact/.

12   Star Staff, "Searches for Accommodations in PR Surge After Announcement of Bad Bunny Residency," *San Juan Daily Star*, February 13, 2025, https://www.sanjuandailystar.com/post/searches-for-accommodations -in-pr-surge-after-announcement-of-bad-bunny-residency.

DISCOGRAPHY

Bad Bunny. *X 100PRE*. Produced by Bad Bunny, Tainy, La Paciencia, and others. Rimas Entertainment. Released December 24, 2018.

Bad Bunny and J Balvin. *Oasis*. Produced by Sky Rompiendo, Tainy, and others. Rimas Entertainment and Universal Music Latin. Released June 28, 2019.

Bad Bunny. *YHLQMDLG*. Produced by Tainy, Subelo NEO, and others. Rimas Entertainment. Released February 29, 2020.

Bad Bunny. *Las Que No Iban a Salir*. Produced by Bad Bunny, Tainy, La Paciencia, and others. Rimas Entertainment. Released May 10, 2020.

Bad Bunny. *El Último Tour del Mundo*. Produced by Bad Bunny, MAG, Tainy, and others. Rimas Entertainment. Released November 27, 2020.

Bad Bunny. *Un Verano Sin Ti*. Produced by Bad Bunny, Tainy, MAG, and others. Rimas Entertainment. Released May 6, 2022.

Bad Bunny. *Nadie Sabe Lo Que Va a Pasar Mañana*. Produced by Bad Bunny, MAG, Tainy, and others. Rimas Entertainment. Released October 13, 2023.

Bad Bunny. *DeBÍ TiRAR MáS FOToS*. Produced by Bad Bunny, MAG, Tainy, La Paciencia, and others. Rimas Entertainment. Released January 5, 2025.

INTERVIEWS

Pablo Batista, head of management/A&R for Neon16. Miami, FL, June 3, 2024.

Eduardo Cabra, music producer. Zoom, June 13, 2024.

Andrew Chow, *Time* reporter. Zoom, July 18, 2023.

De La Ghetto (Rafael Castillo Torres), musical artist. Zoom, July 16, 2024.

Krystina De Luna, Latin music programmer at Apple Music. Zoom, May 24, 2024.

Carina del Valle Schorske, writer and journalist. Zoom, May 24, 2023.

Mariah Espada, former *Time* editor and reporter. Zoom, July 18, 2023.

Alejandro García Padilla, former governor of Puerto Rico (2013–17).
    Zoom, June 20, 2024.

iLe (Ileana Cabra Joglar), musical artist. Zoom, June 13, 2024.

Jeff (pseudonym), celebrity photographer. Los Angeles, CA, March 10, 2023.

Jowell (Joel Muñoz Martínez), musical artist. Chicago, IL, May 26, 2024.

Gustavo Lopez, Latin music executive and CEO of Globalatino (former CEO
    and founder of Machete Music). Woodland Hills, CA, August 17, 2023.

Julyssa Lopez, deputy music editor and reporter at *Rolling Stone*. Zoom,
    June 27, 2023.

Kacho López Mari, film director. San Juan, Puerto Rico, October 9,
    2024; Zoom, December 5, 2024; telephone, January 14, 2025.

MAG (Marcos Borrero), music producer. Zoom, June 13, 2024; Zoom,
    August 19, 2024; telephone, January 14, 2025; Zoom, January 29, 2025.

Marissa Lopez, Latin artist relations at Apple Music. Zoom,
    June 28, 2024; Zoom, March 14, 2025.

Emilio Morales, managing director of Rimas Publishing. San Juan, Puerto Rico,
    October 10, 2024.

Jerry Pullés, Latin music programmer at Apple Music. Zoom, May 20, 2024.

Randy (Randy Ortiz Acevedo), musical artist. Chicago, IL, May 26, 2024.

Angie Romero, former global content lead at Amazon Music and
    former senior editor at Spotify. Zoom, November 17, 2023.

Eddie Santiago, former head of US Latin artist partnerships
    at Spotify. Zoom, June 25, 2024.

Tainy (Marco Efraín Masís Fernández), music producer. Miami, FL, June 4, 2024. Jesús Triviño, senior director of industry relations at
    TIDAL. Zoom, April 23, 2024.

OTHER SOURCES

Abadía-Rexach, Bárbara. "Summer 2019: The Great Racialized Puerto Rican Family." *Society and Space*, February 25, 2020. https://www .societyandspace.org/articles/summer-2019-the-great-racialized -puerto-rican-family-protesting-in-the-street-fearlessly.

Abraham, Jenaro. "Puerto Rico's New Leftist Alliance Poses a Threat to US Imperialism." *NACLA*, December 19, 2024. https:// nacla.org/puerto-rico-left-alliance-imperialism.

Abrams, Zara. "Puerto Rico, Two Years After Maria." *American Psychological Association*, September 1, 2019. https:// www.apa.org/monitor/2019/09/puerto-rico.

Abreu, Christina. *Rhythms of Race: Cuban Musicians and the Making of Latino New York City and Miami, 1940–1960.* Chapel Hill: University of North Carolina Press, 2015.

Aikau, Hokulani K., and Vernadette Vicuña Gonzalez, eds. *Detours: A Decolonial Guide to Hawai'i.* Durham, NC: Duke University Press, 2019.

Alamillo, José M. "A History of Latino/as and Sports." *Oxford Research Encyclopedia of American History*, August 21, 2024. https:// doi.org/10.1093/acrefore/9780199329175.013.374.

Allende Goitía, Noel, "The Profane, the Lewd, and the Misogynistic in Puerto Rican Singing: A Historical and Interpretive Primer to Bad Bunny's Song Lyrics (1900–2022)." In *The Bad Bunny Enigma: Culture, Resistance, and Uncertainty*, edited by Sheilla R. Madera, Nelson Varas-Díaz, and Daniel Nevárez Araújo, 27–44. London: Lexington Books, 2025.

Amaya, Hector. "The Dark Side of Transnational Latinidad: Narcocorridos and the Branding of Authenticity." In *Contemporary Latina/o Media: Production, Circulation, Politics*, edited by Arlene Dávila and Yeidy Rivero, 223–42. New York: New York University Press, 2014.

Aramburu, Diana, and Tania Carrasquillo Hernández. "From Victimization to Feminist Revolution: Performing Decolonized Bodies as Acts of Collective Rebellion in Puerto Rico." *CENTRO: Journal of the Center for Puerto Rican Studies* 35, no. 2 (2023): 7–29.

Arroyo, Jossianna. "Bad Bunny Caribeño." The Bad Bunny Symposium: Thinking with Bad Bunny. Center for Puerto Rican Studies, Hunter College, New York, May 13, 2023. MP4, 01:20:51. https:// centropr.hunter.cuny.edu/media/bad-bunny-caribeno/.

Ayala, César J., and Rafael Bernabe. *Puerto Rico in the American Century: A History Since 1898*. Chapel Hill: University of North Carolina Press, 2007.

Báez, Jillian M. "'En Mi Imperio': Competing Discourses of Agency in Ivy Queen's Reggaetón." *CENTRO: Journal of the Center for Puerto Rican Studies* 18, no. 2 (2006): 63–81.

Bergad, Laird W. *The Dominican Population of the New York Metropolitan Region, 1970–2019*. Center for Latin American, Caribbean, and Latino Studies, CUNY Graduate Center, August 2022. https://academicworks.cuny.edu/clacls_pubs/103/.

Berríos-Miranda, Marisol, and Shannon Dudley. "El Gran Combo, Cortijo, and the Musical Geography of Cangrejos/Santurce, Puerto Rico." *Caribbean Studies* 36, no. 2 (2008): 121–51.

Bonilla, Yarimar. "The Coloniality of Disaster: Race, Empire, and the Temporal Logics of Emergency in Puerto Rico, USA." *Political Geography* 78 (2020): 102–81. https://doi.org/10.1016/j.polgeo.2020.102181.

Bonilla, Yarimar. "Postdisaster Futures: Hopeful Pessimism, Imperial Ruination, and La Futura Cuir." *Small Axe: A Caribbean Journal of Criticism* 24, no. 2 (2020): 147–62.

Bonilla, Yarimar, and Naomi Klein. "The Trauma Doctrine." In *Aftershocks of Disaster: Puerto Rico Before and After the Storm*, edited by Yarimar Bonilla and Marisol LeBrón, 21–37. Chicago: Haymarket Books, 2019.

Bonilla, Yarimar, and Marisol LeBrón, eds. *Aftershocks of Disaster: Puerto Rico Before and After the Storm*. Chicago: Haymarket Books, 2019.

Brisa, Rima, and Isar Godreau. "Dismantling Public Education in Puerto Rico." In *Aftershocks of Disaster: Puerto Rico Before and After the Storm*, edited by Yarimar Bonilla and Marisol LeBrón, 234–39. Chicago: Haymarket Books, 2019.

Burnett, Christine Duffy, and Burke Marshall, eds. *Foreign in a Domestic Sense: Puerto Rico, American Expansionism, and the Constitution*. Durham, NC: Duke University Press, 2001.

Cabán, Pedro. "PROMESA, Puerto Rico and the American Empire." *Latino Studies* 16, no. 2 (2018): 161–84. https://doi.org/10.1057/s41276-018-0125-z.

Cabán, Pedro. "Puerto Rico's Forever Exodus." *NACLA*, February 22, 2018. https://nacla.org/news/2018/02/22/puerto-rico%E2%80%99s-forever-exodus.

Calderón, Tego. "Black Pride." In *Reggaeton*, edited by Raquel Z. Rivera, Wayne Marshall, and Deborah Pacini Hernandez, 324–26. Durham, NC: Duke University Press, 2009.

Castro Pérez, Joel. "La lucha por derecho a ser: Una historia de transfobia institucional 1995–2018." *CENTRO: Journal of the Center for Puerto Rican Studies* 30, no. 2 (2023): 478–501.

Cepeda, María Elena. "'A Cartel Built for Love': 'Medellín,' Pablo Escobar, and the Scripts of Global Colombianidad." In *Critical Dialogues in Latinx*

Studies, edited by Mérida Rúa and Ana Ramos-Zayas, 39–50. New York: New York University Press, 2021.

Cepeda, María Elena. "Marketing, Performing, and Interpreting Multiple Latinidades: Los Tigres del Norte and Calle 13's 'América.'" In *Contemporary Latina/o Media: Production, Circulation, Politics*, edited by Arlene Dávila and Yeidy Rivero, 303–21. New York: New York University Press, 2014.

Cepeda, María Elena. *Musical ImagiNation: U.S.-Colombian Identity in the Latin Music Boom*. New York: New York University Press, 2010.

Chamberlain, Edward. "From Father to Humanitarian: Charting Intimacies and Discontinuities in Ricky Martin's Social Media Presence and Writing." In *Caribbean Migrations: The Legacies of Colonialism*, edited by Anke Birkenmeir, 87–102. New Brunswick, NJ: Rutgers University Press, 2021.

Chavez, Leo. *The Latino Threat: Constructing Immigrants, Citizens, and the Nation*. 2nd ed. Redwood City, CA: Stanford University Press, 2013.

Cintrón-Moscoso, Federico, and Vanessa Díaz. "Photo Essay: The Power of Popular Protest: El Verano Boricua." *Latin American Perspectives* 47, no. 3 (2020): 13–17. https://doi.org/10.1177/0094582X20916217.

Cobo, Leila. *Decoding "Despacito": An Oral History of Latin Music*. New York: Penguin Random House, 2021.

Coddington, Amy. *How Hip Hop Became Hit Pop: Radio, Rap, and Race*. Berkeley: University of California Press, 2023.

Corona, Ignacio. "The Cultural Locations of US 'Latin' Rock." In *The Routledge Companion to Latina/o Media Studies*, edited by Dolores Inés Casillas and María Elena Cepeda, 241–58. New York: Routledge, 2017.

Dávila Ellis, Verónica. "Doing Reggaeton However He Wants: Bad Bunny's YHLQMDLG (Review)." *NACLA*, March 23, 2020. https://nacla .org/news/2020/03/23/bad-bunny-YHLQMDLG-review.

Dávila Ellis, Verónica. "'¿Dónde están las yales?' Reggaetón and Womanhood in the Welfare Island." *Journal of Gender and Sexuality Studies/Revista de Estudios de Género y Sexualidades* 46, nos. 1–2 (2020): 195–214.

de Onís, Catalina. *Energy Islands: Metaphors of Power, Extractivism, and Justice in Puerto Rico*. Berkeley: University of California Press, 2021.

Díaz, Vanessa. *Manufacturing Celebrity: Latino Paparazzi and Women Reporters in Hollywood*. Durham, NC: Duke University Press, 2020.

Díaz, Vanessa, and Petra R. Rivera-Rideau. "'Esta es mi tierra/Esta soy yo': Teaching US Colonialism and Puerto Rican Resistance Through Bad Bunny." *Latino Studies* 22, no. 3 (2024): 562–70.

Dick, Diane Lourdes. "US Tax Imperialism in Puerto Rico." *American Law Review* 65, no. 1 (2015): 1–86.

Dinzey-Flores, Zaire Zenit. *Locked In, Locked Out: Gated Communities in a Puerto Rican City*. Philadelphia: University of Pennsylvania Press, 2013.

Drott, Eric. *Streaming Music, Streaming Capital*. Durham, NC: Duke University Press, 2024.

Duany, Jorge. "Dominican Migration to Puerto Rico: A Transnational Perspective." *CENTRO: Journal of the Center for Puerto Rican Studies* 17, no. 1 (2005): 242–69.

Duany, Jorge. "'May God Take Me to Orlando': The Puerto Rican Exodus to Florida Before and After Hurricane María." In *Caribbean Migrations: The Legacies of Colonialism*, edited by Anke Birkenmaier, 40–58. New Brunswick, NJ: Rutgers University Press, 2021.

Duany, Jorge. *The Puerto Rican Nation on the Move*. Chapel Hill: University of North Carolina Press, 2002.

Erman, Sam. *Almost Citizens: Puerto Rico, the US Constitution, and Empire*. New York: Cambridge University Press, 2018.

Exposito, Suzy. "Fireside Chat on 'Bad Bunny and Resistance in Puerto Rico.'" Lecture, Ahmanson Auditorium, Loyola Marymount University, Los Angeles, March 22, 2023.

Exposito, Suzy. "Mediating Bad Bunny." The Bad Bunny Symposium: Thinking with Bad Bunny. Center for Puerto Rican Studies, Hunter College, New York, May 13, 2023. YouTube, 01:18:09https://www.youtube.com/watch?v=nWIyrjuQabc&list=PLvhJBamtYzrU1kpiRB1EQATrIlH-JEOUS&index=5.

Feil, Ken. *Fearless Vulgarity: Jacqueline Susann's Queer Comedy and Camp Authorship*. Detroit: Wayne State University Press, 2023.

Findlay, Eileen J. Suárez. "Slipping and Sliding: The Many Meanings of Race in Life Histories of New York Puerto Rican Return Migrants in San Juan." *CENTRO: Journal of the Center for Puerto Rican Studies* 24, no. 2 (2012): 20–43.

Findlay, Eileen J. Suárez. *We Are Left Without a Father Here: Masculinity, Domesticity, and Migration in Postwar Puerto Rico*. Durham, NC: Duke University Press, 2014.

Fiol-Matta, Licia. "Pop Latinidad: Puerto Ricans in the Latin Explosion, 1999." *CENTRO: Journal of the Center for Puerto Rican Studies* 14, no. 1 (2002): 26–52.

Flores, Juan. *The Diaspora Strikes Back: Caribeño Tales of Learning and Turning*. New York: Routledge, 2009.

Fussell, Elizabeth, Narayan Sastry, and Mark VanLandingham. "Race, Socioeconomic Status, and Return Migration to New Orleans After Hurricane Katrina." *Population and Environment* 31 (2010). https://doi.org/10.1007/s11111-009-0092-2.

Fusté, José. "Repeating Islands of Debt: Historicizing the Transcolonial Relationality of Puerto Rico's Economic Crisis." *Radical History Review* 128 (2017): 91–119.

Godreau, Isar P. *Scripts of Blackness: Race, Cultural Nationalism, and U.S. Colonialism in Puerto Rico*. Urbana: University of Illinois Press, 2015.

González, Juan. *Harvest of Empire: A History of Latinos in America*. 2nd rev. ed. New York: Penguin Books, 2022.

González Cedeño, Kiana, and Ariana Costales del Toro. "Ballrooms
and the Sacred Runway: Intimate and Public Lamentations
in Cuir Communities of Puerto Rico." *CENTRO: Journal of the
Center for Puerto Rican Studies* 36, no. 2 (2024). https://www
.thefreelibrary.com/Ballrooms+and+the+Sacred+Runway%3a+
Intimate+and+Public+Lamentations+in . . . -a0820017690.

Guevarra, Rudy P., Jr. *Aloha Compadre: Latinxs in Hawai'i.* New
Brunswick, NJ: Rutgers University Press, 2023.

Hernández, Tanya Katerí. "Envisioning the United States in the Latin
American Myth of 'Racial Democracy Mestizaje.'" *Latin American
and Caribbean Ethnic Studies* 11, no. 2 (2016): 189–205.

Hinojosa, Jennifer. "Puerto Rican Exodus: One Year Since Hurricane
María." Research Brief, September 2018, Centro RB2018-
05. Center for Puerto Rican Studies, Hunter College.
https://academicworks.cuny.edu/cpr_pubs/5/.

Hostetler-Díaz, Jean. "Calles de La Resistencia: Pathways to Empowerment
in Puerto Rico." *Latin American Perspectives* 47, no. 3 (2020): 4–12.

Jiménez, Félix. "(W)rapped in Foil: Glory at Twelve Words a Minute." In
Reggaeton, edited by Raquel Z. Rivera, Wayne Marshall, and Deborah
Pacini Hernandez, 229–51. Durham, NC: Duke University Press, 2009.

Jiménez Román, Miriam. "Boricua vs. Nuyoricans—Indeed!" *ReVista:
Harvard Review of Latin America* 7, no. 3 (2008): 8–11.

Jiménez Román, Miriam. "Un Hombre (Negro) del Pueblo: José Celso Barbosa
and the Puerto Rican 'Race' Toward Whiteness." *CENTRO: Journal
of the Center for Puerto Rican Studies* 8, nos. 1–2 (1996): 8–29.

Jiménez Román, Miriam, and Juan Flores, eds. *The Afro-Latin@ Reader: History
and Culture in the United States.* Durham, NC: Duke University
Press, 2010.

Kim, Sujin, and Lisa M. Dorner. "'Everything Is a Spectrum': Korean Migrant Youth Identity Work in the Transnational Borderland."
In *Children and Borders*, edited by Spyros Spyrou and
Miranda Christou, 276–92. London: Palgrave Macmillan,
2014. https://doi.org/10.1057/9781137326317_16.

Kishore, Nishant, Domingo Marqués, Ayesha Mahmud, Mathew V. Kiang,
Irmary Rodriguez, Arlan Fuller, and Peggy Ebner. "Mortality in
Puerto Rico after Hurricane María." *New England Journal of Medicine*
379, no. 2 (2018): 162–70.

Klein, Naomi. *The Battle for Paradise: Puerto Rico Takes on Disaster
Capitalists.* Chicago: Haymarket Books, 2018.

La Fountain-Stokes, Lawrence. "Recent Developments in Queer Puerto
Rican History, Politics, and Culture." *CENTRO: Journal of the
Center for Puerto Rican Studies* 30, no. 2 (2018): 502–40.

La Fountain-Stokes, Lawrence. *Translocas: The Politics of Puerto Rican Drag and
Trans Performance.* Ann Arbor: University of Michigan Press, 2021.

Laguarta Ramírez, José A. "¡Yo no me dejé! Reggaetón Critique and
     Puerto Rico in the Times of Benito Martínez Ocasio." The
     Bad Bunny Symposium: Thinking with Bad Bunny. Center for
     Puerto Rican Studies, Hunter College, New York, May 13, 2023.
     https://www.youtube.com/watch?v=MI9WXGV7CZc&list
     =PLvhJBamtYzrU1kpiRB1EQATrIlH-JEOUS&index=8.
LeBrón, Marisol. *Against Muerto Rico: Lessons from the Verano Boricua.*
     Toa Baja, PR: Editora Educación Emergente, 2021.
LeBrón, Marisol. *Policing Life and Death: Race, Violence, and Resistance
     in Puerto Rico.* Berkeley: University of California Press, 2019.
LeBrón, Marisol. "The Protests in Puerto Rico Are About Life and
     Death." *NACLA*, July 18, 2019. https://nacla.org/news/2019
     /07/18/protests-puerto-rico-are-about-life-and-death.
LeBrón, Marisol. "Puerto Rico and the Colonial Circuits of Policing:
     How Reconsidering the History of Policing in Puerto Rico
     Complicates Our Understandings of the Island's Colonial
     Relationship with the United States." *NACLA: Report on the
     Americas* 49, no. 3 (2017): 328–34. https://nacla.org/news
     /2017/09/27/puerto-rico-and-colonial-circuits-policing.
Leppert, Alice. "Momager of the Brides: Kris Jenner's Management." In *First
     Comes Love: Power Couples, Celebrity Kinship and Cultural Politics*, edited
     by Shelley Cobb and Neil Ewen, 133–50. New York: Bloomsbury, 2015.
Lloréns, Hilda. "Brothels, Hell and Puerto Rican Bodies: Sex, Race, and Other
     Cultural Politics in 21st Century Artistic Representations." *CENTRO:
     Journal of the Center for Puerto Rican Studies* 20, no. 1 (2008): 193–217.
Lloréns, Hilda. "US Media Depictions of Climate Migrants: The Recent
     Case of the Puerto Rican 'Exodus.'" In *Aftershocks of Disaster:
     Puerto Rico Before and After the Storm*, edited by Yarimar Bonilla
     and Marisol LeBrón, 124–37. Chicago: Haymarket Books, 2019.
López Mari, Kacho, dir. *El Apagón—Aquí Vive Gente.* Rimas Entertainment, 2022.
     YouTube, 00:22:00. https://www.youtube.com/watch?v=1TCX_Aqz004.
Marshall, Wayne. "From Música Negra to Reggaeton Latino: The Cultural
     Politics of Nation, Migration, and Commercialization." In *Reggaeton*,
     edited by Raquel Z. Rivera, Wayne Marshall, and Deborah Pacini
     Hernandez, 19–76. Durham, NC: Duke University Press, 2009.
Martin, Ricky. *Me.* New York: Penguin Random House, 2010.
Martínez-San Miguel, Yolanda. "De ilegales e indocumentados:
     Representaciones culturales de la migración dominicana en
     Puerto Rico." *Revista de Ciencias Sociales* 4 (1998): 113–73.
Massol-Deyá, Arturo. "The Energy Uprising: A Community-Driven Search for
     Sustainability and Sovereignty in Puerto Rico." In *Aftershocks of Disaster:
     Puerto Rico Before and After the Storm*, edited by Yarimar Bonilla and
     Marisol LeBrón, 298–308. Chicago: Haymarket Books, 2019.
Meléndez, Edgardo. *Sponsored Migrations: The State and Puerto Rican
     Postwar Migration.* Columbus: Ohio State University Press, 2017.

Meléndez-Badillo, Jorell A. *Puerto Rico: A National History*. Princeton, NJ: Princeton University Press, 2024.

Molanphy, Chris. *Old Town Road*. Durham, NC: Duke University Press, 2023.

Molinari, Sarah. "Authenticating Loss and Contesting Recovery: FEMA and the Politics of Colonial Disaster Management." In *Aftershocks of Disaster: Puerto Rico Before and After the Storm*, edited by Yarimar Bonilla and Marisol LeBrón, 285–97. Chicago: Haymarket Books, 2019.

Morales, Ed. *Fantasy Island: Colonialism, Exploitation, and the Betrayal of Puerto Rico*. New York: Bold Type Books, 2019.

Negrón-Muntaner, Frances. *Boricua Pop: Puerto Ricans and the Latinization of US Culture*. New York: New York University Press, 2004.

Negrón-Muntaner, Frances. "Our Fellow Americans: Why Calling Puerto Ricans 'Americans' Will Not Save Them." In *Aftershocks of Disaster: Puerto Rico Before and After the Storm*, edited by Yarimar Bonilla and Marisol LeBrón, 93–100. Chicago: Haymarket Books, 2019.

Negrón-Muntaner, Frances. "Poetry of Filth: The (Post) Reggaetonic Lyrics of Calle 13." In *Reggaeton*, edited by Raquel Z. Rivera, Wayne Marshall, and Deborah Pacini Hernandez, 327–48. Durham, NC: Duke University Press, 2009.

Negus, Keith. *Music Genres and Corporate Cultures*. New York: Routledge, 1999.

Nieves Moreno, Alfredo. "A Man Lives Here: Reggaetón's Hypermasculine Resident." In *Reggaeton*, edited by Raquel Z. Rivera, Wayne Marshall, and Deborah Pacini Hernandez, 252–79. Durham, NC: Duke University Press, 2009.

Ortiz Valentín, Luis J., and Minet, Carla. "Las 889 páginas de Telegram entre Rosselló Nevares y sus allegados." *Centro de Periodismo Investigativo*, July 13, 2019. https://periodismoinvestigativo.com/2019/07/las-889 -paginas-de-telegram-entre-rossello-nevares-y-sus-allegados/.

Pacini Hernandez, Deborah. "Dominicans in the Mix: Reflections on Dominican Identity, Race, and Reggaeton." In *Reggaeton*, edited by Raquel Z. Rivera, Wayne Marshall, and Deborah Pacini Hernandez, 135–64. Durham, NC: Duke University Press, 2009.

Pacini Hernandez, Deborah. *Oye Como Va! Hybridity and Identity in Latino Popular Music*. Philadelphia: Temple University Press, 2010.

Paíz, Christian O. "Essential Only as Labor: Coachella Valley Farmworkers During COVID-19." *Kalfou* 8, no. 1–2 (2021): 31–50.

Paredez, Deborah. *Selenidad: Selena, Latinos, and the Performance of Memory*. Durham, NC: Duke University Press, 2009.

Pérez, Ileana. "More Than Spanish to English Code-Switching: An Analysis of Bad Bunny's Translanguaging Practices Throughout His Discography." In *The Bad Bunny Enigma: Culture, Resistance, and Uncertainty*, edited by Sheilla R. Madera, Nelson Varas-Díaz, and Daniel Nevárez Araujo, 189–203. Lanham, MD: Rowman and Littlefield, 2025.

Picker, Miguel, and Chyng Sun, dirs. *Latinos Beyond Reel: Challenging a Media Stereotype*. Kanopy Streaming, 2016. https://latinosbeyondreel.com/.

Poblete, JoAnna. *Islanders in the Empire: Filipino and Puerto Rican Laborers in Hawai'i*. Urbana: University of Illinois Press, 2014.

Powdermaker, Hortense. *Hollywood, the Dream Factory: An Anthropologist Looks at the Movie-Makers*. Boston: Little, Brown, 1950.

Power, Margaret. "Seeing the U.S. Empire Through the Eyes of Puerto Rican Nationalists Who Opposed It." *Modern American History* 2, no. 2 (2019): 189–92.

Power-Sotomayor, Jade. "Dancing in Non-English at the Grammys." The Bad Bunny Symposium: Thinking with Bad Bunny. Center for Puerto Rican Studies, Hunter College, New York, May 13, 2023. https://centropr.hunter.cuny.edu/media/bad-bunny-caribeno/.

Prados-Rodriguez, Eva. "Puerto Rico's Fight for a Citizen Debt Audit: A Strategy for Public Mobilization and a Fair Reconstruction." In *Aftershocks of Disaster: Puerto Rico Before and After the Storm*, edited by Yarimar Bonilla and Marisol LeBrón, 213–19. Chicago: Haymarket Books, 2019.

Ragland, Cathy. *Música Norteña: Mexican Migrants Creating a Nation Between Nations*. Philadelphia: Temple University Press, 2009.

Ramírez, Catherine S. *Assimilation: An Alternative History*. Berkeley: University of California Press, 2020.

Ramírez, Catherine S. "Indians and Negroes in Spite of Themselves: Puerto Rican Students at the Carlisle Indian Industrial School." In *Relational Formations of Race: Theory, Method, and Practice*, edited by Natalia Molina, Daniel Martinez HoSang, and Ramón A. Gutiérrez, 166–84. Berkeley: University of California Press, 2019.

Ramos, Iván A. *Unbelonging: Inauthentic Sounds in Mexican and Latinx Aesthetics*. New York: New York University Press, 2023.

Rebollo-Gil, Guillermo. *Writing Puerto Rico: Our Decolonial Moment*. New York: Palgrave Macmillan, 2018.

Reyes-Santos, Alaí. *Our Caribbean Kin: Race and Nation in the Neoliberal Antilles*. New Brunswick, NJ: Rutgers University Press, 2015.

Ríos Ruíz, Elena. "Estado de emergencia ante la violencia del género: Una conversación con la coalición feminista puertorriqueña Coordinadora Paz para las Mujeres." *CENTRO: Journal of the Center for Puerto Rican Studies* 35, no. 2 (2023): 125–36.

Rivera, Eugenio ("Gene"). "La Colonia de Lorain, Ohio." In *The Puerto Rican Diaspora: Historical Perspectives*, edited by Carmen Theresa Whalen and Victor Vázquez-Hernández, 151–73. Philadelphia: Temple University Press, 2005.

Rivera, Raquel Z. "Policing Morality, *Mano Dura Stylee*: The Case of Underground Rap and Reggae in Puerto Rico." In *Reggaeton*, edited by Raquel Z. Rivera, Wayne Marshall, and Deborah Pacini Hernandez, 111–34. Durham, NC: Duke University Press, 2009.

Rivera, Raquel Z. "Will the Real Puerto Rican Culture Please Stand Up." In *None of the Above: Puerto Ricans in the Global Era*, edited by

Frances Negrón-Muntaner, 217–31. New York: Palgrave Macmillan, 2007.

Rivera, Raquel Z., Wayne Marshall, and Deborah Pacini Hernandez, eds. *Reggaeton*. Durham, NC: Duke University Press, 2009.

Rivera-Figueroa, Luis Enrique. "Bad Bunny on the Global Stage: The Network Society, Streaming, and the Latin Music Industry." In *The Bad Bunny Enigma: Culture, Resistance, and Uncertainty*, edited by Sheilla R. Madera, Nelson Varas-Díaz, and Daniel Nevárez Araújo, 75–94. London: Lexington Books, 2025.

Rivera-Figueroa, Luis Enrique. "Bad Bunny's Transgressive Gender Performativity: Camp Aesthetics and Hegemonic Masculinities in Early Latin Trap." *Journal of Latin American Communication Research* 8, nos. 1–2 (2020): 86–108.

Rivera-Rideau, Petra R. "'Cocolos Modernos': Salsa, Reggaetón, and Puerto Rico's Cultural Politics of Blackness." *Latin American and Caribbean Ethnic Studies* 8, no. 1 (2013): 1–19.

Rivera-Rideau, Petra R. *Fitness Fiesta! Selling Latinx Culture Through Zumba*. Durham, NC: Duke University Press, 2024.

Rivera-Rideau, Petra R. "'If I Were You': Tego Calderón's Diasporic Interventions." *Small Axe: A Caribbean Journal of Criticism* 55, no. 3 (2018): 55–69.

Rivera-Rideau, Petra R. "Race, Latinidad, and Latin Pop: CNCO and Reggaetón in the Mainstream." In *Oxford Handbook of Global Popular Music*, edited by Simone Krueger Bridge and Britta Sweers. New York: Oxford University Press, 2021. https://doi.org/10.1093/oxfordhb/9780190081379.013.51.

Rivera-Rideau, Petra R. "Reinventing Enrique Iglesias: Constructing Latino Whiteness in the Latin Urban Scene." *Latino Studies* 17, no. 4 (2019): 467–83.

Rivera-Rideau, Petra R. *Remixing Reggaetón: The Cultural Politics of Race in Puerto Rico*. Durham, NC: Duke University Press, 2015.

Rivera-Rideau, Petra R., and Jericko Torres-Leschnik. "'The Colors and Flavors of My Puerto Rico': Mapping 'Despacito's' Crossovers." *Journal of Popular Music Studies* 31, no. 1 (2019): 87–108.

Rivera-Servera, Ramón H. "Reggaetón's Crossings: Black Aesthetics, Latina Nightlife, and Queer Choreography." In *No Tea, No Shade: New Writings in Black Queer Studies*, edited by E. Patrick Johnson, 95–112. Durham, NC: Duke University Press, 2016.

Rivera Velásquez, Celiany. "Caribbean Kiki: The Cuir Irreverence of Puerto Rican LaBoriVogue and Dominican Draguéalo." *CENTRO: Journal of the Center for Puerto Rican Studies* 36, no. 2 (2024). https://www.thefreelibrary.com/Caribbean+Kiki%3a+The+Cuir+Irreverence+of+Puerto+Rican+LaBoriVogue+and . . . -a0820017689.

Roberto, Giovanni. "Community Kitchens: An Emerging Movement?" In *Aftershocks of Disaster: Puerto Rico Before and After the*

Storm, edited by Yarimar Bonilla and Marisol LeBrón, 309–18. Chicago: Haymarket Books, 2019.

Rodríguez, Juana María. "Getting F****d in Puerto Rico: Metaphoric Provocations and Queer Activist Interventions." In *None of the Above: Puerto Ricans in the Global Era*, edited by Frances Negrón-Muntaner, 129–45. New York: Palgrave Macmillan, 2007.

Rodríguez-Madera, Sheilla L., Mark Padilla, Nelson Varas-Díaz, Torsten Neilands, Ana C. Vasques Guzzi, Ericka J. Florenciani, and Alíxida Ramos-Pibernus. "Experiences of Violence Among Transgender Women in Puerto Rico: An Underestimated Problem." *Journal of Homosexuality* 6, no. 2 (2017): 209–17.

Rosa, Jonathan. "Bad Bunny, Good PR: Race, Language and the Politics of Vernacular Celebrity." The Bad Bunny Symposium: Thinking with Bad Bunny. Center for Puerto Rican Studies, Hunter College, New York, May 13, 2023. MP4, 1:15:51. https://centropr.hunter.cuny.edu/media/bad-bunny-good-pr-race-language-and-the-politics-of-vernacular-celebrity/.

Sanabria León, Waleska, and M. Gabriela Torres. "Colonial Necropolitics in Responding to Gender-Based Violence Amidst Cascading Disasters in Puerto Rico." *Feminist Anthropology* 5, no. 1 (2024): 13–28.

Sandoval-Sánchez, Alberto. *José, Can You See? Latinos on and off Broadway*. Madison: University of Wisconsin Press, 1999.

Santiago-Bartolomei, Raúl. "In Two Caribbean Cities, Digital Platforms Drive Gentrification: With the Help of Apps Like Airbnb, Short-Term Rental Housing Elevates Costs and Fuels Displacement in Havana and San Juan." *NACLA: Report on the Americas* 54, no. 3 (2022): 324–29.

Smith, Stacy L., Katherine Pieper, and Sam Wheeler. "Inequality in 1,600 Popular Films: Examining Portrayals of Gender, Race/Ethnicity, LGBTQ+ and Disability from 2007 to 2022." USC Annenberg Inclusion Initiative, August 2023, 3–4. https://assets.uscannenberg.org/docs/aii-inequality-in-1600-popular-films-20230811.pdf.

Solis Miranda, Regina. "*Bienaventurado el que escuche este liriqueo*: Negotiating *Latinidad* Through Reggaeton." *Latino Studies* 20, no. 4 (2022): 498–526.

Tehranian, John. "Is Kim Kardashian White (and Why Does It Matter Anyway)? Racial Fluidity, Identity Mutability and the Future of Civil Rights Jurisprudence." *Houston Law Review* 58, no. 1 (2020): 151–83. https://houstonlawreview.org/article/18003-is-kim-kardashian-white-and-why-does-it-matter-anyway-racial-fluidity-identity-mutability-the-future-of-civil-rights-jurisprudence.

Thomas, Lorrin. *Puerto Rican Citizen*. Chicago: University of Chicago Press, 2010.

Torres Gotay, Benjamín. "'I'm Quite Comfortable': Abandonment and Resignation After María." In *Aftershocks of Disaster: Puerto Rico Before and After the Storm*, edited by Yarimar Bonilla and Marisol LeBrón, 82–89. Chicago: Haymarket Books, 2019.

Torruella, Juan R. "To Be or Not to Be: Puerto Ricans and Their Illusory US Citizenship." *CENTRO: Journal of the Center for Puerto Rican Studies* 29, no. 1 (2017). https://www.thefreelibrary .com/To+Be+or+Not+to+Be%3A+Puerto+Ricons+and+ Their+Illusory+U.S.+Citizenship.-a0608508782.

Valdez, Elena. "Vivir sin miedo: Las artes contemporáneas ante la violencia de género en Puerto Rico." *CENTRO: Journal of the Center for Puerto Rican Studies* 35 no. 2 (2023): 227–47.

Valle, Ariana J. "Race and the Empire-State: Puerto Ricans' Unequal US Citizenship." *Sociology of Race and Ethnicity* 5, no. 1 (2018).

Vazquez, Alexandra T. "Toward an Ethics of Knowing Nothing." In *Pop When the World Falls Apart: Music in the Shadow of Doubt*, edited by Eric Weisbard, 27–39. Durham, NC: Duke University Press, 2012.

Venator-Santiago, Charles R., and Volodymyr Gupan. "Puerto Rican Population Change in the United States, 2016–2021." UCONN: Puerto Rican Studies Initiative for Community Engagement and Public Policy, Data Report DR 2022-1, September 2022. https://puerto-rican-studies -initiative-clas.media.uconn.edu/wp-content/uploads/sites/3555 /2023/12/UConn_PuertoRicanPopulationChange_FinalPrint.pdf.

Watson, Sonja. "Reading National Identity in Panama Through Renato, a First-Generation Panamanian Reggae en Español Artist." *alter/nativas*, no. 2 (2014): 1–21. https://alternativas .osu.edu/en/issues/spring-2014/essays1/watson.html.

Whalen, Carmen Theresa. "Colonialism, Citizenship, and the Making of the Puerto Rican Diaspora: An Introduction." In *Puerto Rican Diaspora: Historical Perspectives*, edited by Carmen Theresa Whalen and Victor Vázquez-Hernández, 1–42. Philadelphia: Temple University Press, 2008.

Zambrana, Rocío. "Black Feminist Tactics: On La Colectiva Feminista en Construcción's Politics Without Guarantees." *Society and Space*, February 25, 2020. https://www.societyandspace.org /articles/black-feminist-tactics-on-la-colectiva-feminista -en-construccions-politics-without-guarantees.

Zambrana, Rocío. *Colonial Debts: The Case of Puerto Rico*. Durham, NC: Duke University Press, 2021.

INDEX

Page numbers followed by *f* indicate figures.

San Juan, 17, 31, 59, 64–65, 72, 87–88, 102–3, 107, 109, 121, 138, 146, 150; Calle Loíza, 192, 193*f;* Capitolio, 46*f;* Cathedral, 69, 70*f;* Condado, 149; Dominican-owned hookah lounges in, 241n44; Juana Matos caserío, 127; La Perla, 25–26, 142, 240n36; *Nadie Sabe Lo Que Va a Pasar Mañana* listening party in, 200, 202; Old San Juan, 7, 25, 61–62, 65, 69, 71, 149; P FKN R concerts in, 119*f,* 124, 125*f,* 128; Plaza Las Américas, 31; Puerta de Tierra, 149–51; Santurce, 127, 135, 148; short-term rentals and, 282n6 (*see also* Airbnb; gentrification); Verano Boricua protests in, 75*f. See also* El Choli; Rodríguez de Tío, Lola

Santiago, Eddie, 82, 103–5, 118, 167

Santos, Antony, 114

Santos, Romeo, 124

Santos Febres, Mayra, 126

sapo concho, 4, 222, 223*f*

Saturday Night Live (*SNL*), 3*f,* 157–58, 268n6

Sech, 94, 121

Selena, 183, 189, 198, 273n4

Shakira, 165, 183–84, 196

Shirley, Travis, 124

soca, 133

Solá, Sujeylee, 80, 165, 270n35

Solís, Adelaido "Payo," 195, 197. *See also* Grupo Frontera

Sosa, Mercedes, 184

Sotomayor, Sonia, 126

SoundCloud, 11, 28, 32

SoundScan, 167, 271n40

Spain, 6, 11, 82, 216, 219

Spanish language, 7, 35, 49, 81, 177, 248n5; albums, 2, 109, 132; Arnaz and, 161, 268n6; artists, 3, 156–57, 159, 163–64, 166, 183, 268n5; Bad Bunny and, 116, 132, 155–60, 163–64, 169, 171–73, 176, 180, 182, 267nn5–6; Feliciano and, 186; Jersey Club songs, 113; music, 128, 157, 199; performance, 157; pop music, 98; Puerto Rican, 6, 156, 267n5; rap and R&B, 14, 17, 26; songs, 2, 156, 176, 183, 186, 189, 268n6;

trap songs, 27, 29, 241n44. *See also* reggaetón: *roncar* in

Spears, Britney, 114–15

Spotify, 2–3, 29, 36, 119, 120, 128, 132, 167, 247n46; Bieber and, 183; scavenger hunt, 220; US Latin at, 82, 103, 118

Stensby, Wayne, 148

Stillz, 89, 119*f*

streaming: country music and, 201; critiques of, 271n41; Latin artists and, 166; Latin music and, 167–68; platforms, 2, 29, 221, 247n46. *See also* Apple Music; DSPs; Spotify

structural inequality, 97, 122

Suarez, Gary, 111

Taíno people, 6, 126

Tainy (Marco Efraín Masís Fernández), 9, 36, 39, 51–56, 58, 68, 72, 87, 109, 113, 167, 182, 190–91, 247n55; "ACHO PR," 15–16; "Andrea," 134; "Callaíta," 85–86; "Dákiti," 119; *Data,* 51, 52*f; DeBÍ TiRAR MáS FOToS* and, 220, 221*f;* "Estamos Bien," 38, 54–56; Fruity Loops and, 31, 114, 241n49; "I Like It" (Cardi B), 54, 188–89; *Más Flow: Los Benjamins,* 26, 53; "Pam Pam" (Wisin y Yandel), 53; "Una Velita," 215–16; *Un Verano Sin Ti* and, 131, 133–34; "Yo No Soy Celoso," 133–34

Thalia, 184

Three Kings' Day (January 6), 4

Time magazine, 166, 169, 171, 201

Tisci, Riccardo, 84*f*

Tito Flow, 130

Today Show, 157

Tokischa, 102–3

The Tonight Show with Jimmy Fallon, 9, 37–39, 58, 94

Tony Dize, 135

Tony Tún Tún, 53

Torres Gotay, Benjamín, 44

Towers, Myke, 35, 124

transphobia, 69, 97, 103–5

trap music, 4, 27–29, 33, 115, 241n44. *See also* Latin trap